The Politics of Federalism

Constitutional amendment, the control of resources, and the conflict these issues create between Ottawa and the provinces are current preoccupations of Canadian politics. In this study of Ontario's relations with the federal government from Confederation to the Second World War, Professor Armstrong reminds us that almost from the beginning provincial governments have been engaged in a power struggle with Ottawa over the terms of Confederation and the rights to exploit resources.

The British North America Act of 1867 fashioned a Canadian federation which was intended to be a highly centralized union led by a powerful national government. Soon after Confederation, however, the government of Ontario took the lead in demanding a greater share of the power for the provinces, and it has continued to press this case. Professor Armstrong analyses the forces which promoted decentralization and the responses which they elicited from the federal government. He explains Ontario's reasons for pursuing this particular policy from 1867 to the Second World War.

The author's sources are the private papers of federal and provincial premiers and other contemporary political figures, government publications, parliamentary debates, and newspapers. He has identified and developed three separate but related themes: the dynamic role played by private business interests in generating inter-governmental conflicts; Ontario's policy of promoting its economic growth by encouraging the processing of its resources at home; and the tremendous influence exerted by increasing urbanization and industrialization on the growth of the responsibilities of the provinces.

During the 1930s, efforts to restructure the federal system were rejected by Ontario because it preferred to maintain the status quo and was unsympathetic to greater equalization between the regions. Consequently, Ontario took a leading part in opposing the redivision of powers recommended by the Royal Commission on Dominion-Provincial Relations in 1940.

This book provides part of the historical context into which current debates on the question of federalism may be fitted. Thus it will be of importance and interest to historians, students of Canadian history, and the general reader alike.

CHRISTOPHER ARMSTRONG is a member of the History Department at York University.

THE ONTARIO HISTORICAL STUDIES SERIES

The Ontario Historical Studies Series is a comprehensive history of Ontario from 1791 to the present, which will include several biographies of former premiers, numerous volumes on the economic, social, political, and cultural development of the province, and a general history incorporating the insights and conclusions of the other works in the series. The purpose of the series is to enable the general reader and the scholar to understand better the distinctive features of Ontario as one of the principal regions within Canada.

Published

Olga B. Bishop, Barbara I. Irwin, Clara G. Miller (eds.) *Bibliography of Ontario History, 1867-1976: Cultural, Economic, Political, Social*, two volumes (1980)
J.M.S. Careless (ed.) *The Pre-Confederation Premiers: Ontario Government Leaders, 1841-1867* (1980)
Peter Oliver *G. Howard Ferguson: Ontario Tory* (1977)
Christopher Armstrong *The Politics of Federalism: Ontario's Relations with the Federal Government, 1867-1942* (1981)

Forthcoming

David P. Gagan *Hopeful Travellers: Families, Land and Social Change in Mid-Victorian Peel County, Canada West*
Roger Graham *Hon. Leslie M. Frost* (Premier, 1949-1961)
A.K. McDougall *Hon. John P. Robarts* (Premier, 1961-1971)
R.M. Stamp *The Schools of Ontario, 1876-1976*

CHRISTOPHER ARMSTRONG

The Politics of Federalism: Ontario's Relations with the Federal Government, 1867–1942

A PROJECT OF THE BOARD OF TRUSTEES
OF THE ONTARIO HISTORICAL STUDIES SERIES
FOR THE GOVERNMENT OF ONTARIO
PUBLISHED BY UNIVERSITY OF TORONTO PRESS
TORONTO BUFFALO LONDON

© Her Majesty the Queen in right of the Province of Ontario 1981
Reprinted in paperback 2014

ISBN 978-0-8020-2434-3 (cloth)
ISBN 978-1-4426-5146-3 (paper)

Canadian Cataloguing in Publication Data

Armstrong, Christopher, 1942–
   The politics of federalism
   (Ontario historical studies series, ISSN 0380-9188).
   A project of the Board of Trustees of the Ontario
Historical Studies Series and the Government of
Ontario.
   Includes index.
   ISBN 978-0-8020-2434-3 (bound) ISBN 978-1-4426-5146-3 (pbk.)
   1. Federal-provincial relations (Canada) – Ontario –
History.* 2. Canada – Politics and government – 1867–
3. Ontario – Politics and government – 1867–
I. Title. II. Series.
JL19.A75   321.02'3'0971   C81-094067-1

FOR MY MOTHER

Contents

The Ontario Historical Studies Series
  Murray G. Ross, Goldwin French, Peter Oliver, and Jeanne Beck   ix

Preface   *xiii*

Introduction   *3*
  1 Remoulding the Constitution   *8*
  2 Federalism and Economic Development   *33*
  3 Public Power and Disallowance   *54*
  4 Exporting Electricity   *68*
  5 Playing the Federal-Provincial Game   *85*
  6 Financing the Federation in Peace and War   *114*
  7 Social Change and Constitutional Amendment   *133*
  8 Water-power and the Constitution   *160*
  9 The Battle of the St Lawrence   *178*
  10 Revising the Constitution   *197*

Conclusion   *233*

Appendix   *239*
Note on Sources   *241*
Notes   *243*
Index   *273*

The Ontario Historical Studies Series

When discussions about this series of books first arose, it was immediately apparent that very little work had been done on the history of Ontario. Ontario has many fine historians, but much of their work has been focused on national themes, despite the fact that the locus of many of the important developments in the history of Canada – as recent events remind us – was, and is, in the provinces. While other provinces have recognized this reality and have recorded their histories in permanent form, Ontario is singularly lacking in definitive works about its own distinctive history.

Thus, when the Ontario Historical Studies Series was formally established by Order-in-Council on 14 April 1971, the Board of Trustees was instructed not only to produce authoritative and readable biographies of Ontario premiers but also 'to ensure that a comprehensive program of research and writing in Ontario history is carried out.'

From the outset the Board has included both professional historians and interested and knowledgeable citizens. The present members are: Margaret Angus, Kingston; J.M.S. Careless, Toronto; Floyd S. Chalmers, Toronto; R.E.G. Davis, Toronto; Gaetan Gervais, Sudbury; D.F. McOuat, Toronto; Jacqueline Neatby, Ottawa; J. Keith Reynolds, Toronto; and J.J. Talman, London. E.E. Stewart and Raymond Labarge served as valued members of the Board in its formative period. The combination of varied interests and skills of Board members has proven useful. A consensus was soon reached on the need for research in neglected areas of Ontario history and for scholarly and well-written works that would be of interest and value to the people of Ontario. We trust our work will satisfy these criteria.

After much careful deliberation the Board settled on six major areas in which to pursue its objectives: biographies of premiers; a bibliography; a historical atlas; a group of theme studies on major developments (social, economic, and cultural, as well as political) in the province; the recording on tape of the attitudes, opinions, and memories of many important leaders in Ontario; and, as a culmination of these studies, a definitive history of Ontario.

The first edition of the bibliography was published in 1973. Since it was well received, the Board sponsored the preparation of a second, comprehensive edition prepared by Olga Bishop, Barbara Irwin, and Clara Miller, entitled *Bibliography of Ontario History, 1867-1976*. This volume was published in 1980. Our first major publication was *G. Howard Ferguson* by Peter N. Oliver (1977), followed in 1978 by *Ontario since 1867*, a general history of the province, by Joseph Schull. *The Pre-Confederation Premiers: Ontario Government Leaders, 1841-1867*, edited by J.M.S. Careless, the second volume in the biographies series, was published in 1980. *The Politics of Federalism: Ontario's Relations with the Federal Government, 1867-1942*, by Christopher Armstrong, is the first of the theme studies. We hope it will find a large and interested reading audience and that it will be followed each year by one or more equally interesting books, the total of which will inform and illuminate Ontario history in a new and lasting way.

The Board is greatly indebted to its editors, Goldwin French, Editor-in-Chief, Peter Oliver, Associate Editor, and Jeanne Beck, Assistant Editor, for their assistance in the selection of subjects and authors and for their supervision of the preparation, editing, and publication of works in the Series.

MURRAY G. ROSS
Chairman, Board of Trustees
Ontario Historical Studies Series

5 January 1981

For many years the principal theme in English-Canadian historical writing has been the emergence and the consolidation of the Canadian nation. This theme has been developed in uneasy awareness of the persistence and importance of regional interests and identities, but because of the central role of Ontario in the growth of Canada, Ontario has not been seen as a region. Almost unconsciously, historians have equated the history of the province with that of the nation and have depicted the interests of other regions as obstacles to the unity and welfare of Canada.

The creation of the province of Ontario in 1867 was the visible embodiment of a formidable reality, the existence at the core of the new nation of a powerful if disjointed society whose traditions and characteristics differed in many respects from those of the other British North American colonies. The intervening century has not witnessed the assimilation of Ontario into the other regions in Canada; on the contrary, it has become a more clearly articulated entity. Within the formal geographical and institutional framework defined so assiduously by Ontario's political leaders, an increasingly intricate web of economic and social interests has been woven and shaped by the dynamic interplay between Toronto and its hinterland. The character of this regional community has been formed in the tension between a rapid adaptation to the processes of modernization and industrialization in western society and a reluctance to modify or discard traditional attitudes and values. Not surprisingly, the Ontario outlook is a compound of aggressiveness, conservatism, and the conviction that its values should be the model for the rest of Canada.

The purpose of the Ontario Historical Studies Series is to describe and analyse the historical development of Ontario as a distinct region within Canada. The series as planned will include approximately thirty-five volumes covering many aspects of the life and work of the province from its original establishment in 1791 as Upper Canada to our own time. Among these will be biographies of several prominent political figures, a three-volume economic history, numerous works on topics such as social structure, education, minority groups, labour, political and administrative institutions, literature, theatre, and the arts, and a comprehensive synthesis of the history of Ontario, based upon the detailed contributions of the biographies and thematic studies.

In planning this project, the editors have endeavoured to maintain a reasonable balance between different kinds and areas of historical research, and to appoint authors ready to ask new kinds of questions about the past and to answer them in accordance with the canons of contemporary scholarship. Ten biographical studies have been included, if only because through biography the past comes alive most readily for the general reader as well as the historian. The historian must be sensitive to today's concerns and standards as he engages in the imaginative recreation of the interplay between human beings and circumstances in time. He should seek to be the mediator between all the dead and the living, but in the end the humanity and the artistry of his account will determine the extent of its usefulness.

The Politics of Federalism: Ontario's Relations with the Federal Government, 1867-1942, the first theme study to be published, examines a familiar yet highly important subject from a new perspective. The author has shown that the recurring conflict between the governments of Ontario and Canada since 1867 has been fostered by private as well as public economic interests and by the industrialization and urbanization of the province. We hope that this work will enlarge our understanding of the past operation of the federal system and that it will suggest new approaches to the study of the evolution of the federal-provincial relationship in recent years.

GOLDWIN FRENCH
Editor-in-chief
PETER OLIVER
Associate editor
JEANNE BECK
Assistant editor

Toronto
5 January 1981

Preface

This book originated from a suggestion made almost fifteen years ago by Professor Ramsay Cook, that the relations between Ontario and the federal government during the 1920s and 1930s would form an interesting subject for a graduate research paper. Professor Cook has been able to repent his suggestion at leisure; for that paper grew into a doctoral thesis, which he supervised, and ultimately into this book. As a teacher, supervisor, colleague, and friend he has helped me at every stage. Another special debt is to Professor H.V. Nelles. We first met while doing research at the Provincial Archives of Ontario and soon discovered that our interests intersected at many points. I have benefited greatly from innumerable discussions with him and from his splendid book, *The Politics of Development, Forests, Mines and Hydro-electric Power in Ontario, 1849–1941*. I have been able to refer readers to his work where the subject of resource policy overlaps with the study of intergovernmental relations, as it frequently does. Other friends and colleagues such as T.W. Acheson, R.C. Brown, and J.L Granatstein have proffered both good whisky and good advice, and it is not their fault if I have not always taken the latter.

I am indebted to the Board of the Ontario Historical Studies Series, and particularly to the associate editor, Peter Oliver, for support. For access to the papers of the premiers of Ontario since 1919 I must thank the secretary of the provincial cabinet, William McIntyre, and the deputy attorney-general, Rendall Dick, for granting me access to the records of the attorney-general's department. Professor Brown and Mr Henry Borden permitted me to use the diary of Sir Robert Borden, and the literary executors of W.L. Mackenzie King allowed me to examine his correspondence for 1940–1 at a time when it was still closed to other researchers. Willing assistance was provided by the staffs of the Public Archives of Canada and the Provincial Archives of Ontario, in particular by Miss Jackson and Mr Appleby of the PAO, who fetched uncounted boxes without complaint.

Financial support for this study came from the Canada Council, the OHSS, and from York University, whose secretarial services provided speedy and accurate typing. Lorraine Ourom and Catherine Frost of the University of Toronto Press did their best to improve the quality of my prose, for which I am grateful. Any errors are my own responsibility.

CA

*The Politics of Federalism:
Ontario's Relations
with the Federal Government,
1867-1942*

Introduction

Just before six o'clock on the afternoon of 15 January 1941 the premier of Ontario, Mitchell Hepburn, rose for the last time to address the dominion-provincial conference. Under discussion was the report of the Royal Commission on Dominion-Provincial Relations which the year before had recommended a radical restructuring of the Canadian federal system. Hepburn charged that Prime Minister Mackenzie King had seized upon the report,

> dressed it up with the garments of patriotism and cloaked it with the exigencies of war as well, and ... said to those of us who represent the provinces, 'We want you to accept the findings of this report as a war measure in perpetuity.' Now there is where we disagree. We say that we will help you in every conceivable way so far as prosecuting the war is concerned, but we are not going to sell out our respective provinces and generations yet to come under the exigencies of war.[1]

Thus ended, at the hands of the representative of the province of Ontario, the most serious effort to that date to restructure the Canadian confederation.

Almost from the time of the union in 1867 successive premiers of Ontario found themselves embroiled in one conflict or another with the central government. On the face of it this opposition might seem paradoxical. Nowhere in British North America was the initial enthusiasm for Confederation greater than among Upper Canadians. By the 1860s supporters of the dominant political party, George Brown's Reformers, were firmly convinced of the need for a constitutional change to end the unhappy union of 1841 which bound them to the Lower Canadians. On 1 July 1867 hopes ran high that a new era had dawned. To Canadians living in other provinces it has always seemed that the citizens of Ontario have every reason to be pleased with the way in which Confederation has worked. Yet Ontario can lay claim to the title of heart and soul of the movement for provincial rights, of the effort to defend local autonomy against federal interference. Why have the province's leaders become involved in so many disputes with the federal authorities? What have been the issues in dispute? What has been the result of the friction between the two levels of government? This book tries to answer these questions.

The major causes of conflict between Ontario and the federal government became clear during the premiership of Sir Oliver Mowat which lasted an amazing twenty-four years from 1872 to 1896. His successors in office, regardless of party affiliation, continued to pursue similar goals up to the Second World War and after.[2] Mowat recognized that the province occupied a unique place within the Canadian federation, owing to its size, its wealth, and its population. The poorer provinces might look upon federalism as a means of overcoming regional disparities, but Ontario politicians have always valued autonomy more than equality. The province wished to be left alone to develop its bountiful resources, provided that national policies guaranteed it access to markets in other parts of the country. Leaders from Mowat onward, therefore, set out to extend the sway of 'Empire Ontario' and in so doing to increase their own power and authority.[3]

Promoting the economic development of the province has assumed a high priority with every government, and the ownership of lands and natural resources has proved to be a powerful instrument for this purpose. Ontario has generally been satisfied with national development programs such as the protective tariff, which greatly benefited the region; but whenever such policies have failed to meet its needs, the provincial government has not hesitated to try to substitute its own programs for those of Ottawa. The result has frequently been federal-provincial conflict, especially over resource development policies.

Because of its size and wealth Ontario was able to resist any attempts by the federal government to bully or bribe it into line. When other provinces clamoured for 'better terms,' or more money from the federal treasury, Ontario has usually held itself aloof. Mowat and his successors could afford to stay home when other premiers went cap-in-hand to Ottawa and to resist changes in the financial relations between the federal and provincial governments which did not meet with Ontario's approval. The politicians at Queen's Park preferred the greatest possible fiscal autonomy, the right to levy taxes and spend independently.

From an early date Mowat recognized that both his major objectives, managing economic development and securing financial independence, could best be achieved if Ontario possessed a veto over changes in the constitution. He could then block amendments of which he disapproved or demand concessions in return for his assent. Since the British North America Act contained no formula for its own amendment, there was no statutory basis for any such provincial veto. Mowat recognized that the 'compact' theory of Confederation, which contended that the constitution arose from a kind of treaty between the provinces, could be made to serve as a justification of his position. He therefore became an enthusiastic exponent of the compact theory, and his successors followed in his footsteps. Only grudgingly did the federal government concede the right of the provinces to be consulted formally about constitutional amendments, so that later premiers continued to press the case long after Mowat's retirement.

Two other factors helped to create and intensify conflicts between the two levels of government. First, there were private interests who wished to secure their own ends and often turned to one level of government or the other for assistance. If rebuffed, they naturally looked to the other level for what they had been refused: should provincial regulations stand in the way, it was only natural to look to Ottawa for help. Sometimes governments could be played off against one another in a kind of federal-provincial 'game.' Each level of government acquired groups of clients with their own interests, which transformed intergovernmental relations from a simple bilateral relationship into a complex and confusing mixture of public and private ends. In addition, friction was sometimes created by competing bureaucrats who strenuously resisted any loss of authority. Sincerely believing in their ability to do a better job than their counterparts in the other capital, they would press their political masters to stake claims to a broader jurisdiction and draw their governments into clashes.

Economic development, fiscal policies, and constitutional change were not the only causes of conflict between Ontario and the federal government before the Second World War, but other issues did not usually involve the first ministers nor did they threaten to disrupt relations seriously. It must be remembered that social welfare policies were not of major significance to governments in this period. Only the relief of unemployment became a major source of negotiation and discussion during the 1930s. A whole range of issues on which the two levels of government now routinely consult received minimal attention in the period discussed here. Hence the narrow focus in this study on economic growth and the division of public revenues.

Political parties are also not dealt with at length. The stances adopted by successive premiers demonstrated striking similarities and continuities regardless of their party labels. Ideology does not seem to have played a critical role. The premier of Ontario, by virtue of his office, was almost compelled to resist federal interference in local affairs whatever the rights and wrongs of the matter. Party loyalties, however, had an undeniable influence on the creation and solution of differences. Members of the same party at Ottawa and Queen's Park naturally enjoyed closer and more confidential relations than did political rivals. Both federal and provincial ministers of one party shared the desire to settle their disagreements quickly and quietly so as not to provide their opponents with ammunition. By the same token, provincial ministers were quick to charge their federal counterparts with partisan motives when they did not get their wishes, if the two governments were of different political persuasions. Rather than analyse the role of parties in isolation, I have tried simply to note those instances in which partisanship or party loyalty exercised a significant influence upon intergovernmental relations.

Likewise, political skills could affect both the tone and the substance of these relations. Between Confederation and the Second World War Ontario had four premiers who made a particular impact upon the political life of the province.* Mowat, of course, won six general elections and dominated the conduct of affairs from 1872 until his retirement to the federal scene in 1896. Sir James Whitney finally unseated the long-entrenched Liberals in 1905 and held power through four general elections before he died in office in 1914. Howard Ferguson ousted the Farmer-Labour coalition in 1923 and demonstrated his mastery over a divided opposition until he resigned to become Canada's high commissioner in London in 1930. The most flamboyant of all, Mitchell Hepburn, brought the Liberals back to power at long last in 1934 and kept the pot boiling until his abrupt retirement in 1942. The relations between such forceful personalities and the incumbent federal prime minister could not fail to have an impact upon federal-provincial relations. This was particularly true when feelings of personal bitterness arose as between Mowat and Sir John A. Macdonald and Mitchell Hepburn and Mackenzie King. I have sought to point out this personal dimension where it affected the relations between governments.

For the sake of clarity I have approached this subject from the point of view of the provincial government. At Queen's Park what issues aroused discontent with Ottawa? How did the local ministry seek to achieve its objectives? But this does not mean that this book is intended as a defence of provincial policies on every count. On occasion the premiers behaved with scant regard for their avowed principles. Both federal and provincial ministers acted sometimes from partisan motives or with a view to bolstering their chances of victory at the next election. That was and is the nature of Canadian politics.

One may ask, however, to what extent Mowat and his successors commanded the popular support of Ontarians in their wrangles with Ottawa. As a study in intergovernmental relations this book can provide few direct answers. Indeed, it seems almost impossible to divine public opinion on such questions. At one time a majority of the provincial electorate might respond to claims that the federal government was seriously violating provincial rights, at another they might display indifference or a healthy cynicism. Sometimes the majority of Ontarians clearly did accept that the national interest required the sacrifice of local desires; on other occasions they did not. It might be pointed out that the most successful provincial politicians like Mowat and Whitney were among the most forthright defenders of provincial rights, but it could well be argued that their electoral appeal did not depend heavily upon this fact. So the degree to which Ontario politicians actually reflected popular feeling about the operations of the federal

---

* See appendix for a list of premiers and prime ministers.

system must remain a moot point. The people of Ontario were swayed by the tug of conflicting views; for they recognized that both levels of government had claims upon their loyalty. The very consciousness of separateness from those in other provinces confirmed the reality of Canadian diversity upon which the strength of the provincial rights movement rested.

1 Remoulding the Constitution

The British North America Act made the Confederation agreement law. In 1867 the compromise arrived at by the colonial politicians during the Quebec Conference of 1864 became a British statute which divided jurisdiction between two levels of government. Surprisingly, the Upper Canadian leaders had agreed to the creation of a highly centralized federation. John A. Macdonald, of course, had long believed in the superiority of a unitary state (or legislative union), but George Brown had for years complained vehemently about the interference of Lower Canadians in local affairs under the unhappy union of the two Canadas formed in 1841. Yet Brown's Reformers, who dominated Upper Canadian politics, consented to the terms of Confederation because they believed that an acceptable balance had been struck by which local interests would be safeguarded while the national government was given power to manage economic development. Moreover, they expected that the new province of Ontario would dominate the federation, owing to its size and wealth.

These expectations were not to be realized; for Sir John A. Macdonald, as first federal prime minister, vigorously exercised the powers of the central government. Before long, the Ontario Reformers, now led by Edward Blake, began to express dissatisfaction at Macdonald's failure to consult the provinces and to demand a provincial veto over important constitutional changes. When Blake retired as Ontario premier in 1872, to be succeeded by Oliver Mowat, the forces of the 'provincial rights' movement acquired a leader of extraordinary longevity and superior political skill. Mowat had much to do with altering the shape of the Canadian federation in the late nineteenth century.

The most contentious issue between Ottawa and Toronto during Mowat's premiership was the dispute over the northwestern boundary of Ontario. Macdonald was eager to whittle down the size and influence of the province by awarding as much of the contested area as possible to the more compliant Manitobans. Mowat was equally determined to retain all the lands and their valuable resources lying west from the Lakehead to the Lake of the Woods. Efforts to secure an agreement between 1873 and 1878 with the more friendly administration of fellow-Liberal Alexander Mackenzie were allowed to drag on until Macdonald regained office in time to block a settlement. Bickering continued throughout the early 1880s until the courts sustained Ontario's claims. Even then the Judicial Committee of the Privy Council had to be appealed to a second time before Macdonald finally gave way in 1889. This dispute was also marked by personal bitterness between the two leaders, each one determined to extract the last ounce of political advantage from the conflict.

Oliver Mowat was determined to widen provincial powers, to raise the province, in fact, to a co-ordinate sovereignty with the central government, each supreme within its own sphere. In the effort to achieve this end he worked to extend the powers of the lieutenant-governor and, in particular, to resist the exercise of the federal cabinet's power to disallow provincial legislation. Here again Mowat's political skills proved an asset as he condemned Macdonald and his ministers for flouting the will of the duly elected representatives of the people. In 1887 he quickly seized on the idea of an interprovincial conference to review the state of the constitution and persuaded those premiers who attended to endorse his position. In this instance, however, Macdonald simply ignored the conference, and no changes were made in the BNA Act. Nonetheless, the interaction of political pressure, institutional change, and legal decisions which often bore little relationship to the intentions of the Fathers of Confederation combined by the end of the century to remould the constitution of Canada. In this process Ontario's influence was of paramount importance.[1]

I

For nearly fifteen years prior to the Quebec Conference George Brown and his Reform supporters from Canada West had been calling for constitutional change to put an end to 'French Canadian domination.' When Brown agreed to enter the 'Great Coalition' of 1864 with the Liberal-Conservatives under John A. Macdonald and George-Etienne Cartier, the new ministry pledged 'to bring in a measure ... for the purpose of removing existing differences by introducing the federal principle into Canada.' At the conferences in Charlottetown and Quebec that same year a general federation of the British North American colonies was agreed upon. With the Civil War in the United States much on their minds, the Fathers of Confederation determined to create a strongly centralized union to avoid any occurrence of a tragedy such as the Americans had suffered. In Macdonald's mind, 'The fatal error which they have committed ... was in making each State a distinct sovereignty, in giving to each a distinct sovereign power except in those instances where they were specially reserved by the constitution and conferred upon the general Government. The true principle of a Confederation lies in giving to the general Government all the principles and powers of sovereignty and in the provision that the subordinate or individual State should have no powers but those expressly bestowed upon them.' Hence section 91 of the BNA Act granted parliament power 'to make laws for the peace, order, and good government of Canada, in relation to all matters not coming within the classes of subjects by this Act assigned exclusively to the Provinces,' and sections 92 and 93 of the act enumerated the seventeen areas in which the provinces would possess jurisdiction. The new federal government, however, was also given power to nullify any piece of provincial legislation within one year of its passage by disallowing it or to prevent any bill from becoming law by refusing formal assent. Canada, the Fathers were determined, should never be plagued by a disruptive 'states' rights' movement.²

The leading Upper Canadian Reformers heartily approved of these provisions. George Brown thought: 'we have thrown on the localities all the questions which experience has shown lead directly to local jealousy and discord, and we have retained in the hands of the General Government all the powers necessary to secure a strong and efficient administration of public affairs.' To Oliver Mowat fell the task of introducing the resolution setting forth the limited provincial powers at the Quebec Conference. Delegate E.B. Chandler of New Brunswick immediately objected: 'You are adopting a Legislative Union instead of a Federal. The Local Legislatures should not have their powers specified but should have all the powers not reserved to the Federal Government, and only the powers to be given to the Federal Government should be specified. You are now proceeding to destroy the constitutions of the Local Governments and to give them less powers than they have had allowed them from England, and it will make them merely large municipal corporations.' But the Canadian coalition stood firm on the question of where the 'residual' power should rest, although Brown admitted, 'I should agree with Mr Chandler were it not that we have done all we can to settle the matter with sufficient powers to Local Legislatures.' The conference, therefore, accepted the wishes of the Upper and Lower Canadians.³

By section 92 of the British North America Act the provinces were given exclusive jurisdiction over sixteen specified areas, including natural resources, local public works, prisons, charities, the administration of justice, 'property and civil rights in the province,' and 'generally all matters of a merely local or private nature.' To carry out these responsibilities the provinces were permitted to levy direct (but not indirect) taxes, to borrow money, to sell or lease their public lands and resources, and to impose various kinds of licence fees. In addition, the new province of Ontario would receive a fixed annual grant of $80,000 for the support of its government plus a yearly subsidy of 80 cents per head of population for each of its 1,396,091 residents according to the census of 1861 or $1,116,872.80 in all.

The debate at the Quebec Conference revealed that the Upper Canadian Reform leaders accepted Chandler's claim that the provincial governments would be 'merely large municipal corporations.' In the interests of economy and simplicity Brown wanted to abandon parliamentary responsible government and create unicameral legislatures elected for a fixed three-year term. A small executive would be selected to advise the lieutenant-governor, a federal official appointed to 'bring these [provincial] bodies into harmony with the General Government.' This proposal, however, was too radical for the leader of the Lower Canadian *bleus*, George-Etienne Cartier, who thought it smacked of republicanism. Other delegates supported Jonathan McCully on Nova Scotia, who argued, 'We must have miniature responsible Governments.' The BNA Act, therefore, provided that Ontario should have a legislative assembly of eighty-two members with a responsible executive committee (or cabinet) consisting of an attorney general, a provincial treasurer, a provincial secretary, a commissioner of crown lands, and a commissioner of agriculture and public works. Yet there was little in these constitutional debates upon which to base the bold claims of co-ordinate sovereignty for the provinces made subsequently when Oliver Mowat had assumed the premiership.[4]

Why did the Upper Canadian Fathers of Confederation accept such narrowly circumscribed provincial powers? For John A. Macdonald, a believer in legislative union, the outcome was quite satisfactory. Within his lifetime he expected to see the provincial governments 'absorbed in the General Power.' 'My own opinion,' he wrote in 1868, 'is that the General Government or Parliament should pay no more regard to the status or position of the Local Governments than they would to the prospects of the ruling party in the corporation of Quebec or Montreal.' George Brown was equally happy; he wrote jubilantly to his wife from Quebec in 1864, 'all right!!! Conference through at six o'clock this evening – constitution adopted – a most creditable document – a complete reform of all the abuses and injustice we have complained of!! Is it not wonderful?' Later he would argue that 'the scheme now before us has all the advantages of a legislative union and a federal one as well ... By vesting the appointment of the lieutenant governors in the General Government, and giving a veto for all local measures, we have secured that no injustice shall be done, without appeal, in local legislation ... [A]ll matters of trade and commerce, banking and currency, and all questions common to the whole people, we have vested fully and unrestrictedly in the General Government.'[5] Was this the same George Brown who had spent the past fifteen years railing against Lower Canadian interference in the affairs of his province and demanding 'rep. by pop.'?

Brown, it must be remembered, spoke not only for the farmers of the western peninsula of Upper Canada but also for the ambitious businessmen of Toronto. The latter believed that a strong central government was a prerequisite for economic growth and western expansion, hence Brown's emphasis on the economic authority granted the central government. But the Reform leader was also convinced that the new constitution included safeguards for the vital interests of his locality. The composition of the Senate proved to be the most contentious and time-consuming subject at the Quebec Conference, precisely because that body was to represent regional interests and be selected on a regional basis to balance the House of Commons, where representation by population would rule. Seventy-two senators would be appointed by the federal cabinet, twenty-four from Ontario, twenty-four from Quebec, and twenty-four from Nova Scotia and New Brunswick. Defending himself against charges that he had abandoned the principles of representative government in consenting to this arrangement, Brown argued that 'our Lower Canada friends have agreed to give us representation by population in the Lower House, on the express condition that they shall have equality in the Upper House ... If from this concesson of equality in the Upper Chamber we are restrained from forcing through measures which our friends in Lower Canada may consider injurious to their interests, we shall, at any rate, have power, which we never had before to prevent them from forcing through whatever we may deem unjust to us.' The Senate, then, was intended to represent and defend regional interests against outside interference.[6]

Two other factors must have helped to still any fears which Brown may have harboured that a strong central government might use its power to work against the sectional interests of Upper Canada. Ontario would elect 82 members of parliament in a House of Commons totalling 181. Moreover, the province's population was rising steadily, by almost 225,000 between 1861 and 1871. (Quebec's population, by comparison, rose less than 80,000 in that decade.) In 1867 Brown told a convention of Reformers that in the redistribution following the 1871 census Ontario could expect to have 94 or 95 seats in the Commons, and ten years later, if the rate of population growth were maintained, it would have a majority in that body. (In the event, Ontario was allotted only 88 of 200 seats in 1872 and its representation peaked at 92 of 211 members in 1882.) Brown also naturally assumed that the vast majority of Ontario representatives would be loyal Reformers, ready to rally round whenever the province's interests were at stake. In an age when party lines were fluid, with Brown himself in a coalition including his leading opponents and many independent 'loose fish' among the legislators, he probably assumed that most of the Ontario representatives would respond to a call to protect the rights of the province. In addition, Ontario's twenty-four senators could be relied upon to see that justice was done.[7]

As a result, George Brown and his Reform supporters had no qualms about leading Upper Canadians into a highly centralized federal union, almost a legislative union of the type desired by John A. Macdonald. Ottawa would wield wide authority, especially in the field of economic policy, while exercising close supervison over provincial affairs through the lieutenant-governors and the power of disallowance. Cheap and simple provincial governments would manage local matters such as education, which had caused so much ill-feeling under the union of the Canadas between 1841 and 1867. And there were institutions and individuals who would see to it that Ontario's interests were not neglected at the federal level.

This easy confidence about the terms of Confederation did not survive many years after 1867. The Great Coalition began to fall apart following Brown's withdrawal in 1865, and within a few years an opposition party had coalesced around the Upper Canadian Reform tradition. It was not long before the Reformers began to raise objections to Sir John A. Macdonald's management of national affairs, including his conduct of relations with the provinces.

In 1869 Edward Blake, who had assumed the leadership of the Reformers in the Ontario legislature in opposition to the government of John Sandfield Macdonald, protested strongly against the granting of 'better terms' to Nova Scotia by the Conservative federal cabinet. To pacify the angry Nova Scotians Macdonald had given them a larger subsidy, and Blake promptly introduced in the assembly a series of thirteen resolutions attacking any alteration in the terms of the BNA Act without consultation with the other provinces. These thirteen resolutions articulated a view of provincial rights which Blake's successor, Oliver Mowat, was to elevate to the status of received truth. Reviewing the constitutional history of the Canadas, Blake argued that the union of 1841 had failed because Upper Canada had been unfairly treated. Confederation had remedied that situation, but now the federal government was unilaterally amending the terms of an agreement accepted by the provinces only a few years before 'in full settlement of all future demands on Canada.' Not only was this action unjust to Ontario, but as a result, 'the former evils so far from being removed by Confederation will be intensified, the just expectations of the people will be disappointed, sectional strife will be aroused, the Federal principle will be violated and the Constitution will be shaken to its base.' The consent of all the provinces, Blake insisted, was required for any alteration in the terms of Confederation.

What Blake had provided was the first classic statement of the 'compact theory' of Confederation, the contention that the federal union was the result of a compact or treaty among the provinces and could not be altered without their consent. Sandfield Macdonald's majority turned back Blake's first twelve resolutions but permitted the thirteenth to pass, fearing that many of the government's supporters would desert. This final resolution demanded legislation, presumably by the British parliament, 'to remove all colour for the assumption by the Parliament of Canada of the power to disturb the financial relations established by the Union Act as between Canada and the several provinces.'[8]

In 1871 Blake forced Sandfield Macdonald to resign. Blake explained his government's policy regarding the 'external relations' of the province this way: 'that there should exist no other attitude on the part of the Provincial Government towards the Government of the Dominion than one of neutrality; that each Government should be absolutely independent of the other in the management of its own affairs. As citizens of the Province of Ontario we are called upon to frame our own policy with reference to our Provincial rights and interests and to conduct our own affairs.' Although he pledged non-interference in the affairs of other jurisdictions, he referred specifically to his resolutions attacking the grant of 'better terms' to Nova Scotia as evidence of the fact that 'Occasions may arise ... in which the rights of the Province have been infringed, and upon such occasions, of course, it becomes the duty of the Province to act ... in order to prevent the infringement of the Provincial interests, of which we believe ourselves to be the guardians.'[9]

Blake's statement served notice that the Ontario Reformers had abandoned their previous acquiescence in a highly centralized federal system. This new attitude arose largely from partisanship. The Great Coalition of 1864 had dissolved, and Reformers like Brown, Blake, and Alexander Mackenzie were working to create a competing national party which would take office in Ottawa in 1873. If Macdonald's Conservatives were the party of centralism, then its opponents would become the party of localism and provincialism, recruiting the anti-Confederates of the Maritimes to the Reform cause. In 1872 the decision was taken to abolish dual representation, by which men like Blake, Mackenzie, and Sandfield Macdonald held seats in both the national and the local legislatures. Faced with the choice, Blake and Mackenzie decided to make their careers in Ottawa, and the Reform leaders persuaded Oliver Mowat to leave the judicial post he had held since the end of 1864 and return to active politics. On 25 October 1872 he was sworn in as premier, a post he would hold until 14 July 1896.

Mowat fully accepted the new Reform view of the federal system. Circumstances had changed since 1864 when he had moved the Quebec resolutions setting forth the powers of the general and local governments, content with a system in which the provinces would possess only a narrow range of specified powers. Now he shared the views of Blake, Brown, and Mackenzie, 'that if the province was to be governed from Ottawa, as it had been formerly from Quebec, the chief object of Confederation would be thwarted and provincial autonomy would become a delusion and a sham.' In his first address to the legislature he promised to follow the course already charted by Blake a year earlier. This marked the culmination of a process which had begun even before Confederation when George Brown resigned from the Great Coalition: 'Building on the deep Upper Canadian commitment to self-government and local authority and the developing grass-roots concept of majoritarian populist democracy, he and other Reform leaders began to articulate the relatively alien doctrine of classical federalism.' The compact theory of Confederation was the intellectual link provided by Edward Blake between the well-springs of Reformism and Mowat's day-to-day conduct of relations with Ottawa after 1872.[10]

II

When Oliver Mowat became premier he found the provincial government already embroiled in a serious dispute with Ottawa which had important implications for the future development of Ontario. The issue was the determination of the western boundary of the province.[11] The frontier between the old Province of Canada and the territories of the Hudson's Bay Company had never been clearly defined. In 1869 the new Dominion of Canada purchased all of the company's lands, and in 1870 created the province of Manitoba, a small area surrounding the Red River settlement near the present-day site of Winnipeg. In July 1871 Sandfield Macdonald and Sir John A. Macdonald agreed to appoint two commissioners to settle the problem, and William McDougall and E.E. Taché were chosen by the respective governments. Nothing had been achieved by the time Edward Blake became premier in December 1871, however, although the importance of reaching an understanding had already been pointed up by applications from private parties for mining licences west of Lake Superior. In the spring of 1872 the Ontario government received a confidential report from McDougall on his preliminary discussions with federal officials. He predicted that Ottawa would try to fix the same boundary as that stipulated in the Quebec Act of 1774, a line drawn due north from the confluence of the Mississippi and Ohio rivers crossing the north shore of Lake Superior in the vicinity of Port Arthur and extending to the height of land around Hudson Bay. However, McDougall argued that a review of the documents had convinced him that the western boundary of the province should be fixed at least as far west as the 'North-West Angle' of the Lake of the Woods, which was about 300 miles beyond the point proposed by the federal government. If Taché stuck to his position, no agreement between the commissioners would be possible, and the likely result would be 'protracted and angry discussion' between the governments.[12]

Within months of taking office, Blake was confronted with a major federal challenge to the rights of Ontario, in his mind an attempt to pare down the size and influence of the province and seize a vast quantity of resources which rightly belonged to it. The accuracy of McDougall's predictions was quickly confirmed when Joseph Howe, the secretary of state for the provinces, forwarded to Toronto his draft instructions to Commissioner Taché. The provincial government promptly ordered McDougall to have nothing further to do with the negotiations and passed an order-in-council, declaring it could not 'consent to the prosecution of the Commission for the purpose of marking on the ground the line so defined.'[13] The government of Sir John A. Macdonald complained that this policy of non-cooperation might mean that crimes committed in the disputed area would go unpunished. However, when Ontario replied by demanding that its boundary should run due north from the source of the Mississippi, slightly west of the Lake of the Woods, Macdonald hastily proposed that the whole matter should be referred to the Judicial Committee of the Privy Council in London, the highest appeal court of the empire, for a final interpretation of the treaties and documents. 'The mineral wealth of the country is likely to attract a large immigration into these parts,' wrote the prime minister; so a speedy settlement was required. Perhaps doubtful of the legal basis of the provincial case, Premier Blake would have

nothing to do with a reference to the Privy Council. Instead, he proposed that efforts to settle the matter by negotiation should continue and, in the meantime, that Ontario should be given jurisdiction over the entire disputed territory to avoid confusion over mining and timber licences and law enforcement. The federal government refused to make such concessions, and there the matter rested when Mowat became premier late in 1872.[14]

The new government preferred to do nothing rather than risk losing a case before the courts, and this patience was rewarded in the fall of 1873 when their fellow-Liberals under Alexander Mackenzie took power in Ottawa. Now Mowat could hope for a respectful hearing for the province's claims, and in the spring of 1874 the legislature passed a resolution calling for a settlement by arbitration. In the fall Provincial Treasurer Adam Crooks visited the capital and arranged that Ontario Chief Justice W.B. Richards (selected by the province) and Lemuel A. Wilmot of New Brunswick (chosen by Ottawa) should be appointed arbitrators with power to secure a third party as chairman. Meanwhile, the two administrations arrived at a temporary arrangement by which Ontario would handle all land grants as far west as longitude 91°30', near the headwaters of the Rainy River, at a point roughly half-way between the boundary proposed by Macdonald's government near Port Arthur and the province's claim that the north-west angle of the Lake of the Woods should form the limit. Once a final agreement had been arrived at, all grants could be ratified by legislation, but meanwhile development might proceed.[15]

Both governments placed their faith in negotiation rather than the arbitration, however; for it appears that Richards and Wilmot never bothered to choose a chairman. Mowat relied upon David Mills, a Liberal member of parliament and law teacher, to draw up the provincial brief. Mills suggested that a line drawn due north from the source of the Mississippi (just west of the Lake of the Woods) might form the boundary, but that the province was entitled to demand compensation for a huge area stretching as far west as the forks of the Saskatchewan. This bold claim was too much for even a friendly federal government, and the prime minister wrote privately to the premier in the fall of 1876, 'I think it is likely that we can agree to the western boundary [proposed by Mills], but it is utterly useless to talk of compensation for something upon a suppositious claim west of that. That cannot under any circumstances be even spoken of by us.' All the land within the watershed of Hudson Bay would also have to remain federal property, Mackenzie declared. As a result, the negotiations bogged down because the Ontario government was reluctant to abandon any of its claims without compensation, while Ottawa could not make such concessions without arousing protests in other provinces.[16]

Having arrived at a modus vivendi on land granting in 1874, neither government seemed eager to press for a quick settlement. The death of Lemuel Wilmot and the appointment of Chief Justice Richards to the Supreme Court of Canada stalled the arbitration completely. Not until 1878 did the two governments get around to naming their replacements. Chief Justice Robert A. Harrison of Ontario was then appointed by the province and Sir Francis Hincks by the Mackenzie government, and they chose the British minister in Washington, Sir Edward Thornton, as the third member of the board. Both governments committed themselves to accepting the arbitrators' findings as 'final and conclusive' and agreed to implement them by concurrent legislation. Fear of a Liberal defeat in the forthcoming federal election probably provided the necessary spur to action, and the arbitrators obligingly summoned the two parties for a hearing on 1 August 1878.[17]

Ontario was represented by the premier (and attorney general), Oliver Mowat, while Hugh MacMahon and E.C. Monk were retained by the Dominion. The province argued that its boundaries should be those claimed from the Hudson's Bay Company by the Canadas prior to Confederation and pointed to a statement made by Commissioner of Crown Lands J.E. Cauchon in 1857 that if Canadian territory did not extend all the way to the Pacific then it was bounded by a line due north from the source of the Mississippi to the shores of the Bay. These claims, it was noted, had been reiterated by federal negotiators when Rupert's Land was purchased in 1869. At the very least Mowat argued, Ontario extended to the north-west angle of the Lake of the Woods and perhaps even as far west as the Rocky Mountains. MacMahon stuck by the federal position that historical precedents validated a line running north from the confluence of the Ohio and Mississippi rivers and passing through the Port Arthur area to the height of land around Hudson Bay. The failure of the provincial government to object to the acquisition of Rupert's Land by Ottawa in 1869, he contended, debarred it from claiming additional territory later on. In rebuttal Mowat pointed out that 'there is no evidence that Ontario even knew anything about the matters which are said to estop her before these matters were finally concluded. In fact, they all took place without any reference to the Local Government.'

After three days of hearings the arbitrators produced a unanimous report which accepted almost all the province's claims: the western boundary should run due north from the north-west angle of the Lake of the Woods to the English River, then along the Albany River to the shore of Hudson Bay and follow the shore to a point north of the head of Lake Temiscaming. Ontario, it seemed, would have its way. A report to the government published in 1879 rejoiced that 'this fine region contains within its limits timber lands of great value, rich and varied mineral deposits, rivers and lakes of noble proportions ... the treasure of which, when sought with the ardour and appliances of modern enterprise, may yield a return not even dreamed of by those old explorers who were most sanguine of its resources.'[18]

On 17 October 1878, however, Sir John A. Macdonald once more assumed the prime ministership after a federal election, and when Provincial Secretary Arthur S. Hardy informed the federal authorities of his intention to introduce legislation to take possession of the disputed territory he received no response. The provincial legislature at its 1879 session duly passed 'An Act respecting the Administration of Justice in the Northerly and Westerly parts of Ontario,' but Macdonald continued to ignore requests by the province to bring down concurrent legislation to confirm the award of the arbitrators. The provincial government repeatedly claimed to have accepted the award, 'not because it was believed to have accorded to this Province all that was claimed on its behalf, or all that the Province might within its strict legal rights have had awarded to it, but because the tribunal appointed jointly by the two governments was one to whose competency and character no one could take exception, and because according to the judgement of the people of Ontario neither party to the arbitration could consistently with good faith refuse to abide by the decisions.' To the Mowat administration it might seem 'embarrassing and injurious' to have the award ignored, but to Macdonald's Conservatives the appointment of the arbitrators by Mackenzie and Mowat had been a 'solemn farce,' since only one of the three men chosen to resolve this complex legal tangle was a lawyer. The prime minister did not bother to answer the letters from Toronto calling upon him to act.[19]

In January 1880, however, the federal government at last took the offensive. Justice Minister James McDonald recommended that the recent Ontario legislation should be disallowed, because it concerned the administration of justice in territory which had not been recognized as provincial property. Mowat introduced a series of resolutions in the legislature setting out the Ontario case and again demanding that the federal government recognize the award of the arbitrators. Caught in a difficult political situation, provincial Conservative leader W.R. Meredith felt compelled to support the motion. Mowat responded to the threat of disallowance with the claim that 'there is far more reason for maintaining that the award gave us too little, than for maintaining that it gave us too much; and it gave us considerably less than Dominion Ministers had claimed before the purchase of the rights of the Hudson's Bay Company.' In the House of Commons the prime minister defended his actions by arguing that only the Judicial Committee of the Privy Council could finally determine the legal boundaries of Ontario, although he did support the appointment of a select committee of the House to look into the whole matter. Predictably, this committee found that the arbitrators' award did not set forth the true boundaries of Ontario. Meanwhile, the Ontario legislation was disallowed, and Mowat was able only to persuade Justice Minister McDonald to introduce a bill to provide for the enforcement of criminal law within the disputed territory. Moreover, in May 1880 Mowat took advantage of a petition from some businessmen in Rat Portage (Kenora) to create a divisional court there to administer justice in the area.[20]

The premier continued to press James McDonald to pass further legislation regarding the administration of justice. In February 1881 he wrote, 'I trust also that authority will be given to the Ontario Government to deal with the land and timber in the disputed territory, subject to our accounting therefor in case our right to the territory should not be maintained.' Another series of resolutions calling upon Ottawa to recognize the award of the arbitrators passed the legislature by a vote of seventy-five to one. The prime minister still paid no attention. In fact, he deftly countered in March 1881 by placing before the Senate a bill to extend the boundaries of Manitoba as far east as Port Arthur including the whole of the disputed territory. 'The effect of settling the boundary between these Provinces,' Sir John told the House of Commons, 'will compel, I do not say the Province of Ontario, but the present Government of Ontario, to be reasonable, and not to insist upon a boundary which cannot be supported in any Court or tribunal in the world. They will come to terms quickly enough when they find they must do so. To use an expression which is common in Scotland, it is land hungry they are for that country, and they are resolved to get it rightly or wrongly.' An additional reason for granting the entire territory to Manitoba was that the Dominion would still control all of the valuable lands and minerals. Macdonald frankly admitted that the area 'must be given either to Ontario or to Manitoba, and we cannot afford to give it to Ontario, if it belongs to the Dominion, because the lands would belong to Ontario. Keeping it as a portion of Manitoba, the lands belong to the Dominion.'[21]

The Ontario government immediately registered an 'earnest and vigorous protest' against this move. Dragging Manitoba into the fight between the province and Ottawa was 'an act of direct antagonism and hostility to the interests and rights of the Province of Ontario ... calculated to aggravate all existing difficulties and to prove most prejudicial to the harmony and accord which should prevail between the provinces of the Dominion.' The prime minister paid no more heed to this complaint than to any of the previous ones. He had put himself one up on Oliver Mowat and was confident that once Manitoba confirmed the extension of its boundaries by legislation the matter would be out of his hands. If anyone subsequently challenged the boundary the courts would have to settle the problem. Within a few months the provincial government objected that the federal government was granting land and timber rights to private parties within the disputed area, thus confirming Mowat's worst fears.[22]

In 1881 the premier decided to seek a private meeting with Macdonald in an effort to reach a settlement. But he gave warning beforehand that the province was not prepared to settle for anything less than the full award of the arbitrators, and he rejected the claim that the additional territory would make Ontario too big and give it 'undue weight' within the federation. On the contrary, he argued, with the award added Ontario's area would total about 200,000 square miles as compared with Quebec's 193,355 square miles; without the addition Ontario would occupy only 110,000 square miles. Why, he asked, should Ontario be only a little more than half as big as Quebec or about a quarter the size of British Columbia? The premier lectured Ottawa on how it ought to have behaved: 'It was the duty of the Federal authorities to protect the just rights of all its Provinces; to render unnecessary inter-provincial conflict for the maintenance of such rights; to employ the constitutional powers of the Dominion Parliament and Government respectively in minimizing the evils of a disputed boundary pending the settlement of the dispute; and to take such steps for determining such evils at the earliest possible date. Unhappily, the present Federal authorities have not chosen to discharge these manifest duties.[23] Not surprisingly, the negotiations with the prime minister in November 1881 proved fruitless, since he insisted that the whole matter be referred to the Supreme Court for a binding decision on the documents in the case. Ontario would have nothing to do with this idea.

Mowat repeated his attacks on the federal government in the 1882 throne speech, provoking Macdonald to complain that the premier really had no interest in a settlement: 'Mowat is thoroughly hostile. He is the mere jackal to Blake's lion and must be met in the same spirit.' The Ontario legislature discussed the boundary question on several occasions during the assembly's sitting and Mowat went so far as to threaten secession if he did not get his way: 'if they could only maintain Confederation by giving up half of their Province, then Confederation must go, ... and if they could not demand the large amount of property to which they were entitled without forgoing the advantages of Confederation, then it was not worth maintaining.' Before the House rose, however, Mowat introduced a resolution approving the idea of a reference to the British Privy Council, but only on condition that complete control of the disputed territory be handed over to the province in the meantime. Macdonald countered by having Manitoba pass an act incorporating Rat Portage (Kenora) as a Manitoba town during the summer of 1882, ignoring Ontario protests that the area had been under its control since 1871.[24]

The result was the great 'battle' of Rat Portage in the summer of 1883. Both provinces had appointed a number of constables who promptly set about arresting one another, arousing expectations that a general riot would ensue when the citizens released the Manitoban officers from the Ontario jail. In the end the violence petered out, but apparently it convinced the politicians that a settlement was overdue. Mowat, for instance, had called a provincial election in February 1883, and despite the fact that the Liberals had made much of the unjust treatment received by Ontario at the hands of the federal Conservatives, he had seen his majority reduced as the Tories won nine additional seats. Evidently, translating federal-provincial conflict into votes was no simple matter.[25]

In the fall of 1883 negotiations between the provincial governments of Ontario and Manitoba finally produced an agreement to refer the whole matter to the Judicial Committee of the Privy Council; in the meantime the disputed territory would be administered jointly. The Manitobans undertook to try to persuade Macdonald to join in this reference case so that any decision would be binding on all the parties concerned. In the spring of 1884 the prime minister agreed to participate in the reference to fix the boundaries, but at the last moment he withdrew, apparently content to let Manitoba bear the burden of making the federal case. The Judicial Committee undertook to hear the joint reference from the two provinces in the spring of 1884, with Mowat appearing personally for Ontario. The decision, rendered in July, was a satisfying victory for the province, since the Privy Council upheld the award of the arbitrators in 1878 on almost every point, fixing the western limits of Ontario at the north-west angle of the Lake of the Woods.[26]

This decision, however, was not binding until ratified by legislation, and Macdonald steadfastly refused to act. To increase the size of Ontario so greatly would unbalance the union: 'History will repeat itself and posterity will find out that the evils that exist in other federations from the preponderance of one or more members will again happen.' In the end, Mowat was forced to launch a suit against the St Catharines' Milling Company which was cutting timber in the disputed area under a federal licence. The Judicial Committee of the Privy Council found for the province in 1888, holding that the territory had been part of the Province of Canada prior to 1867 and thus had passed into the provincial domain at Confederation. At long last, in 1889, parliament adopted an address requesting the British to pass legislation fixing the western boundary of Ontario at the north-west angle of the Lake of the Woods, extending north-easterly along the English River to Lac Seul and the Albany River flowing into James Bay. The province thus secured not only the huge disputed territory west of the Lakehead but a considerable area north of the height of land separating the Great Lakes from the Hudson Bay watershed, precisely as the arbitrators had recommended over a decade earlier.[27]

The tenacity with which Oliver Mowat prosecuted the Ontario claim to the vast territories west of Port Arthur, including two trips to the Privy Council in London, reflected the value which he placed upon the territory to be gained for the province and its forests, minerals, and waterpowers and the partisan advantage he hoped to extract from the issue. Sir John A. Macdonald may have been right when he argued that the operation of the federal system might be impaired if one province became too big and too powerful, but the premier refused to make any concessions, particularly since his case had been upheld by the arbitrators – which made concessions politically impossible. He remained determined to secure control of all the resources of the province and manage them in the interests of Ontario citizens. Neither he nor the prime minister would give way, with the result that the wrangle lasted for fifteen years and embittered other aspects of the relations between the province and the central government.

III

The bitterness engendered by the Manitoba boundary dispute was most evident in the Mowat government's resistance to federal interference in Ontario affairs through the use of disallowance and the powers of the lieutenant-governor. During the 1880s there occurred a series of acrimonious disputes over the way in which the federal system should operate, disagreements which were settled mainly on Ontario's terms with a consequent diminution of federal powers. As a result, the federal system did not function in the way that the Fathers of Confederation had envisaged, because the provinces through political activity and through the decisions of the courts were gradually recognized as co-ordinate jurisdictions with the central government, fully sovereign within their sphere of authority and not at all like the glorified municipalities originally envisaged.

These disputes involved the authority of the lieutenant-governor, because Mowat perceived that the scope of provincial authority depended in part upon this official's prerogatives and powers. The Fathers of Confederation had intended that the lieutenant-governors should be officials appointed by the federal cabinet, whose function was to keep provincial policies in harmony with national objectives. To do so the governors were given power to nullify any provincial legislation by refusing assent or to reserve any bill for reference to Ottawa where the cabinet could decide whether or not it would come into force. Thus the governors were supposed to act at the bidding of the central government, but Mowat refused to accept this situation. He contended that the governor was the Crown's representative at the local level and hence was possessed of all the prerogative powers of the monarch which fell within the provincial sphere of authority. Not only was this role necessary if the provinces were to enjoy full responsible government, he argued, but it reflected the fact that the provinces were claiming to be co-ordinate sovereignties with the federal power, not subordinate entities.[28]

Thus, much of the debate over the office of the lieutenant-governor was concerned with whether or not he possessed certain prerogative powers of mainly symbolic importance. Should the governor receive royal salutes? Did he have the power to pardon offenders? Could he appoint lawyers as queen's counsel? In themselves almost trivial questions, they acquired their significance from their context as a part of Ontario's struggle to achieve wider provincial powers and to create a descentralized federation. In addition, patronage was at stake; in 1872 Oliver Mowat appointed a number of QCs. At that time Macdonald refused to be drawn into a conflict with the province, but in 1886, with relations soured by the conflict over the Manitoba boundary and other issues, a dispute did occur. The administration of justice was a provincial responsibility, and Mowat therefore argued that the governor had full prerogative powers to create QCs: 'The position of my Government is that the Lieutenant-Governor is entitled, *virtue officii* and without express statutory enactments, to exercise all prerogatives incident to Executive authority in matters over which the Provincial Legislatures have jurisdiction.'[29] The federal authorities rejected this contention and the issue was eventually referred to the courts. However, in 1888 Mowat passed legislation giving the lieutenant-governor authority to pardon offenders against the laws of the province. When Justice Minister Sir John Thompson objected to this act, a reference case was also submitted to the courts. Before a final decision could be given in either case, the Privy Council decisively settled these issues in another decision. In the matter of *The Liquidators of the Maritime Bank of Canada v. the Receiver-General of New Brunswick* (1892) the judicial committee upheld the full extent of the provincial claims which Mowat had been making over the past two decades: 'The British North America Act, 1867, has not severed the connection between the Crown and the provinces; the relation between them is the same as that which subsists between the Crown and the Dominion in respect of the powers, executive and legislative, public property and revenue, as are vested in them respectively.' In ringing phrases Lord Watson's decision sustained the notion that the central government and the provinces were co-ordinate sovereignties, separate but equal to one another: 'The object of the Act was neither to weld the provinces into one, nor to subordinate provincial governments to a central authority, but to create a federal government in which they should all be represented, entrusted with the exclusive administration of affairs in which they had a common interest, each province retaining its independence and autonomy.' The Supreme Court of Canada's subsequent decision on the reference case concerning the appointment of QCs reflected this new view of the constitution by upholding Mowat's claims on the grounds 'that the Lieutenant-Governor of a province is as much the representative of Her Majesty the Queen for all purposes of provincial government as the Governor-General is himself for all purposes of the Dominion Government.' With a vital assist from the Privy Council Mowat had gotten his way.[30]

About the power of disallowance there could be no doubt. By sections 56 and 90 of the BNA Act the federal cabinet was given authority to nullify any piece of provincial legislation within one year of the date upon which it was formally received by the secretary of state. This provision had been conceived by the Fathers of Confederation as another means of ensuring that local legislatures acted in harmony with national policies. No restrictions were imposed upon the exercise of this power by the constitution, but disputes soon arose, in which Ontario took a leading part, when the provinces claimed that disallowance violated local autonomy and substituted the will of a small group of federal ministers for that of the elected representatives of the people.

As the first minister of justice it fell to Sir John A. Macdonald to set forth the circumstances in which he would intervene, and in 1868 he reported: 'In deciding whether an Act of a provincial legislature should be allowed or sanctioned, the government must not only consider whether it affects the interest of the whole Dominion or not; but also whether it be unconstitutional, whether it exceeds the jurisdiction conferred on local legislatures, and in cases where jurisdiction is concurrent, whether it clashes with the legislation of the general Parliament,' Macdonald added that there should be as little interference with provincial legislation as possible and suggested that the provincial governments should first be advised of objections and asked to make the necessary changes in their acts.[31]

During the first fifteen years or so after Confederation the federal authorities pursued this relatively cautious policy. Almost all the acts disallowed were believed by successive justice ministers to be ultra vires, or beyond the constitutional powers of the provinces, and to interefere with federal policies in a significant way. Edward Blake, minister of justice in Alexander Mackenzie's government, stated the principles which guided him this way:

I maintain that under our Constitution ... the provinces have the uncontrollable power of passing laws, valid and binding laws, upon all those matters which are exclusively within their competence, except, perhaps, in the rare cases in which such legislation may be shown substantially to affect Dominion interests. If you are to admit the view that the Dominion Cabinet may veto and destroy your legislation on purely local questions, you make your local legislatures a sham, and you had better openly, honestly and above-board ... create one central legislative power and let the parliament at Ottawa do all the business.

The only appeal, Blake added, against clearly valid provincial legislation was to the local electorate rather than the federal cabinet.[32]

Despite this policy of non-interference by the central government, friction over the question of disallowance did arise with some provinces, including Ontario. In 1869 Sir John A. Macdonald nullified two acts passed by the province on the grounds that they were beyond the competence of the legislature. Protests from Attorney-General Sandfield Macdonald were ignored. In 1874 Oliver Mowat's government passed an act by which escheated and forfeited estates would become the property of the provincial treasury. The premier argued that the old Province of Canada had possessed these privileges and that it was 'undeniable that all rights of the provinces as they existed before Confederation have, by the Confederation act, been divided between the Dominion and the provinces, and that whatever has not been given to the former is retained by the latter.' This claim to all residual jurisdiction, quite contrary to the intentions of the Fathers of Confederation, was rejected by the Mackenzie administration and the act was nullified. When Edward Blake was minister of justice he did not hesitate to threaten disallowance of a number of Ontario acts which he believed were ultra vires of the province, and the Mowat government complied with his demands for amendments in each case.[33]

When Sir John A. Macdonald returned to power in 1878 he immediately became embroiled in the dispute over the north-western boundary of Ontario. In 1880 he disallowed an act passed by the province providing for the administration of justice in the disputed territory, pointing out that the boundary was far from settled. This intervention reflected the growing tension between the two levels of government. And the same kind of tensions apparently underlay the disallowance of the Ontario Rivers and Streams Act in 1881.

This legislation originated in a dispute between private parties. In 1879 Boyd, Caldwell and Company began lumbering on the Mississippi River, a tributary of the Ottawa, and floated their logs down that stream. Peter McLaren of Carleton Place attempted to prevent them on the grounds that he alone had financed the dams and improvements which made the river usable for driving logs, and in 1880 McLaren secured an injunction against Boyd, Caldwell and Company. In 1881 the Mowat administration, doubtless influenced by William C. Caldwell, Liberal member for Lanark North, introduced 'An Act for Protecting the Public Interests in Rivers, Streams and Creeks,' which permitted anyone to drive logs on a waterway upon payment of a fee to those responsible for any improvements. Peter McLaren, a Conservative, promptly appealed to the federal government to protect him by disallowing this legislation, claiming that his rights had been unjustly violated. Macdonald responded instantly; without even consulting the Ontario government he nullified the act. 'I think the power of the local legislatures to take away the rights of one man and vest them in another, as is done by this Act, is exceedingly doubtful,' wrote the prime minister, 'but assuming that such right does, in strictness, exist, I think it devolves upon this government to see that such power is not exercised in flagrant violation of private rights and natural justice.'[34]

Adam Crooks, the acting attorney-general, protested angrily at this swift intervention on behalf of a political ally. He defended the Rivers and Streams Act and denounced the disallowance of a measure clearly within the competence of the provincial legislature. 'The Confederation Act,' he reminded Macdonald, 'was intended to give practical effect to the exercise of the fullest freedom in the administration and control in local matters within each province, which was the main object of Quebec and Ontario, especially, in seeking such union.' Now local self-government was to be overturned 'on the private statement of a private individual.' So strongly did the provincial government feel that it reintroduced the legislation at the 1882 session of the legislature, doubtless with the enthusiastic support of the Caldwell interests.[35]

In disallowing the Rivers and Streams Act Macdonald undoubtedly departed from the principle generally adhered to during the previous fifteen years that only legislation beyond the jurisdiction of the provinces might properly be disallowed. 'Property and civil rights' as well as the natural resources of the province were clearly under the control of the local legislature, but the prime minister was sufficiently angry at Oliver Mowat to interfere. Indeed, he promptly disallowed the Rivers and Streams Act again in 1882 and once more in 1883 when the province persisted in repassing it. In 1884 the act was approved by the legislature for a fourth time, but by then the Judicial Committee of the Privy Council had found in favour of the Caldwell interests in a suit against McLaren. The judges held that the Rivers and Streams Act merely declared to be law certain principles which had been in force even prior to Confederation. Unrepentant, Macdonald continued to defend his action in 'protecting a man from a great wrong, from a great loss and injury, from a course, which if pursued, would destroy the confidence of the whole civilized world in the law of the land.' But he did not disallow the Rivers and Streams Act a fourth time.[36]

The rhetorical violence produced by the repeated disallowances of the Rivers and Streams Act can be explained partly by the pressure from competing private interests and partly by the desire of the politicians to make some capital. Mowat was happy to have an additional weapon with which to bludgeon Ottawa at the height of the dispute over the north-western boundary. He certainly attempted to capitalize on his role as defender of provincial rights in the provincial election of 1883. Similar considerations of politics and patronage also explained the row over Ontraio's new liquor licensing legislation. In 1883 Macdonald passed an act imposing federal liquor licensing, after strongly criticizing Mowat as 'a little tyrant who had attempted to control public opinion by getting hold of every office from that of Division Court bailiff to a tavern-keeper.' Even when the Privy Council upheld provincial authority in this area, Ottawa continued to enforce the new law. Mowat retaliated by bringing in legislation requiring those holding federal licences to pay additional fees to the province – a kind of fine for taking out a federal licence. This act was speedily disallowed by the federal government, but the courts eventually upheld Mowat's contention that the province had exclusive powers in the field of liquor licensing.[37]

After this rash of disagreements in the early 1880s, however, the power of disallowance ceased to be such an important factor in the relations between Ontario and the federal government. In part this change reflected Macdonald's recognition that the political price of such interference in local affairs was too high. Disallowance was a blunt instrument, and its use provoked cries of outrage. Except in the case of provincial legislation which clearly ran contrary to federal policy, it was better to leave the courts to decide upon the constitutionality of provincial statutes. J.S.D. Thompson, who became Macdonald's justice minister in 1885, was inclined to obey Edward Blake's dictum that disallowance could not properly be used on acts clearly within provincial jurisdiction.[38] The partisan bitterness aroused by the boundary dispute was probably more important in creating this conflict between the province and the Dominion than any clash of principles. Sir John A. Macdonald, ever the political pragmatist, used whatever weapon he had to hand to resist Mowat's pretensions, and Mowat, for his part, did all he could to arouse so much antagonism towards Ottawa that the use of disallowance against Ontario came to seem ill-advised.

IV

The combination of these grievances over the north-western boundary, the office of the lieutenant-governor, and the power of disallowance explains Ontario's enthusiastic participation in the interprovincial conference of 1887.[39] The idea that the provinces should meet and discuss changes in the federal system came from the new premier of Quebec, Honoré Mercier. Mercier's primary concern, however, was not so much with federal interference in local affairs but with financial matters. Quebec had not engaged in a series of wrangles with Ottawa of the sort which had embittered Ontario-federal relations, but the province was short of funds, heavily in debt, and constantly pressing Macdonald to concede better financial terms. In the spring of 1887 the Quebec premier suggested to Mowat a meeting to discuss 'the autonomy of the Provinces and their financial arrangements with the Dominion.' Although Mercier mentioned the need for the provinces to organize 'a system of common defence' against 'the centralizing tendencies manifested of late years by the Federal Government,' his real concern was clearly 'the inadequacy and injustice of the financial arrangements' in the BNA Act. In 1867, he pointed out, the provinces had given up customs and excise revenues worth $12,000,000 (which had doubled over the past twenty years) in exchange for subsidies of only $2,750,000 (now increased to $3,340,000).[40]

Better terms had little appeal for Mowat's government. Sandfield Macdonald had accumulated a large surplus while in office, and the Liberals had succeeded in balancing the province's books almost every year thereafter, partly through the sale of timber limits. Ontario did not need financial assistance, and its citizens would have to contribute the lion's share of the funds to provide larger federal transfer payments to the other provinces. Yet Mercier's approach found Mowat in a receptive frame of mind. The dispute over the boundary and the role of the governor was still dragging on, and the dust had barely settled from the row over the repeated disallowance of the Rivers and Streams Act and the liquor licensing legislation. A conference of the provinces, Mowat perceived, might be the perfect body to endorse the compact theory of Confederation and suggest constitutional changes to outflank the centralizing ambitions of Sir John A. Macdonald. Accordingly the Ontario premier replied that 'with regard to the financial arrangements this Province was satisfied with the provisions of the BNA Act and would still prefer them to any change,' but that his cabinet recognized the financial problems of the other provinces and agreed on 'the importance of resisting encroachments on provincial rights.' If new financial terms could be agreed on, this might stop Macdonald from dipping into the federal treasury whenever a province became so importunate as to threaten political damage. To Mowat and his ministers the $2,500,000 in railway subsidies granted to Quebec in 1884, under the threat that MPs from that province would withold their support for government measures, was only the most flagrant example of a practice against which Edward Blake had protested as early as 1869. In 1885 Commissioner of Public Works Christopher Fraser told the legislature:

we who have charge of Ontario affairs would be recreant to our trust if in the face of what we see going on, and what is absolutely certain to occur again, we made no sign and did not indicate that Ontario would not continue submitting to these raids by the other Provinces.

(Cheers) I say again, let there be any needful readjustment, and when such a readjustment does take place, let it be understood as an absolute and final settlement. That is the attitude of the Province of Ontario. We do not care to get these indirect and unwarranted grants, and that Ontario shall be the milk cow for the whole concern.

Mowat eagerly accepted Mercier's invitation.[41]

The interprovincial conference met in the fall of 1887 after much preliminary manoeuvring. Macdonald had brusquely refused Mercier's invitation to attend, and he succeeded in inducing the premiers of Prince Edward Island and British Columbia to decline as well. Thus, only the Liberal governments of Ontario, Quebec, Nova Scotia, and New Brunswick sent delegates to be joined by representatives from Manitoba's Conservative administration, angered by repeated disallowances of their railway legislation. When the conference opened on 20 October, Honoré Mercier addressed the delegates at length, pointing out the problems which had arisen during the past twenty years. Oliver Mowat was then chosen as chairman and the delegates settled down to a week of closed-door deliberations. On 28 October the meeting broke up after unanimously endorsing a list of twenty-two resolutions.[42]

Most of these resolutions bear the clear stamp of Mowat's influence. In opening the gathering Mercier had placed readjustment of the federal subsidy first among the necessary amendments, but in the final list it was relegated to seventeenth place, coming after changes in the direction of greater provincial autonomy desired by Mowat's government. First on the list, not surprisingly, was a demand for the abolition of the power of disallowance, and second came a proposal for the reference of constitutional issues to the courts for a determination of jurisdiction. Next came the call for Senate reform on the grounds 'that a Senate to which appointments are made by the Federal Government, and for life, affords no adequate security for the provinces.' Half the senators should be chosen by the provinces. In addition, the BNA Act should be amended to give the lieutenant-governor the full prerogative authority of the Crown within the sphere of provincial jurisdiction. This series of constitutional changes was clearly designed to give the provinces a larger role in national affairs of the kind for which Ontario had been contending over the past fifteen years.[43]

The other resolutions agreed to by the provincial delegates also concerned issues over which Ontario had clashed with federal authorities: local works should not be withdrawn from provincial jurisdiction by being declared for the general advantage of Canada without the concurrence of the province concerned; lists of electors should be drawn up solely by provincial enumerators; members of legislative assemblies should have the same privileges and immunities as members of parliament; the provinces should have some authority over bankruptcy and insolvency. Finally, all the delegates approved a demand that the northern and western boundaries of Ontario, as determined by the Privy Council, should be enacted into law by the British parliament. In each case Mowat's interest in these issues was well-known and was endorsed by his fellow premiers.[44]

Their interest, of course, was focused primarily upon the seventeenth resolution of the conference dealing with the revision of the subsidies. Existing payments were declared 'totally inadequate' and a hefty increase was demanded in the scale of grants for the support of government. In addition, the annual sum of 80 cents per capita was to be tied no longer to the population of 1861 but to the most recent census, with provinces receiving 60 cents per head for all population in excess of 2 million. This 'basis for a final and unalterable settlement' would have cost Ottawa almost $1 million more than the $3.2 million it had paid out in 1887 for these purposes, with Ontario alone receiving an additional $580,000. Any reluctance Oliver Mowat may have felt at supporting such large additonal subsidies, primarily funded by Ontario taxpayers, was overridden by three considerations: he had the support of the other premiers for the constitutional changes he desired; this act would be a final settlement to the subsidy question; and his government could doubtless put the additional money to good use. The conference concluded by agreeing to submit its resolutions to the provincial legislatures for approval and then to press Britain for appropriate amendment of the BNA Act.[45]

For all the fanfare which surrounded the interprovincial conference of 1887 (Mercier compared it explicitly to the 1864 Quebec Conference which had hammered out the Confederation agreement) its practical results were meagre. Macdonald refused to take any notice of it whatever, insisting it was no more than a Cabal of disgruntled Grits. When Mowat asked him to meet the premiers and formally receive the resolutions of the conference, he refused.[46] Nothing was done. But in a larger sense that was not important; for Macdonald had already abandoned the practice of aggressively disallowing provincial legislation of which he disapproved. In 1884 the Judicial Committee had upheld Ontario's boundary claims and in 1888 it again found for the province in the *St Catharines Milling Company* case, so that in 1889 Macdonald finally agreed to support legislation to grant the disputed territory to the province. The authority of the lieutenant-governor still remained unclear, but that issue, too, would eventually be settled in favour of the provincial claims by the Privy Council in the *Martime Bank* case in 1892. Although the BNA Act was formally unaltered, it hardly mattered.

By that time, too, Sir John Thompson had acquired more influence over legal and constitutional affairs at Ottawa. The Nova Scotian seemed more willing than Macdonald to allow the provinces to go their own way, an attitude demonstrated by a less aggressive use of the power of disallowance.[47] In 1890 Edward Blake proposed amendments to the Supreme Court Act to facilitate reference cases so that many jurisdictional disputes could be settled by the courts. Earlier legislation had permitted references to the Supreme Court, but since the judges were not required to give reasons for their decisions they simply gave categorical answers to questions put to them. In 1891 Thompson introduced the necessary amendments, permitting the court to take additional evidence and hear representations from all interested parties before issuing a reasoned decision.[48] The relationship between Mowat and Thompson was not marred by the kind of animosity that existed between Macdonald and Mowat,[49] and the Ontario premier readily agreed to the justice minister's suggestion in mid-1891 that he frame a reference case on the issue of provincial control over the inland fisheries. This proved to be the first of a series of important reference cases on matters such as prohibition and company law which were ultimately dealt with by the Judicial Committee of the Privy Council.[50]

Thus the trend towards greater respect for provincial rights was evident even before Sir John A. Macdonald's death in 1891, and in the words of one historian, 'After 1896 provincial rights and the compact theory attained a position close to motherhood in the scale of Canadian political values. It would be difficult to find a prominent politician who was not willing to pay at least lip-service to the principle of provincial rights and its theoretical underpinning, the compact theory.' Following the *Maritime Bank* decision, the Judicial Committee held in 1895 that 'the exclusive powers of the provincial legislatures may be said to be absolute.' Regarding the duty of the federal government to intervene through the power of disallowance to protect private rights the Privy Council declared, 'The supreme legislative power in relation to any subject-matter is always capable of abuse, but it is not to be assumed that it will be abused; if it is, the only remedy is an appeal to those by whom the legislature is elected.'[51] As we shall see, this doctrine was to assume a vitally important place in the relations between Onatrio and the federal government over the succeeding fifteen years.

In bringing about this constitutional revolution, which converted the provinces from glorified municipalities into co-ordinate sovereignties with the federal government, Sir Oliver Mowat had considerable help. In particular, the favourable decisions of the Privy Council provided the legal underpinning for the positions he fought for, yet he was also greatly assisted by his own political canniness. In his conduct of federal-provincial relations he mapped out the methods which his successors would follow up to the Second World War and after.[52] He placed the highest priority on achieving the widest possible independent control over the development of Ontario's resources, and for that reason he fought long and hard with Macdonald over the north-western boundary. He displayed little enthusiasm for increased federal payments from Ottawa to the provinces, preferring to levy and spend his own taxes, but he showed at the interprovincial conference in 1887 that he understood how to rally the other provinces behind him in his constitutional demands by making concessions in the financial field. The key to his defence of provincial rights was the compact theory of confederation, adumbrated by Edward Blake in 1869 but raised to a first principle of federal-provincial relations during Mowat's long tenure of office. It was the compact theory which provided the basis for claiming a veto over any constitutional changes, giving Ontario a strong weapon with which to defend its interests, which Mowat's successors would not hesitate to use. In 1896 Mowat resigned the premiership in response to Wilfrid Laurier's pleas to bolster up the new Liberal government in Ottawa; when the Ontario legislature met in 1897 his roly-poly figure was missing from the leader's chair for the first time in a quarter-century. Andrew Pattullo provided a glowing valedictory: 'In this long series of constitutional victories lies perhaps Oliver Mowat's highest claim to enduring fame and everlasting gratitude of his countrymen. For it was essential to the stability and very existence of Confederation that the rights and privileges of the Provincial and Federal Governments should be clearly and justly defined. Without such just consideration and protection of the rights of the Provinces by the Privy Council, it is quite certain that the Provinces would not have remained in the same union.'[53]

2 Federalism and Economic Development

In the late nineteenth century promoting economic growth seemed all-important to Canadians. Their country was underdeveloped, economically backward in light of the existing technological knowledge,[1] and comparisons with the United States provided incessant reminders of this fact. From the time of Confederation the federal government's chief instrument for promoting economic development was the protective tariff. No province benefited from the tariff more than Ontario which underwent rapid industrialization, and the 'National Policy' received hearty support from many in the province from the time of its inception in 1878.

Gradually during the 1890s, however, Ontarians began also to look to the provincial government to assist in promoting economic development. Dissatisfaction mounted in some quarters at being mere producers of raw materials to be manufactured elsewhere, at being 'hewers of wood and drawers of water.' Could the resources so painfully wrested from the Canadian Shield not be processed inside the country, thus creating further industrial activity? This sense of discontent came to a head as a result of changes in the American tariff in 1897 designed to encourage the importation of raw materials and discourage processed products from entering the United States market. The lumbermen and miners of Ontario looked first to the federal government for assistance but found the Laurier administration unwilling to act. They therefore began to press the provincial cabinet to help them.

After some initial hesitation the government of Arthur S. Hardy agreed to impose a 'manufacturing condition,' requiring all pine logs cut on crown lands to be sawn into lumber in Canada. This action by the province created conflict between Toronto and Ottawa. American lumbermen who had purchased timber limits in Ontario, intending to raft logs across the upper Great Lakes to American mills, put pressure on Ottawa to intervene and disallow the manufacturing condition. Pressure was also applied from Washington and London, but the provincial government stood firm. The apparent success of the new regulations in promoting growth in the lumber industry soon sparked demands for the extension of the manufacturing condition to minerals. It was claimed that this would lead to the creation of a nickel refinery in Ontario.

When the provincial government acted in 1901 there was an even more violent outcry by American nickel interests with operations in the Sudbury basin. This time Laurier proved more sympathetic than he had previously to those who complained that their rights had been violated. The minister of justice threatened to disallow the provincial act as an interference with trade and commerce. Although a compromise was eventually negotiated, the government of George Ross was sufficiently chastened that they never brought the manufacturing condition on nickel into force. The threats of the mining interests to close down completely their operations at Sudbury evidently had an effect.

After the defeat of the Liberals in 1905 by the Conservatives under James P. Whitney, the federal-provincial friction generated by resource development policy intensified. When the province reserved some choice mining limits on the bed of Cobalt Lake and sold them to a syndicate, a group calling themselves the Florence Mining Company attempted to overturn the transaction. Whitney promptly introduced legislation to confirm the deal and, later, another act banned any challenges to the sale through the courts. Once more, the aggrieved parties turned to Laurier for assistance. Although the federal government exerted considerable pressure to change the legislation Whitney stood firm, and the courts ultimately upheld the constitutionality of the provincial measures. In the case of both the manufacturing condition and Cobalt Lake what was significant was the role of private interests in provoking intergovernmental conflict as rival parties sought support either in Ottawa or at Queen's Park.

I

During the 1890s Ontario lumbermen began to abandon their traditional commitment to continental free trade in forest products and toy with the notion of a manufacturing condition. At the root was a shift in the popular conception of the province's future. That 'New Ontario' would one day be immensely valuable was clear: that was why Mowat had fought so long and hard with Macdonald over the northwestern boundary. The discovery of vast stands of timber, of new metals, and of huge expanses of arable land reinforced the belief that the area was a treasure-house. Lumber, pulpwood, nickel, copper, gold, and silver – all would find a ready market in the burgeoning factories and cities springing up throughout North America. Technology would at last overcome the obstacles which stood in the way of their exploitation. A combination of new resources and entrepreneurial talent would provide the underpinnings of a mighty 'Empire Ontario,' an industrial state which could become as rich and powerful as Germany or the United States itself. But none of these goals would be achieved without a struggle, and government must be prepared to aid in the task of building up 'Empire Ontario.'[2]

The Dingley tariff of 1897 served only to confirm this view of the world. The election of President William McKinley signalled the turn of the United States towards increased protection. Ontario lumbermen were shocked by the reversal of the trend towards free trade in forest products which had begun with the McKinley tariff of 1890. The Wilson-Gorman Act of 1894 had removed all American duty on logs and lumber imported from Canada. But the bill introduced into Congress by House Ways and Means Chairman Nelson Dingley in the spring of 1897 would impose a duty of $2 per thousand board feet upon sawn lumber imported from Canada. Logs would still be permitted free entry, but any effort by the Canadian government to encourage home manufacture by imposing export duties would be nullified by an ingenious provision: The amount of any new Canadian duties would simply be added to the American levy, thus closing the market to the imported lumber altogether. Ontario lumbermen, it seemed, must either be prepared to compete at a great disadvantage or resign themselves to shipping unprocessed raw materials to the United States. Imperial ambitions could never be fulfilled by becoming mere 'hewers of wood' for their rich southern neighbours; selling goods abroad to which maximum value had not been added by final processing meant 'pumping the life blood out of our country and sending it to vitalize the artisans and labourers of another country.'[3]

The sense of anger and frustration felt by Ontario lumbermen was fuelled by two additional factors. Export sales failed to increase as expected after 1894, in part because of the depression. Along the north shores of Lake Huron and Lake Superior, now the heart of the industry, Michigan operators began to purchase limits, towing booms of logs across the lakes to mills in their home state. The Dingley tariff threatened to reinforce this trend while destroying the export trade in sawn lumber from the province. If Ontario became the major source of pine timber for the north-eastern United States, another problem would loom before long: the need for conservation. White pine and even spruce were becoming increasingly scarce south of the border, and local lumbermen insisted that 'the granting of special facilities or privileges to Americans to come here and slaughter our forests should not be given.'[4]

The immediate reaction to the Dingley bill was strenuous lobbying in Washington by Canadian lumbermen. That action failed to produce results. In July 1897 the new duties came into force. Since trade policy was recognized as a federal responsibility, Ontario operators turned at once to Ottawa for help, demanding that the old export duty of $2 per thousand board feet on logs should be reimposed to force the Americans to negotiate. In June 1897, after leading businessmen within the Liberal party had applied pressure to the cabinet, the government was induced to put through a bill giving it power to impose export duties on sawlogs, pulpwood, and minerals by order-in-council as retaliation for the Dingley tariff. But the ministers were divided on whether or not to proclaim the new act for fear of further provoking the United States. Moreover, the prime minister was already sounding out the McKinley administration on the possibility of a reciprocal free trade agreement on natural products as part of a general settlement of outstanding Canadian-American differences. Laurier refused to endanger these negotiations by imposing new trade barriers.[5]

Here the dynamic role of private interest groups in intergovernmental relations became clear. The lumbermen of Georgian Bay, bankruptcy staring them in the face, could not afford to await the outcome of bargaining with Washington. They needed protection against American policy at once, and if Ottawa refused to grant it, then the province must be made to do so. The BNA Act, after all, conferred ownership of lands and natural resources on Ontario. Upon these proprietary rights provincial management of resources depended: the Ontario government was landlord to the lumberman. Why not insert in the annual timber licence a regulation requiring all logs cut on crown lands to be sawn in Canada? Such a manufacturing condition had an additional advantage: since it was not an export duty it would not lead to retaliation under the Dingley act. As John Bertram, a prominent Liberal businessman, put it in a letter to the *Globe* early in August, the manufacturing condition 'would be purely a domestic matter for Ontario to deal with and would meet the exigencies of the case in a way that would be fair to all parties.' Bertram and E.W. Rathbun took the lead in reviving the moribund Ontario Lumbermen's Association in order to put pressure on the government of Arthur S. Hardy.[6]

Convincing the province to act was no easy task. As early as 1886 Conservative leader W.R. Meredith had complained that Mowat was making no effort to have Ontario timber manufactured locally, and in 1887 he had proposed a manufacturing condition for timber licences. In reply Education Minister George W. Ross clung to laissez-faire: 'The Government was prepared to sell timber to the highest bidder. It was not prepared to impose conditions that would debar American millionaires from paying high prices for Canadian limits.' Arthur Hardy, then provincial secretary, argued that the matter had nothing to do with the province: 'The question has been considered by the Government, and they have decided to let the Dominion Govenment take the responsibility of foreign policy.' In 1890 the crown lands department did sell a few limits subject to a manufacturing condition, but it was dropped for the 1892 sale. Restrictions were proposed in both 1893 and 1894 by Conservative MPP Andrew Miscampbell but were voted down by the Liberals. An 1894 election pamphlet entitled 'Export of Saw Logs to the United States' unequivocally stated the Mowat government's position: the matter was 'one with respect to which the Dominion Government has recognized its responsibility by dealing with it frequently both by legislation and by regulation,' so 'it is advisable that the Provincial Government should not interfere.' So determined were the Liberals to remain uninvolved that the anonymous pamphleteer sounded like a confirmed centralist: 'Is it advisable under these circumstances that any individual province should undertake to interfere with a question which is purely one of trade and commerce, and by its action seriously and adversely affect this great trade with which the welfare of the commercial interests of the whole Dominion are interwoven and bound up?'[7] Governments do no more than they are compelled to.

By 1897 the pressure was mounting. On 19 August the Ontario Lumbermen's Association voted by forty-eight to eleven to change the Crown timber regulations, although Ottawa valley lumbermen were much less enthusiastic than their counterparts in Georgian Bay. J.M. Gibson, the commissioner of crown lands, regarded any alteration in the timber licence as a breach of faith with limitholders. Yet he admitted that 'there was such a jingo wave and feeling ran so high that in view of the near approach of the election they might be obliged to move in that direction.' During September the cabinet was besieged by delegations from the Lumbermen's Association and the American limitholders whose interests were threatened. Buffeted to and fro, Hardy stalled for time. On 16 October the Association reiterated its demands by a vote of forty-two to four, and when the legislature met, Conservative leader James P. Whitney took the floor to denounce the Michigan operators: 'Are we,' he roared, 'to stand like cravens and allow these men from Michigan to work their will?' In December the lumbermen met the cabinet again. Rathbun put their case succinctly: 'If it were a condition that the timber should be manufactured in this country, the transfer of capital and enterprising men from the United States to Canada would be greater than ever before.'[8]

The demand for action became irresistible. Without consulting federal authorities, Hardy himself announced that the Crown Timber Act would be amended. Many Liberals, like J.S. Willison of the *Globe*, believed that continued failure to act would have cost the Liberals the coming election. So effective had the public relations efforts of the lumbermen been that the bill passed without a division. The people of the province had been persuaded by a small private interest group that the manufacturing condition represented a significant step in the creation of 'Empire Ontario,' compelling the government to take action. With an impending provincial election on 1 March 1898 the Liberals took what credit they could for the new policy,[9] and the narrowness of their victory erased any thought of retreat. On 30 April 1898 the embargo on exporting pine sawlogs came into force; henceforth all timber cut on crown lands had to be manufactured in Canada. Yet the Hardy administration would soon discover that this foray into the field of development policy had its cost.

In June 1898 the federal cabinet agreed to the creation of a joint high commission to deal with all outstanding Canadian-American problems. In the negotiations for free trade in natural products the manufacturing condition proved central. Sir Wilfrid Laurier wrote: 'Lumber is really the key of the whole situation. It ought to be free between the two countries, and if it were free all the other little troubles would be speedily removed.' But the Michigan limitholders were determined that there would be no agreement as long as the embargo remained in force. On 11 June lawyers Don M. Dickenson and Robert Lansing petitioned the secretary of state on their behalf, claiming that the new regulations were confiscatory, since they had destroyed the value of limits in which their clients had invested some $12 million. They suggested that the embargo should be suspended until the high commission could deal with the trade question. Two days later they discovered an even better solution: Washington should ask Ottawa to disallow the legislation.[10]

Secretary of State William R. Day endorsed their protest and forwarded it to the British ambassador, Sir Julian Pauncefote, with the suggestion that the colonial office use its influence to have the embargo suspended. Meanwhile, through Sir Louis Davies, Dickenson made a direct approach to the federal government asking for disallowance. The matter was discussed in cabinet and Justice Minister David Mills was requested to make a formal report on the constitutionality of the legislation. Davies, however, did not hold out much hope to the Americans. He pointed out that the Dingley tariff which had led to the embargo 'placed Canadian lumbermen at an intolerable disadvantage and practically deprived Ontario of the benefits which she would derive from the cutting of her own timber in her own territory.' As for disallowance, timber licences were a provincial matter, and

The law advisers of the Dominion Government have consistently held that it is not proper for us to veto any Statute of a Provincial Legislature, even if unconstitutional, leaving the point of unconstitutionality to the courts, unless such act contravenes some settled policy of the Central Government ...

From what I have said you will see that it would be a very drastic and dangerous step for the Central Government to veto the legislation of the character such as you call to my attention. The Provinces certainly would never submit to it, and it would give rise to something akin to a social revolution.[11]

Nonetheless Arthur Hardy soon found himself under heavy pressure to withdraw the embargo in order to assist the commissioners in their task. Acting Prime Minister Sir Richard Scott suggested that the premier should offer to suspend it in return for free trade in forest products. Joseph Chamberlain, the colonial secretary, added his voice to those calling for the whole matter to be left to the high commission. But Hardy proved obdurate: using the embargo merely as a bargaining counter had been discussed with the lumbermen in the fall of 1897, but the expectations aroused by the manufacturing condition had now rendered such tactics impossible:

It is ... quite obvious that whatever the American tariff may be in future, an unlimited right of lumbermen, American or Canadian, to cut and carry away logs from the lands of the Crown to be sawn in the United States would not satisfy public opinion. A few years of general and unlimited cutting for American mills ... would make such vast inroads on our forest reserves as virtually to overturn the policy heretofore pursued by the Province of reserving sufficient white pine forests to answer the requirements of the country and of Canadian mills, and to provide Provincial revenues for all time to come ... The Government therefore do not see their way to assent to the suggestion no matter what may be offered by way of a reduction or abolition of duty on Canadian lumber.[12]

Having imposed the embargo reluctantly, Hardy was now determined to reap every possible ounce of political benefit from its popularity.

To demonstrate his soundness on this issue the premier proposed to make reference to the American and British pressure in the throne speech at a session of the legislature called for 5 August 1898. Laurier sought to restrain him from giving further offence to the United States. 'At present,' he wrote to Scott, 'the best policy on this point is to keep absolutely silent.' Scott evidently succeeded in convincing Hardy, since the throne speech referred only to the depression in the lumber trade caused by the Dingley tariff. When the opposition pressed him to table all correspondence with Washington regarding the embargo, he refused, stating only that in his reply to Day's note 'the contention of the American lumbermen is opposed throughout.' But he promised that if the matter was dealt with by the high commission, Ontario would be represented.[13]

In a formal response to the petition from the Michigan limitholders, Hardy as attorney-general defended both the legality and the propriety of the manufacturing condition as one of many crown timber regulations. Ontario's forests, he noted, had netted the province an average of $750,000 every year since Confederation or a third to a quarter of the provincial revenues. Never before had control of this provincial domain been challenged. What right had Ottawa or anyone else to interfere with resource management? The Crown Timber Act of 1898 was indubitably constitutional, and 'The justice or otherwise of the act in question is not to be determined by the Dominion Government. There is scarcely a general law affecting civil rights in this Privince now on the Statute books which has not at its introduction been objected to on grounds that it worked injustice or hardship to some class affected by it.' Only the legislature could lift the embargo.[14]

Privately Hardy warned the prime minister that he would insist on being present if the high commissioners discussed the embargo; for he was much concerned that Ontario's interests might be sacrificed in the drive for reciprocity. 'If the statement is true that the American Commission require the abandonment of certain lines of policy of your Government prior to even entering into negotiation it would be fatal if their views were complied with. That does not appear to me to be negotiation of any form – it is a stand and deliver demand; and just so, too, if they take that stand in relation to our Timber Act.' Although Joseph Chamberlain was equally determined to exclude provincial representatives from the commission's deliberations, Hardy and his senior colleague, George Ross, journeyed to Quebec City in September to be present at the first session as observers. They achieved little, although they did meet Congressman Tawney, chief lobbyist for the Michigan lumbermen, who also held a watching brief.[15] Before long they returned to Toronto. To the relief of the provincial ministers it soon became clear that the enthusiasm for freer trade on both sides had largely evaporated. Although the commission met twice more in Washington, it made no substantial progress on this issue. Ontario apparently had defied successfully the pressure of the United States to establish control over the development of its forest industries.

Yet the deadline for disallowance did not expire until 24 April 1899, and as the date approached, pressure upon Ottawa to intervene increased. John Charlton, one of the high commissioners and a lumberman with extensive interests on both sides of the border, took the extraordinary step of drafting a petition for his friends, the Michigan limitholders, asking Treasury Secretary Lyman J. Gage to use his power to declare the manufacturing condition a de facto export duty and thus bring the retaliatory provisions of the Dingley Act into force. This move would effectively close the American market to Canadian lumber and force Laurier to nullify the embargo. When the news arrived in mid-April that Gage was about to act, Charlton was delighted. Laurier hastened to protest this 'most unfriendly' step, and enquiries in Washington ultimately revealed the rumour to be unfounded. The prime minister remained adamant in his refusal to intervene: 'Our American friends can fight it in the law courts, as suggested to them in the interview we had with them, but evidently they have set their hearts upon obtaining from us a promise that we would disallow the Ontario Act, which certainly would have been a very summary but not very liberal way of restoring them to their position.'[16] Finally the deadline passed.

The Michigan limit-holders refused to give up. They sought to persuade congress to amend the Dingley Act to cover the manufacturing condition. Laurier dispatched Edward Farrer to Washington to find out what was going on, and he reported that while the administration would oppose such a move, congress might take matters into its own hands. Perhaps, Farrer suggested, Laurier could take the steam out of these attacks upon Ontario policy by inducing Hardy to suspend the embargo until it had been tested in the courts. The prime minister agreed. In mid-May he suggested to Premier Hardy that any new legislation which would exclude all Canadian lumber from the American market would be 'most detrimental if not absolutely fatal to the Ottawa lumbermen, and both to the lumbermen of Quebec and the Maritime provinces.' Why not a suspension to deflect congressional criticism? The premier, a good Liberal was pained: "There is scarcely anything that we would not do to meet your views on political questions within the compass of our authority, and what might be thought to be practicable.' But he could not safely accede. Any reference to the courts would immediately be attacked as a backhanded method of withdrawing the embargo: 'A dozen constituencies could not be carried today if we were to declare a policy hostile to the Act, or even one which would leave us open to a large measure of suspicion in that area.' Hardy could spare no sympathy for the lumbermen in other provinces: 'Self preservation is a very strong law, as you know, and just at this moment we may have several by-elections coming on, and we cannot afford to place in the hands of the enemy a club such as that we have voluntarily allowed the case to go to the courts, as they will say or insinuate with a direct view of giving the case away. they would assuredly say so if the opinion of the Court was against us.'[17] If the Michigan lumbermen wanted to test the law, let them sue.

When they finally did prepare a suit, however, they suffered another rude shock. Hardy as attorney-general refused them the necessary fiat to take the Crown to court unless they dropped all claims for damages. Their lawyer wrote angrily, 'Attempting to deal with the Hardy Goverment is simply ludicrous ... [I]f this attitude is insisted upon by the Ontario Government I shall urge the American Government to at once put an end to negotiations with a country possessing a government which acts like this.' Laurier suggested a compromise, but the premier had already had second thoughts and early in July granted the fiat. Laurier also tried to persuade the lumbermen to cease their pressure upon congress for retaliation, but they refused to do so unles the embargo was suspended during the summmer towing season when log booms could cross the lakes. Since the provincial government would have nothing to do with this idea, the matter was dropped.[18]

John Charlton was not ready to leave the courts to decide. Instead he took the unusual step of writing to the British chargé d'affaires in Washington to ask the colonial office to use its influence upon 'the very queer specimen of a Government at Toronto.' When this letter was forwarded to Ottawa for comment, the reply contained a reminder that the Americans had acted first in imposing the Dingley tariff. As a result, 'public opinion in Ontario would not sustain the government in suspending the Act.' Still, Charlton, a Liberal member of parliament, and his brother William, a Liberal MPP, persisted owing to their large personal interests. Because of the Charltons' party connections the provincial cabinet agreed to grant them a hearing. John argued that the Michigan men had already filed damage claims totalling more than $1 million with Washington. Suspension of the embargo would mean that these claims would be dropped. William added that Laurier 'had directed him to state that he was extremely desirous that the law should be suspended.' The ministers ignored them. Then the two brothers proposed that log exports be permitted during the 1899 season, the limitholders to post a $2 million bond to be paid as penalty if the courts rejected their suit. Nothing came of this proposal either.[19]

During the summmer of 1899 a planned session of the joint high commission was first postponed then abandoned altogether. The final failure to reach a free trade agreement naturally meant that the sawlog embargo steadily declined in importance as an issue in Canadian-American relations. By then the manufacturing condition appeared to be an unqualified success. Lumber prices rose throughout 1899 and new mills sprang up along the Canadian shores of the upper Great Lakes, providing 1,000 new jobs. The government of Ontario, once so reluctant to act, could now pose as the inventor of a potent new engine for economic development. Their triumph was complete when the Ontario supreme court upheld the constitutionality of the embargo, a decision with which the Privy Council ultimately concurred. By the time of the 1902 election the Liberals were even claiming that they, not the Conservatives, had had the idea in the first place.[20] The plight of the Michigan limitholders was forgotten.

With the zeal of converts the cabinet now set about applying the manufacturing condition to other resources. An obvious candidate was pulpwood, upon which similar regulations were soon imposed. True, this action did not prove an immediate success, but that was because the province of Quebec refused to introduce similar restrictions, which offered American paper-mills an alternative source of supply.[21] Nonetheless, as the demand for Ontario's resources in the continental market steadily grew, the province's future seemed to be lit by the rosy glow of prosperity.

II

The manufacturing condition might appear to be the key to unlock the immense treasure-house of 'New Ontario,' but it had already proven a source of federal-provincial friction as well. And that lesson would be repeated unmistakably when the Ontario government, still in the first flush or enthusiasm, sought to extend a similar condition to the nickel ores of the Sudbury basin. Here, too, the ability of businessmen to mobilize government for their own ends was made quite clear, and it was this factor more than anything which propelled the two governments into conflict with one another, despite the mediating ties of party solidarity.

Discovered in 1883 during the construction of the CPR, Ontario's nickel-copper mines attracted only mild interest at first. Gradually the properties of nickel-steel alloys, particularly for armour-plating, became widely known. Suddenly there was a new interest in this vital strategic material. By the 1890s, however, the province had already sold most of its choicest nickel-bearing lands outright. The industry was dominated by the Candian Copper Company, whose entire output was shipped to the plant of R.M. Thompson's Orford Refining Company in Constable Hook, New Jersey. Only Orford (which would amalgamate with Canadian Copper and the Canadian Mining and Metallurgical Company in 1902 to form International Nickel) possessed the technical skill and the capital resources to handle successfully the refractory ores of the Sudbury basin. Most of the rest of the world's demand was supplied from the French penal colony of New Caledonia in the southwestern Pacific. As the demand for nickel rose during the last decade of the century, shipments of ore and partly smelted matte from Canada to the United States rose steadily.[22]

The Dingley tariff of 1897 placed ore and matte on the free list but imposed a duty of 15 cents per pound on fine metal. Since there were no refineries in Canada, the immediate effects were minimal. The loudest protest against the new tariff came from Samuel J. Ritchie, recently ousted as a member of the Canadian Copper syndicate. Ritchie's plans to found a nickel-steel complex in Canada were many and varied, and in due course he joined with a group of prominent Hamilton businessmen, John Patterson, A.T. Wood, and J.M. Gibson. Leading Liberals all, they supported Ritchie's demand that the Laurier government should assist them by imposing an export duty on nickel. The cabinet took power to impose such a levy on ores and metals in the summer of 1897, but the promoters of the Nickel Steel Company, like the lumbermen of Georgian Bay, found that the prime minister was unwilling to jeopardize the pending trade negotiations with the United States. R.M. Thompson warned Laurier in no uncertain terms that any increase in duty would lead Canadian Copper to close its Sudbury operations, throwing 1,500 men out of work, and get its nickel from New Caledonia instead. The government refused to impose any duty on nickel.[23]

Rebuffed in Ottawa, Ritchie and his friends did precisely what the Ontario lumbermen had done: in the fall of 1899 they turned for help to the province. They could be certain of a sympathetic hearing at Queen's Park, since one member of the syndicate, J.M. Gibson, had just become attorney-general in the new administration of George W. Ross. Although an opponent of the sawlog embargo at the outset, Gibson now took quite a different view where his own interests were involved; and the province's civil servants were equally enthused by the apparent success of the manufacturing condition in laying the foundations of 'Empire Ontario.' In November Archibald Blue, director of the bureau of mines, suggested that government take steps to encourage nickel refining. First of all the federal government was formally requested to impose an export duty on ore and matte; once again Laurier refused. It was decided that all future mining licences should contain a manufacturing condition, but this point was largely academic, since the best claims had long since passed into private ownership. Accordingly, the provincial cabinet decided in the spring of 1900 to amend the Mines Act and impose a prohibitive tax on all ore exported from Canada and refined outside the British Empire. Mine operators would be charged a licence fee of $7 for every ton of ore raised and $50 for every ton of matte smelted, but these sums would be rebated entirely if the nickel were refined in Canada. The Conservatives made no objection to these changes, grumbling only at the government's belated conversion to a policy which they had first suggested. The new tax would come into force only when proclaimed by an order-in-council.[24]

Whether or not Gibson's colleagues understood exactly what they were getting into with the new Mines Act (and there is some question about whether the other ministers recognized the full implications of the legislation), they were swiftly reminded of the ability of rival interests to use the federal system for their own ends. The Canadian Copper Company was already preparing its defences. It had claimed that it was impossible for it to undertake refining in Canada because R.M. Thompson would not permit it to use certain patents which he owned if it were in competition with his Orford Refining Company. When it was pointed out that Orford had carelessly allowed its Canadian patents to lapse, freeing all comers to use them, notice was hastily given in the House of Commons of a private bill to revive them. Premier George Ross protested that Canadian Copper was simply trying to protect itself from competition. Laurier's reply was soothing: 'There seems to be no reason, at first sight, to pass such legislation, and I fully agree in all the reasons you state, but it may be preferable to wait until the Bill is formally introduced before formally deciding on any course.' When A.T. Wood of the Hamilton syndicate raised the matter in the House, however, Sir Louis Davies was equally non-committal. The nervous Ross put through the legislature a resolution condemning the patent bill which received Conservative support. But the Thompson interests were not without their own influence in high places. When the bill came up it was not opposed by the Liberals and soon passed.[25]

Thus fortified, Canadian Copper could turn its attention directly to the new provincial legislation. Company counsel Wallace Nesbitt warned Gibson that he would ask the American secretary of state to intervene with the colonial office if the tax were imposed. Ross became concerned that the company might use its influence in Ottawa to have the new Mines Act disallowed. Defensively he wrote to Laurier, arguing that the federal government itself would have imposed an export duty had it not been for the trade negotiations with Washington. He promised that the act would not be proclaimed law without a 'reasonable certainty that nickel can be refined in Canada as easily as in the United States.' Once more the prime minister's reply seemed reassuring: 'we have no intention of disallowing your Mines Act, though representations made to us have been rather vociferous, and I may tell you that I have not paid much attention to the strength of the complaints, as by tradition as you know we are not in favour of disallowance.' Yet the representations continued. In September 1900 lawyer W.R.P. Parker formally petitioned for disallowance. Nominally representing a group of mining claim owners, Parker was really speaking for Canadian Copper, and he argued that the new tax would in fact be an export duty and thus an unconstitutional attempt by the province to regulate trade and commerce. If not nullified it would destroy vested rights and cause investors to withdraw.[26]

It fell to Gibson as attorney-general to reply formally to Parker's petition. In December he forwarded to Ottawa a strong defence of the legislation. Drawing upon the example of the sawlog embargo, he denied that the tax was an effort to regulate trade and commerce. Rather, it was designed to regulate the use of the province's resources and to raise revenue. When nothing further was heard from the justice department, Gibson assumed that the matter had been settled: there would be no disallowance. But as the deadline for such action, 18 May 1901, approached, the assaults upon the legislation continued. Indeed, they redoubled. Two British concerns with small Canadian operations, the H.H. Vivian Company and the Mond interests, now entered protests, probably at R.M. Thompson's behest. Acting for Dr Ludwig Mond, J.M. Clark reiterated the points raised by Parker's petition, and also noted that while the act remained unproclaimed it could not be tested in the courts. Once the deadline for disallowance had passed, the federal government would be unable to prevent it taking effect by a simple order-in-council.[27]

Other letters began to rain in upon the prime minister, most harping upon the danger of a flight of capital form Canada. Parker, for instance, returned to the fray with the claim that the act had struck 'a very great blow ... to the credit of Canada.' The general manager of the Bank of Montreal, E.S. Clouston, delivered an equally dire warning:

The inevitable result, if it is permitted to remain on the Statute Book, will be the closing of the doors to the flow of English capital into this country. Dr. Mond is a very prominent man not only in the scientific but also in the manufacturing world, and if it is known in the London markets that after investing very largely in this country his property was practically confiscated by the Ontario legislature, it will have a very serious effect on future English enterprises here.

A cabinet committee including the prime minister, Clifford Sifton, and A.G. Blair heard a delegation of mine-owners make similar points during April. Stevenson Burke, the president of Canadian Copper, warned Sir Richard Cartwright against the siren song of those behind the manufacturing condition: 'They have theory, theory, theory – nothing else. Let them produce something marketable before you destroy by your orders this industry you now have.' John Bertram, an enthusiastic supporter of the sawlog embargo, warned Laurier that along with many other Ontario Liberals he disliked the mining legislation and believed that disallowance would help the party. Businessmen, he claimed, hesitated to come out openly against the act for fear of vengeance by the provincial government.[28]

Ross and his ministers were now forced to defend their new Mines Act against all of these charges: that it was not only confiscatory and unconstitutional but inexpedient and ineffective as well. Yet had they been inclined to back down and see the legislation scrapped, they could hardly have done so. Ontario was enjoying a healthy mining boom, which only increased the popularity of the policy. The provincial Conservatives kept up the pressure; on 1 January 1902, they introduced a resolution in the legislature calling for the proclamation of the tax. If such a tax were levied, they predicted, Onatrio would have a nickel-steel refinery within two years.

If it could not retreat, the government found it even harder to go forward. Canadian Copper seemed in earnest about its threat to close down the Sudbury works if the act was proclaimed. Thus E.J. Davis was forced to propose an amendment to the Conservative motion declaring immediate proclamation 'premature and not in the public interest.'[29] Whatever Gibson's hopes of controlling his own nickel refinery, Premier Ross appears to have concluded that the interests of the province might be served more effectively by using the manufacturing condition to force the company to build a Bessemer smelting plant at Sudbury. This plant would cost $250,000 to construct, would employ an additional 250 men, and would be some improvement on the present situation. Unfortunately, Stevenson Burke had dug in his heels and refused to proceed unless the Mines Act was repealed, a concession it was politically impossible for the premier to make.

Justice Minister David Mills brought matters to a head. On 11 April 1901 he warned Ross that he had examined the act and intended to recommend its disallowance, unless it was amended before the deadline of 18 May. To Mills the tax seemed a clearly unconstitutional attempt by the province to regulate trade and commerce through an export duty. It must go. Why, the agitated Ross demanded, could the province's power to levy such a tax not be left to the courts to pronounce upon? He even offered to take the political risk of commencing a reference case. Until the act was proclaimed, replied the implacable Mills, the courts had no authority to pronounce upon it. Why, asked Ross, had Mills not revealed his objections to the legislation sooner? Gibson had delivered his formal defence of the act in the previous December and received no response from Ottawa. Now the provincial legislature had adjourned for the year, so that amendments were impossible before the deadline. Mills was not moved.[30]

In desperation Ross pleaded with the prime minister to come to his aid: 'This disallowance would lead to a rupture between the two levels of government that might lead to disastrous results. We could not, you can easily see, acquiesce in disallowance now any more than we did when the "Rivers and Streams" Bill was disallowed by Sir John.' Gibson also complained that public opinion in Ontario would condemn any disallowance as 'an outrage on the best interests of the province.' Moreover, Gibson mentioned that rumour had it that disallowance had been promised to Canadian Copper only in return for a hefty contribution to Laurier's 1900 campaign.[31]

The prime minister certainly had no taste for interfering in the affairs of a Liberal government in the country's largest province. The sawlog embargo had shown that. But he was becoming uneasy at what he had heard about the Ontario Mines Act: 'I would like to know what induced Ross to put such an extraordinary legislation on the Statute Book. There must be another side to the question which has not yet been made apparent to me.' The premier's explanations failed to satisfy him. Unwilling as he was to disallow except in 'very extreme cases,' he warned that this legislation seemed 'absolutely prohibitory.' He told Gibson abruptly that the act could not 'successfully be defended on general principles.' As for the notion that there had been a pre-election deal with Canadian Copper regarding disallowance, that was 'sheer nonsense.'[32]

With the deadline only days away and Mills determined not to budge, things looked black for the provincial government. Once again, however, the prime minister came to the rescue. At an Ottawa meeting to which they had been hastily summoned, Ross and Gibson were able to explain the political predicament in which they found themselves. The justice minister was with difficulty persuaded to accept a reference to the Supreme Court on the constitutionality of the act prior to 18 May as an alternative to disallowance. Somewhat ungraciously the Ontario politicians agreed to this course of action, the premier complaining to Laurier, 'I must say I was not a little surprised at the position taken by some members of the Government. It would seem that they were resolved upon a course with regard to the political effect of which they were indifferent.' But back in Toronto the other members of the cabinet refused to go along with the deal. Not only would the reference indicate their wavering on the principle of the manufacturing condition and be sure to draw fire from the Conservatives, but the stated case would force the province to admit publicly that the licence fees were higher than the value of the ore itself. Fears were raised that the validity of the act as a tax might be undermined.[33]

Laurier did his best to arrange a compromise so Mills would not insist upon disallowing. All the province needed to do, he informed Ross, was to pass an order-in-council agreeing to the reference before the 18 May deadline. On 17 May the issue was still undecided as telegrams flew back and forth between Ottawa and Toronto. A reproachful Laurier warned Ross that he had better whip his unruly colleagues into line: 'I rely on you to have the understanding between us carried out in good faith.' At last the ministers gave way; they would consent to the reference only in the vaguest and most general terms in an order backdated to 14 May. Having conceded this much, they refused to budge any further. With the deadline safely past there was nothing more Mills could do. By the end of the month Laurier was still pressing the provincial cabinet to agree to the precise terms of the reference case. Although Ross also feigned displeasure at the delay, he pointed out that the lawyers were still negotiating. But these discussions soon lapsed and the case was never brought to trial.[34]

The provincial government seemed to have got its way, despite the pressure brought to bear by Canadian Copper and the hostility of David Mills. But the victory was more illusory than real. Whether or not the mining taxes were constitutional (and there is reason to think that they were) the provincial government was sufficiently chastened not to proclaim the legislation. What if Canadian Copper were to carry out its threat to close the Sudbury works and leave the cabinet to cope with 1,500 angry, unemployed miners? What would the Conservatives make of the fact that the attorney-general had a personal financial interest in a rival nickel refining concern? What if the manufacturing condition were held unconstitutional by the courts? Better forget the whole thing and allow the Mines Act of 1900 to gather dust unproclaimed. The Canadian Copper interests were thus able to thwart provincial policy, in part through the aid of the Laurier government reinforced by David Mills's conviction that the mining taxes represented an unconstitutional interference with trade and commerce. This situation remained unchanged until 1916, when emotional charges that vital strategic materials were being shipped to Canada's enemies from the International Nickel Company's plants in the neutral United States compelled Inco to yield to the pressure to construct a refinery at Port Colborne on Lake Erie.[35]

III

The same kind of friction with Ottawa sparked by private interests plagued James P. Whitney's Conservative administration, which took office in 1905. The construction of the provincially owned Temiskaming and Northern Ontario Railway, begun by the government of George Ross in 1902, had opened wide areas of the Canadian Shield to mineral exploration.[36] In 1904 the discovery of silver near Cobalt sparked a mad rush northward, and the Conservative government became convinced that new policies were required to claim the 'people's share' of this bonanza. The province's bureau of mines therefore reserved a number of choice mining locations from all staking in the hope that the province could reap extraordinary revenues from them by auctioning them off. Included in reservation under an order-in-council dated 14 August 1905 was the bed of Cobalt Lake. Nonetheless a sharp operator named W.J. Green decided early in 1906 to try to establish a prior right to the lake-bed by hook or by crook. Knowing of Green's activities, the Whitney government promptly introduced legislation to confirm the prohibition upon staking in that location. Green, by now part of a syndicate calling itself the Florence Mining Company, immediately protested that the act would deprive the company of its rights. He demanded that Ottawa disallow it. The company solicitor, while admitting that the legislation concerned property and civil rights, argued that it would exercise 'a prejudicial effect on Canada at large by destroying the credit that should attach to the Public Acts of the Provinces and to the rights that have been legally obtained thereby.' This assertion ignored the fact that Green had been warned from the very outset that his claims were invalid and would not be accepted. Justice Minister A.B. Aylesworth rejected the petition for disallowance on the grounds that the Ontario act did not clearly affect any vested right.[37]

By the time this decision was rendered in May 1907, the Florence Mining Company had become embroiled in an even more bitter wrangle with the provincial government. A company organized by the prominent Toronto stockbroker Sir Henry Pellatt had purchased the mineral rights to the bed of Cobalt Lake from the province for $1,085,000. The Florence Company promptly entered suit to block this sale in the hope of forcing Pellatt to make a quick cash settlement with them to drop the action. But the Ontario government rushed through legislation giving Pellatt's Cobalt Lake Mining Company undisputed title to the lake-bed, and to prevent any further nuisance suits barred all further appeals to the courts on this subject. The Florence Company's backers were convulsed with rage at seeing their holdup foiled. Company secretary H.H. Maw wrote to the premier, 'if a South American republic treated a European investor as we have been treated, his Government would undoubtedly send a gunboat to prevent the confiscation of his rights.' Lacking naval support, the aggrieved entrepreneurs could do little but appeal to the federal government for disallowance. Novelist Ralph Connor (Reverend C.W. Gordon) pompously lectured the prime minister on his duty:

If any Province in the Dominion can by sheer weight of majority override the courts of justice, then a serious blow is given to all security in property in Canada ... [I]f any Legislature can step in and without reference to courts of law make or break titles, what inducement can be offered to capitalists to invest? There is an end to all security in property. At this particular crisis in our history when our very future depends upon our ability to persuade foreign investors as to the security of investment an Act of this kind would, to my mind, be an unparalleled calamity.[38]

Laurier received these appeals sympathetically. He believed that barring access to the courts was 'iniquitous' and called the act 'confiscation, nothing else.' 'If the legislation passed by the Whitney government or anything approaching it had been passed by Ross when he was in Office or by us at Ottawa,' he later complained, 'the whole Conservative press, the 'Mail,' the 'News,' the 'Telegram,' the whole Conservative party, Foster, Borden and the rest, would have made the country ring with their indignation.' But he was not inclined to disallow. He told Ralph Connor, 'Whilst on the merit of the petition is seems to me that you have made a very strong case, I need hardly tell you that the disallowance of a Provincial Act is a very serious exercise of authority and one which has never been favoured by the Liberal party.' Since control of property and civil rights lay clearly with the provincial assembly, 'the remedy under the circumstances is with the people of the Province themselves.' The prime minister might also have pointed out that provincial Liberal leader George P. Graham had told the legislature in January 1907:

The idea getting abroad that there was any possibility of defective titles had injured the Cobalt country. One company had taken the circumstances as an excuse to rob – that was too strong a word perhaps – to depress a certain stock through which millions were lost by the public. 'The Government have a duty to perform,' he said, 'not only to protect the investor even if the necessary inspection should take weeks or months, but to make their titles absolutely good against the attack.'[39]

Although the local Liberals opposed the Cobalt Lake legislation because it barred access to the courts, they clearly sensed the popular appeal of a policy designed to secure a larger share of the mineral wealth of Ontario for the citizens.

Even if Laurier were reluctant to intervene, the provincial government could not be certain that he would not use this threat to force concessions from them. Sir Henry Pellatt therefore hired a former Liberal minister, F.R. Latchford, to represent his company in its dealings with the federal government. On 15 November 1907 Latchford travelled to Ottawa to meet with the prime minister and was told that no disallowance was contemplated. He returned to Toronto to inform the directors (and almost certainly the premier as well), but when he requested Laurier to put this assurance in writing he was fended off with excuses. Laurier claimed, 'You have been altogether too previous. My conversation was confidential and I gave you my views, but this is a matter which is primarily in the hands of Mr. Chief Justice, and I would not deal with it in his absence.'[40] What role Sir Louis Davies could have played beyond advising upon the constitutionality of the Ontario legislation is not clear. Most likely, the prime minister simply wished to prevent the angry Florence Mining Company crowd from discovering he had decided not to disallow. In any event, Latchford seems to have remained confident that the undertaking he had received would ultimately be carried out.

Laurier evidently found it politic to proceed deliberately because of the pressure which the supporters of the Florence Mining Company were bringing to bear. Company counsel J.M. Clark (who had acted for the Canadian Copper Company during the wrangle over the nickel manufacturing condition in 1901) harked back to that controversy in reminding the prime minister that 'Old Country investors relied largely on the power of disallowance and on the protection of our Courts ... Mr Clouston of the Bank of Montreal recently pointed out that property is not as well safeguarded in Canada, particularly in Ontario, as in Mexico, and I would submit that it would be inopportune for you to decide to allow to be taken away this remaining safeguard.' Clark insisted that the company sought disallowance only so that the courts might pronounce upon its claims. Laurier admitted that other important Liberals also felt it was 'very urgent to have us disallow this law.' As a result, he requested the province to put forward a formal defence of the legislation.

Whitney positively relished this opportunity to deride the backers of the Florence Mining Company as 'persons having pretended claims good, as it is believed, neither in morals or law.' Their lawsuit, he charged, had been intended simply 'to embarrass the company who had paid over one million dollars to the Government for their patent,' since it was not uncommon for 'parties to institute lawsuits against mining companies or individuals vexatiously attacking their rights on unsubstantial grounds, and simply for the purpose of inducing the attacked party to pay the attacking party for peace and to avoid the embarrassment of their property being in litigation when they may wish to dispose of it or work it.' W.J. Green had never established any claim to the bed of Cobalt Lake, and even had he done so it was no business of the federal government. Disallowance, Whitney claimed, had never been intended as a means of supervising the justness of provincial actions, and since the legislation was clearly constitutional, Ottawa should keep its nose out of the matter.[41]

In January 1908 the courts refused to hear the Florence Mining Company's suit until the issue of disallowance was settled. The premier confidently told a reporter from the *Globe* afterwards, 'I can tell you this, the Act will not be disallowed.' Frantically J.M. Clark wrote to the prime minister demanding to know whether he had given Whitney such an assurance, since rumours 'were being most assiduously used by the Ontario Government and its friends who are endeavouring to create the impression in the public mind that [t]his legislation has your approval.' Laurier's reply was soothing: 'I have had no correspondence with anybody upon the subject of the Cobalt Lake Bill, nor do I remember that I have had any confidential communication on the same. I presume Mr Whitney in using the words, "I can tell you this, the Act will not be disallowed," was relying on the record of the Liberal party against interference with local legislation.'[42]

At last, however, this charade was played out; in April 1908 Justice Minister Aylesworth formally rendered his decision against disallowance. He accepted 'the general view that it is not the office or the right of the Dominion Government to sit in judgment considering the justice or honesty of any Act of a provincial legislature which deals solely with property and civil rights within the province.' The framers of the BNA Act might have intended disallowance to be used in such cases as this, but, Aylesworth said proudly, since 1896 Liberal justice ministers had refused to interfere with legislation within the sphere of provincial authority. Nonetheless, Aylesworth did not conceal the distaste which he and the prime minister shared for Ontario's actions; in a bow to the powerful forces within the party and the business community who had criticized Whitney's legislation, he pronounced the Cobalt Lake act a 'confiscation of property without compensation and so an abuse of legislative power.'[43]

Laurier's prudence in refusing to intervene in the dispute was made clear in June 1908 when Mr Justice Riddell found a claim for damages by the Florence Mining Company wholly unfounded. Riddell went so far as to say, 'In short, the legislature, within its jurisdiction, can do everything that is not naturally impossible and is restrained by no rule, human or divine. If it be that the plaintiffs acquired any rights which I am far from finding – the legislature has the power to take them away. The prohibition, "Thou shalt not steal," has no legal force upon the sovereign body, and there would be no necessity for compensation to be given.'[44] Here indeed was a broad definition of provincial power over property and civil rights, a definition far too sweeping for the taste of Laurier or Aylesworth. Although firmly convinced of the wisdom of refusing disallowance, the prime minister still wanted to alert the people of Ontario to the subversive nature of the development policies being pursued by the Whitney administration. In the spring of 1909 he decided to table all the correspondence between the federal authorities and the Florence Mining Company in the House of Commons. To J.M. Clark he confided that since 'no greater efforts have been made to give publicity to the iniquitous legislation enacted against you ... I hope we shall have a debate upon it, which might be a good opportunity for the press to start a campaign and to show the matter in its full iniquity, for iniquity it is without any equivocation.' Aylesworth led off the debate in the House. While admitting that under the Canadian constitution the supremacy of provincial rights was 'a principle of greater importance to the welfare of the Dominion as a whole than even the sacredness of private rights or private ownership,' the justice minister was sharply critical of the province's effort to prevent the Florence Mining Company from having its day in court. On that principle, he maintained, the government might go around confiscating farms from their rightful owners and perhaps even repeal Magna Carta altogether. The only remedy, he warned, lay in the hands of the voters of Ontario.[45]

Whitney responded the next day with a free-swinging attack upon Aylesworth in the Ontario legislature. He dismissed 'the remarkable and violent outbreak of the Minister of Justice' on behalf of the 'swindlers' and 'adventurers' behind the Florence Mining Company: 'He may vilify the Provincial Government and the people of Ontario, but I am glad to know that the people don't pay much attention to what Mr Aylesworth may say or do in his capacity as a statesman except as a curiosity. (Government laughter and renewed applause.)'[46] A few weeks later the premier was gratified when the Court of Appeal totally rejected the Florence Mining Company's appeal against Riddell's decision. Chief Justice Sir Charles Moss found that W.J. Green had no claim whatever to the minerals on the bed of Cobalt Lake, and that provincial legislation of both 1906 and 1907 was entirely constitutional. Whitney was elated that the decision showed 'in conclusive language that there was no good faith or honesty of purpose behind the claims. Further, it defends and approves the Statutes passed by us. This, I think, will settle the pirates for a while.' He ordered 1,000 copies of the judgment printed as a pamphlet. Believing this 'a pill' which should 'knock Aylesworth out' for some time, he arranged to have Conservative A.C. Boyce read the decision to the House of Commons. Boyce was delighted to oblige: 'As you know it was rubbed into us pretty hard here about this frightful violation of private rights by your Government, and it will be a very pleasurable incident indeed when we are able to retaliate upon Mr. Aylesworth, who as you know, went out of his way to abuse your Government in this connection, quite unwarrantably and unjustifiably as the Court of Appeal has found.' The premier's triumph was complete in March 1910 when the Judicial Committee of the Privy Council abruptly rejected the appeal of the Florence Mining Company on grounds they had 'completely failed to establish their claim to have made a discovery.' Whitney gave himself the pleasure of twisting the knife once more by mailing a copy of the judgment to the justice minister.[47]

The dispute between the Ontario government and the Florence Mining Company, which the federal authorities allowed themselves to be drawn into, demonstrated the extent of provincial jurisdiction over property and civil rights by 1910. The courts entirely confirmed the constitutionality of Whitney's decision to assume title to the minerals on the bed of Cobalt Lake and dispose of them to the highest bidder while barring all legal challenges to this action. Deeply offended as they were by the thrust of this 'nefarious' legislation,[48] Laurier and Aylesworth recognized that it was well within provincial authority. Although they may have been tempted to disallow, they sensed that the political costs would be too high. Not only had the Liberals harped upon their respect for provincial rights since Mowat's time, but they did not wish to be forced to nullify a popular action by the provincial government which had netted the treasury over $1 million. Even if the federal Liberals sometimes failed to live up to their reputation as defenders of provincial rights, they were wise enough not to tackle James Whitney head-on. Their efforts to discredit his policies in other ways also failed, because of his own political astuteness and the soundness of his constitutional position, which was sustained by the courts. In this contest Ottawa was clearly outclassed.

The role of the state in capitalist society includes the provision of assistance to private interests. When jurisdiction is divided by federalism, both levels of government may be looked to for certain kinds of assistance. These interests do not consider the abstract virtues of centralized administration versus local control but concern themselves with which level is able and willing to provide what they seek. Should the central government refuse assistance, then it is likely that the provinces will be approached and vice versa. Likewise, opponents of new policies will seek protection from the other level of government where possible. The friction between Ontario and the federal government over the manufacturing condition and the Cobalt Lake case clearly illustrated these significant characteristics of Canadian federalism.

3 Public Power and Disallowance

During the early twentieth century popular enthusiasm for provincial policies designed to promote the development of Ontario resources continued to grow. The Royal Ontario Nickel Commission, which reported in 1917, summed up their appeal this way:

There is, first, the natural desire to have all the work on raw material which is produced here done at home, up to the point of turning out the finished article. Employment is given to Canadian workmen, Canadian chemists and Canadian experts. The rewards of this labour are spent in Canada and swell the volume of Canadian business. There is a feeling of impatience at seeing Canadians hewers of wood and drawers of water, while in another country technical and skilled work is performed in refining an article of Canadian origin.[1]

But in an age when industrial might rested upon iron and coal, Ontario's mines produced little of either. The future development of the province thus seemed to rest upon a supply of cheap energy.

Beginning in the 1890s, experiments with the generation and long-distance transmission of hydroelectricity pointed towards a day when this new source of power might be widely available. And in this respect Ontario seemed highly favoured, since the vast potential of Niagara Falls lay near the centre of its populated area, while in the north and west rivers leapt through the rocky canyons of the Shield surrounded by minerals and forests. Perhaps the promise of freedom from imports of Pennsylvania anthracite would be found in water-power. Once the silent, the inexhaustible, and the infinitely flexible power of 'white coal' became available, Ontario would be transformed into one of the industrial workshops of the world.[2]

With so much at stake it is hardly surprising that hydroelectric development policies sparked intense political controversy, particularly after 1905, when they took a new direction under the Conservative administration of James P. Whitney.

Soon after his election the premier declared that 'The water power at Niagara should be free as the air, and more than that, I say on behalf of the government that the water powers all over the country shall not in future be made the sport and prey of capitalists and shall not be treated as anything but a valuable asset of the people of Ontario whose trustees the government of this people are.'[3] This note of radicalism may have been more rhetorical than real, but it reflected a rising concern that private power developers might channel most of the power of Niagara across the river into the lucrative United States market or else to Toronto, the metropolitan centre of the region. The power barons were certain to demand high rates for their product, rates which might nullify the potential advantages of cheap and abundant energy supplies in the drive to industrialize Ontario. These concerns led to the foundation of a political movement seeking public control of hydroelectric development. This group wanted to ensure that the power from Niagara Falls was retained in Canada and distributed throughout south-western Ontario at rates low enough to be attractive to consumers, particularly those engaged in manufacturing.

The success of the public power movement created friction between federal and provincial governments. Private entrepreneurs who saw their interests threatened by state intervention appealed to the federal government for protection. And Sir Wilfrid Laurier continued to display the sort of sympathy for the 'sacred rights of private property' which had led him to offer consolation to the promoters of the Florence Mining Company.[4] Moreover, the development of power at Niagara Falls involved the relations between Canada and the United States, in which the federal authorities naturally had an interest. Whitney's government resisted all demands for disallowance of Ontario's power legislation and insisted on the right of the province to manage the development of this new source of energy. In the end, despite much acrimony, the Laurier government conceded to the province most of the premier's demands.

I

The first steps towards the creation of the public power movement were taken by a group of businessmen and industrialists in south-western Ontario, from Waterloo, Berlin (now Kitchener), Preston, Hespeler, Galt, and Guelph. They were alarmed because two American-controlled power companies had already secured provincial approval to begin building power plants on the Canadian side of the falls by 1902, and they appeared to have little intention of distributing current in Canada. In 1903 the Ontario Power Company and the Canadian Niagara Power Company were joined by a new syndicate headed by three prominent Canadian businessmen, William Mackenzie, Henry Pellatt, and Frederic Nicholls. Since this group already controlled the franchised lighting and traction concerns in Toronto, it was clear that they intended to channel the output of their Electrical Development Company to that city. Only through co-coperative action could the dream of cheap hydro for other parts of the province be realized.[5]

Yet the administration of George Ross failed to respond to demands for action to assist the public power cause. The premier refused to help, even though members of the Toronto branch of the Canadian Manufacturers Association, painfully familiar with the high rates and poor service offered by Mackenzie-Pellatt-Nicholls syndicate, joined in the agitation. Ross merely authorized the creation of an Ontario Power Commission to investigate the potential of long-distance transmission lines owned exclusively by a municipal co-operative. Direct competition between public and private utilities remained barred by the so-called 'Conmee clause' of the Municipal Act, which required the purchase of any existing private utilities by new public undertakings. At first the Conservative opposition seemed little more responsive, but one man, Dr T.E. Kaiser, sensed the political capital to be gained from support for public power. In 1902 he persuaded his party's leadership to move a resolution in the legislature endorsing the generation and distribution of power for the municipalities at cost. Yet during the next three years the issue was little discussed by the Tories, perhaps because they were afraid that Ross might steal their policy, as had happened with the manufacturing condition. However, Whitney's victory in 1905 opened the way, and Adam Beck of London, an increasingly prominent figure in the public power movement, was made minister without portfolio.[6]

Beck lost no time in making his position clear:

The interest of the Government ... is two-fold. It has first, an interest in the water power resources of the Province as a source of revenue to the public treasury. It has also an interest in the commercial development of the Province, and ... a very great influence upon the commercial development of the Province will be exercised by the furnishing of cheap power. It is the duty of the Government to see that the development is not hindered by permitting a handful of people to enrich themselves out of these treasures at the expense of the general public ... The Government has the same right over the Provincial water powers to which it holds the title that it has over the timber, minerals and Crown lands of the Province.[7]

The execution of this policy, however, soon embroiled the provincial government in conflict with Ottawa, just as in the past they had collided over provincial plans for the development of Ontario's lands, forests, and mines.

In May 1906 Beck was chosen head of the newly created Hydro-Electric Power Commission; the Commission was established to regulate private utilities and to undertake the distribution of electricity to the municipalities by means still to be decided upon. The setting up of the HEPC did not mean that the Whitney cabinet was firmly wedded to a policy of public ownership of the transmission lines and generating stations. Far from it. In the premier's words, his government was 'pledged to get cheap power for this Province, but it is not pledged as to the means of doing it.' Nonetheless, the fact that the HEPC possessed powers of expropriation created alarm among the managers and security-owners of the province's private utilities. Whitney did his best to calm them by assuring them that there was no immediate intention to use this authority, and even if it became necessary, full compensation would be paid. But so edgy had the bond-holders in Britain become that the premier found it necessary to advise Laurier in the spring of 1906 that 'there has been no justification for the alarm manifested in some quarters with reference to the consequences of this legislation. We have no doubt that we will be able to meet the views of the public on this great question without any recourse to the necessary powers contained in this Act.'[8]

Indeed, Whitney's major problem was to keep the enthusiasts in the public power movement under control. Beck and his tame pressure group, the Municipal Power Union of Western Ontario, were insistent that only a publicly owned transmission line to distribute Niagara power could ensure low rates. The premier was more concerned with Ontario's financial reputation in the London money markets, and during a visit to the British capital in the summer of 1906 he devoted his efforts to calming the fears of investors. Unfortunately for him, the Electrical Development Company was equally assiduous in spreading anti-Hydro propaganda at home and abroad. Whitney complained to his brother that the Mackenzie-Pellatt-Nicholls bunch 'has endeavoured to get our legislation disallowed at Ottawa; it has spread rumours abroad, without a shadow of a foundation that we were interfering with vested rights, etc.'[9] This campaign continued even after Sir Henry Pellatt purchased the Cobalt Lake mining property and ironically became an ally of the provincial government in the fight with the Florence Mining Company. Despite a shaky financial situation, the Electrical Development Company continued to lead the struggle against the government's policy. Whitney and Beck refused to be intimidated. A number of municipalities received the approval of their ratepayers to enter into power contracts with the HEPC, and at long last, in March 1908 the provincial cabinet ratified an agreement between the Commission and the Ontario Power Company to supply current from its Niagara generating station to be distributed over a publicly owned transmission line. When the HEPC came to sign final agreements to supply power to each municipality the terms differed slightly from those approved by local ratepayers. Beck was therefore permitted to rush through a bill during the final hours of the 1908 session of the legislature empowering the mayors alone to sign 'sufficient, valid and binding' contracts with Ontario Hydro without further reference to the ratepayers.[10]

These contracts did not specify the exact price at which the power would be delivered, because the cost of the transmission line was not yet known. As a result, the mayor of Galt refused to sign, and individuals in both London and Toronto launched suits to overturn the contracts on grounds that such an unlimited commitment had never been approved by local ratepayers. Realizing that another round of municipal voting might require a year or more, Adam Beck decided to put through further legislation validating all the contracts. This act passed without even a division of the assembly at the 1909 session. In order to prevent nuisance suits to block Hydro's plans Beck included a clause which stated the municipal contracts should 'not be open to question and shall not be called into question on any ground whatever in any court but shall be held and adjudged to be valid and binding.'[11]

Like the Cobalt Lake legislation of 1907, this act provoked a storm of protest and embroiled the Ontario government in conflict with Ottawa. Private power interests refused to relax their hostility towards the HEPC; they now saw to it that the prime minister was deluged with requests for disallowance of this act. The opponents of the Hydro trotted out many of the same arguments raised by the Florence Mining Company and its supporters. The very repetition of the ban on legal challenges intensified Canadian and British financial opinion. The premier, however, professed unconcern in a letter to his London financial adviser: 'We are not at all exercised here over the question of disallowance. It, or rather our legislation, is the key of the whole power scheme, and ... the real object which our opponents have in view is the destruction of the power scheme. They care very little about the constitutional question.' Any move in the direction of federal intervention would help rather than hurt the political prospects of the Conservative government. 'From a Party point of view,' wrote Whitney, 'nothing could be better for us.'[12]

Yet he was probably more concerned than he appeared. Laurier and Justice Minister Aylesworth had made it clear when tabling the correspondence with the Florence Mining Company in the spring of 1909 that their sympathies lay with the critics of such high-handed provincial policies. The forces now massing against Ontario's power policy were far more formidable than that rather shady crew of mining promoters. Suppose that the private power developers succeeded in persuading the prime minister that Canada's financial reputation in London had been seriously damaged by Ontario's actions. E.R. Wood of Dominion Securities put the case forcefully to Laurier:

The right of Federal veto was incorporated in our constitution as a safeguard of private property, and it may serve at the same time to save the credit of the Dominion in the financial centre of the world. The wealth of this country must be developed, and our great transportation and other enterprises must be financed by British and foreign capital. This is absolutely essential. And it will be absolutely impossible if there is as much as a suspicion that our government will break faith with investors. Save the credit of the Dominion by exercising the power of veto.

On a visit to London Finance Minister W.S. Fielding was warned that the federal government might find it impossible to borrow there if it did not intervene.[13]

Other opponents of the power scheme attacked the legislation on constitutional grounds, arguing that it went beyond mere control of property and civil rights. Denial of access to the courts was denounced as a 'high-handed and mischievous use of legislative power' which, according to a group of stockbrokers, might 'become a precedent for all sorts of reckless or partisan legislation.' Some saw this as a clear violation of equity and natural justice. The president of the Home Bank, for instance, was confident that 'The general desire must be for protection of vested rights and security from legislation that would interfere with right and justice.' A prominent clergyman declared that the federal government had a clear duty to protect the citizens of Ontario against an act 'dangerous and suicidal in character' which had 'grievously wronged' them. Denunciations of every kind and description were collected by the lawyers for the Mackenzie-Pellatt-Nicholls syndicate and reprinted as a pamphlet entitled *The Credit of Canada, How It Is Affected by the Ontario Power Legislation: Views of British Journals and of English and Canadian Writers and Correspondents*. Numbered among these were constitutional expert A.V. Dicey, historian Goldwin Smith, and the Duchess of Marlborough's estate manager.[14]

Faced with this onslaught, the premier decided he must counter-attack. Whitney undertook a series of speeches in which he defended the power legislation as necessary to carry out the will of the people. Municipal councils had been eager to get on with the plan and fully supported the government's decision to forbid harassing suits. 'All the watered-stock experts and stock gamblers in Canada,' he charged, 'are on the side of our opponents in this matter.' In dealing with the British critics he was more circumspect. During the summer of 1909 he gave only a single interview to the *Economist* in which he deplored the fact that reputable British journals should permit themselves to be used as propagandists for a gang of self-interested promoters. He was delighted to learn that most efforts to arouse hostility towards his government had failed; if anything, financial opinion had begun to sympathize somewhat with the province because of the behaviour of its leading critics in London.[15]

Justice Minister Aylesworth requested Whitney to make ready his formal response to the disallowance petitions by the end of 1909. Meanwhile, the plaintiffs kept up a barrage of criticism directed at the power legislation. In early October a pair of lawyers representing the private utilities secured an interview with the prime minister and the minister of public works. F.H. Chrysler tried to convince them that the province lacked all jurisdiction over Niagara power since it was situated upon a navigable, international river. Not only investors but the municipalities themselves, he argued, were threatened by the terms of the HEPC contracts, which were good for thirty years with no right of appeal. Even if the 1909 act did not violate the BNA Act, it was 'unconstitutional' in the sense that it was contrary to natural justice. A transcript of this meeting speedily appeared as a pamphlet under the title *A Question of Disallowance, Argument before the Privy*

Council on the Petitions for Vetoing of the Power Legislation, the Credit of Canada the Supreme Issue.[16] This production irritated Whitney, if only because it attempted to portray a bit of lobbying as a judicial proceeding, but Justice Minister Aylesworth hastened to reassure him that he regarded the pamphlet as 'an entirely gratuitous piece of work.'[17]

Ontario's formal response to the disallowance petitions was prepared by Whitney, Beck, and Attorney-General J.J. Foy and was handed to Aylesworth in December 1909. It included not only a history of the public power movement but copious citations from previous justice ministers regarding the proper use of disallowance. Then the objections raised by the petitioners were taken up one by one. Since the act dealt with property and civil rights, it was clearly constitutional. Just legislation or not, the province felt entitled to rely upon Aylesworth's own statements regarding the Cobalt Lake case that this was no longer a ground for disallowance. If the Ontario government lacked the freedom to act, then the province's citizens had less than the full democratic rights of British subjects. The validation of municipal by-laws by parliamentary enactment was commonplace in Canada, while the claim that barring access to the courts was a denial of natural justice was simply nonsense; in Britain itself during the previous year no less than thirty-four statutes had limited such appeals. The suits had been stayed because they were simply harassing: 'No vested right, nor right of or to property of any kind, is in any way affected by the Act in question ... Delay would have occurred until the Legislature had an opportunity to deal with the question ... And the delay would have been disastrous to the whole Power Scheme which had been endorsed by the Province.' Those who argued that the legislation had damaged Canadian credit in London were referred to statements by the likes of William Mackenzie regarding the buoyant financial condition of the country; the Electrical Development Company, it was pointed out, was not even among those petitioning for disallowance. Finally, the claim that the federal government had exclusive jurisdiction over the Niagara River was dismissed with a jest apparently added by Whitney himself: 'The rights of the Dominion over the River are only so far as it is navigable, and the River's non-navigability at the point referred to is apparent and notorious.'[18]

The premier was well satisfied with this presentation of the case: 'I make bold to say that no man who has an open mind on this question can condemn our legislation from any possible point of view if he understands the whole situation.' Whitney was particularly pleased when several members of the Liberal government of Quebec, in Toronto on a goodwill tour, spoke out strongly in support of provincial rights. He thought L.A. Taschereau's remarks

regarding the encroachments of Federal power on provincial jurisdiction were very pointed, and, indeed, were almost extreme. You may depend on it that from that day forward the Provinces of Ontario and Quebec will be looked upon as standing together for the protection of everything relating to the Provinces.

The universal belief here is, and I suppose the same belief obtains elsewhere, that Gouin and I have been making arrangements for this, and all the little details [were] arranged for some time. Of course, this is not true, but there is no doubt whatever that there is the fullest and frankest agreement between the two Governments ...[19]

Conservative MP Andrew Broder suggested this interprovincial amity would 'make Sir Wilfrid and Aylesworth think twice before interfering with our power legislation,' while opposition leader Robert Borden was confident that Ontario 'should not apprehend the slightest interference' from Ottawa.[20]

And indeed, Laurier and Aylesworth found themselves on the horns of precisely the same dilemma which had confronted them the previous year over the Cobalt Lake case. Genuinely offended by the thrust of the hydro legislation they nevertheless had to face up to the consequences of a disallowance. The prime minister wrote fretfully, 'I am sorry to say that whilst the legislation is abominable, the reasons for disallowance are not as strong as I would like them to be.' His justice minister gloomily concurred that the 1909 act was 'undoubtedly monstrous, but I cannot see that it is ultra vires, and if the people of Ontario *want* that sort of a Government and legislature, the difficulty to my mind, is to see why *we* should rush to rescue them from their own chosen rulers, and at the same time rescue the rulers from a situation which by this time, I think, very possibly they themselves would be glad to be relieved from.'[21] Laurier agreed. 'The more I think of it the more difficulties I see in the way of disallowance,' he wrote to one Liberal MP in September 1909, and to the president of the North American Life Assurance Company he explained,

Everybody must admit that your qualification of this legislation is not too severe, and that it is highly improper and prejudicial to the best interests of the country. Such, at all events, is my opinion of it, but we have already refused to disallow legislation of a similar character. My opinion still is that the power of disallowance should not be exercised, except in cases of extreme emergency, and where the interests of the Dominion at large are likely to suffer. If the evil complained of is simply confined to private individuals, I think this should not be a reason for interference.[22]

Only if peace, order, and good government were endangered would federal intervention be justified, although Laurier admitted to the president of the Bank of Commerce that if Canada's credit were seriously affected,' 'it may then be held to be against good order, and, as such, subject to disallowance.' But he really did not believe that that situation would occur. How, he asked an angry New York financier, could Ontario's action 'affect all Canadian securities any more than a repudiation by a state of the Union could affect the securities of the United States?' Recalling the principles of Blake and Mowat, he insisted that 'the remedy was not in the exercise of the power of disallowance by the stronger government at Ottawa, but by the people of the province themselves.'[23]

The Liberal leader was equally terse with those who advised him that disallowance would reap great political gains for his party. After all, the act had been passed without a word of objection from the provincial Liberals: 'Were we now to disallow this legislation, it would be re-enacted again by Whitney, disallowed again, re-enacted once more, and where would that end?' Laurier wrote to another Grit: 'One thing surprises me, in all this: I receive letters from political friends almost every week on this subject, all advising disallowance or telling me the province is unanimously for it. If such be the case it would certainly help the matter to have meetings and resolutions passed to denounce the local government, to denounce their action and ask them to repeal their own legislation. So far nothing of the kind has been done.'[24] Even lifelong Conservatives like Henry O'Brien promised him 'the great silent vote of the country (even in Toronto, the most ignorant and prejudiced city in the Dominion),' if he would intervene. 'A larger number of Conservatives than you have any idea of' would rally behind disallowance; they had kept silent only 'because the people realize it is quite useless to appeal to Sir James Whitney, who refuses to listen to anybody on the subject and have preferred to voice their sentiments on the subjects by appeal to the Dominion government.' But Laurier preferred to trust his own shrewd political instincts. He could see the broad popular appeal of the public power policy, and the unhappy consequences of federal interference: 'I would feel it a calamity,' he wrote, 'to come to a clash with the Legislature of the Province.'[25]

Yet the provincial government could not feel entirely certain that Ottawa would not interfere. They knew how repellent both Laurier and Aylesworth found the hydro legislation, how powerful was the pressure upon them to intervene. In January 1910 the ministry was waited upon by a delegation from the Canadian Bankers Association, then by a group of Liberal MPs from Ontario. One supporter of the private power interests told the press afterwards: 'If we are not much misinformed there was a very strong feeling in the Cabinet in favour of disallowance.'[26] Whitney himself admitted that a majority of the federal ministers probably supported disallowance. What if the prime minister became convinced that the credit of Canada really had been undermined? By the spring of 1910 the premier was ready to make a small tactical concession in order to gain the larger victory. Provincial Secretary W.J. Hanna was dispatched to Ottawa to see Laurier near the end of March; the two men discussed a possible amendment to the 1909 legislation which would lift the total ban on lawsuits regarding the hydro contracts. Although the validity of the agreements themselves would still be exempt from challenge, those who claimed to have suffered damages would now be entitled to try to recover them in the courts.[27]

Whether or not this peace offering was necessary, the suspense was soon at an end. By mid-April 1910 the federal cabinet had received Aylesworth's report recommending that the Ontario legislation be left to stand. In reality the decision not to intervene had probably been taken months before, but the justice minister noted the provincial government's offer to make amendments. In explaining his refusal to disallow Aylesworth emphasized constitutional considerations: the act was clearly within the powers of the province and it was not the place of the federal authorities to pronounce upon the justice of all provincial statutes. He recalled his own comments on the Cobalt Lake legislation, nothing that even if there had been an 'unwise or indiscreet' use of authority or even 'practical confiscation of property,' the only court of appeal was the provincial electorate. As for the claim that the credit of Canada had been impaired, the justice minister expressed scepticism. Such injury, if it had indeed occurred, arose from 'the general scheme for furnishing through the Hydro-Electric Power Commission electrical power or energy in competition with the business of existing companies rather than [from] any natural consequences of the amending legislation which is the subject of this report.' Acts passed before 1909 were long since immune from disallowance. The hydro legislation would stand.[28]

Although less jubilant than at the time of the Cobalt Lake decision, which, after all, made the hydro disallowance case something of an anticlimax, Premier Whitney was still well satisfied. 'We have had our anxious moments,' he confided to a friendly British newspaperman, 'as we well knew that probably a majority of the Dominion cabinet were anxious to disallow the legislation, but the Justice Minister, partisan as he is, held very strong views in our favour and was able to override the others.' In public the premier proudly proclaimed 'the beginning of a new era in constitutional development under the British North American Act. It is now certain that in future there will be no further attempts – at any rate, no successful attempts – to minimize or destroy the power of a Provincial Legislature acting within the limits of its jurisdiction.' Even past bitterness towards Aylesworth was forgotten: the justice minister had now become 'a tower of strength' on the side of Ontario, a man of views 'lucid and unanswerable.'[29]

Thus the federal government had confirmed its refusal to intervene against the province's development policies by nullifying them through disallowance, despite the clearly expressed distaste of both Laurier and Aylesworth for what they regarded as improper interference with the rights of private property by the Whitney administration. To some this seemed tantamount to a constitutional revolution which would, it was said, permit a provincial legislature to repeal Magna Carta if it chose to. The conviction grew that there must be greater legal protection for the rights of property and the propertied classes. Wallace Nesbitt, a well-known corporation lawyer who had acted for Inco in the dispute over the nickel manufacturing condition, argued that the hydro legislation demonstrated the need for an amendment to the BNA Act to guarantee the inviolability of contracts as the constituion of the United States did. While sympathetic, Laurier was clearly conscious of the political obstacles to reversing the course of constitutional development of the preceding forty-five years.[30] It fell to Governor-General Earl Grey, a tireless busybody, to take up this cause in earnest. Sir James Whitney would have none of it. The threat to private rights posed by his government had been grossly exaggerated, he declared, for he was 'a straight-out champion ... of the rights of property and of vested rights.' He added: 'Asking the assent of the provinces would in effect be asking them to hand back and deliver up a portion of the jurisdiction given them by the BNA Act – and for the reason that they, the people of the Province, cannot be trusted with such power and jurisdiction.' Sir Edmund Walker of the Bank of Commerce explained frankly why he and his kind lacked heart for such a struggle: 'I do not know of any prominent person who would publicly avow the necessity of an amendment to the British North America Act because of such Provincial legislation, although there are many who think such an amendment necessary. Men like [William] Mackenzie have too many dealings with the Government to be willing to act, although they are precisely the ones who are interested in the status of Canadian securities abroad.'[31] No more was heard of the matter.

II

The evolution of the constitution, both legal and customary, since the 1880s had resulted by 1910 in a redefinition of the circumstances under which it was felt proper for Ottawa to intervene in local affairs. In disallowing the Rivers and Streams Act in 1881 Sir John A. Macdonald had argued that 'the power of the local legislatures to take away the rights of one man and vest them in another ... is exceedingly doubtful, but assuming that such right does ... exist I think it devolves upon this government to see that such power is not exercised in flagrant violation of private right and natural justice.'[32] During the next three decades, however, the courts steadily broadened the sphere of provincial powers, and in 1898 the Judicial Committee of the Privy Council concluded that 'The supreme legislative power in relation to any subject matter is always capable of abuse, but it is not to be assumed that it will be abused; if it is, the only remedy is an appeal to those by whom the legislature is elected.'[33] By 1909 this had become accepted doctrine and Chief Justice Falconbridge of Ontario ruled:

We have heard a good deal recently about the jurisdiction of the Province, a good deal of complaint about the exercise of its power; but there is no doubt that the highest authority has declared that within its own jurisdiction it is supreme; in fact, while it seems rather severe I suppose that there is not any doubt it has been conceded in recent cases that if the Legislature had chosen to confiscate – the word that is used – the farm of the plaintiff without any compensation, they would have a perfect right to do it in law, if not in morals.[34]

Macdonald had also discovered in the case of the Rivers and Streams Act that the political cost of disallowance could be heavy. While the federal government's power to nullify any and all provincial statutes might remain untrammelled in law, practice was a very different matter. A powerful and determined provincial administration might set up such an outcry that Ottawa would be deterred from interfering. Nonetheless, when private interest groups found themselves in conflict with the Ontario government, they still turned to the federal authorities as readily as in Macdonald's time. Even the disputes over the manufacturing condition, which clearly demonstrated Laurier's reluctance to disallow, did not alert them to the changing times. With regard to the Cobalt Lake and Ontario Hydro legislation they found the prime minister and the justice minister extremely sympathetic to their objections but unwilling to intervene directly. This reluctance stemmed partly from respect for constitutional niceties and partly from the Liberal party's oft-proclaimed (if not always honoured) respect for provincial rights but also from a clear sense of the popularity of Whitney's policies. The premier himself had been taken aback by the acclaim which had greeted his rather timid efforts to secure for the people a larger share in the mineral wealth of the province in the Cobalt Lake case, but the lesson had not been lost upon him. And Adam Beck's skill at organization and public relations sustained popular enthusiasm for public power. Thus, as Laurier warned one angry critic of the hydro legislation, 'The remedy is primarily in the hands of the people of Ontario. So far I have seen no evidence that they in any way resent this legislation. There have been no protests, no meetings, no recourse to other methods which under our constitution can be taken to testify to the wants and wishes of the people.'[35] As long as that was true he refused to interfere.

Nevertheless, poorly disguised sympathy of the federal ministers for the critics of Whitney's policies had its own effect. As Professor Nelles points out:

The ability of vested interests to mobilize one level of government against another necessarily discredited the federal power of disallowance. In the Rivers and Streams, Manufacturing Condition, Cobalt Lake and ... the Hydro disallowance cases, the federal government's threatened use of the power confronted sound, just, and what is more important, popular provincial legislation ... [N]othing could have been more ill-advised than to be put into the position of even contemplating disallowance of the Cobalt Lake and Hydro bills. Yet the federal government was seen to have submitted to the special pleading of the allegedly victimized parties. The Cobalt Lake and Hydro cases did not develop into another Rivers and Streams knock-down, dragged-out fight between the province and the dominion ... But the Laurier government just as effectively compromised itself in both cases. Its partisan animus confirmed the suspicion of the Ontario government that no federal government could be expected to possess the high-minded impartiality required in the exercise of the disallowance power.[36]

Despite occasional appeals to Ottawa by aggrieved private interests during the next few years, disallowance (and even the threat of disallowance) largely ceased to be a means by which the federal government could exercise discipline over the provinces after 1910.

Why did a prime minister as politically astute as Laurier permit himself to be drawn into the controversies surrounding the Ontario Hydro legislation and the Cobalt Lake case – controversies which could do little but damage his authority? His party, after all, was supposedly committed to respect for provincial rights. In part he acted out of ideological commitment: Laurier did believe strongly in the need to defend the rights of property. On one occasion he wrote: 'The provision of the American constitution protecting the sacredness of contract has been a source of incalculable strength to the Union. I have always regretted such a provision had not been thought of by the Fathers of our own Confederation.'[37] Thus, appeals for help against the rather high-handed legislation passed by Whitney's government did not fall upon deaf ears. But it might also be argued that as his stay in office lengthened, his concern for provincial rights diminished. Confronting a long-entrenched Conservative administration during the 1890s, the Liberal leader had concluded that he needed the support of the Liberal provincial premiers to dislodge that government. And this, in turn, meant emphasizing his respect for provincial rights. (Robert Borden, facing a similarly well-entrenched administration, would follow precisely the same course after 1905.)

When Laurier won office in 1896, the visible symbol of this reverence for provincial rights became the presence in the cabinet of four former provincial premiers. But symbols should not be mistaken for substance. During his first decade in office Laurier did nothing to alter the formal constitutional relationship between the provinces and the Dominion. In 1899 he toyed briefly with the idea of reforming the Senate but quickly abandoned it when the British government objected.[38] The longer he remained in office the less concerned the prime minister seemed to be with provincial sensibilities. In Ontario's case the problem was made more acute by the lack of an effective local lieutenant after Sir William Mulock retired in 1905. The political bungling of A.B. Aylesworth almost justified Whitney's acerbic observation that 'the idiotic talk of "Baby" Aylesworth' made him 'without exception the most infantile specimen of politician or statesman that ever came to my notice.'[39]

Typical of the clumsiness with which relations between Ottawa and Toronto were too often handled after 1905 was the dispute which blew up over the Petawawa lands. For some years the militia department had been seeking a larger training ground, and negotiations for a 73,000 acre site in the Ottawa valley were begun during the Ross administration. Some of these lands were licensed to lumbermen, but 55,000 acres remained entirely in provincial hands. Early in 1907 Whitney and Frank Cochrane, the minister of lands, forests, and mines, met with Sir Frederick Borden, the minister of militia and defence, and agreed to lease the lands for ninety-nine years for 25 cents an acre annually, provided that the private interests were compensated by the federal government for their timber rights. On 22 March 1907, however, the militia department abruptly seized the lands by order-in-council under section 117 of the BNA Act, which permitted the dominion to take 'any lands or public property required for fortifications or for the defence of the country.'[40]

When Whitney complained, he was told that Cochrane had failed to carry out the agreement to execute the lease, while the timber licensees had demanded $112,000 in compensation for the loss of their privileges. The premier denounced this use of federal power as 'unnecessary, unwarranted and arbitrary.' Since the province and the lumbermen had no means of redress, Whitney was undoubtedly delighted to point to this 'strange condition of affairs to obtain in a British country.' But Laurier simply ignored all protests, even when the legislature unanimously passed a resolution condemning Ottawa's action. In the House of Commons several federal ministers were critical of the Ontario government for bad faith in the negotiations.[41] Since Whitney was uncertain that any consitutional challenge would be sustained by the courts, he allowed the matter to drop. A good deal of bad feeling had been created, in part because Whitney seized the opportunity to make some politcal hay, but this situation might have been avoided by a more conciliatory approach on the part of the federal government.

Despite his public posture of respect for provincial rights, Laurier did not cease the vigorous exercise of the power of disallowance. During his fifteen years in power thirty pieces of provincial legislation were nullified, though admittedly eighteen of them were anti-Oriental statutes passed by British Columbia. Macdonald himself had disallowed forty-one provincial acts from 1878 to 1891, a dozen of which were Manitoba railway charters. Between 1891 and 1896 and from 1911 to 1921 successive Conservative administrations disallowed only two provincial laws.[42] The depth of Laurier's devotion to local autonomy might thus be questioned. On other occasions, as with the manufacturing condition on nickel ore, Laurier and his ministers threatened disallowance in order to secure agreement to changes, and in the case of the Ontario Hydro legislation Whitney offered to make amendments in order to head off any federal interference.

At the same time the presence of a Conservative government at Queen's Park after 1905 brought these disputes into the public eye. Unlike the negotiations over the manufacturing condition, which were conducted in private, Whitney lost no opportunity to try to reap political benefit by resisting federal interference with popular provincial policies. Indeed, the skill he displayed in doing so made it all the more difficult and politically risky for Laurier to bend the province to his will. The political popularity of such policies as the manufacturing condition, the sale of Cobalt Lake, and the development of a publicly controlled electrical system reflected the enthusiasm of Ontario's voters for efforts to develop the economic strength of their province.

4 Exporting Electricity

Provincial policies designed to regulate the production and distribution of Ontario's natural resources, such as the manufacturing condition and the creation of Ontario Hydro, had an obvious appeal to the voters. Upon this base of primary products and cheap energy supplies might be built the economy of an industrial giant. But one danger existed: the export of electricity to the United States might undermine the objectives towards which successive provincial administrations had worked. The danger was a real one, owing to the historical development of the hydroelectric industry in Ontario. American promoters had been early in the field, and by 1900 had secured the only two development franchises from the province's Queen Victoria Niagara Falls Parks Commission, which controlled the waters of the Niagara River. After the turn of the century, however, it began to be realized that permitting large-scale exports of power would mortgage the economic future of Ontario in two ways: not only would it curtail the supply of cheap energy but it would permit adjoining New York state to preserve and enhance its economic superiority at the province's expense. Not surprisingly, controlling exports of power soon became a major concern of the government of James P. Whitney and its successors.

That electricity exports should become a source of federal-provincial conflict is hardly to be wondered at. First, there was the federal government's acknowledged responsibility for international trade. Import-export policy was clearly Ottawa's preserve. Second, the largest power developments in southern Ontario, actual or potential, lay on the St Lawrence–Great Lakes system. But that system was both a navigable waterway and an international boundary, and navigation and international relations were also clearly federal responsibilities. If electricity were developed through construction of a canal project, could Ottawa claim the right to sell that power wherever it wished, even in the United States? Could these power exports be permitted on liberal terms in the hope of promoting an accommodation between the two countries on other outstanding issues?

Finally, Whitney and his successors discovered that certain decisions taken when the hydroelectric industry in Canada was in its infancy further complicated the situation. The Canadian side of Niagara Falls had been willingly handed to American entrepreneurs by the province for development in the 1890s, and these entrepreneurs not unnaturally intended to transmit most of the power produced to the lucrative market in their homeland. The lax conditions imposed upon Niagara's development had been one of the concerns which fuelled the public power movement from the beginning. Should later provincial governments interfere with long-term export contracts, the power company managers were certain to appeal for assistance not only to Ottawa but to Washington, thus creating federal-provincial friction. In fact, this problem became acute during the First World War, when industrial mobilization produced a serious power shortage.[1]

I

Fear that industries located in New York state would absorb the lion's share of Niagara's power was a vital factor in rallying the Ontario business community behind the public power movement. Aware of this situation, the Conservatives sponsored a resolution in the legislature as early as 1902 calling upon the government to take the power to ban the export of electricity. Whitney's election in 1905 made early action on this issue likely. In fact, the first moves came from private interests in the United States. Operators of thermal generating stations disliked competition from cheap, imported hydroelectricity. The generating companies on the American side of Niagara Falls also were quick to see the advantage to them of limiting imports from Canada. Working through various civic-minded associations concerned with preserving the scenic beauties of Niagara Falls, the alliance of American power producers drummed up a campaign to forbid any further diversions of water from the Niagara River for power purposes. If successful, such a restriction would be a severe set-back to the public power movement. The new Ontario government waited to see how the Laurier cabinet would respond to this pressure.

In the spring of 1906 Congressman T.E. Burton, prodded by the coalition of beautifiers and power producers, introduced a bill in congress to empower the secretary of war to limit electricity imports from Canada. The Burton Act restricted the two American-owned companies on the Canadian side of Niagara to exports of 60,000 horsepower. President Theodore Roosevelt also directed the American section of the International Waterways Commission to investigate the question of diversions at Niagara. Secretary of State Elihu Root hoped that some agreement on that topic could be incorporated into a general treaty on Canadian-American relations.

This flurry of activity caught both levels of government in Canada unprepared. The federal cabinet hastened to draw up legislation to regulate the export of electricity from Canada and to license all exporters. A copy of the bill was sent to

Premier Whitney before being introduced in parliament in April 1906, but he made no formal reply. Nonetheless, a number of Conservative MPs from the province strongly criticized the bill in the Commons debate. They argued that it might interfere with the efforts of the newly created Hydro-Electric Power Commission to purchase Niagara power.[2] In the face of this opposition Justice Minister Charles Fitzpatrick agreed to let the bill stand until the provincial government gave its verdict. Both Deputy Attorney-General J.R. Cartwright and lawyer Aemilius Irving studied the legislation and reported that a provision in the bill exempting all existing contracts from control would make it impossible for the HEPC to regulate power exports by altering the agreements between the companies and the Niagara Park Commission. As it stood, they advised Whitney, the legislation might even permit the power companies to evade any limitations on exports, thus undermining provincial power policy completely. As a result of Ontario's protests the bill was shelved pending further discussions between Ottawa and the province.[3]

Premier Whitney was in a quandary. Undeniably, the federal government had the authority to regulate exports. If it would do so in accordance with provincial wishes it could greatly assist the HEPC in dealing with the private power companies. But Ottawa's reluctance to interfere with existing agreements convinced him that the legislation was more likely to benefit the private power companies than the Hydro. In fact, George Gibbons, head of the Canadian section of the International Waterways Commission and a staunch Liberal, was at work on just such a scheme. He believed that revised export legislation combined with a treaty with the United States would take the steam out of the public power movement and gain the credit for securing cheap electricity supplies for the Laurier government.[4]

In the spring of 1906 the International Waterways Commission agreed to recommend that the 200,000 cubic feet per second (second-feet) flowing over Niagara Falls should be divided as follows: up to 18,000 second-feet could be diverted on the American side for power production while Canada got 36,000 second-feet. (The disparity was due to the 10,000 cubic feet per second removed from the Great Lakes to the Mississippi at Chicago and lost.) The diversion of 54,000 second-feet at Niagara should produce 485,000 horsepower, enough to meet three times the existing demand, and Gibbons hoped that the Roosevelt administration would accept the recommendation as the basis for a treaty. Such a treaty would give the existing generating companies a virtual monopoly at Niagara and the growing American market for power should increase the value of each horsepower exported by $5 per year. In return for these favours, Gibbons believed, the companies would be prepared to supply low cost power to the Canadian side, thus taking the wind out of Adam Beck's sails and averting 'the socialistic progress in Ontario.'[5]

After consulting the Toronto financial community, already deeply alarmed by Beck's Hydro legislation, Gibbons set about revising the power export bill with the help of the new justice minister, A.B. Aylesworth. In December 1906 a copy of the bill was forwarded to Whitney. Because the act now gave the federal cabinet power to decide how much electricity was surplus to the needs of Ontario and to fix the price of exported current, many provincial ministers apparently approved of it. They hoped that it might make the private power companies less hostile to the HEPC. All things considered, Whitney confided to Beck, he felt inclined to approve the proposed legislation. But the Hydro chairman was not satisfied; he wanted the provincial cabinet to be given power over all export licences and the right to impose terms and conditions of its own. Only such authority would ensure that 'the interests of the Province would be safe.'[6]

Owing to this difference of opinion, the provincial government made no formal comment on the revised bill, which was submitted to Parliament in January 1907. Yet a number of Conservative back-benchers promptly denounced it as a clear violation of the right of the province to manage its own energy supplies. Because of the outcry, both Opposition Leader Borden and Justice Minister Aylesworth again requested Whitney's views. After a month's delay, apparently because Beck was still not content, the premier could respond only with some vague generalities about the need for careful consultation between province and dominion. As a result Aylesworth decided to proceed with the bill in March 1907 and it speedily passed. The new export licensing system probably satisfied the more moderate elements in the provincial cabinet, including Whitney, who were eager to avoid a direct confrontation with the private power interests.[7]

Both Whitney and Beck seem to have been more concerned about the proposed treaty between Canada and the United States than about the export legislation. They feared that if the monopoly of the power companies at Niagara were confirmed by international agreement the companies would become more intransigent. A draft treaty along the lines proposed by Gibbons was ready by the fall of 1907, giving Canada the right to divert about 36,000 second-feet at Niagara – twice as much as the United States was permitted. When the terms of the agreement were revealed by the press early in 1908, Adam Beck was greatly alarmed. If no new franchises could be granted at Niagara, he warned Whitney, 'it would undoubtedly prove fatal to industrial interests throughout western Ontario.' Should the province consent to the treaty, 'our hands will be tied, and we will practically be at the mercy of the corporations to whom charters have been granted, and our only weapon of defense will be beyond our grasp.' The premier requested that Laurier arrange a meeting at which the British ambassador to Washington, formally in charge of the negotiations, might hear the province's case. In February 1908 Attorney-General J.J. Foy, accompanied by the Hydro commissioners, Beck, J.S. Hendrie, and W.K. McNaught, went to Ottawa to state their case to James Bryce.[8]

It is not clear how effective this provincial intervention in international relations was, but it may have strengthened the determination of the Canadian negotiators not to concede the American demand that the treaty state explicitly that the power companies on the Ontario side at Niagara could export up to half their production. Not including such a provision at least left open the possibility that exports might be recaptured at some future date, and with this the province had to be content. But when George Gibbons claimed that Whitney had given his approval to the terms of the treaty, the premier was quick to correct him. He did not even know what the treaty provisions were, he insisted, 'and I am distinctly and unmistakably positive that I not only never agreed to anything, but that I was never asked to do so.'[9] Still, when the Boundary Waters Treaty was finally signed in January 1909, the province made no protest. Yet Beck and Whitney remained wary, and their suspicions seemed confirmed when the United States Senate added a rider to the agreement giving the Americans control over three-quarters of the flow of the St Mary's River at the Sault. The premier complained that 'The point is that while we agree by the Treaty to tie ourselves up at Niagara and elsewhere in consideration of the Americans tying themselves up also elsewhere, we now find that at the last moment a change is to be made, and the old condition of affairs is to spring up again and remain in existence at Sault Ste Marie.' He protested formally to Ottawa against approving the change. In the end, however, Justice Minister Aylesworth's opinion that the rider would not seriously affect Canadian rights was accepted, and the treaty came into effect in 1910,[10] giving Ontario the right to divert up to 36,000 second-feet at Niagara, and the Americans half that amount.

Because control over both exports and treaty-making lay so clearly in federal hands, the provincial government could do little more than offer advice to Ottawa and seek to ensure that its interests were not seriously compromised. The 1907 power export legislation at least ensured that electricity sales to the United States were made under annual licences and were subject to control. The 1909 Boundary Waters Treaty established the principle that each nation was entitled to an equal share of the waterpower on international streams, about which the province could scarcely complain. By 1909 it hardly mattered so much that the limited diversion at Niagara might strengthen the hands of the private power companies, since Beck and Whitney were by then fully committed to a publicly owned distribution system. Their dominance over the private entrepreneurs had increased by the time the treaty went into effect in 1910 with the threat of disallowance gone. Nevertheless, the issue of which level of government in the final analysis possessed the authority to regulate power exports remained unsettled. When the war created a serious electricity shortage, the confict between the two levels of government would flare up again with increased intensity.

II

The other factor which created friction between the two governments over energy policy was the constitutional ambiguity regarding the ownership of water-power on navigable and international rivers. An 1898 decision by the Privy Council granted ownership of the beds of all inland waterways to the province of Ontario. Part of that proprietary right seemed to be the beneficial use of the power of the flowing waters. Yet it was not clear how far the right of use was limited by federal jurisdiction over navigation. Premier George Ross made one effort to settle this issue by persuading the federal government to agree that all the water not required for navigation belonged to the province. But no such formal understanding was ever reached.[11]

In 1907, with the question of electricity exports in mind, Premier Whitney was outraged to learn that an American concern, the St Lawrence Power Company, had applied to the federal government for permission to dam the entire St Lawrence River near Cornwall. He felt that 'the proposition to hand over control of the St. Lawrence to a private corporation – and an alien one at that – is so startling as to take away one's breath ... [T]he mere mention of the scheme is enough to secure condemnation.' George Gibbons agreed. He pointed out to the prime minister that the company had already had one application turned down since it had proposed to export more than half its power production to the United States. He recommended that the federal government should have nothing to do with any scheme to dam the St Lawrence which involved the export of Canada's half share of the power. But the Aluminum Company of America, which had instigated the plan, refused to drop the idea and continued to press for approval in Washington and Ottawa.[12]

The danger to provincial interests became more acute in 1908 when the Ontario Court of Appeal decided that grants to private owners of crown lands lying on navigable rivers included the river-beds to the middle of the water courses. While this judgment was in accordance with English common law Ontario had always proceeded on the assumption that river- and lake-beds remained in crown hands unless specifically alienated. Should the decision stand, the province's legal adviser warned: 'It further follows that all the great water powers of this province and the right to use the water of the St Lawrence River, the Ottawa River or any of our navigable waters, the shores of which have been granted away, is in [sic] private owners.' A private concern like the Aluminum Company might simply buy up the lands along the bank and deprive the province of its control over this vital resource.[13]

Moreover, Sir Wilfrid Laurier took the view that the federal government alone had the right to authorize development on navigable rivers. Discussing the case of the Rainy River, the prime minister told the House of Commons in 1909 that 'insofar as a navigable river is concerned the local legislature has not the power to create a corporation which would exercise any rights over a navigable stream.' While admitting that the law was vague on this point, he insisted that the provinces had no authority 'to create any work interfering with a navigable river ... The authority to deal with a navigable river is left exclusively with parliament.'[14]

Fortunately for the province, the St Lawrence Power Company's plans required approval by the International Waterways Commission which held hearings on the proposal in March 1910. Adam Beck represented Ontario Hydro; he argued that the danger of granting such privileges to private interests had been made plain at Niagara Falls: '[I]f any water power trust should get hold of power of that kind, it could deliver the energy produced on its own terms and to that extent could practically enslave the people for all time to come.' Public ownership was the only way to ensure effective regulation. Lawyer Irwin Hilliard, an old crony of the premier, put the case for the province of Ontario. He complained that the efforts of the St Lawrence Power Company to obtain a federal charter were designed simply to evade provincial control: '[W]hat we say, speaking on behalf of the Government, is that any power which is developed from the water of the River St. Lawrence belongs, as to the proprietary rights, to the Province of Ontario.' And the newly created Commission of Conservation, which included Frank Cochrane, Ontario's minister of lands, forests, and mines, also came out strongly against the company's plan.[15] Nonetheless Laurier failed to prevent the chief Liberal whip, F.F. Pardee, from introducing a private bill to incorporate the St Lawrence Power Company. Although supporters of the bill argued that it merely chartered a harmless transmission company which must make a contract with a non-existent generating company in order to obtain power, others were less sanguine. Premier Whitney was determined to block the bill rather than see 'the Dominion ... give another pinprick to Ontario.' Beck reiterated his attacks upon the company's plans and lawyer George Lynch-Staunton was briefed to appear before the Private Bills Committee on behalf of the province. In the Commons debate Conservative MPs aired the same objections and pointed out the suspicious fact that the company would possess sweeping powers of expropriation. Robert Borden bluntly denounced the scheme as an attempt to undermine the HEPC.

The prime minister refused to intervene. He insisted that the bill was a private measure of no concern to the government. Nonetheless, he allowed the House to debate the bill all through the night of 14–15 March 1910 and until noon the following day. During the discussion Public Works Minister William Pugsley criticized the province's pretensions.

[T]he Ontario Government has no power on earth to develop this water power. It is a power contained in a navigable river, which under the British North America Act is absolutely under the control of this parliament. Another insuperable obstacle is that it is an international river ... I do not think that any province has the power to engage in the construction of a work which of necessity extends outside the limits of the province.[16]

But the opposition was so bitter that the sponsors were eventually forced to accept an amendment specifically stating that the bill did not constitute approval for damming the St Lawrence. Then the Senate struck out the declaration that the company's works were for the general advantage of Canada. As a result the bill was dropped.[17]

Laurier was not dismayed by this outcome. He had already warned George Gibbons not to let the International Waterways Commission announce its findings without consulting the federal government. After the parliamentary debate he wrote to Gibbons: 'Nothing done at this moment over all this question is the best policy.'[18] But the prime minister apparently resented the province's interference; he called it 'a clear case of obstruction engineered by Beck to keep the monopoly of the Hydro-Electric Commission.' Near the end of 1910 he grumbled in a letter: 'You know as well as I do that the local Government has attempted to exercise jurisdiction over navigable waters, which is clearly outside the power vested in the Province ... Our policy during Sir Oliver Mowat's time was to prevent the Dominion Government from encroaching upon the powers of the Provinces. We may now have to prevent the Province of Ontario from encroaching upon the powers of the Dominion.'[19]

For the time being, however, open conflict was averted, because the International Waterways Commission refused to approve the damming of the St Lawrence unless the plans clearly specified that one-half the power produced would be sold in Canada.[20] In the aftermath of this affair the Whitney government sought to ensure the province's control over water-power on navigable rivers by passing an act in 1911 'for the Protection of the Public Interest in the Bed of Navigable Waters.' This legislation provided that in the absence of the express grant of a water-lot the Crown should retain all the riparian rights. Those who had already developed water powers without such a grant were permitted to apply for patents to their water-lots to be granted at the cabinet's discretion.[21] Prior to its defeat in the fall of 1911 the Laurier administration made no comment upon this move, but to Whitney's surprise and annoyance the new Conservative justice minister, C.J. Doherty, criticized it severely. He declared that it was general, retroactive legislation designed to recover, without compensation, rights previously granted away by the Crown. Attorney-General J.J. Foy's heated reply expressed regret at again being 'called upon to defend the rights of a Provincial Legislature within the limits of ... section 92 ... to enact such laws as it may deem expedient.' What right had the federal cabinet to question the propriety or justness of the actions of the provincial legislature? Disallowance would involve 'the substitution for the judgment of the people of Ontario as final arbiters, the judgment of a body in no sense representative of, and having no responsibility to, the people of Ontario, and a return to the system of government which obtained before the establishment of responsible government in Canada.'

Doherty's spirited answer was that disallowance could be exercised 'for the purpose of preventing ... irresparable injustice or undue interference with private rights or property through the operation of local statutes.' He admitted that no private parties had registered complaints, however; so he lamely concluded that the act would be left to operate.[22] Why he should have become embroiled in such a dispute, particularly in light of the close ties which existed between Whitney and the new prime minister, Robert Borden, is far from clear. Perhaps it simply reflected the inexperience of a fledgling minister. In any event Doherty appears to have recognized that the political cost of such a fight was too high, and he permitted the matter to drop.

The province made a number of other attempts to settle the matter of ownership of water-power on navigable rivers. In 1911 Lands, Forests, and Mines Minister Frank Cochrane demanded that Ottawa hand over all rents received for water used for power purposes on the Welland and Trent canals. To Justice Minister Aylesworth it seemed that the province was claiming title to 'everything except (I suppose) any [water] that may still be in the clouds.' He advised that the claim be ignored.[23] In 1912 the provincial government again sought to bring the matter to a head by starting two suits against the federal government in the Exchequer Court. While these suits were being prepared, several meetings were held during 1913 between Borden and Lands, Forests, and Mines Minister W.H. Hearst in an effort to negotiate a settlement. Nothing resulted, and the matter was dropped until 1915 when Hearst, by then premier, raised it once more. Despite further meetings no final settlement was ever reached.[24] By that time the war effort had begun to cause serious power shortages in Ontario and attention focused upon the friction between the two governments caused by this problem during the next five years.

III

The First World War not only quickened the pace of industrialization in Ontario but also accelerated the integration of the province into the North American economic system. This made it more difficult for the province to establish its own set of priorities in energy policy, and such efforts led to friction with both the federal government and American authorities. Thus the policies of Ontario Hydro under the leadership of Adam Beck frequently embroiled the provincial government in conflict with Ottawa during the war.

The success of the Hydro-Electric Power Commission in attracting customers had already threatened to exhaust the supply of power available to it from private producers before war broke out. Compounding this problem were the efforts of the three companies at Niagara Falls to increase their right to export to the United States. In the spring of 1914 Beck advised a member of the federal cabinet that 'the question is a very important and most vital one to the province of Ontario, and there is no doubt that within a very short time we shall require all of the water and available power therefrom from [sic] Niagara Falls for the supplying of industries in western and central Ontario ... We strenuously object to increasing the amount of power allowable for export.' As a result the Borden government refused to license increased exports and actually reduced the Canadian Niagara Power Company's quota by 6,500 horsepower annually.[25]

As another means of controlling the private generating companies at Niagara, Beck procured from the Ontario cabinet an order-in-council in June 1914 formally dividing up the 36,000 cubic feet per second of water which Canada could divert at the Falls for power purposes. Canadian Niagara was granted 8,225 second-feet, the Ontario Power Company 11,180 second-feet, and the Electrical Development Company, 9,985 second-feet. The remaining 6,500 second-feet were thus available for future use. By July 1915 Beck claimed that the demand for power required new generating facilities at Niagara. He proposed that Ontario Hydro itself should build a huge new plant with an ultimate capacity of 500,000 horsepower. Water would be diverted above the Falls into a canal and used at Queenston, where the greater head would make for more efficiency. This ambitious undertaking, he said, would take three years to build and cost $10 million. The provincial cabinet was extremely reluctant to embark on such a project in wartime, but eventually it buckled under pressure from the membership of the Ontario Municipal Electric Association, a pro-Hydro pressure group. A bill rushed through during the final hours of the 1916 session of the legislature empowered the HEPC to begin construction once the cabinet gave permission.[26]

This legislation immediately provoked a protest from Washington. The diversion of 6,500 second-feet around the Falls to Queenston, argued Secretary of State Robert Lansing, would interfere with a proposed dam across the Niagara River in the gorge between the Falls and Queenston. The Borden government hastily forwarded this note to Toronto for comment. Consultations took place between the prime minister and Ontario Attorney-General I.B. Lucas as well as officials from the External Affairs Department and engineers from the Hydro. Since the 1909 treaty clearly gave Canada the right to divert 36,000 second-feet at Niagara, both governments agreed that the American objections should be ignored. Washington allowed the matter to drop.[27]

The private power companies were even more unhappy with Beck's plans to enter into direct competition with them. Under the agreements between the companies and the Niagara Park Commission, the commissioners had bound themselves not to take water from the Niagara River for power purposes. Sir William Mackenzie, who controlled the Electrical Development Company, was convinced that the Queenston project was a violation of this undertaking, despite a clause in the Niagara Development Act of 1916 specifically exempting it. But when the Electrical Development Company tried to take the matter to court, it found the way blocked by the refusal of the attorney-general (who was also a Hydro commissioner) to permit it to sue the HEPC. As a result, the company petitioned the federal government in the spring of 1917 to disallow the Niagara Development Act of 1916 and certain amendments made to it at the 1917 session of the legislature. The grounds for disallowance were that by entering into illegal competition with the private producers the Hydro would harm the credit of Canada and violate the contractual rights of the companies to their serious detriment.[28]

In reply Attorney-General Lucas argued that the Hydro had not been authorized to violate the rights of the companies. No work at all had been done as yet, but the province had a duty to make the most efficient possible use of the limited amount of water available for power purposes. In addition, he repeated all the arguments against disallowance which had become familiar over the past couple of decades. Justice Minister Doherty refused to interfere with the provincial legislation on the company's behalf.[29]

Because of his long-standing conflicts with the private producers Adam Beck experienced serious difficulties when he attempted to purchase additional supplies of power to meet the growing demand from war industries. The Canadian Niagara Power Company would provide additional power only if the provincial government formally agreed to permit it to export half of its total production in perpetuity. By 1 May 1916 Beck had only 100,000 horsepower available to meet a demand of 114,000 horsepower and was forced to curtail deliveries to munitions makers.[30] He persuaded Premier Hearst that Ottawa must be approached to cut back power exports, and by early July the province was insisting that *all* power exports must be stopped to meet domestic needs. A black-out in Toronto on 18 July created such an uproar that Canadian Niagara gave in, apparently fearing cancellation of its export privileges, and agreed to sell 50,000 horsepower to the HEPC. Yet by the fall of 1916 a further shortage had developed, and American firms warned the Imperial Munitions Board that they would be unable to fill British orders if power exports from Ontario were cut further.[31]

In April 1917 the Hydro purchased the Ontario Power Company outright to secure its generating capacity, although included among the company's obligations were long-term export contracts for over 50,000 horsepower per year.[32] In 1916 and 1917 the legislature also passed two Water Powers Regulation Acts which permitted the province to investigate the generating capacity of any private plant, fix an authorized maximum, and order the company to deliver any excess production to the Hydro. Beck knew, for instance, that the Electrical Development Company had in its plant eleven generators rated at 150,000 horsepower. Since the company was authorized to produce only 125,000 horsepower, it might be compelled to deliver the excess to the HEPC. The company's management resisted and demanded that the two Water Powers Regulation Acts be disallowed (along with the two acts authorizing construction of the Queenston plant). Company solicitor D.L. McCarthy charged that Adam Beck was making himself a virtual dictator: 'It has already become widely understood that no candidate for a seat on either side of the House has any chance whatever of being elected until he arrives at an agreement with the Chairman of the Hydro-Electric Commission.' The aims of the public power movement had been utterly subverted: 'Under the name of "public ownership" small groups of persons have been endowed by the legislature of Ontario with powers of an exclusive and monopolistic character, without adequate constitutional checks upon their proceedings.'[33]

Again Lucas defended the legislation and reiterated that the federal government could never really judge the justness of the province's actions. He added that far from being an injured party the company had illegally appropriated large amounts of water without paying for it and had 'up to the present done nothing to assist the Hydro-Electric Commission or the Government of Ontario in solving the problem of an adequate supply of power to meet the extraordinary demands occasioned by the war.' To this veiled charge of disloyalty, Lucas added the warning that disallowance might 'have the effect of intimating to such companies ... that they may with impunity defy any control on the part of the Executive Government or Legislature of the Province while at the same time disregarding the fulfillment of their contractual obligations.' On 4 May 1917 Justice Minister Doherty refused to disallow the Water Powers Regulation Act of 1916, although reserving the 1917 act for later consideration. He suggested that the issues in dispute ought to be settled in court, and the provincial government promptly filed suit against the Electrical Development Company for breach of contract. In addition, a commission of enquiry under the 1917 act was set up on 25 July to inspect the operations of the company.[34]

The company renewed its petition for the disallowance of this legislation in November 1917, and in January 1918 the province delivered its defence of the act in the customary terms. The influence of Sir William Mackenzie and his associates, however, secured a personal hearing before the justice minister in April 1918. Lawyer G.H. Kilmer, who represented the province, reported that the company's solicitors simply 'rehashed the matters covered by their petition and indulged in a tirade of vulgar abuse of the Provincial authorities, the Hydro-Electric Commission and the Commissioners appointed ... under the Water Powers Regulation Act.'[35] The Ontario government must have been dismayed by Doherty's report. He severely criticized the 1917 legislation for leaving it to a commission of three Supreme Court judges to determine the capacity of a power plant. Such matters were best left to the courts to decide, if the HEPC believed that a company was violating its contractual agreements. 'Beyond this', remarked Doherty sourly, 'the undersigned is unable to offer any suggestions favourable to the course which the legislature had adopted, and it is with very great hesitation that he has concluded that in view of the precedents and principles which have governed the Ministers of Justice in their recommendations upon local legislation that he ought not to advise the disallowance of this statute.' Nonetheless, the federal authorities once more allowed Adam Beck to have his way. On the following day, 25 April 1918, the investigative commission ordered the Electrical Development Company to deliver 25,000 horsepower from its excess capacity to the Hydro.[36]

By that time the power shortage had become acute. In June 1917 the Carborundum Company of Niagara Falls, New York, had reported that it was unable to deliver abrasives ordered by the British government. An enquiry by the Imperial

Munitions Board revealed that 'everything points to the Ontario Hydro Electric Commission refusing to allow power to be exported to the United States.' Both Britain and the United States held the federal government responsible for straightening out these problems. On 27 June Sir Joseph Flavelle, chairman of the Imperial Munitions Board, met with Beck and the power company executives at Toronto. The gathering proved unproductive. The representatives of the Electrical Development Company and the Canadian Niagara Power Company complained bitterly that while they exported 22,000 and 36,000 horsepower respectively, the Ontario Power Company, now owned by Hydro, continued to fulfil contracts for the supply of 50,000 horsepower to American customers. Beck wanted their export sales to cease completely without giving up his own agreements, while the private companies wanted any reductions in exports to be shared among all three producers.

Flavelle sympathized with this point of view. But Adam Beck categorically refused to enter into any tripartite agreement on redistributing power supplies, on the grounds that Hydro, as a governmental body, was already acting entirely in the public interest. The meeting broke up without any result, and within a week there were further complaints that power supplies for Allied munitions plants had been curtailed.[37] At Flavelle's suggestion, Borden approached Premier Hearst directly in the hope of winning his co-operation. But Hearst responded with a strong defence of the Hydro. Unlike the private companies it was not a profit-making operation but was designed to serve the public; already it had curtailed industrial supplies for this reason and could meet the needs of the munitions makers only by recapturing power that was being exported to the United States. 'In view of what I have said above,' wrote the premier, 'I cannot see what this Province or the Commission can do more than we are doing to economize in power, and to utilize it to the very best advantage for war purposes.'[38]

In the light of Hearst's cool response, Borden and Flavelle dropped plans to convene a conference of Canadian and American officials to set power supply priorities during the summer of 1917. But in September another wave of telegrams from American munitions makers protesting rumoured cuts in power exports descended upon Flavelle. The Imperial Munitions Board feared that 'there would be a serious danger of strong retaliatory measures if such diversions were actually effected.' The British ambassador in Washington was warned that vital coal and steel supplies from the United States might be cut off. He, too, suggested a conference with the American authorities. However, the Borden government, fearful of Beck's disruptive presence at such a meeting, showed no enthusiasm for the idea. Instead, it was decided to set up a one-man royal commission to investigate the problem; Sir Henry Drayton's enquiry would at least provide an excuse to fend off the Americans for a few months.[39]

Drayton set to work promptly. He soon discovered that a critical power shortage did exist and would probably reach a peak of 102,000 horsepower by 1 December

1917. Cancellation of export contracts was no solution as this would only hamper munitions production in the United States. While critical of the performance of the private power companies, Drayton's comments about the Hydro's record were even more scathing. In acquiring the Ontario Power Company in April 1917 the HEPC had foolishly agreed to use its 'best endeavours' with both federal and provincial governments to keep the company free at all times to fulfil its export commitments. No wonder, then, that Beck was pressing Ottawa to ban all exports by the privately owned companies while leaving Ontario Power alone, In fact, Drayton suggested, Beck was not even being straightforward about his objectives; he really hoped to induce Ottawa to ban *all* power exports from Canada. In anticipation of this prohibition he had inserted in the purchase agreement a clause providing that if the federal government interfered with Ontario Power's export contracts, the company would not be liable for any damages. Drayton therefore recommended that the three Canadian generating companies should continue to export 108,000 horsepower annually. Meanwhile, a power controller should be appointed by Ottawa under the War Measures Act with authority to fix priorities for electricity supply in Canada and to compel the companies to obey them.[40]

When a cabinet committee met to consider Drayton's report on 26 October 1917, it already had before it a demand from Beck that *he* should have this kind of power. In an effort to get his way the Hydro chairman sent a warning to Customs Minister J.D. Reid that he would put up a 'Beck-Hydro' candidate to oppose every Unionist running in Ontario in the December general election. The ministers decided to temporize; Dratyton was appointed power controller and directed to draw up a list of priorities to which the private producers but not the Hydro would be subject. Drayton quickly ordered all generating stations to run at full capacity and to take as much water from the Niagara River as they required. After meetings with American officials he decided that exports could not be reduced below an average of 108,000 horsepower without harming the overall war effort. The power controller used every means he could think of to keep the Hydro chairman under control: 'It was whispered that Sir Henry went so far as to tell Adam Beck if he were not more co-operative the public might have to be told that Adam Beck had a pro-German relative in the United States.'[41]

The power shortage in Ontario became even more acute on 21 December 1917 when a surge of current severely damaged several generators at the Canadian Niagara Power Company's plant. The fault was traced to a short circuit in the HEPC system to which that equipment had been connected. Convinced that Hydro engineers had been guilty of sloppy practices Canadian Niagara refused to reconnect its generators after repairs and began exporting the power to Buffalo for street lighting. Sir Joseph Flavelle complained: 'We have had a singular experience: the United States was denied power for necessitous plants; the British Government was denied power for ferrosilicon plants; while this power was being exported to the United States because a difference between the Hydro Commission and the

Canadian Niagara Power Company could not be composed.' Drayton was forced to intervene in February 1918 and order Canadian Niagara to resume supplying power to the Hydro system.[42]

Adam Beck still refused to co-operate. Ottawa learned in January 1918 that Washington was extremely upset because vital supplies of carbide and explosives were being held up, because power had been denied the producers by Ontario Hydro. Unless this situation was rectified, the United States fuel controller might cut off indispensable coal exports to Canada. Borden appealed to Hearst to rein in his headstrong, self-willed Hydro chairman but he got little response. Hearst not only refused to come to Ottawa to see the prime minister, but when interviewed by Newton Rowell at Queen's Park, he admitted he knew little about the matter. A fortnight later the premier did agree to go to the capital, and Reid and Flavelle later journeyed to Toronto to meet with Beck. But the Hydro chairman remained obdurate.[43]

American officials became more and more annoyed. Borden left for Washington at the end of February 1918 to try to sort out these and other wartime problems. Before his departure he 'arranged with Rowell to see Press in Toronto on Power question as Beck is evidently determined to fight us.' R.J. Bulkley, the American fuel controller, bluntly informed the Canadian delegates that they were handling both Beck and the private producers much too tentatively. The Toronto Power Company, for instance, had a 14,000 horsepower steam plant standing idle which could supply the HEPC with much-needed power. Borden promised immediate action and Bulkley agreed to release an additional 250 tons of coal per day to run the plant. On his return to Ottawa the prime minister ordered Drayton to do everything necessary to see that American munitions suppliers suffered no power shortages in future.[44]

By early April, however, the Americans were again complaining. Once more the problem was the friction between Beck and the private producers. He refused to supply the American Cyanamid Company with all the power it was entitled to under its contract, because the Toronto Power Company was supplying current only to its own customers and not Hydro. Eventually the federal cabinet had to give Drayton wider authority so that he could compel Toronto Power to provide 11,000 horsepower to the Hydro at peak hours. Nonetheless, the power controller still lacked authority to fix priorities for power distributed by Hydro. Beck alone decided how much current would be made available for domestic uses, exercising an independent authority which continued to disrupt relations between Canada and the United States.[45]

Just as the war was coming to an end Beck cut off all supplies to certain munitions-makers in October 1918. Other customers began to receive only irregular service. A deputation of angry industrialists descended upon the power controller, demanding protection; a meeting of the Toronto branch of the Canadian

Manufacturers Association was convened on 18 October with both Beck and Drayton present.[46] Publicly the power controller praised the Hydro chairman, but privately federal officials were convinced that he had been negligent in selling current and promoting electric appliances without an assured source of additional power. When extension of the Ontario Power Company's plant was delayed, he blamed everything on them, charging that the power controller had permitted urgently needed power to be exported while the Imperial Munitions Board had placed orders without being certain energy was available. Sir Joseph Flavelle was infuriated. Beck, he complained to Newton Rowell, could never admit to being at fault: 'True to his type he charges his troubles to the incapacity and inconsiderateness of others, and probably hoped that, as before, if sufficient storm were raised, he would some way secure temporary assistance which would carry him over the trying period until his new power is developed.' Another federal official remarked that the Hydro chairman's behaviour was such 'that those familiar with his acts wonder whether he is intentionally and boldly interfering with war work or simply an unreasonable being.'[47]

Flavelle wanted a complete embargo on civilian electricity consumption except for lighting. Drayton, however, was unwilling to save Beck's neck and incur the odium which such a move would provoke. He proposed across-the-board cuts for all consumers in an effort to muddle through till spring. Fortunately, the Armistice solved the problem. Within a fortnight some American war contracts had been cancelled, all British orders were terminated on 11 December, and the remaining American orders ceased at the year's end.[48] The steadily worsening post-war recession put a temporary end to the severe shortage of electricity, although by the fall of 1920 Ontario Hydro again found itself short of power. Once more Adam Beck tried to force the Electrical Development Company to supply him with additional current by requesting Ottawa to cancel all of the company's export privileges. Trade and Commerce Minister George Foster refused to intervene.[49] In fact, the province had already decided to purchase Sir William Mackenzie's utility empire including the Electrical Development Company. Even the opening of the world's largest hydroelectric station at Queenston in 1922 did not fully satisfy Ontario's ever-growing appetite for power, which explains the attention paid to the development of the lower St Lawrence and the Ottawa rivers during the 1920s.

Throughout the period from 1905 to 1920, then, the issue of controlling the exportation of electrical energy was a particular source of friction between the federal and provincial governments. Because of clear federal responsibility for controlling exports and the management of international relations, Ontario found itself in a difficult position when it tried to go its own way. During the war the scope for independent action was further narrowed by ever-increasing economic integration with the United States. Once the Americans entered the fighting in

1917, their claim to a share of Canadian energy supplies to support the war effort could hardly be denied by the federal government, which eventually asserted its authority by appointing a power controller under the War Measures Act.

After 1914 Adam Beck assumed the key role in shaping provincial policy, in part because of the ineffectiveness of Hearst, Whitney's successor as Premier. The Hydro chairman was both devious and aggressive in his dealings with his cabinet colleagues, as evidenced by the way in which he entangled them against their better judgment in commitments to build the huge Queenston plant as well as a system of electrified railways. Brooking no opposition and freed from the close control once exercised by Sir James Whitney, Beck went about his business with scant regard for any interests but his own and those of his organization. The wartime power shortage presented him with a golden opportunity to acquire more generating capacity and to place his rivals, the private power producers, at a serious disadvantage. Federal officials found that they had to be ready to fight their hardest if they wished to interfere with the Hydro, Beck's personal fiefdom.

The legacy of this conflict proved extremely important to the future conduct of federal-provincial relations. There survived in Ottawa the conviction expressed by Sir Wilfrid Laurier that only the federal parliament could authorize power development on navigable international or interprovincial rivers. To this belief Laurier's successors clung, as we shall see. Moreover, considerable bitterness was engendered among Hydro officials and provincial politicians by the wartime clashes. Ontario's leaders became prejudiced against all proposals for the exportation of electrical energy, and were convinced that every effort to retain control over power development on the provincial and international boundary waters was justified by this consideration alone.

5 Playing the Federal-Provincial Game

Federal interference in provincial affairs was not confined to policies concerning natural resource development. As Ontario's economy grew, control of corporate business became another source of friction. As in the cases of the Hydro and Florence Mining Company, private interest groups in pursuit of their own objectives often provoked the conflict between governments. In addition, a bureaucratic imperative existed, with provincial officials defending their sphere of authority against what they saw as federal interference. Ontario civil servants became fearful that the central government might encroach upon their power to incorporate and regulate companies. They enlisted in this battle both their political superiors, who feared the loss of authority and revenues, and certain private interests who, for reasons of their own, preferred to come under local rather than national jurisdiction.

Such conflict arose out of a certain ambiguity in the BNA Act regarding the incorporation of companies and, hence, their regulation and taxation. Local legislatures were given the right to incorporate companies with 'provincial objects,'[1] but these objects were nowhere specifically defined. Obviously, small undertakings whose dealings were confined to a limited geographical area could perfectly well operate under provincial charters. But as the nineteenth century drew to a close, the scope and extent of corporate business steadily expanded. Now a manufacturing concern based in Ontario might service a national market, while an insurance company might be writing policies on property located in another province or even another country. Once those undertakings entered the interprovincial or international sphere did they cease to have 'provincial objects' and fall under federal control? Or were 'provincial objects' to be defined according to the other subsections of the ninety-second clause of the BNA Act which included 'property and civil rights,' an all-encompassing category which the courts showed every disposition to define in a broad and generous way?

Ottawa, however, was not without its own authority in the field of company incorporation. Since undertakings such as banking and shipping fell under exclusive federal jurisdiction, parliament had the sole power to incorporate companies engaging in such activities. Moreover, under its general authority to regulate 'trade and commerce' the central government appeared to have broad powers to incorporate, regulate, and tax companies, wherever chartered. The BNA Act also conferred on parliament the power to legislate with regard to shipping, railway, and telegraph lines which crossed provincial boundaries. Even more sweeping was the authority to declare any 'local works and undertakings ... although wholly situate within [one] Province ... before or after their execution ... to be for the general advantage of Canada.'[2] Obviously, operators of such works would be entirely free from local control and regulation. As the range of corporate enterprise increased, a clear division of jurisdiction became more and more imperative. As early as 1881 the Judicial Committee of the Privy Council held that the central government's authority to regulate trade and commerce 'did not include the regulation of the contracts of a particular person or trade, such as the business of fire insurance, within a single province.' Ontario's regulations regarding insurance contracts were thus a proper exercise of jurisdiction over 'property and civil rights.'[3] At the beginning of the twentieth century clashes over company regulation occurred on several fronts.

I

The conflict was primarily provoked by private interests eager to exploit the profit potential of the new hydroelectric technology in supplying power and transportation services. Like other utilities' promoters, these men realized that if they could secure local monopolies for the provision of electrical service, they might reap a very generous return on their investment. And it was, of course, that same realization which helped persuade Whitney to embark upon the experiment of public ownership. Faced with a provincial government determined to regulate utility companies, ambitious entrepreneurs sought to escape local control for the more hospitable climate of Ottawa, which seemed less disposed to interfere in their affairs. By playing off one level of government against the other, in a kind of federal-provincial 'game,' they hoped to secure special privileges, which the local assembly would be unlikely to grant in the face of pressure from municipalities and individuals desiring low-cost, efficient services.

The most persistent of these entrepreneurs were those interested in light electric railways, whose development blurred the distinction between long-distance steam lines and municipal tramways. By the turn of the century electrified lines could carry passengers and light freight over considerable distances. Ontario municipalities, creatures of the province, had long since franchised and regulated transit companies operating within their boundaries. While in most cases these franchises were for fixed terms and carried annual rentals, federally incorporated railway companies received charter privileges in perpetuity and often possessed broad powers of expropriation. Before the First World War municipal transit systems, particularly in larger cities, were usually extremely profitable, and the temptation to try to crack such a lucrative market using federal protection to avoid franchise restrictions proved irresistible to some businessmen.

From an early date Ontario officials were aware of these activities. In 1882 the legislature passed a resolution protesting against the parliamentary practice of declaring steam railway lines built under provincial charters for the general advantage to Canada, thus permitting them to 'escape' provincial supervision, a complaint reiterated at the interprovincial conference in 1887.[4] In 1895 the Mowat administration passed an Electric Railway Act which imposed restrictions upon the promotion of such companies to prevent financial speculation and stock watering. Fares were limited to a level which would provide an 8 per cent annual dividend on shares, and rights of way through municipalities and powers of expropriation were regulated. E.H. Bronson, the minister responsible for this legislation, pressed federal Railways Minister John Haggart to oppose all efforts by electric railway promoters to evade these restrictions by obtaining federal charters. At least Bronson urged Ottawa to amend the national Railway Act to impose similar limitations.[5] The federal government failed to act upon Ontario's request, and in 1896 the issue was raised again when the Hull and Aylmer Railway Company sought to extend its lines across the river into Ottawa despite the Ottawa Street Railway's thirty-year exclusive franchise with the city. The solicitor-general in the new Liberal government, Charles Fitzpatrick, pointed out to the House of Commons that it was a dangerous principle to adopt that this 'House may simply declare a work to be for the general advantage of Canada without its being in reality work for the general benefit of Canada, taking it in that way out of the power of the local legislature and making it one of Dominion concern.' As a result, the promoters withdrew the request for such a declaration, and an understanding was reached that the Hull company's lines would extend no further than a terminus inside Ottawa.[6]

Nevertheless, the problem remained. In 1897 E.H. Bronson again complained to Railways Minister A.G. Blair that the spread of light electric railways was causing problems:

The promoters of some of these schemes, on account of the special provisions in the Ontario Act, have been looking to the Federal parliament for charter powers. It is, of course, true that the undertakings are purely local, and should in every instance be left to the jurisdiction of the provincial legislature, but it is unfortunately so easy under the terms of the British North American [sic] Act to declare an enterprise of this kind as being 'for the general advantage of Canada,' that these men under cover of that provision have been, some of them at least, seeking incorporation in Ottawa.

He again urged Blair to amend the federal Railway Act to conform with Ontario's, or to adopt a fixed policy of requiring applicants to apply to the provincial legislature for their charters. Still, however, nothing seems to have been done.[7]

During the next few years more than a dozen entrepreneurs obtained declarations of general advantage at each session of parliament, almost all of them for railway schemes. In principle the Laurier administration remained committed to the defence of local autonomy, but in practice it turned a sympathetic ear to the demands of businessmen for broad corporate powers. In 1902, for instance, a group calling themselves the North Shore Power, Railway and Navigation Company applied for a charter to permit them to operate (among other things) a pulp and paper mill, a power station, and a railway in Quebec. Conservative leader Robert Borden protested that to grant these requests and declare the works for the general advantage of Canada would mean 'invading the jurisdiction of the legislature of the province of Quebec.' The prime minister, however, saw no danger. The first duty of government was to promote economic growth; refusing the requests of entrepreneurs 'might restrict the development of the company and put a damper upon the use of capital.' A federal charter would give the North Shore Company 'more extensive power and more elasticity,' he argued, and the bill passed easily with government backing.[8]

A few days later an application was received to charter the Toronto and Niagara Power Company, an enterprise controlled by William Mackenzie and Henry Pellatt. This concern would transmit the current developed by the Electrical Development Company to Toronto for use by the Toronto Electric Light Company and the Toronto Railway Company. Two Conservative MP s from the city protested that the new company would be in a position to force the renewal of the lighting and transit franchises (held by the latter concerns) on favourable terms by threatening to cut off the power from Niagara and refusing to supply anyone else. With a federal charter the province would be unable to intervene effectively. Once again, however, the company's backers proved strong enough to push its application through.[9]

But so broad were the powers granted this company that the provincial government of Ontario became concerned. In March 1903 Attorney-General John M. Gibson complained to Justice Minister Fitzpatrick that 'the power assumed to be given to this company is at variance with the well-understood control which municipalities exercises [sic] over streets and public roadways within their limits.' Gibson complained that the declaration of general advantage had been inserted merely for the purpose of giving jurisdiction, and if jurisdiction can be assumed in that way in one case, it can be in any other case. Who is to determine whether any particular work is or is not "for the general advantage of Canada"?' Noting that the problem was likely to become more acute as electric railways spread out across the province, the attorney-general argued that if Ottawa were to take control of all the new lines, there would be a vast interference in municipal rights. Undertakings of limited magnitude should be left to the province, he insisted.[10]

Fitzpatrick replied that municipal rights were fully protected under the federal Railway Act, which required the consent of the local government to use highways or public places. But parliament must retain unlimited discretion to make declarations of general advantage. If the province opposed any charter application it was perfectly at liberty to make its case before the Railway Committee or the Private Bills Committee, and he promised in future to forward all applications for works in Ontario to the attorney-general. Still dissatisfied, Gibson tried to persuade Railways Minister Blair to act: 'The view of our Government is that this matter should not be allowed to drift on in the loose way as between the two jurisdictions which has hitherto been pursued. Some sort of legislative declaration on the subject appears to be necessary.' Blair promised his co-operation, and Gibson sent lawyer Aemilius Irving off to Ottawa to confer with the railways minister in May 1903.[11]

Irving toyed with the notion of having a Supreme Court judge examine all applications for a declaration of general advantage and report upon the proposed undertakings. But the issue was not really a judicial one, nor was the justice minister prepared to curtail the independence of parliament, and the idea was soon dropped. All that Irving could suggest was an amendment to the Railway Act to make clear that a provincially chartered railway did not fall under the control of Ottawa simply by virtue of intersecting a federally incorporated road. Blair raised no objections to this idea, but debate in the House of Commons soon revealed that many MPs wanted all railways, electrified or otherwise, to come under the jurisdiction of the newly created federal regulatory body, the Board of Railway Commissioners. To make the board's powers clear some members even suggested that all railways in Canada simply be declared for the general advantage. Alarmed, two Liberal back-benchers in the Ontario legislature hastily introduced a resolution condemning declarations which violated municipal and provincial rights, particularly in the case of light electric railways. The motion passed with bipartisan support.[12]

Provincial concern was increased by section 184 of the proposed Railway Act, which appeared to give the Board of Railway Commissioners authority to permit any existing railway to enter the streets of a municipality without its consent. Based upon the assumption that the success of a railway project might depend upon access to a municipal terminus, this proposal was intended to provide an appeal against unreasonable local demands. But the Conservatives, led by members from Ontario, mounted a strong attack on the bill. E.F. Clarke, member for West Toronto, denounced it as an attempt to destroy the value of all municipal traction franchises by permitting unlimited competition from railways. Clarke, a former mayor of Toronto, complained that electric railway promoters had come to the federal parliament in an effort 'to escape the obligations which the provinces and the municipalities would impose on them ... If the right to operate a street railway is to be declared for the general advantage of Canada, where will legislation of this kind stop?' Where, too, asked Dr T.S. Sproule, were those Liberals who had so vehemently defended provincial rights in the past? Now the unsupported word of any businessman was sufficient to 'deprive the provinces of their constitutional rights in that corporation.' The colourful W.F. Maclean of East York detected a 'constitutional revolution' in the direction of a legislative union, since 'the provinces are being stripped of many of their powers, and especially have we seen during this session and during the past session, a general raiding of municipal rights, particularly in the province of Ontario.'[13]

Railways Minister Blair was taken aback by the violence of this assault. His only aim, he insisted, had been to meet objections made by a few companies that the new Railway Act would restrict their charter rights by making their works subject to municipal approval. They could now appeal to the Board of Railway Commissioners. In future, all railways would require civic approval to enter a municipality, so that there was no intention to interfere with local jurisdiction. It was irrelevant whether or not declarations of general advantage had been properly granted in the past, and he charged that the Conservatives were simply trying to make political capital by representing themselves as defenders of provincial autonomy. The Liberals rallied behind the minister to pass the bill.[14]

As though to point up the dangers which the opposition had predicted however, the House turned its attention that same afternoon to the incorporation of the Toronto and Hamilton Railway Company. Four or five suburban railways were to be amalgamated, and the centrepiece of the new system would be an electrified line between Toronto and Hamilton. The whole system would be declared for the general advantage of Canada and placed under the control of the Board of Railway Commissioners. In the debate over the Railway Act this application had been referred to as a blatant example of the kind of abuse complained of by the Conservatives. E.F. Clarke complained that the Mackenzie-Pellatt interests who controlled the undertaking were seeking to 'override by legislation from this parliament the old obligations, the duties, the conditions, which the legislature of the province of Ontario imposed upon them and which the municipalities imposed upon them.' The railway lines were to be chartered in perpetuity, not franchised, and were to run into the centre of Toronto to connect with the syndicate's street railway system, against the wishes of the civic authorities. The Ontario Union of Municipalities and the mayors of Toronto, Hamilton, and St Catharines all joined in opposing the application.[15]

Blair responded cautiously. Both sides would get a full hearing in the Railway Committee, he insisted, with the result, one observer noted, that a veritable 'cloud of lobbyists' immediately settled upon Ottawa. The promoters insisted that they were being maligned: electrification of their main line did not make them mere tramway operators. They represented the wave of the future, when a network of electric railways would criss-cross the entire nation. Toronto politicians were attempting to secure control of all public transportation between the city and its suburbs, they claimed. Fred Markey, a prominent Liberal backer of the company, complained that the Ontario government was also using this application as a pretext to try to force all railways which operated only within the province to seek local charters. In private discussions the promoters were franker. They admitted that the city of Toronto wielded enough power in the provincial legislature to block any bill and had secured passage of a resolution opposing their scheme in the assembly. Mayor Thomas Urquhart, himself a Liberal, maintained that the syndicate had then turned to the federal authorities for help, arguing that there was nothing to be lost electorally by granting the application, since 'Toronto is Tory anyway.'[16]

So hot did the dispute become that the prime minister and the rest of the cabinet were drawn in. Laurier received a petition from the municipalities involved, endorsed by Aemilius Irving on behalf of the Ontario attorney-general, and another from the Canadian Union of Municipalities. The ministers were forced to listen to formal representations from both sides. It was decided that the application must go back to the Railway Committee for further hearings, and E.F. Clarke again took the lead in criticizing it. Eventually Postmaster-General Sir William Mulock, who represented a constituency in the Toronto area, concluded that there was so much opposition that the bill must not pass without the city's approval. He called representatives of company and city together and demanded that they agree upon 'provisions guaranteeing the company's complete liability to provincial legislation, present and future.'[17] When the revised bill was finally presented to the House of Commons late in August 1903, it still did not escape criticism. Mulock admitted that declarations of general advantage might have been misused in the past, but pointed out that the local authorities were now satisfied. After that the Toronto and Hamilton Railway charter passed without a division.[18]

Why did the bill pass? The syndicate, which had many other interests, obviously had considerable influence with the cabinet. Afterwards, Laurier argued that in ordinary circumstances his government would have opposed the legislation, but once the promoters and the municipal authorities had reached a compromise it was safe to permit a free vote in the House. George Ross's provincial administration also failed to take a strong stand on the issue, perhaps because the Mackenzie-Pellatt interests had close ties with it, too. In the fall of 1903 the premier did complain in general terms about the government's decison to reject certain Senate amendments to the new Railway Act which would have widened provincial and municipal control over lighting, heating, and power franchises, and particularly over electric railways, even if federally chartered. But his protests were ignored.

No agreement was ever reached between the two Liberal administrations on the proper divison of authority in this area. In the spring of 1904 Ross suggested to Laurier that the problem might be solved simply enough: 'Where a charter is for purely provincial purposes the Dominion might direct the applicant to the Provincial Government concerned.' But the old practice continued, and that summer Attorney-General Gibson complained angrily that it was still 'left to the whim of the applicant, who may say in his application, no matter how entirely local or how strictly provincial his proposed company may be – that he seeks incorporation for a company with "Dominion objects." It is very much like the case of a short line of railways between two towns in the interior of the province being declared "*a work for the general benefit of Canada.*"'[20]

After the defeat of the Ross government in 1905 and the election of Whitney and the Conservatives, the stakes in the federal-provincial 'game' seemed to increase. On the one hand, social change and technological advance imparted ever greater value to franchises for the supply of electricity and public transportation. At the same time, members of the Whitney administration tried to exercise tighter control over Ontario utilities than their Liberal predecessors had, in the belief that the public was entitled to a larger share in the profits earned. This development in turn made some businessmen increasingly determined to obtain federal protection against these violations of 'the sacred right of private property.' The result was to propel the two levels of government into a series of collisions with one another.[21]

E.W. Backus, a legendary figure in the resource industries of northwestern Ontario, was one who faced the new provincial government with a challenge from the moment it took office. In February 1904 his provincially chartered Ontario and Minnesota Power Company had signed an agreement with the Ross government to dam the Rainy River between Fort Frances, Ontario, and International Falls, Minnesota. Half the power produced was to be made available for use in Canada, but during the election campaign Backus persuaded the newly appointed commissioner of crown lands, A.G. MacKay, to alter these terms without informing the local citizens. Arguing that the amount of power to be developed varied greatly according to the season, Backus promised that a fixed quantity, 1,000 horsepower, would be reserved for use in Canada. Having secured a monopoly on power development in the area, Backus was in a position to delay construction until his enterprises in the United States required the current, since the province could do nothing except threaten to cancel the whole agreement.[22]

As soon as these terms were agreed to, Backus quickly requested a federal charter for the Ontario and Minnesota Power Company and a declaration that its works were for the general advantage of Canada. Once granted, and embodying the arrangement with the province, the charter would provide a powerful defence against interference by Queen's Park. What did it matter if the development of Fort Frances was held back because all but 1,000 horsepower of electricity was being channelled to Backus's extensive American operations? The ground for seeking a federal charter was that the Rainy River was both the international boundary and navigable in places. Postmaster-General Mulock defended the propriety of the request, and despite strong criticisms from Borden and the Conservatives, the charter passed the Commons.[23] Not until the bill came up for second reading in the Senate did Whitney, not yet two months in office, rouse himself to offer opposition. He requested Laurier to delay the legislation until his government could study it, then briefed an Ottawa lawyer, R.G. Code, to appear before the Private Bills

Committee of the Senate. Under pressure from Code, James Conmee, the Liberal MP from the area, and the solicitors for the town of Fort Frances, it was agreed that the declaration of general advantage should be dropped, so that the rights of the province under its agreement with the company would be protected.[24]

Thus the new provincial government was warned at the outset of the need to keep a sharp eye out for entrepreneurs playing the federal-provincial 'game.' Provincial Treasurer A.J. Matheson told the legislature: 'This Province must watch what the Dominion does ... I say that the Dominion has no right to deprive this Province of valuable rights. It is not to the advantage of the Dominion and Province that there should be this wholesale giving of charters by the Dominion in the manner in which they have been given in the past.' Whitney concluded that Ontario needed somebody in Ottawa to hold a watching brief over all federal legislation, and R.G. Code, a prominent Conservative who had performed effectively in the fight with Backus, was chosen. In May 1905 the premier directed him to examine all pending bills 'with a view to informing me whenever you discover anything which you think needs the attention of the Provincial Government.' Since the parliamentary session of 1905 was already well advanced, Code could do little at first except keep his eyes and ears open. Gradually, however, he worked his way through all the private bill applications involving Ontario and appeared to oppose any declarations of general advantage for essentially local works before the Private Bills Committee or the Railway Committee. Other legislation he promised to refer to Toronto for instructions. Later that year the arrangement was made permanent, and Code was placed on a retainer by the provincial government. He held this position for the next five years, until the election of a Conservative administration in Ottawa restored direct, confidential communication between federal and provincial ministers.[25]

Meanwhile, attempts to evade provincial regulation had reached such proportions that the Whitney government created the Ontario Railway and Municipal Board in 1906. This regulatory tribunal had the power to enforce its decisions upon municipalities, local railways, and utilities, and it promptly ruled that all franchises should be limited to a term of twenty-five years. But the board's power to control federally chartered undertakings was questionable, thus leading board members to urge the government to try to persuade Ottawa to declare only interprovincial railways to be for the general advantage of Canada, and to place all other lines within the province under its control. Like his predecessor, Railways Minister H.R. Emmerson refused to commit himself, promising only that the matter would be taken up at the interprovincial conference in the fall of 1906. Premier Whitney cannot have had high hopes for an understanding with Ottawa on this issue, since Code had warned him that 'There appears to be a somewhat general opinion prevailing, both in the Commons and in the Senate, that all railways, save local electric roads, should be under Dominion jurisdiction – this regardless as to whether jurisdiction properly belongs to the Dominion or not.' The conference did discuss briefly the question of a uniform company law, but no agreement was reached.[26]

At every session of parliament, however, these disputes between Toronto and Ottawa were renewed.[27] Early in 1907 an application was received to incorporate the Hamilton Radial Electric Railway as a work for the general advantage of Canada. The leading promoter of this concern was none other than John M. Gibson, erstwhile staunch defender of provincial rights. He argued that the proposed line would ultimately extend to the international boundary at Niagara and Windsor, and would connect with other federally chartered lines to obtain freight traffic. Moreover, he pointed out that the line of the Hamilton Radial, begun as a provincial undertaking in 1894, had crossed the Grand Trunk Railway's tracks in 1897. In 1903 a legal decision had held that this connection placed the Hamilton Radial under federal jurisdiction. Gibson insisted 'that so far from our wanting to escape supervision or control by the Provincial [Railway and Municipal] Board, we would rather have to deal with that Board than the Dominion Railway Board, both on the ground of convenience and because we have been strongly impressed with the view that Mr Leitch and his colleagues are honestly endeavouring to deal with cases that come before them fairly.' But Gibson urged Whitney not to oppose his application at Ottawa since the provincial legislature lacked the power to grant his request.[28]

Premier Whitney was not impressed. In February 1907 he told the assembly something must be done to stop 'the perfect stream' of applications for declarations of general advantage. If companies could escape provincial jurisdiction so easily, then 'our control over own affairs is merely nominal ... I certainly think it is time for us to enter a protest. Now, I say ... and I am weighing my words, that our Government will not submit to this unless it is compelled.' Even the embarrassed opposition leader, George Graham, promised full Liberal support for the defence of provincial rights.[29] The government introduced legislation providing that any public utility company in Ontario which secured a federal charter could lose all its 'powers, rights, privileges and franchises' at the discretion of the cabinet. All municipal franchises could be terminated and all bonuses or subsidies cancelled, and in future municipalities were forbidden to enter into contracts with federally chartered companies without express approval from the cabinet. Whitney told the legislature: 'True, this is serious legislation; we intend it to be so. It is designed to resent [sic] and put a stop to the insuperable barriers and obstacles with which officious legislators at Ottawa seek to embarrass the Province. It is aimed against the trend of affairs at Ottawa to trample upon Provincial rights.' The premier must have enjoyed the discomfiture of the local Liberals, particularly at a time when he was being much criticized for his Hydro legislation. Having made similar protests against federal charters prior to 1905, they could not now oppose his bill and permitted it to pass without a division, although privately Graham referred to the act as the 'Big Club' and hinted that it might be ultra vires. 'In order to protect the Liberal party,' he told Laurier, 'I made the announcement ... that the party in Ontario were prepared to adhere to the policy which had always been theirs and in doing this I prevented the present Ontario government appropriating something that is very important in party politics.'[30]

Nevertheless, the promoters of the Hamilton Radial bill refused to let it drop. Gibson shuttled back and forth to the capital, exerting his influence in high places (and provoking even the loyal *Globe* to complain of 'the touts of the interested corporations haunting the lobbies of Parliament'). He appealed once more to Whitney to drop his opposition, but the premier instructed Code to go before the Railway Committee and denounce the bill as 'a distinct outrage on the civil rights of the Province.' At the committee stage in the Commons a number of Conservatives sharply attacked the bill, and after a lengthy debate it died when the session of parliament ended before it was passed.[31]

Gibson was not deterred, however, and he let it be known in the fall of 1907 that he intended to revive his application the following year, despite the embarrassment of George Graham, now federal railways minister. He disliked the thought of going before the Railway Committee and giving his opinion of the bill. 'Should I do this in a way that will look at all as if I have forsaken the Liberal principle of Provincial Rights,' Graham confided to the prime minister, 'I fear my influence as a political factor in Ontario will be in a great measure destroyed.' To avoid this awkward situation he suggested a meeting of all the provincial governments to try to reach an agreement on the proper division of jurisdiction over companies: 'If some amicable arrangement could be come to the difficulty would be obviated, and railway enterprises would be unhampered, and all the opportunity for the Tory party in Ontario to make political capital out of the Provincial Rights cry would be crushed.'[32]

Whitney was also ready to consider compromise. Following the suggestion of the chairman of the Railway and Municipal Board, the cabinet agreed that all steam railways should be under federal control and all electrified railways under provincial jurisdiction. Gibson remained determined to ram his bill through parliament by collecting political debts from his fellow Liberals. As one Toronto Conservative summed it up, the attitude of the promoters was: 'We have the pull in this parliament to get this change, and we are going to get it without rhyme or reason.'[33] Gibson himself became convinced that Whitney and his friends were simply obstructing him in order to demonstrate their own influence. Whitney, Gibson warned the prime minister, would simply try to bulldoze him at any conference: 'He is better at bull-dozing than anything else.' Caught in the middle, Laurier was well aware of the need to proceed cautiously, but he and his ministers could not accept the division of control over railways proposed by the province. Finally, the cabinet decided that they would permit the bill to pass only if the cities of Toronto and Hamilton were satisfied. Eventually, civic officials gave their approval, and when the bill reached the Commons, Graham dutifully defended it. He also promised vaguely to continue discussions with Ontario but specifically rejected the suggestion that all electrified lines should fall under provincial authority. The Conservatives tried vainly to make the company subject to the Railway and Municipal Board, but eventually they gave in to the weight of the government's majority and permitted the charter to pass.[34]

Certainly, the Hamilton Radial scheme was a classic 'case of short line of railway between two towns in the interior of the province being declared "a work for the general benefit of Canada,"'[35] something Gibson had strongly opposed at the time he had written those words in 1904. But the Hamilton entrepreneur refused to be swayed by the reluctance of the federal government to get involved and the embarassment he caused the local Liberal party. He knew how to collect his political IOUs to obtain his objectives. Other businessmen were not slow to receive the message that a federal charter might permit a corporation to secure freedom from provincial interference. When similar applications for electric railway charters were debated in the Commons in 1910, Conservative T.S. Sproule complained: 'We are provoking the antagonism of the provinces by our invasion of provincial rights with regard to water powers and chartering provincial railways and in many other directions, and that feeling of ill-will is bound to grow until ultimately it may cause a good deal of trouble.' Graham defended the federal government, arguing that Canada would one day have a nationwide system of electric railways which ought to be under central control. This assertion provoked T.W. Crothers to observe: 'I suppose in one sense an industrious old lady who keeps a cabbage garden is carrying on an industry for the general advantage of Canada ... I would like the minister to give a case where this government would not grant a charter on the ground of provincial rights. It would be a great saving of time if the government would announce its policy in this matter.'[36]

The activities of James Conmee seemed to demonstrate the appositeness of Crothers's view. In 1906 the Liberal MP for Thunder Bay and Rainy River devised a grand scheme for his personal benefit. The Nipigon River, running south from Lake Nipigon into Lake Superior, had a hydroelectric potential estimated at 200,000 horsepower. Conmee determined to secure control of this power and develop it. Unfortunately, the Ontario government possessed a one-chain reserve along both banks, making it the riparian proprietor and owner of the power. Conmee hoped, nonetheless, to take over these rights and set up a power company free from the regulation of the Ontario Hydro-Electric Power Commission. He concluded that the most effective method would be to organize a federally chartered company which might be able to use its power of expropriation to oust the province from control. In 1906 Conmee had a bill introduced in the Senate to charter the Port Arthur Power and Development Company. This concern sought authority to develop power on both Nipigon and Pigeon rivers, and since the

Pigeon River formed the international boundary, Conmee argued, it was imperative that the company should have a federal charter. With the charter in hand Conmee could set about his planned coup.

Although the bill passed the Senate, Whitney soon spotted the danger and alerted federal Conservative leader Robert Borden, who deputed Sproule to obstruct the bill so that it did not reach the floor before the end of the session.[37] Undaunted, James Conmee returned in 1908, this time calling his undertaking the Ontario and Michigan Power Company to emphasize its internationality. Whitney promptly advised George Graham that 'the Province must fight any such legislation,' but the railway minister ignored his warning. The premier therefore gave notice of a motion in the Ontario legislature denouncing the bill. Opposition leader A.G. MacKay hastily wired the prime minister to ascertain the government's view of the charter. But Graham had failed to brief his colleagues, and Laurier could reply only in generalities: if the bill proved on investigation to interfere with provincial rights it would be turned down. Whitney, meanwhile, did his best to kick up a storm. His motion referred to the 'unwarranted and illegal interference with the territorial sovereignty of the province,' and he insisted that his government would use all means to resist this 'aggression and encroachment' by Ottawa, including an appeal to Britain. The local Liberals, caught off balance, could only move an amendment noting that Conmee's bill was not a government measure; but MacKay expressed support for the principle of provincial rights and called for a conference to discuss the matter, a suggestion rejected by the large Conservative majority in the legislature.[38]

With the political dangers of the proposed charter clear, Laurier at once ordered Senate leader Richard Scott to bury the bill in committee. So swiftly was this done that James Conmee complained of the 'scant courtesy' shown him. But Laurier stood firm, putting off his importunate supporter with a tale about the danger to the negotiations with the United States over the Boundary Waters Treaty posed by the charter. George Graham was sent to talk to Conmee and to try to calm him down. Ontario Liberal leader MacKay was reproachful about the whole affair; he thought passage of the bill could have cost Laurier ten seats in Ontario if the party had failed to defend the provincial rights cause.[39]

Conmee proved irrepressible, however. At the 1909 session of parliament he was back again with another bill to charter the Ontario and Michigan Power Company. When he brought it before the Commons, the Conservatives attacked it fiercely and took the unusual step of opposing its reference to the Private Bills Committee. Yet Graham, Aylesworth, and Laurier all defended the request for a federal charter on the grounds that one of the rivers to be developed was both navigable and international. The bill was finally dispatched to the Committee. Whitney could not understand the ministers' actions: 'I cannot help being astonished,' he wrote to his brother, 'that Laurier does not turn down Conmee without any more fuss. The matter is a nuisance and has any amount of cheek, and Laurier is not adding to his reputation by letting him even attempt the outrageous legislation which he proposes.'[40]

The premier again mobilized his forces to try to block the bill. Lawyer G.T. Blackstock was sent to Ottawa to assist R.G. Code in representing the province before the Private Bills Committee. But Liberal whips made sure that thirty MPs were present to approve the application, although a good many Ontario members took care to stay away. Back in the Commons, Aylesworth stoutly defended the principle of issuing federal charters to all concerns whose operations extended beyond a single province. A.C. Boyce summarized the Conservative view of the issue:

The Ontario government takes control of certain powers in certain rivers and streams in Ontario and provides for regulating and developing of those powers and the rates that shall be charged that public for their use. That policy is a popular one, endorsed by the people of that province. This Bill cannot be regarded as other than a direct and flagrant interference with that policy and an attempt to wrest from the province of Ontario the jurisdiction given it by our constitution.

Haughton Lennox colourfully suggested that Conmee's attitude was 'If me and me learned friend, brother Aylesworth, read the British North America Act right, we kin give a man a charter to take the furnace out of your cellar for the general advantage of Canada.'[41]

In an effort to defuse the opposition, the prime minister intervened in the debate to suggest that the declaration of the company's works for the general advantage of Canada should be eliminated. He admitted that if Ontario had a policy of not granting water powers to private concerns, the company's proposed powers of expropriation might involve interference with provincial rights. Perhaps restrictions should be imposed upon the company's right to export its power. Until these matters were settled, the House would suspend action on the bill. The opposition was jubilant. Code believed Laurier's intervention had 'practically killed' the bill, since 'without the right of expropriation the charter would be of little use.' Boyce was delighted that Laurier had 'so certainly exposed his Minister of Justice to very severe censure and ridicule.'[42]

Everyone underrated Conmee's determination. He immediately set about redrafting the bill to meet Laurier's objections without surrendering the all-important power of expropriation. He pleaded with the prime minister not to block the charter, arguing that if the bill were dropped altogether, he would face humiliating jibes from the Conservatives. Laurier wavered and eventually agreed to let the bill come up once more, provided the company was shorn of its more sweeping powers of expropriation. Along the Nipigon River only lands needed to construct transmission lines could be purchased compulsorily, although the right to develop power at one site there and on the Pigeon River was granted.[43]

With the parliamentary session nearing its end, Conmee did his utmost to put his bill through. After agreeing to let it stand over a weekend, he tried to slip it past during the private bills' hour on Friday. Ontario Conservatives stalled, arguing that the provincial government must have a chance to pronounce upon the changes. Code spent the weekend briefing opposition MPs on Whitney's views. The premier was still concerned about the misuse of the power of expropriation and was opposed in principle to the federal government granting a private company power to seize provincial crown lands. On the following Monday and Tuesday the Conservatives continued to drag their feet on the pretext of awaiting a formal pronouncement from Toronto. The prime minister remarked acidly upon the Conservatives' new-found reverence for provincial rights: 'There was a time when they ignored provincial rights. I welcome their conversion and I rejoice that they now recognize the error of their ways. We are all at one upon the question of provincial rights.' But he made it clear that the House was not going to prorogue before some kind of charter went through.[44]

The matter was left to stand until the end of the week. On Friday House leader W.S. Fielding received a letter from Ontario Attorney-General J.J. Foy which reiterated the province's objections and rejected each of the justifications advanced for a federal charter. The Pigeon River might be navigable and an international boundary, but the Attorney-General claimed that half the power still belonged to the province. Foy pointed out that the Canadian Niagara Power Company had been operating at the Falls since 1892 with only a provincial charter. His strongest objections he reserved for the expropriation rights which the company sought. Clearly they were intended to be used to thwart provincial policies concerning hydroelectric development.[45]

In the debate which followed Laurier argued that parliament had always chartered railway companies with expropriation powers which could be used on the public lands of the provinces. The bill marked no departure in principle. Conservative leader Robert Borden replied that this principle should then be reciprocal: the provinces ought to be able to take over Dominion property. But he did admit that the bill had now been shorn of its most objectionable features. Nevertheless, the House formally divided on the act, the Liberals lining up solidly behind it. On Whitney's instructions Code kept the bill tied up in the Senate Private Bills Committee for a couple of days, and Sir Mackenzie Bowell led a fight against it on the floor. Eventually, however, the charter became law, but without the declaration of general advantage or the wide powers of expropriation originally sought. On the whole, opposition members were well satisfied with the fight they had put up on Ontario's behalf.[46]

Undaunted, James Conmee was back again the next year. In 1910 his scheme was called the Nipigon-Albany Canal and Transportation Company, which had modest plans to connect Lake Superior with Edmonton via canals along the Rainy River, Lake Winnipeg, and the Saskatchewan River. The real object of the undertaking was, of course, to pick up all the water powers along the route. Blocking such a scheme was difficult for the province, Whitney admitted, if the federal government was prepared to support Conmee 'or any other robber.' Fortunately, Ontario's lands and forests and mines minister, Frank Cochrane, persuaded the newly created Commission of Conservation to denounce Conmee's plans. Its chairman, Clifford Sifton, brought his considerable influence to bear with the prime minister: 'No one can read the Bill or listen to the discussion without coming to the conclusion that the Bill is without bona fides, that is to say that the incorporators have no serious intention whatever of constructing the canal which is the ostensible object of the Bill. This being so, it becomes clear that the Bill is a cloak for some other ulterior object.' On orders from the Cabinet the bill was drastically amended by Public Works Minister William Pugsley and then buried in the Railway Committee.[47]

In the first decade of the twentieth century the efforts of promoters like John Gibson and James Conmee to escape provincial control provoked serious friction between the two levels of government. The election of a Conservative government at Ottawa in 1911 put an end to the federal-provincial 'game' of playing off one level against the other. As opposition leader, Robert Borden had frequently expressed his distaste for such activities. In anouncing the new Halifax Platform in 1907 he complained that 'Promoters ... have come to the Dominion Parliament for charters which should have been granted by the provincial legislatures. One charter, obtained nearly twenty years ago, was brought before the Dominion Parliament under some flimsy pretext and was renewed by the Dominion Parliament in defiance of provincial rights, simply for the reason that no further renewal could be obtained from Ontario.'[48] The message was clear, and in any case, the influence which Sir James Whitney exercised upon the new prime minister after 1911 was such that no measures which the provincial government objected to stood much chance of passing the House of Commons.

II

The conflict over regulation and control of companies was not confined to those enterprises declared for the general advantage of Canada. There remained the larger issue of defining a company with 'provincial objects.' If these objects were territorially limited, many enterprises would suddenly require federal charters, while a functional definition of 'provincial objects' would leave many large undertakings content with local incorporation. And beyond that lay the question of the extent to which the provinces could regulate and tax federally chartered concerns and vice versa. While private interest groups obviously were concerned with such issues, the debate was conducted primarily at the legal and bureaucratic level. In the final analysis, it was up to the courts to define 'provincial objects' and to decide to what extent each jurisdiction could control companies incorporated elsewhere. Meanwhile, bureaucrats at both levels manoeuvred to maintain or increase their share of authority in this area. Occasionally they would call upon allies within the business community who saw an advantage in placing themselves under one set of regulators rather than another; although the wrangling was largely left to the judges, lawyers, and bureaucrats, whenever the friction became too intense, politicians were also drawn into the fray.

Since central Canada was the most highly developed region of the country, it was in Ontario and Quebec that this debate over the power of incorporation became most significant during the late nineteenth century. Successive federal ministers of justice criticized provincial acts for granting extra-provincial powers. In 1889, for instance, Sir John Thompson declared bluntly that 'A provincial legislature cannot authorize a company to do business beyond the limits of the province.' In 1897 Sir Oliver Mowat as minister of justice insisted that a province had no right to impose restrictions upon federal companies doing business there.[49] In 1899 Justice Minister David Mills introduced legislation permitting any five persons to constitute themselves as a loan company by letters patent. J.H. Hunter, Ontario's registrar of loan companies, hastened to alert the provincial government. The new bill, he told Premier Arthur Hardy, was intended to permit Zebulon A. Lash to amalgamate a number of provincially chartered loan companies into a single federal conglomerate with a minimum of trouble. Hunter believed there was 'no time to be lost in making a stand for Provincial Rights.'[50]

Hardy agreed. He complained to Mills that if companies were permitted to pull up stakes and move their place of incorporation, the province would be 'thrust aside' and become powerless to control them. Proceeding with the bill, he warned, would lead to 'a constitutional fight at every step which certainly should be anything but agreeable with your government in power.' Prime Minister Laurier tried to soothe the angry premier without giving ground: 'Mills is very much inclined to the opinion that he is in the right, and, consequently, that you are in the wrong. This is a nice point, as to which I offer no opinion. Suffice it to say that we do not want to, and will not, quarrel with our friends.'[51] But Hardy was not mollified; he persuaded the Libral premiers of New Brunswick and Quebec and the attorneys-general of Nova Scotia and British Columbia to support his protest.[52] Despite the publication of the full text of Hardy's objections, Mills refused to give in. He was convinced that the federal jurisdiction over trade and commerce included control of money-lending companies. In the House of Commons he argued that companies doing business in more than one province ought to be federally chartered. The legislation was passed, and lacking clear grounds for a legal protest, the province could do little.[53]

As a result, the government of Ontario turned its attention to other means of controlling corporate business, including those firms with federal charters. The Ontario Companies Act of 1897 required all concerns doing business in the province to obtain licences from the provincial secretary. In 1900, however, licence fees were imposed for the first time. The Extra-Provincial Corporations Act fixed the fee at $25 if the capital stock was under $100,000 and at $50 if it exceeded that sum. The business community became agitated; the secretary of the Canadian Manufacturers' Association demanded that Ottawa ensure that federal companies had an unhindered right to do business in all parts of the country. Federal officialdom was sympathetic. Under-Secretary of State Joseph Pope complained of this 'audacious invasion of the Federal domain,' and warned: 'It cannot be expected that commercial men will go to the trouble and expense of taking out Dominion charters when they are obliged to take out provincial licences as well. They will assuredly go direct to Toronto and give us the go-by.' He recommended that the act be disallowed.[54]

Justice Minister Mills concurred. Like his predecessor, Mowat, he believed that the provinces had no authority to impose conditions upon federal companies wishing to do business. He demanded that the provincial government amend the legislation. Premier George Ross defended the act. Any federal company had an unconditional right to a licence once the fees were paid. The prohibition on the operation of unlicensed companies was simply intended to compel payment. But Mills was adamant. The act must provide that all companies, wherever incorporated, be treated exactly alike. After all, he wrote, 'The government of Canada is not a foreign government; the corporations that it creates are not foreign corporations; they are as much at home in the province of Ontario as those called into existence by the local legislature, and violent hands ought not be laid on them. If this is done it is our duty to protect them ... In my opinion, all legislation of this kind ought to be disallowed if persisted in.'[55] Although alarmed by this threat, the Ontario cabinet dug in its heels, and the legislature was prorogued in 1901 without making any changes in the act. Mills stood his ground. The premier and his attorney-general, John Gibson, travelled to Ottawa in May to discuss the matter with the justice minister, but they were compelled to promise amendments to be introduced in 1902 taxing all corporations at an identical rate in order to avert disallowance.

Premier Ross complained that he 'was not a little surprised at the position taken by some members of the Government. It would seem that they were resolved on a course with regard to the political effect of which they were indifferent.'[56] So he adopted Fabian tactics. The promised amendments were not brought down during the 1902 session; in fact, in 1903 the general statute law amendment act included a clause which provided that every corporation requiring a provincial licence should pay a fee fixed by order-in-council. This change was apparently made without a full appreciation of its significance, but it soon attracted the critical attention of Charles Fitzpatrick, who had succeeded Mills as justice minister. He pointed out that increases in the nominal fees fixed by the 1900 act could be used by the cabinet to discriminate specially against federally chartered companies. In June 1904 he threatened to disallow the entire statute law amendment act, covering a wide range of matters, if the province did not immediately agree either to drop all licence fees for federal companies or to fix a uniform scale for all undertakings.

Attorney-General Gibson insisted that there had been no discrimination but claimed that Ottawa could not limit the right of the province to raise money through direct taxation. In the end he renewed Ross's promise of 1901 to amend Ontario's legislation so that all companies would be treated alike.[57] By the time the legislature met in 1905, however, James Whitney's Conservatives had taken office. Whether or not they were aware of Gibson's promise, they took no action.

Attention now shifted to the question of whether provincially incorporated companies could do business outside their home jurisdictions. In the case of *Hewson v. Ontario Power Company* in 1905 the judge remarked in passing that a provincially chartered concern had no right to connect its power lines with those of a company in another province or another country. The same view was shared by A.B. Aylesworth, the new justice minister. In 1907 the issue came before the Supreme Court. The case of the *Canadian Pacific Railway Company v. Ottawa Fire Insurance Company* revolved around the right of a provincially chartered insurer to make a contract covering property in another jurisdiction. Ontario alone might stand to lose $200,000 a year in licence fees if it were decided that all such companies required federal charters. Recognizing the importance of the case, Chief Justice Charles Fitzpatrick invited the province to take part in the appeal.[58]

Attorney-General J.J. Foy readily accepted the invitation. Ontario's counsel took the line that 'provincial objects' included everything not specifically granted to the federal authorities under section 91 of the BNA Act. While the court did not go that far, its decision in May 1907 upheld the right of provincially chartered insurers to write coverage anywhere in Canada. Federal officials were surprised and dismayed. Early in 1908 the deputy minister of justice argued that the 'unsatisfactory state' of the law made a further reference to the courts desirable. Would Ontario take part? The province, content with its recent victory, remained cool to the idea. This lack of enthusiasm was reinforced by the list of questions Ottawa proposed to ask the Supreme Court, which seemed 'to be shaped with the view of putting it up to the Provinces as hard as they know how to put it.' The province's lawyer agreed that the questions had been 'chosen as a short cut towards limiting provincial jurisdiction.'[59]

This reluctance was powerfully reinforced when Sir Robert Finlay, a London barrister who often represented the province before the Privy Council, gave his opinion that the term 'provincial objects' was intended to be interpreted geographically. Preferring the status quo to the risk of an adverse decision along those lines, Attorney-General Foy simply ignored the federal proposal.[60] Instead, in 1909 Ontario and the other provinces began to press Ottawa to consider an amendment of the BNA Act to confirm their jurisdiction. Aylesworth was violently opposed to the idea; he thought it would 'upset the whole fabric of Confederation.' While agreeing that the provinces had 'not a leg to stand on, in my humble judgment,' the prime minister felt it would be wise to agree to hold a conference on the matter, 'not with a view of yielding to their pretensions, but simply to discuss them ... The political effect would be better.' But Aylesworth and Secretary of State Charles Murphy, who was responsible for administering federal company law, continued to drag their feet.[61] Ontario stepped up the pressure. In December 1909 licence fees were increased by order-in-council under the 1903 legislation for federal companies operating within the province. This action, together with legislation passed by British Columbia in 1910 to prohibit unlicensed companies from doing business altogether, convinced the federal cabinet that a conference was required.

In March 1910 delegates from British Columbia, Saskatchewan, Manitoba, Ontario, Quebec, and New Brunswick gathered in Ottawa. Ontario was represented by Provincial Secretary W.J. Hanna and Deputy Attorney-General Edward Bayly. Their mood was intransigent. The provincial delegates swiftly rejected the idea of further reference to the courts on the grounds that the *Ottawa Fire Insurance* decision of 1907 had already upheld their contentions. If any ambiguities remained, an amendment to the BNA Act should be drafted to remove them. These proposals were received by Laurier, Aylesworth, and Murphy. The justice minister wated no time in pointing out that he and his predecessors had consistently criticized local charters which included extra-provincial powers, and the three ministers refused to consider any constitutional amendments.[62] Instead, Ottawa decided to force the issue by pressing ahead with a reference case on its own. On 9 May 1910 a list of questions was formally referred to the Supreme Court and a hearing fixed for mid-summer. The provincial governments were greatly alarmed at this high-handed move, and all except British Columbia supported Foy's suggestion that they seek an idefinite postponement of the hearing. Laurier and Aylesworth were unmoved. Indeed, they decided upon a second reference case to settle the division of jurisdiction over insurance companies. Among the key provisions of the new federal Insurance Act of 1910 was a requirement that all provincial insurance companies doing business outside their home province should obtain licences from and make deposits with the federal superintendent of insurance, who was authorized to inspect them. But these clauses had promptly been declared ultra vires by a Montreal magistrate as an interference with provincial control of property and civil rights.[63]

When the Supreme Court opened its hearings on the reference cases in October 1910, Wallace Nesbitt representing Ontario (in conjunction with Manitoba, Alberta, and the three maritime provinces) immediately moved to stop the action on the grounds that the whole reference procedure was unconstitutional. The court rejected this. The provinces then met to reconsider their strategy. At a meeting chaired by Premier Whitney they decided to appeal this decision to the Privy Council immediately. If turned down, they would then defend their case on its merits in the Supreme Court. Costs were to be shared according to population.[64]

Meanwhile the government of Ontario kept up the pressure on Ottawa. In January 1911 new regulations were introduced under the Extra-Provincial Corporations Act. Licence fees were now to be based 'on the amount of capital authorized to be used in Ontario.' This rather vague phrase seemed to imply that federal companies with head offices in the province might pay on their total authorized capital, while foreign concerns need only pay on the amount of capital actually used there. Aylesworth thought this discrimination intolerable and demanded that the government live up to its repeated promises to treat all companies alike. But because the new regulations were imposed by order-in-council under legislation last changed in 1909, he was powerless to disallow them. The Whitney administration simply ignored his complaints.[65]

Not until May 1912 did the Privy Council decide the provincial appeal regarding reference cases. It upheld the Supreme Court's finding and preparations began for hearings on the Companies and Insurance References in October. Ontario hoped that the newly elected Borden government might prove more responsive to the wishes of the provinces than Laurier had been. Deputy Attorney-General Edward Bayly suggested that the province agree to co-operate in the Insurance Reference provided Ottawa dropped the Companies case: 'The Dominion had little to gain and the Provinces have a great deal to lose by the status quo not being maintained. The Corporations [sic] Reference raises more questions than would arise in concrete cases, in all probability, in a hundred years, and if the Provinces have all these questions answered in their favour they will be about where they are now.' The Borden cabinet discussed this idea, but even the influence of the powerful Conservative government in Ontario was not sufficient to persuade them to drop the Companies Reference.[66]

The Supreme Court heard the two reference cases in late 1912 and early 1913. In both instances Ontario's counsel argued that the province's jurisdiction over property and civil rights gave it wide powers to regulate companies operating there. Naturally, it was claimed that provincially chartered companies could operate anywhere in Canada and the rest of the world, if not forbidden by other jurisdictions. The decisions were handed down in the fall of 1913. In the Insurance case the rights of the provinces were endorsed and the 1910 Insurance Act held to be ultra vires as an interference with provincial authority to regulate the making of insurance contracts. In the Companies Reference the outcome was very confused. All six judges answered each of the seven questions, but no clear consensus emerged. Each side felt that its position had been sustained. Ottawa therefore wanted to appeal only the Insurance Reference to the Privy Council, but Ontario insisted that if there was to be an appeal, both cases must go forward together.[67]

Frank Cochrane, the province's liaison man in the federal cabinet, soon reported that the federal insurance department was determined to pursue its appeal, since it could hardly continue to function if the courts held many of its activities unconstitutional. Federally chartered insurance companies were also supporting the appeal, in order to avoid competition from provincially chartered concerns operating under less stringent regulations. But Justice Minister Charles Doherty was dithering about what to do with the Companies Reference.[68] Before long the Privy Council was expected to hear the case of *John Deere Plough Company v. Wharton* which would raise many of the same issues. The *John Deere* case dealt with the right of a federal company to operate in British Columbia without the licence required by the province's 1910 legislation. In 1915 the Judicial Committee held that the provinces could regulate companies through general laws concerning matters like taxation but could not 'legislate so as to deprive a Dominion company of its status and powers.' The provincial statute was declared invalid. Having sought such a decision for a long time, the federal authorities lost any desire to pursue the Companies Reference further, particularly in view of the well-known dislike of the Judicial Committee for answering abstract questions in reference cases. Now it was federal bureaucrats who displayed a lack of enthusiasm for pursuing a settlement in the courts.[69]

The provinces, however, with Ontario in the lead, insisted that the matter should be cleared up. It was finally decided to revive a concrete case, long dormant, which dealt with the same issues and to appeal it to the Privy Council, together with the two references on Insurance and Companies. The dormant case was *Bonanza Creek Gold Mining Company v. the King*, in which an Ontario chartered concern had sued the Crown in 1908 for refusing to grant it certain mining licences in the Yukon which were available only to companies 'incorporated under Canadian charter.' The Supreme Court had upheld the government's action. Now all three cases would go to the Judicial Committee to be argued together.

The decision, announced in 1916, was a satisfying victory for the provinces. The Privy Council found that the only 'actual powers and rights' which they could grant by charter were those which could be 'exercised within the province.' However, provincial companies could be provided with the 'capacity to accept extraprovincial powers and rights,' extending their 'provincial objects' beyond the province's territorial limits where permitted by other jurisdictions.[70] Although this was less certain, the provinces also seemed to be permitted to tax federal companies if all such concerns were required to take out licences to do business. Edward Bayly, Ontario's deputy attorney-general, jubilantly summed up these findings as 'a win for ... the Province's contention, a complete recognition of the rights of Provincial Companies to do business outside the Province and recognition of the right of the Provinces to tax Dominion and other companies.' His pleasure was derived not simply from the vindication of his interpretation of the constitution by the Privy Council, but from the knowledge that many companies, whatever the scale of their operations, would continue to seek provincial incorporation. And company charters meant revenues: 'The result in money in the Companies Reference and the Bonanza Case between an unfavourable and favourable judgment to this Province alone would be the difference between the annual average income and almost no income at all, which for Ontario amounts to $250,000 or more per annum.'[71]

III

This 1916 decision by the courts not only legitimized provincial incorporation of companies with interprovincial or international operations, but the Insurance Reference ended federal efforts to regulate provincially chartered insurance companies. The squabbling between the two levels of government over company law might thus have been expected to come to an end. But it did not. The degree to which Ottawa could still control federally or foreign-chartered insurers operating in the provinces remained unclear. In the late 1920s and early 1930s further wrangling broke out over this issue, and it will be discussed here because it forms a loud and discordant coda to the whole conflict. Moreover, it demonstrates how bureaucrats fighting to preserve their spheres of influence, as well as private interests seeking favours from one level of government at the expense of the other, could create friction between Ontario and the federal government.[72].

The federal department of insurance had been created in 1875. George D. Finlayson, a crusty Nova Scotian who had entered the department in 1907, became superintendent of insurance in 1914, only to be deprived of many of his responsibilities by the Privy Council just two years later. But Finlayson's determination not to surrender any of his authority to regulate insurance companies seems never to have wavered. He promptly set about devising a new federal Insurance Act. Passed in 1917, this legislation made failure to take out a federal licence a criminal offence for Canadian- or foreign-chartered companies; provincial concerns could secure these if they wished. This claim of jurisdiction over foreign insurers was founded upon rather tortuous construction of federal control over 'aliens' and 'immigration.' It had been devised by the deputy minister of justice, who allegedly told the cabinet that 'this was the only way it could be done, if it could be done at all.'[73] Some provisions of the act were invalidated by the Privy Council in 1924, however, and in 1926 the Ontario Court of Appeal found the key licensing provisions unconstitutional.

At an interprovincial conference held that summer, Ontario's attorney-general, W.F. Nickle, moved a resolution calling upon the federal authorities to recognize 'the binding character' of this series of legal decisions and to withdraw altogether from the field of insurance regulation. The motion was seconded by the premier of Quebec and received the support of all the other first ministers.[74] George Finlayson was unmoved; he set about drafting new legislation to require insurers operating in Canada to be licensed by Ottawa. When the new bill was presented to parliament in 1927, Edward Bayly wrote angrily: 'The Provinces have won almost steadily in the courts but the Dominion Departments have to a great extent disregarded the law.' Ontario's superintendent of insurance, R. Leighton Foster, was particularly annoyed by one section of the bill. Foreign-based companies were now required to deposit $100,000 worth of securities in Ottawa in order to obtain a licence, twice the amount previously required. This change had the enthusiastic support of the joint-stock insurance companies chartered by the federal government, who viewed it as a stiff protective tariff to exclude low-cost foreign competition, which had recently increased greatly, particularly from American mutual insurers. Aware of the possible loss of provincial licence fees and angered by what he considered Finlayson's favouritism to the joint-stock insurers, Foster persuaded the 1927 annual meeting of the Association of Provincial Insurance Superintendents to condemn the new act.[75]

Foster also induced Ontario Premier Howard Ferguson to challenge the new legislation directly. Ontario and Quebec agreed to issue provincial licences to some twenty New England fire insurance mutuals which had refused to put up federal deposits. These companies were promised legal support if charged by Ottawa with failure to obtain the required licence. Meanwhile, Finlayson insisted that both common sense and actuarial experience required that foreign companies should make deposits in order to secure the rights of their policy-holders in Canada. 'It is safe to say,' he wrote, 'that the officials of the province are aware of the unsoundness of the system they have proposed, and that the action has been taken merely for the purpose of again throwing insurance legislation into the chaos of litigation in the hope that, in the outcome, some support may be obtained for provincial claims to jurisdiction.'[76]

Only an agreement between the political leaders at the 1927 dominion-provincial conference seemed to offer any solution to the impasse short of another protracted legal battle. Ontario's new attorney-general, W.H. Price, raised the issue, and Prime Minister Mackenzie King promptly suggested that a subcommittee be set up, chaired by Solicitor-General Lucien Cannon, to thrash the matter out. But the discussions were dominated by the officials, not by the politicians. The federal superintendent took the offensive with a forty-five-minute harangue in which he denounced provincial pretensions, repeating his allegation that Ontario 'had at times shown a disposition to go out of its way to negative [sic] everything the Dominion has done. This has not been to the benefit of the public, but has, on the other hand, involved expense which ultimately falls on the company and thus on the insuring public.' He was frequently interrupted by Deputy Attorney-General Bayly of Ontario, who reminded the superintendent that he was not a lawyer and severely criticized his 'ridiculous' views on the constitution. When Finlayson finished, Foster took the floor to suggest that the best thing his federal counterpart could do would be to shut up shop altogether. Finlayson's response, recorded Foster, was to laugh, wave his hand, and make 'a dirty remark about my looking for another job ... [saying] by inference that there was no use talking to me.' In this unpromising atmosphere it was clear that the bureaucrats would not get far. Attorney-General Price believed that 'If we are to make any progress the Ministers will have to meet without the Deputies and decide what can be done.' If such a meeting was held it did not prove fruitful, and in the end the subcommittee could report only that the matter needed more study.[77]

This failure apparently convinced Premier Ferguson that the provinces would have to resort to the courts. Although a Conservative, he did not hesitate to seek the co-operation of his Quebec Liberal counterpart, L.A. Taschereau, on this as on other issues. They agreed to refer the new 1927 federal Insurance Act to the Quebec Court of Queen's Bench for an opinion on its constitutionality. A hearing was held in November 1929. Counsel for the provincial government claimed that Ottawa had been invading the autonomy of the provinces 'in the insurance field because, apparently, the officials of the Insurance Department are more pugnacious and grasping than the others – with regard to jurisdiction, of course.' Although the Quebec court was divided, an appeal to the Privy Council produced a firm declaration that federal efforts to regulate foreign-based insurers constituted 'intermeddling' in the business of insurance. The key provisions of the 1927 Insurance Act were declared unconstitutional and the federal licence was dismissed as 'an idle piece of paper.'[78]

Nonetheless, Superintendent Finlayson remained undaunted. Despite repeated protests from Ontario Attorney-General Price, Finlayson succeeded in persuading the Bennett administration in 1932 that Ottawa could regulate insurance companies incorporated both by the federal government and abroad. The latter would be controlled under federal jurisdiction over aliens, bankruptcy, and insolvency. Price was outraged when he learned of this scheme. Why, he asked the prime minister, did Ottawa refuse to concede defeat? The head offices of 90 per cent of all Canadian companies were located in Ontario and Quebec, and those provinces 'could not, if they would, sidestep and avoid responsibility for the regulation of the business of insurance within their jurisdiction.'[79] Bennett was aware, however, that some Canadian insurers did not wish the federal government to cease regulation altogether. Life insurance companies found the certificates of solvency issued by Ottawa useful when doing business abroad, business which was of significant value to them. These concerns preferred to seek some compromise which would satisfy the provinces, so the Canadian Life Insurance Officers Association retained Newton W. Rowell as counsel to help in drawing up new federal legislation. Senator Arthur Meighen, who had charge of the bills, entrusted their drafting largely to Rowell.[80]

Despite many meetings between Rowell and Ontario officials, the provincial government remained adamantly opposed to any federal role. Such intransigence led Finlayson to induce Finance Minister E.N. Rhodes to include in his 1932 budget a 10 per cent tax on insurance premiums paid to foreign insurers lacking federal licences. This prohibitory levy would, of course, compel them to submit to regulation by Ottawa or lose business. Price denounced this measure as another 'invasion of provincial rights;' even Senator Meighen thought it 'patently and defiantly unconstitutional.'[81] Nevertheless, Finlayson had his way: the premium tax was retained and new insurance legislation was passed requiring all Canadian, British, and foreign companies to register with the insurance department in order to do business.[82]

Ontario would have none of it. After meetings between Price and Premier Taschereau it was agreed that Quebec would issue a provincial licence to Lloyd's of London, which had never applied for a federal permit. Efforts by Arthur Meighen to convene a conference in September 1932 to avert a confrontation were rebuffed by Price. The attorney-general demanded that Ottawa admit that it lacked authority in this area and cease interfering. Meighen could only grumble that if the attitude of Ontario and Quebec was

to fight to their limit regardless of all claims of economy or the general public good, and to feel that a great victory is gained if these claims are acknowledged by the courts, then surely it would have been better if there had been no Confederation at all. Without Confederation there would be one hundred percent provincial rights in everything, and if the attitude of the Province of Ontario ... is correct one hundred percent provincial rights would be a constitutional paradise.[83]

Price paid no attention. In October 1932 he and Taschereau met in Montreal and it was agreed that he would seek an interview with Meighen and demand the repeal of all federal insurance legislation. If Ottawa agreed, the provinces would offer to support the creation of a federal insurance bureau to administer the regulations, although the actual licensing would still be done at the provincial level. Meighen and Price met in Toronto on 7 November, and the attorney-general warned that if this offer were refused, the provinces would move towards the American system, in which the jurisdiction where the head office was located handled all regulatory activity.[84] Outraged federal officials denounced the provincial proposal as 'a plain demand for the complete abdication of the field,' and the cabinet rejected the plan. Instead, the whole matter was referred to the dominion-provincial conference to be held in January 1933. Price thought that any further discussion was a waste of time, but Meighen hoped that the other seven provinces would rally to Ottawa's side.[85]

Despite more pressing questions, the conference of first ministers devoted almost an entire day to the question of insurance. As Meighen had hoped, all the provinces except Ontario, Quebec, and British Columbia expressed support for some continuing federal role. Bennett even suggested that this might be sufficient grounds for Ottawa and the other six provinces to apply to Britain for a constitutional amendment to clarify federal authority. No decision was reached, but after the conference Premier George Henry took steps to prevent the insurance industry from endorsing such a move by warning a group of executives that he would retaliate against any action by the other provinces to interfere with Ontario's jurisdiction.[86] Nevertheless, the life insurance companies renewed their pressure for a revised federal insurance act in the fall of 1933. Newton Rowell once again set to work drafting new legislation with the help of federal civil servants. Despite objections from Superintendent Finlayson, the constitutional experts were now convinced that Ottawa had the authority to do little more than issue certificates of solvency to Canadian-incorporated companies. Rowell warned that if a security deposit were demanded of Lloyd's of London under the new legislation, as Finlayson wished, the famous underwriters would join with Quebec and Ontario (where they were already doing business) in another legal challenge to federal authority. Meighen at first disagreed: 'I think the Bill without the Lloyd's provisions will be much more vulnerable before the Privy Council, and if we lose there again we are through.'[87] Eventually, however, Rowell, Bennett, and Meighen agreed privately to drop altogether the provision requiring Lloyd's to obtain a federal licence. Finlayson protested, but to no avail, and by the summer of 1934 the new legislation was passed by parliament. Henceforth, effective regulation of the business of insurance for companies not chartered by Ottawa rested with the provinces, although if they wished, companies could go abroad with certificates of solvency issued by the government of Canada.[88]

This struggle between Ontario and the federal authorities over the control and regulation of corporate business reveals several things about the nature of intergovernmental conflict in Canada. First, as in the case of natural resource policy, private interests played a significant role in creating friction. Pursuing their own objectives they turned to the level of authority which seemed most responsive, particularly when the provincial authorities embarked upon efforts to tighten regulatory controls upon utilities after 1905 and in the process intensified the animosity between Ottawa and Queen's Park. On occasion, it should be noted, private interests could defuse such conflicts. In the 1930s Newton Rowell, as lawyer for the Canadian Life Insurance Officers Association, participated in the drafting of new federal insurance legislation, which it was hoped would stand up in court while retaining some federal jurisdiction. This effort won him the enmity of Insurance Superintendent Finlayson, who was determined to make no concessions to provincial pretensions. Such incidents demonstrate the danger of conceiving of intergovernmental relations too narrowly, of seeing the provinces on one side and the federal government on the other. Sometimes the politicians on both sides had relatively little interest in the issues involved and merely hoped the problems would go away, but private interests refused to let that happen.

On the other hand, a kind of bureaucratic imperative must be taken into account.

Civil servants sometimes were reluctant to see their spheres of authority diminished, their duties assumed by a competing authority. Bureaucrats frequently pointed out to their political masters the dreadful consequences of permitting Ottawa (or Toronto) to take over this matter or that. And the politicians usually supported their civil servants, for they too disliked seeing their power and their revenues diminished at the expense of others. While the reasons advanced for federal or provincial regulations were always couched in the language of efficiency, effectiveness, or the public interest, the true wellsprings were sometimes less noble. On occasion the politicians might conclude that the struggle was no longer worth pursuing. After a string of adverse legal decisions had severely restricted the jurisdiction of the central government over insurance, Superintendent Finlayson merely set about redrafting the legislation in the hope of salvaging something, but the prime minister wondered if it was not time to give up. In January 1934 Bennett wrote: 'We might as well face the fact that it [the federal insurance department] has no jurisdiction, and there is an enormous waste of money and time for stationery and other purposes. Is it not a suitable time to have the matter disposed of?'[89] But no self-respecting bureaucrat could easily subscribe to such a view, and a good deal of the heat in the conflict between the two levels of government arose from that fact.

Private interests were always ready to make use of the diffusion of power inherent in federalism. This was true of both Canada and the United States, where during the early twentieth century

business advocacy of *federal* regulation was motivated by more than a desire to stabilize industries that had moved beyond state boundaries. The needs of the economy were such, of course, as to demand federal as opposed to random state economic regulation. But a crucial factor was the bulwark which essentially conservative national regulation provided against state regulations that were either haphazard or, what is more important, far more responsible to more radical, genuinely progressive local communities.[90]

Yet the independent authority retained by the American states also had its value to entrepreneurs. In 1888 New Jersey liberalized its company law to permit corporations to hold stock in other concerns and to do all of their business outside of that state. Other jurisdictions followed suit with the result that 'The late nineteenth century saw the emergence of the state which by design made its law a special haven for businessmen who wanted a kind of corporate organization such as the law of most states denied them.'[91]

Thus, in the United States

A federal structure with significant decentralization inherently provided two routes of escape for business interests that were 'caught' in a particular state's policy of discrimination or stringent regulation. One escape route was *lateral*. That is, a business could remove its legal domicile or its operating facilities from a 'hostile' state to a 'benign' one ...

The other escape route provided by federal structure was *upward*; that is, the private business interest that experienced stringent regulation could ... seek legislation from Congress that would supplant state authority with a more benevolent national policy.

The railways were among the enterprises which sought such federal regulation, and

A similar movement occurred in the insurance industry. Confronted with increasingly severe state regulation, many leading insurance company executives came to favour federal regulation. Although they won President Theodore Roosevelt to their point of view and a powerful move was made in Congress to obtain a national law, their campaign was blocked by conservative as well as reform opposition.[92]

By the 1930s, however, a powerful trend had been set in the direction of national control of corporate enterprise in the United States based upon an extended interpretation of the authority over interstate commerce.

In Canada events took a different course. The courts construed the power of parliament to regulate 'trade and commerce' very narrowly. The Canadian federal system developed in a more decentralized way than the American. Provincial legislatures did not find themselves bound by the constraints of due process, and within their sphere of exclusive jurisdiction parliamentary sovereignty permitted decisive action. The provinces, rather than the federal government, eventually came to be responsible not only for the business of insurance but also for the regulation of the securities industry. Although some businessmen might continue to seek protection from parliament or the federal bureaucracy, their success was slight.

The limited role played in these conflicts by ideological notions about centralism versus local autonomy should also be noted. The bureaucrats involved were sincerely convinced that they could do a better job than their counterparts at another level. For private interests it was simply a matter of looking to the government which would give them what they sought. It may be concluded that in the conflict over regulation of companies neither side covered itself with glory. Yet it is difficult to disagree with the Ontario official who wrote in 1916 to protest that in the matter of company charters it was really a case of 'attacks by the Dominion upon Provincial rights and not attacks by the Provinces upon the Dominion.'[93] It was fitting, therefore, that the provincial cause, under the leadership of Ontario, should ultimately prevail.

6 Financing the Federation in Peace and War

The province of Ontario fully shared in the rapid growth which Canada underwent during the first two decades of the twentieth century. Economic development and population increase (in Ontario's case from 2.2 to 2.9 million people) caused a rapid rise in government spending. As late as 1899 the province spent a total of only $3.7 million – less than the Mowat administration had disbursed in 1874. Thereafter, however, spending mounted steadily (see Table 1). After 1915 the rate of increase was markedly enhanced by wartime inflation. In 1900, for instance, the Department of Education required $758,466.26, while by 1920 it absorbed $5,568,146.55, more than a sevenfold rise. Maintaining and staffing public institutions such as lunatic asylums cost the province $828,201.34 at the turn of the century and $3,399,021.82 twenty years later, while grants for hospitals and charities rose from $184,898.32 to $743,661.78 in the same period. The cost of new public buildings was a mere $163,631.10 in 1900 compared to $1,057,784.55 in 1920, and the Department of Agriculture spent only $209,168.66 at the beginning of that period but $1,273,708.68 at the end.

Despite such rapid increases in total spending, however, those functions of government actually required a smaller percentage of the supply bill at the end of the period than at the beginning, so steep was the rise in total government expenditure (see Table 2). Education, for instance, took over 20 per cent of Ontario's expenditure in 1900 but only 17 per cent in 1920. A similar pattern may be discerned for most other items. The cost of maintaining public institutions fell from 22 per cent of spending to just over 10 per cent while aid to hospitals and charities dropped from 5 per cent to a little over 2 per cent. Expenses for new public buildings fell from 4.4 per cent of the supply bill to 3.3 per cent, for agriculture from 5.6 per cent to 4 per cent.

What then accounts for the very sizable increases in the provincial budget beyond the requirements of population increase and wartime inflation? The answer appears to be the creation of an infrastructure upon which future industrial development might rest, in particular the creation of a publicly owned system of

TABLE 1
Expenditures,[a] government of Ontario, 1900–20 (ordinary and capital accounts)

Item	1900	1905	1910[b]	1915	1920
civil government	265,347.53	374,975.69	565,527.36	807,832.50	1,421,868.17
legislation	142,773.45	211,107.09	249,511.29	291,171.83	333,936.17
administration of justice	427,854.72	501,524.78	659,414.74	774,897.97	795,993.65
education	758,466.26	1,131,799.17	1,700,797.48	2,067,740.63	5,568,146.55
public institutions:					
maintenance	828,201.34	907,307.19	1,131,019.58	1,389,932.87	3,399,021.82
immigration & colonization	6,257.46	32,225.42	75,196.57	48,579.81	99,830.80
agriculture	209,168.66	405,534.76	621,514.94	685,970.19	1,273,708.86
hospitals & charities	184,898.32	268,182.68	352,834.86	480,639.25	743,661.78
repairs & maintenance	89,040.34	73,333.88	252,830.51	189,898.91	402,279.89
public buildings	163,631.10	234,977.40	643,092.59	1,633,197.17	1,057,784.55
public works	25,944.01	69,853.29	154,808.74	151,996.45	311,795.10
colonization roads	143,845.51[c]	178,313.02	452,745.33	220,262.26	451,808.59
crown lands	162,861.27	321,731.28	569,507.50	490,672.66	[d]
game & fisheries	—	—	—	130,859.50	429,593.07
public highways	—	—	—	—	378,144.38
attorney-general	—	—	—	—	39,742.44
treasury	—	—	—	—	397,600.83
provincial secretary	—	—	—	—	331,347.69
labour & health	—	—	—	—	405,364.63
lands & forests	—	—	—	—	1,104,202.31
mines	—	—	—	—	218,641.45
HEPC	—	—	—	—	12,313,500.00[e]
T&NO Railway Commission	105,860.54	35,930.52	62,438.36	77,280.48	346,587.35
refunds					136,817.14
miscellaneous	234,008.70	238,699.47	2,438,677.62[d]	2,811,747.58[f]	145,658.63
total supply bill spending	3,748,159.41	4,985,495.64	9,929,917.47	12,252,680.06	32,107,035.85

[a] Supply bill spending; omits certain statutory items
[b] End of Fiscal Year switched from 31 Dec. to 31 Oct.
[c] Includes mining roads
[d] See lands & forests
[e] Includes 2,175,000.00 for HEPC
[f] Includes 2,600,000.00 for HEPC

SOURCE: Ontario, Public Accounts, *Sessional Papers*, no. 1, 1901, 1906, 1911, 1916, 1921

TABLE 2
Per cent of supply bill expenditures by item, government of Ontario, 1900–20

Item	1900	1905	1910	1915	1920
civil government	7.1	7.5	5.7	6.6	4.4
legislation	3.8	4.2	2.5	2.4	1.0
administration of justice	11.4	10.1	6.6	6.3	2.5[a]
education	20.2	22.7	17.1	16.9	17.3
public institutions:					
maintenance	22.1	18.2	11.4	11.3	10.6
immigration & colonization	0.2	0.6	0.8	0.4	0.3
agriculture	5.6	8.1	6.3	5.6	4.0
hospitals & charities	4.9	5.4	3.6	3.9	2.3
repairs & maintenance	2.4	1.5	2.5	1.5	1.3
public buildings	4.4	4.7	6.5	13.3	3.3
public works	0.7	1.4	1.6	1.2	1.0
colonization roads	3.8	3.6	4.6	1.8	1.4
crown lands	4.3	6.5	5.7	4.0	—[b]
game & fisheries	—	—	—	1.1	1.3
public highways	—	—	—	—	1.2
attorney-general	—	—	—	—	0.1
treasury	—	—	—	—	1.2
provincial secretary	—	—	—	—	1.0
labor & health	—	—	—	—	1.3
lands & forests	—	—	—	—	3.4
mines	—	—	—	—	0.7
HEPC	—	—	—[c]	—[c]	38.4
T&NO Railway Commission	—	—	—	—	1.1
refunds	2.8	0.7	0.6	0.6	0.4
miscellaneous	6.2	4.8	24.6[d]	22.9[d]	0.5

a See also attorney-general below.
b See lands and forests below.
c Included in miscellaneous
d Includes HEPC
SOURCE: Table 1

generation and distribution of electricity. The political appeal of an assured supply of cheap and abundant hydroelectricity and his empire-building proclivities quickly led Sir Adam Beck into the acquisition of the Ontario Power Company and the commencement of construction on the vast Queenston plant during the First World War. As early as 1910, 21.9 per cent of provincial spending was alotted the HEPC, a level maintained in 1915, but rising to 38.4 per cent by 1920. In addition, there was the money invested in the provincially owned Temiskaming and Northern Ontario Railway, which by 1920 was indebted to the provincial government to the tune of $20,700,000.00.[1] In fact, so rapidly did these expenditures rise that social services actually absorbed a diminishing portion of provincial spending between 1900 and 1920.

Having taken on these new obligations, Ontario soon joined in the search for additional provincial revenues. Naturally enough, this movement led to the idea that more money ought to be secured from the central government. After all, Ottawa had access to the bountiful receipts from the protective tariff, steadily rising in this period of unprecedented prosperity. By contrast subsidies to the provinces remained at the levels fixed in 1867. Sir John A. Macdonald's refusal to approve the increases demanded by the premiers at the interprovincial conference in 1887 had crushed the first concerted move in that direction, and during the 1890s little more was heard of the matter.

I

Beginning in 1899, however, the Liberal government of Quebec once more began to press Sir Wilfrid Laurier to grant an increase in the subsidy. At first the prime minister temporized, although he did concede some special allowances to the maritime provinces in 1901. This move provoked an angry complaint from Premier George Ross of Ontario: 'The effect of these grants will, undoubtedly, be to call the attention of the Province of Ontario to what is, in a modified sense, better terms to the other Provinces, and if the leader of the Opposition raises the war-cry that Ontario has been sacrificed for the other Provinces it would put us in a very embarrassing position.'[2] His reaction, was, of course, entirely in keeping with the hostility to piecemeal grants which the Mowat administration had displayed in the 1870s and 1880s. Successive Ontario governments were inclined to disapprove of such grants of 'better terms' because so much federal revenue was raised from Ontario taxpayers. If there were to be increases, then they should be made across the board to benefit all provinces, not granted as special treatment to one discontented region of the country or another. Needless to say, however, exceptions could arise when the provincial government believed that it alone should receive special assistance from Ottawa for some particularly worthy purpose. The Temiskaming and Northern Ontario Railway was a case in point.

In the early twentieth century Canada was in the throes of a vast railway-building boom, fuelled in part by generous subsidies granted by the Laurier government to private entrepreneurs. The role of the state was to assist in creating the framework upon which future growth depended, and in 1901 the Ross administration also took up this task. The discovery of thousands of acres of arable land in the Clay Belt of the Canadian Shield focused attention upon 'New Ontario' after 1900. Facing an election, George Ross decided in November 1901 that the province itself would construct a railway from North Bay to the head of Lake Temiskaming, and at the 1902 session of the legislature the Temiskaming and Northern Ontario Railway Commission was created. Ross was confident that the T & NO, like every other new line in Canada, would be eligible for a federal subsidy of $3,200 per mile, but when the premier approached Laurier, he received an unexpected rebuff: 'The financial relations between the Dominion and the Provinces are regulated by the British North America Act, and any subsidy given to one Province will be sure to raise a heavy crop of protests and demands from the other Provinces.' The prime minister refused to budge from this position, despite repeated protests from Toronto that the T & NO ought to be treated as a special case.[3]

Nevertheless, the province pressed ahead with its plans. No one questioned the wisdom of this project after blasting by construction crews uncovered the fabulously rich silver strike at Cobalt in 1903. By 1905 the rush of prospectors was prodigious. Early in 1904 Ross renewed his request for a subsidy. Another refusal, he claimed, would make it certain that the Liberal party would 'be attacked because of ungenerous treatment to the Province ... and that would not be desirable in the face of a general election.' Not even this telling argument, backed up by a visit to Ottawa from the commissioner of crown lands, F.R. Latchford, could sway Laurier. In an effort to escape criticism from the provincial Conservatives, Ross attempted to shift the blame to the federal government by introducing a resolution in the legislature formally demanding the money. Laurier countered by preparing a reply to be tabled in the assembly, repeating his arguments against a grant, adding that 'One of the constituent members of the Confederation cannot be treated as an ordinary railway company.' Privately, he rebuked Ross for pressing the matter so far. The chastened premier hastily modified his resolution simply to point out the obvious virtues of the provincial railway and its extreme worthiness to receive the usual subsidy of $3,200 per mile. The motion proposed by the premier was passed, but Ross then permitted the issue to drop.[4]

After the Conservative victory in 1905, the Whitney government renewed this application, more as a matter of form than from any conviction that Laurier would retreat from his earlier refusal to assist a Liberal administration. The only new argument which could be advanced to justify a subsidy was that it would permit the extension of the T & NO tracks as far north as Cochrane on the proposed National Transcontinental, enabling savings to be made on the construction costs of that road. Receiving no response to this request, Whitney and his treasurer, Colonel

A.J. Matheson, journeyed to the capital early in 1906 to put the province's case personally. They failed. Whitney reported that 'Laurier's remarks at that time showed me conclusively that the matter had been thoroughly talked over among them. It may be that their supporters in Quebec and in the Lower Provinces would have kicked against a subsidy, or they may have felt that they could not do so after having refused the Ross Government.' And there, for the time being, the matter rested.[5]

Discontent on the part of all the provinces, including Ontario, mounted after 1900, as their financial problems intensified. In November 1902 Premier S.N. Parent of Quebec took the initiative in calling the other provincial leaders together for a conference. The invitation came at an unfortunate time for George Ross. The general election of May 1902 had given the Liberals a narrow victory, but protests had unseated three members and the by-elections were called for January 1903. Should the Conservatives sweep these seats, they would outnumber the Liberals forty-nine to forty-eight. Thus the Ontario ministers were fully occupied on the hustings, and the premier did not attend the gathering in Quebec City.

Nonetheless, the Ontario government prepared a memorandum, setting forth its position, to be tabled at the first session of the conference. The Fathers of Confederation, this document argued, had failed to take account of the steady rise in the financial needs of the provinces when they based the annual per capita subsidy of 80 cents on the population of 1861. Ontario was now spending four times as much on education, on the administration of justice, on hospitals and charities, and on agriculture as it had done in 1861. More money had to be found, but since the subsidy was unchanging, provincial taxes must be raised. Ontario, therefore, proposed a solution similar to that adopted by the 1887 conference, tying the susidy to the most recent census and including a generous increase in the fixed grants for the support of civil government. The other premiers quickly accepted this proposal, although they scaled down the proposed grant for civil government from the level suggested by the Ross government to that agreed upon in 1887.[6]

This meeting seems to have aroused little popular interest in Ontario, where attention was then focused on the prohibition referendum in December and the forthcoming by-elections. The delegates to the conference had agreed that their resolutions should be presented formally to the federal cabinet. On 27 January 1903 George Ross, safely confirmed in office by the voters, travelled to Ottawa with his colleague, F.R. Latchford, to do so. The premier spoke optimistically to reporters of the many good uses to which the $626,484.89 due Ontario under the conference resolutions could be put. Laurier handled the provincial request firmly but diplomatically. He did not reject the change out of hand but imposed two conditions. Nothing would be done unless the provinces accepted this as an absolutely final solution to the subsidy question and the legislature of every province had endorsed it.[7]

By 1903 the Ontario government had become deeply interested in a general subsidy increase. Politically shaky, George Ross wished to do everything he could to woo the voters who had almost put an end to the thirty-year reign of the Liberals. But the rising cost of new programs threatened to create a serious budget deficit. 'More money we must have,' he wrote to Laurier, 'and with your superabundant surplus you could supply the needs of all the Provinces without impairing the political value of your financial standing.' But the plea fell on deaf ears. The prime minister refused to take the matter up with his cabinet, and Ross could do no more than put through the legislature a resolution endorsing the conference's decision and hope that the other premiers would do likewise.[8]

By 1904 the Ontario budget deficit had risen to $800,000, and Ross again begged for help. Once more he was turned down. Such aid was 'quite impossible' in an election year, Laurier replied: 'Your finances are in good condition, so far as I can see, and, therefore, there is no pressing necessity for you to have this additional revenue.' When the premier suggested holding an interprovincial conference, he was told that a subsidy increase could be granted only as part of a settlement covering all the issues in dispute between the dominion and the provinces, including company incorporation, regulation of local railways, and so forth.[9] After the Conservatives under James P. Whitney assumed power in 1905, they also found that additional provincial revenues were needed for new programs. By this time pressure was increasing from the less affluent Maritimes and from Quebec for a revision of the subsidies. Since these administrations were controlled by Liberals, their views were more likely to be considered in Ottawa, so Whitney left it to others to make the provinces' case. When the attorney-general of Nova Scotia enquired about his views, however, the new premier replied that he was quite ready to co-operate.[10] In the fall of 1905 Lomer Gouin of Quebec also sounded out Whitney and finding him receptive suggested that he write directly to Laurier. The Ontario premier did so, but received no encouragement. Sir Richard Cartwright, the senior Ontario Liberal, was unsympathetic to such requests; he advised the prime minister that Ontario, 'which contains nearly half the population of the Dominion, is at present possessed of ample funds for all legitimate purposes. It is a most questionable policy to load down the Dominion with a heavy additional subsidy to be paid by Ontario and expended by its government for objects which it had much better leave alone, but which the acquisition of such a windfall will inevitably stimulate it to undertake.' When Gouin continued to press the matter with Laurier he received a sharp rebuke from the Liberal leader.[11]

By the spring of 1906, however, all the provincial legislatures except British Columbia's had formally approved the resolutions of the 1902 interprovincial conference. Public bodies like the Montreal Chamber of Commerce and Board of Trade had endorsed an increase in the provincial subsidies. Lomer Gouin toured Ontario, Manitoba, and the Maritimes to drum up more support. Eventually Laurier gave in and summoned the premiers to a meeting in October 1906.

Whitney announced publicly that his government would not be bound by the 1902 resolutions. A memorandum signed by him, along with Provincial Treasurer A.J. Matheson and Attorney-General J.J.Foy, put forward the ingenious argument that the level of subsidies agreed upon in 1864 had been governed primarily by the central government's ability to pay. Current subsidies should be adjusted to the same standard, and since the dominion revenues had increased enormously, the provinces should get a larger share of the funds. Whereas the present annual subsidy to Ontario totalled only 61 cents per captia, it would immediately rise to 97 cents if tied to current population.[12]

When the conference met, Gouin was chosen as chairman and a committee was set up, including Foy, to draft the critical resolution on subsidies. The provincial leaders soon agreed that the soundest basis for their demands would be the 1902 resolutions. The subsidy should be increased to 80 cents per capita of current population up to 2,500,00, 60 cents per head beyond that. The only controversy arose over Whitney's determination that individual provinces should be prevented from submitting demands for financial assistance over and above the agreed levels – a natural position, since Ontario would bear about half the cost of such special grants without sharing in their benefits. The other premiers were insistent, however, and eventually the Ontario leader gave way. The provincial demands were submitted immediately to the federal cabinet along with a request for special assistance from British Columbia because of its sparse population and rugged terrain. The prime minister promptly referred that demand back to the conference, doubtless hoping that Whitney would use his influence to torpedo it; one journalist reported that the ministers were flattering the Ontario premier 'in the most barefaced terms.' Over Premier Richard McBride's opposition Whitney suggested British Columbia should only get an extra $100,000 per year for ten years. In the end, the federal government agreed to accept the provincial request, including the special grant to British Columbia.[13]

Laurier wished to make this a 'final and unalterable' settlement of provincial demands. Indeed, he inserted these words into the amendment of the BNA Act embodying the changes which was forwarded to the British parliament in 1907. The phrase was dropped from the bill in the British House of Commons, however, on the grounds that parliament could not properly be bound in this way. Despite strong pressure from Laurier and Finance Minister W.S. Fielding, the Asquith government refused to restore the phrase, and the amendment passed without difficulty.[14]

II

Although Laurier hoped to make the 1907 subsidy increases a 'final and unalterable' settlement, neither he nor anyone else could check the social forces which were relentlessly inflating provincial spending. Within a few years pressure began to mount for further changes in the BNA Act. As long as the Liberals remained in power at Ottawa, however, they refused to give way to provincial demands. Not until 1911, when the Conservatives took office, did the provinces receive a more sympathetic hearing.

The allotment of governmental responsibilities in Canada has always been a part of the political process, not merely the result of abstract deliberations on the role of the state. For a long time Robert Borden enjoyed scant success in his efforts to unseat the popular and well-entrenched government of Sir Wilfrid Laurier. Gradually he came to recognize that the provincial Conservative parties might provide vital assistance at election time. In order to court premiers like Douglas Hazen of New Brunswick, Richard McBride of British Columbia, Rodmond Roblin of Manitoba, and James Whitney of Ontario, the opposition leader had to listen attentively to their grievances. This, he admitted, was a new departure for the party of Macdonald: 'In very many matters touching the everyday life of the people, the policy and aims of any provincial administration are of the greatest interest and importance. The Liberal-Conservative party for many years past has been inclined to regard Provincial issues as of somewhat minor consequence; and the provincial Conservative leaders have not received from the party as a whole the support and encouragement to which they were justly entitled.' The Party's Halifax platform of 1907 promised 'The unimpaired maintenance of all powers of self-government which have been conferred on the Provinces of Canada under the Constitution.' And in the House of Commons, as we have seen, Borden frequently criticized the centralizing tendencies of the Laurier administration in matters like the chartering of companies and the use of declarations of general advantage to Canada.[15]

Borden's reward for attention paid to the premiers' wishes came in 1911 when the local leaders threw their full weight behind him in the campaign against reciprocity. Nowhere did this involvement prove more important than in Ontario. One study on the 1911 election in that province suggests that the Conservative organization was so powerful that it would have scored a substantial victory even without the emotive issue of future relations with the United States. True or not, the seventy-two members from Ontario made up more than half of the new government's majority. Close, confidential relations existed between federal and provincial ministers. Premier Whitney had considerable influence with the new prime minister, having helped him overcome several challenges to his leadership in the past. Whitney also permitted Frank Cochrane, his minister of lands, forests, and mines, to play a leading organizational role in the election and to become minister of railways and canals. Cochrane became the main channel for communication between the two administrations.[16]

During the election campaign Whitney charged that the Quebec-dominated Liberal government had persistently ignored Ontario's interests. In particular, he cited the matter of the extension of the province's boundaries to the north and west beyond the height of land marking the watershed of Hudson Bay. When Alberta and Saskatchewan were created in 1905, Manitoba had begun to agitate for an extension of its restricted area. Whitney's government also sought to claim a share of this vast territory and at the interprovincial conference of 1906 proposed that the eastern boundary of Manitoba should be extended northward to the Churchill River and along it to Hudson Bay, so that both provinces would have access to the only usable port on the western shore (see map, p. 16). Nothing came of this proposal because the Manitoba government opposed such a huge addition to Ontario, and Laurier was loath to alter the boundaries of Manitoba, since such an action would reopen the separate school question.[17]

Negotiations dragged on in a desultory fashion over the next five years. In 1909 Whitney sought to persuade Manitoba to agree to the Nelson River as the boundary, some one hundred miles south-east of the Churchill River. Ontario would still have access to the less desirable harbour at York Factory. Eventually, however, Whitney and Roblin agreed to drop the matter because they recognized that Laurier was unwilling to act. The Ontario premier complained: 'We tried to get our proposition accepted, but Sir Wilfrid Laurier, and I am sure I am not prepared to blame him altogether, William Patterson [sic], George P. Graham and Mr. William Lyon Mackenzie King from the Province of Ontario turned the Province down.' Whitney made no secret of the fact that he expected a Conservative ministry to take a very different view. Once the results were known he wrote jubilantly: 'The situation and prospect of Ontario under the new Dominion Government will be entirely altered and altered very materially for the better.'[18]

Whitney was irritated to discover in November 1911 that Rodmond Roblin had lost no time in putting Manitoba's case for a boundary extension before the cabinet. Frank Cochrane was sharply warned to see that no decision was made until Ontario was heard from. In the unlikely event that his views were ignored, the premier bluntly advised Cochrane: 'although I shall be sorry to do so, yet, if necessary, I shall feel compelled to call upon every one of the seventy-two Government supporters from Ontario to take an active and individual part in assisting us in this matter.' To the prime minister Whitney wrote: 'now that our friends are in power at Ottawa we will be compelled to explain to the people why it is that the unfair treatment which we claimed we received from the Laurier Government is continued.' Chastened, Borden and Cochrane quickly sought to reach a compromise acceptable to both of their provincial allies. It was finally agreed that Ontario's boundary demands could not be granted, but the province's territory was extended due north from the Lake of the Woods then north-east to the shores of Hudson Bay and it was granted a railway right-of-way to either York Factory or Port Churchill. With this decision Whitney had to be content.[19]

The Ontario government also insisted that a subsidy should be awarded to the Temiskaming and Northern Ontario Railway, the subsidy which Laurier had steadfastly refused to grant. The premier reminded Frank Cochrane within a month of taking office that 'During the campaign, while we did not say we had a promise, we declared that we expected to get a subsidy and as you know it is a reasonable expectation.' The provincial treasurer submitted a formal request for aid of $12,000 per mile for some 300 miles of track. The cabinet approved the subsidy, although only at the usual rate of $6,400 per mile or about $2 million in all. When the Commons debated the appropriation, Liberal D.D. McKenzie summed up the situation accurately: 'Ontario has given a large majority to the present government, and it has only to present its claim and get any amount of money it may require.'[20]

Although passed by the House of Commons, the subsidy bill ran up against the large Liberal majority in the Senate which voted it down. The renewal of the application received the backing of both parties in the provincial legislature the following year, and Cochrane agreed to try again to get it through parliament. Although criticized as a payoff to Whitney, the grant now secured the support of the Liberal leader in the Senate, Sir George Ross, who as premier had made the first application to Ottawa back in 1901. The bill was finally passed and a cheque for $2,134,180 went out to the province.[21]

Two other federally funded programs came into existence at the same time, largely as a result of pressure from Ontario: aid to agricultural education and aid to highway construction. Although these services clearly fell within provincial jurisdiction, nonetheless they became the first of a wide range of conditional grants or grants-in-aid for specific purposes which the federal authorities would provide in later years. They came about because Whitney had extracted certain promises from Borden in return for his support, and the Conservative victory made these debts due and payable. Any doubt about this situation was removed when the new cabinet included references to grants for agriculture and highways in the first throne speech but omitted immigration for which funds had also been discussed. The premier quickly reproved Frank Cochrane: 'Of course, this may be inadvertence but it is a serious matter, as it was plainly stated by Mr Borden in speeches, and it has been repeated by me on every platform.' However, aid to immigration was not restored.[22]

So impatient was Whitney to see the conditional grants for agriculture begin that he refused to wait, while Agriculture Minister Martin Burrell collected information and laid plans, before bringing in legislation in 1913. The premier insisted that the funds be made available at once, so that the provincial throne speech of 1912 could mention them as practical evidence of Ontario's newly acquired influence with Ottawa.[23] Burrell had to improvise a bill appropriating $500,000. Ontario's deputy minister of agriculture, C.C. James, was then made a special commissioner to plan a permanent program. He recommended that the federal money be spent on improving agricultural education. Whitney had no objection as long as the federal government did not interfere with the autonomy of the province. When

Martin Burrell came to Toronto to explain his plans, he informed the cabinet that some federal supervision of the spending would be required. Whitney hastened to warn Borden that 'great importance will be placed upon the payment of this aid to the Provinces to be expended by them. I hope that there will be no question whatever as to this, because I am afraid if this aid were to be expended by the Dominion Government complications would ensue and great harm would be done.'[24]

Eventually, Frank Cochrane suggested that both sides might be satisfied by a formal agreement between the two governments covering the projects to be financed with federal funds. Some persuasion was necessary, but Whitney eventually accepted that this was a reasonable way to ensure that the funds were used for proper purposes without violating provincial autonomy. Over the next decade $10 million was budgeted for this program. Whitney was delighted with the arrangement, but because of his insistence on local control, the federal government found it almost impossible to exercise effective supervision, particularly once the First World War broke out. When the Liberals assumed power at Ottawa in 1921 they allowed the program to lapse.[25]

Federal grants for highway construction, another of Borden's election promises, created similar problems. Frank Cochrane hurriedly introduced a measure which would have granted $1 million to the provinces in 1912, $350,000 of which was allotted to Ontario. The Liberals denounced the bill on the grounds that roads were clearly a local responsibility, and that such grants would seriously undermine the division of powers. Moreover, the bill left it to the discretion of the minister to distribute the funds among the provinces. The House of Commons eventually approved the act, but in the Senate the Liberals attacked all-out. Sir Richard Cartwright trumpeted, 'Were I to suggest a short title for the Bill, I would recommend the following – that this should be declared a Bill to make the British North America Act so much waste paper and to provide a permanent corruption fund for the government of the day.' The bill was soundly defeated.[26]

Under pressure from the Ontario government, Cochrane promised to reintroduce the legislation in 1913. He even increased the amount of aid to $1.5 million. Should the Senate vote the bill down again, they would make themselves increasingly unpopular in Ontario. Cochrane confided to William Hearst, his successor as lands, forests, and mines minister: 'I intend every year that I am here to continue to increase the amount every time so that they will have an increasingly larger responsibility to swallow and greater difficulty defending their course in the country.' But the Grits returned to the attack as vigorously as ever, and Sir George Ross led his fellow Senators in rejecting the bill again. In the end, Cochrane's plan was thwarted by Finance Minister Thomas White, who convinced the prime minister that there was no use swelling the estimates in a time of recession with a twice-defeated measure. The bill was not reintroduced in 1914.[27]

In addition to the boundary extension, the T & NO subsidy, and aid to agricultural education, Premier Whitney hoped to secure from the Borden government an across-the-board increase in the federal subsidy to the provinces. When Sir Lomer Gouin suggested to the Ontario leader in the summer of 1913 that another interprovincial conference should be convened, Whitney readily agreed that such a gathering was 'very necessary.' Before the meeting in October he asked the prime minister to set forth his cabinet's views on any issues likely to be raised, so that the Ontario delegation could 'go into the Conference prepared to discuss the matter from the point of view of the Dominion Government.' Borden ordered all the federal government's position papers summarized and forwarded to Toronto so that the provincial ministers would be well briefed. In return for protecting Ottawa's interests Whitney evidently expected a sympathetic hearing on the subsidy increase, a further return upon the close relations between the two governments.[28]

The Ontario ministers left for the conference in October 1913 prepared to argue that recent social and economic developments made new financial arrangements urgently necessary. Only one-quarter of the Ontario budget could now be met from the subsidy as against three-quarters at the time of Confederation. By contrast, the federal government was enjoying steadily growing revenues from tariffs and customs duties. Whereas 35 per cent of federal income had been required to pay the subsidies in 1868, by 1912 only 10 per cent of a vastly larger revenue was now needed for that purpose. 'The Confederation bargain' was nothing sacred, ran the provincial argument: 'It was admitted at the time to be a bundle of compromises .... And there is no reason why the Confederation bargain with respect to subsidies is not a proper subject for periodical revision.' The Fathers of Confederation had never expected all the money from the customs duties to go to Ottawa: 'That would be as much as to say that they expected all the increase in the important functions of the Government would enure to that part of the functions allotted to the Dominion Government, and that none of the Provincial functions would increase in importance. Now the exact opposite is the case.'

The present subsidy arrangements, the Ontario government declared, needed 'radical revision' because they were 'grossly unfair' to that province in particular. For each citizen of Ontario only 97 cents worth of aid was received, while for every Albertan Ottawa paid over $3.37. Not only should subsidies be paid on a strict population basis, adjusted decennially, but the provinces should have some share in the buoyant tariff revenues, too. Above some fixed sum allotted to Ottawa, the provinces should get a percentage of the customs in addition to the fixed subsidy. Such an arrangement 'would have the element of finality about it, and under such an arrangement, the provinces would share proportionally in the increased revenue.'[29]

This ingenious scheme apparently appealed to all the provincial leaders at the conference. Their only difficulty lay in agreeing upon the cut-off point beyond which revenue-sharing should occur. A conference committee, including Ontario's treasurer, I.B. Lucas, therefore suggested instead that the provinces should simply ask for a flat 10 per cent of all tariff revenues. The money would provide for a 50 per cent increase in grants to civil government, and the remaining $13,321,214.37 (available in 1913) would then be divided according to population. Such a scheme naturally attracted the Ontario politicians, because it did not mean any increase in taxes paid by its residents to support the poorer provinces, and with 2,523,274 inhabitants the provincial government could expect a hefty share of the money.[30]

Borden had tacitly approved the calling of the conference because he did not wish to offend his powerful allies, the Conservative Premiers. Nor could he reject their demands outright, but he clearly saw the dangers inherent in this plan. Every tariff revision would generate federal-provincial conflict. A decline in the customs revenues might push the poorer provinces to the brink of bankruptcy. Indeed, Canada was already slipping into just such a dangerous recession. Thus, when Whitney and Gouin explained the provinces' demands to him, he returned a non-committal answer, saying merely that 'he saw no objection to the Provinces coming at stated intervals – say every ten years – to discuss and conclude any financial arrangements as between Canada and the provinces, if circumstances warranted.'[31] Even Whitney seems to have recognized that the provincial request was unlikely to be met. Writing privately to Borden he admitted that his government would be content with much less than 10 per cent of federal tariff revenues, but he left no doubt of the urgency of his government's financial needs since highway improvements were under way which alone would cost between $10 million and $15 million: 'I desire to press upon you with great earnestness the necessity of granting the application to the extent you think you can go. Speaking for Ontario ... *we must have some* aid on this application. Consider, too, what will be said by our opponents at the different political treatment given the Provinces by the two political parties. *I do feel* that I may rely upon you in this, that you will make a public statement *this year or next year*, but in the latter case *let the announcement be made this year without fail.*'

Borden ignored this plea. His finance minister had already advised him that Canada would have much difficulty in borrowing during the coming months, and that all unnecessary expenditures should be curtailed.[32] The recession of 1913 and outbreak of war in 1914 together dashed all hopes of an across-the-board subsidy increase. Indeed, the subsidy granted in 1907 has remained substantially unchanged ever since. The Conservative prime minister did pay off some political debts to his provincial allies, but he refused to be pushed into accepting all or their demands. Perhaps the most important product of the Whitney-Borden alliance was the first conditional grant programs, which certainly benefited the province significantly. In the future such grants would prove of much greater significance than subsidy increases in providing financial assistance to the provinces.

III

The outbreak of the First World War made the responsibilities of the central government literally those of life and death. By contrast, the role of the provinces seemed unimportant, and as federal spending spiralled upward, passing $1 million a day, Ottawa was in no position to grant further financial assistance to the provincial governments. Indeed, it soon became evident that stiffer federal taxes would have to be imposed, leaving the provinces with less and less room to manoeuvre. Any hopes which the premiers might have had for larger subsidies or broader conditional grant programs thus were doomed to disappointment.

As long as the war could be financed by borrowing in London and granting the British dollar credits to purchase Canadian supplies, Finance Minister Thomas White did not make any drastic changes in the taxation system. In 1915, however, consideration was given to an income tax. White was aware that such a move would be both unpopular and administratively complex, but what really deterred him was the likelihood of provincial protests. In January 1915 the cabinet discussed the idea, but as the prime minister recorded, 'Objection that direct taxation should be left to the Provinces seems strong.' In the House of Commons the finance minister pointed out that many municipalities and some of the provinces already depended on revenue from income taxes. The Dominion should not intrude in this field of taxation, he argued.[33] Once the London money market was closed to foreigners in November 1915, White decided to float a domestic war loan of $25 million. Apprehensive about the response, the finance minister suggested to the premiers that the bonds should be exempt from all provincial taxes and succession duties (as well as federal taxes) to make them more attractive to buyers. William Hearst of Ontario refused to consider this idea because of the loss of tax revenues which his province would incur. The suggestion was dropped, but the loan proved an enormous success anyway.[34] Yet increasing military costs also forced White to impose new taxes. In 1916 he introduced the business war profits tax on excess profits and early in 1917 he raised it although he firmly resisted Liberal demands for an income tax, on the grounds 'that until it is clear that it is in the national interest, having regard to our needs, to impose that taxation, the policy would be to trench as little upon the field to which the provinces alone can resort.'[35]

The decision to impose conscription was what finally convinced White that an income tax was necessary, not so much financially as politically. The new tax was initially designed mainly to counter demands for conscription of wealth along with conscription of manpower. White did not consult the provinces over this move, but in the parliamentary debate he emphasized that provincial needs had made him reluctant to take such a step. The Liberals welcomed the new tax, and there was no criticism of interference with local autonomy from any of the members. Nor did the premiers protest this supposedly temporary impost. In the charged atmosphere of 1917 no sacrifice seemed too great for the war effort.[36]

Even these new taxes proved insufficient to meet wartime financial needs; in 1917, 1918, and 1919 three Victory Loans were floated to raise an additional $1.7 billion. So massive was this borrowing that the government decided in 1917 to close the Canadian capital market to all other borrowers, 'to conscript or expropriate the right of competition of new securities with Dominion loans.' Without consultation with the provinces, an order-in-council was passed in December 1917 under the War Measures Act, making it a criminal offence to issue or sell any new securities in Canada without the approval of the minister of finance. On this occasion the provincial leaders did react strongly. Premier Hearst joined in the objections raised by Sir Lomer Gouin of Quebec and others. So loud were the protests that the order was modified in Janurary 1918 to require approval only after issues went on the market. Moreover, White promised to lend the provinces the funds they needed to meet issues maturing abroad during the next five years at 6.5 per cent to keep the provinces out of the market. Attorney-General I.B. Lucas still argued that however laudable the federal government's objectives might be, not even the War Measures Act could give Ottawa the power to abrogate provincial power under the BNA Act to borrow money for provincial purposes. He promised, however, that Ontario would abide by the order-in-council on the understanding that the province refused to surrender any of its legal rights. Within a few months Ontario did take advantage of White's offer and borrowed some $2,000,000 to pay off foreign creditors.[37]

In February 1918 a dominion-provincial conference was held; the major topics of discussion were means of increasing food production and the treatment of returned soldiers. Ontario was represented by Premier Hearst and Lands, Forests, and Mines Minister Howard Ferguson. This gathering produced the first serious rumblings of discontent about the new wartime taxes, and Premier George Murray of Nova Scotia was directed by other provincial delegates to formulate a draft resolution to be forwarded to the federal government. This brief noted that the subsidies had not been increased since 1907 and that Ottawa had now introduced income taxes. The provinces suggested, therefore, that half the receipts from income taxes should be turned over to them on a per capita basis to help meet their new obligations until peace was restored, when a thorough revision of the financial arrangements within Confederation could be made.[38]

This proposition was submitted to the prime minister in the spring of 1918 by Hearst and the other premiers. Within the federal bureaucracy, however, thinking was already running on quite different lines: the prevalent assumption now was that the income tax would not be merely temporary. The income tax, wrote the finance minister's private secretary 'is to be more sharply graded and will certainly be permanent.' There seems to have been no official response to the provincial proposal.[39]

With the end of the fighting in sight, Borden summoned another dominion-provincial conference in October 1918. By the time the premiers had gathered in Ottawa on 19 November he had already sailed for the peace conference, so White was left to preside. The prime minister had warned his cabinet before leaving for Europe to expect a demand for an all-round subsidy increase, and it developed out of the discussions of the return of lands and natural resources to the prairie provinces. Hearst of Ontario raised no objection, but he did object to a federal proposal to turn over the resources to the three provinces while continuing to pay them a subsidy in lieu of the lands. The other six premiers insisted that in that case they also must have an increased subsidy. It was not, Hearst argued, a matter of 'subsidy-grabbing': 'The representatives of this Province simply demanded what was Ontario's right and fair play in the distribution of Dominion Subsidies. Ontario wants no advantage over any other Province, or anything that is not her just due, but this Government is determined to see that this Province that contributes nearly half of the whole revenue of the Dominion is not discriminated against in favour of any other Province.' But the federal cabinet refused to grant an increase to all of the provinces. When Thomas White tried to revive the negotiations near the end of 1918, he found the Ontario premier opposed to mixing up the prairie resource question with subsidy readjustment, and the matter was dropped.[40]

Borden and White had already made up their minds that no general subsidy increase could be conceded. The finance minister bluntly explained the federal government's position to the premier of Prince Edward Island early in 1919: 'In view of the enormous burden of indebtedness and pension and other obligations necessarily imposed by the war upon the Dominion Government, I think it is extremely improbable that any increase in provincial subsidies will be considered.' He added: 'It appears to me that all the provinces are really in better positions to meet their financial requirements than the Dominion as their public debts are very small. I think the difficulty of most provincial governments has been that they hesitate to resort to direct taxation to meet their deficits.' When the premiers pressed White at the November 1918 Conference to promise to refrain from further invasion of the field of direct taxation, particularly with income and inheritance taxes, he could suggest only that another meeting should be held later to discuss the division of tax fields. No such conference was ever held, and it soon became apparent that Ottawa now regarded the Income Tax Act as a permanent and indispensable feature of its fiscal arrangements.[41]

In fact, the only financial concessions which Ottawa made to the provinces were some new conditional grants, including the aid to highway construction which had been blocked by the Senate Liberals in 1912 and 1913. At the dominion-provincial conference in November 1918 it was suggested that a road-building scheme would provide jobs for returned soldiers, and after a brief discussion of the principle of conditional grants, the provinces expressed enthusiasm for the idea. In March 1919 legislation was introduced to provide $20 million over the next five years. Each province would get a block grant of $80,000, and the remainder of the funds would be allotted in proportion to population. For the first time the provinces were required to put up matching funds, since Ottawa agreed to meet only 40 per cent of the total cost. Under this act Ontario drew $5,877,300 to construct 638 miles of roads, mostly hard-surfaced intercity highways. At the same time, conditional grants were also introduced to create a nationwide unemployment service run by the provinces, to combat venereal disease, and to encourage technical education. Thus by 1920 conditional grants had become an established feature of federal-provincial financial relations, although the sums of money involved were not yet large.[42]

The First World War brought other changes in social and economic conditions which forced the federal government to take some responsibility for another matter which lay within provincial jurisdiction. By mid-1918 there had developed serious public concern about the shortage of urban housing. Boards of trade, veterans' organizations, and organized labour joined in a chorus of complaints, particularly in Ontario. Premier Sir William Hearst argued that 'Insofar as the present situation has been brought about by the War, it might well be considered a War problem, and that its solution along with other War problems, rested with the Federal Government.'[43] But Ottawa did not respond at that time. In November 1918, however, the province renewed its proposal. Sir John Willison, chairman of a provincial housing committee, suggested that the federal government should spend up to $10 million on housing. Finance Minister White refused to agree but offered to consider loans to the provinces for this purpose. At the dominion-provincial conference White bowed to further pressure from Hearst and agreed to lend up to $25 million to the provinces under the War Measures Act.[44]

The implementation of this program, however, was hampered by serious conflicts between bureaucrats in Toronto and Ottawa. Thomas Adams, the town planning adviser to the Commission of Conservation, soon clashed with J.A. Ellis of the Ontario Railway and Municipal Board. The province wanted as little federal control over the use of the funds as possible, whereas Adams had not only drawn up regulations specifying the cost of the houses, the size, and the construction materials to be used, but demanded that each have an adequate water supply and face onto a paved street. Premier Hearst, who had formed a low opinion of Adams, complained that there would be 'no end of trouble if the Dominion [is] going to have a set of regulations over and above those of the Province.'[45] Meetings between Ellis and Adams failed to solve these differences, and in the end, the federal cabinet decided that it would impose only a few general conditions, provided each province submitted an acceptable outline of planning principles. Hearst made it clear to the ministers that he would not go ahead with the program unless there was 'a clear and absolute understanding ... that when our scheme is approved by your Government there will be no interference on the part of your Government, or any official thereof.' This condition was accepted by the federal government in February 1919, and concurrent legislation was speedily passed. Ottawa loaned $8 million to Ontario municipalities and over 5,000 houses were constructed. In the spring of 1920 Arthur Meighen decided that the federal government should withdraw from this field of responsibility, which properly belonged to the provinces, but he was persuaded to grant some additional loans in 1921 in light of the serious recession. Thereafter the program lapsed and the loans were gradually repaid.[46]

Between 1900 and 1920 Canada's provinces underwent significant economic and social changes which produced demands for new government services. One response to this development was to look towards Ottawa for financial assistance. Even the province of Ontario, which had not previously shown much enthusiasm for increased federal transfer payments, primarily funded by Ontario taxpayers, now was ready to accept them in exchange for its share of the money. In 1907 the basic subsidy was increased and tied to population, but even that amount proved inadequate, and in 1913 Premier Whitney led the provincial leaders in seeking a share of federal tariff revenues. Although the Borden government refused to grant this concession, it tried to pay some of its political debts to Whitney by introducing conditional grants for agricultural education and highway construction. Borden also speedily conceded Whitney's request for an extension of the boundaries of his province northward and eastward to Hudson Bay and a subsidy to the provincially owned T & NO Railway.

The onset of the First World War negated any possibility of further federal grants, and it stimulated a significant invasion of the fiscal domain previously reserved to the provinces when the income tax was introduced during 1917. But in the wartime crisis even Ontario's leaders had to abandon their long-standing commitment to local autonomy in the pursuit of national goals. Once the fighting ended, however, efforts by the provincial premiers to recover the exclusive right to levy an income tax or to obtain some share in the receipts from it were stymied by Ottawa on the ground that wartime borrowing and war-related expenses had left it burdened with such debts that such sharing could not be contemplated. The provinces received only a few crumbs from the federal table in the form of new conditional grant programs and loans for housing construction. While the federal government was prepared to admit some responsibility for problems directly created by the war, it kept its cash commitments to a minimum and sought to end the new programs as speedily as possible. Thus the provincial financial outlook at the beginning of the 1920s was not bright. New and expensive services were sure to be demanded by the voters; the federal subsidies were becoming an increasingly insignificant part of their budgets. New sources of revenue would have to be found.

7 Social Change and Constitutional Amendment

The economic crisis of the early 1930s convinced a great many Canadians that their country's constitution had to be changed. But how? To most people it seemed obvious that the central government needed wider authority to deal with the problems of mass unemployment. Ontario's political leaders, hard-pressed as they might be by the cost of providing relief to those out of work, rejected this conventional wisdom. They would have been content to shift the heavy burden of relief payments onto a national program of unemployment insurance, but beyond that they were unwilling to surrender any jurisdiction or any sources of revenue to Ottawa. Instead they demanded that the federal government should yield to them the field of income taxation and permit the Provincial government establish its own priorities. Less fortunate provinces might have to look to Ottawa for assistance, but Ontario preferred to go its own way.

Since the BNA Act itself contained no provision for constitutional amendment the first step towards any constitutional change was agreement upon an amending formula. But successive Ontario premiers, loyal as ever to the compact theory of Confederation, were insistent that they should have a veto over any proposed alterations. Until this was definitely conceded they preferred to stand pat and oppose all changes. Neither level of government, federal or provincial, demonstrated much enthusiasm about implementing new social welfare programs during the 1920s, although both provincial spending and provincial debt rose rapidly in Ontario's case (see Tables 3 and 4). For his part, Mackenzie King, the prime minister during most of that decade, was content to let the constitution rest unaltered. He was determined not to hand over to the provinces the revenues raised by taxation on incomes, considering the vast debts accumulated by the central government during the First World War and the continuing cost of military pensions. So despite periodic discussions about amending the BNA Act, nothing was done prior to 1930.

The election of R.B. Bennett in that year coincided with the steady decline of the economic situation. Unemployment relief became so costly that it could no longer be left to the municipalities and provinces. But relief was not managed

TABLE 3
Expenditures, government of Ontario, 1925–40 (ordinary account)

Item	1925	1930	1936[a]	1940
agriculture	2,239,616.86	2,723,788.09	1,531,781.13	2,121,697.54
attorney-general	2,510,723.12	3,106,207.00	2,247,319.22	3,330,139.57
education	9,259,464.03	11,558,179.55	9,835,581.81	12,837,444.08
game & fisheries	357,476.46	558,836.50	434,902.08	558,103.12
health	606,306.58	880,032.42	6,187,596.83	11,102,181.04
highways	3,534,911.91	4,968,625.75	4,236,782.41	9,944,296.12
insurance	48,621.99	64,172.23	66,943.87	58,389.93
labour	2,299,403.04	3,945,903.01	274,492.71	664,175.61
lands & forests	3,055,277.88	2,408,332.57	1,303,038.85	2,140,467.71
legislation	365,933.51	371,770.85	257,237.58	285,479.91
lieutenant-governor	5,450.00	6,350.00	9,217.06	9,583.33
mines	278,115.27	488,746.46	259,079.38	372,506.38
municipal affairs	—	—	77,825.67	4,654,432.64
northern development	—	2,104,834.09	2,290,098.87	—
prime minister	327,473.97	231,745.02	160,817.45	178,788.62
provincial auditor	89,862.90	109,466.28	112,341.98	114,047.31
provincial secretary	6,216,616.65	8,448,205.75	740,907.56	1,599,630.06
provincial treasurer	2,134,584.17	1,913,247.12	784,193.45	1,273,731.87
public welfare	—	1,955.51	4,507,892.18	8,964,446.64
public works	805,181.26	955,657.57	552,120.71	843,136.96
miscellaneous	88,983.12	1,150,689.19	98,391.91	4,694.00
public debt	17,238,175.78	11,992,617.73	21,287,759.40	21,325,721.96
subtotal	51,462,178.50	57,989,352.69	57,256,322.11	82,365,094.40
unemployment: direct relief & administration	—	—	21,813,368.20	9,041,953.41
total	51,462,178.50	57,989,352.69	79,069,690.31	91,407,047.81

[a] End of fiscal year changed from 31 Oct. to 31 March in 1934–5.
SOURCE: Ontario, Public Accounts, *Sessional Papers*, no. 1, 1926, 1931, 1937, 1941

TABLE 4
Gross debt, province of Ontario, 1915–40

Year	Gross debt	HEPC	Per capita net debt
1915	50,275,000	12,316,000	3.48
1920	127,262,000	65,717,000	7.90
1925	332,391,000	141,717,000	42.32
1930	473,372,000	176,799,000	62.49
1936	689,559,000	172,735,000	112,76
1940	737,078,000	145,319,000	135.58

SOURCE: *Budget Statement of the Honourable James N. Allan, Treasurer of Ontario, 1963* (Toronto: King's Printer, 1963), appendix, 66–7

through a sweeping redistribution of constitutional responsibilities. Instead the system of federal grants-in-aid worked out during the depression at the end of the first World War was simply extended. Bennett and the premiers continued to discuss constitutional change during the early 1930s, but even in such critical times there seemed to be little disposition to make the concessions needed to secure agreeement. At long last, with the popularity of his government steadily ebbing away, Bennett finally abandoned the search for consensus and introduced his 'New Deal' without regard to the provinces. Thus, in both good times and bad, Canada failed to adapt its 'horse and buggy' constitution to the demands of the new age. A good part of the responsibility for that failure may be ascribed to the conservatism of Ontario's leaders, who preferred the devil they knew to the one they did not.

I

In the months immediately after the war ended it appeared that the federal government did intend to embark upon a new series of social programs to meet the needs of an urban and industrial society. Canada became a signer of the labour clauses of the Treaty of Versailles and a member of the International Labour Organization. These commitments included support for the principle that all workers should have the right to organize and bargain collectively; that minimum wage levels should be set so as to ensure a reasonable standard of living; that men and women should get equal pay for equal work; that child labour should cease; that the working day should be eight hours and the working week forty-eight; and that there should be a weekly day of rest. Such matters had always been believed to be provincial responsibilities since they concerned 'civil rights in the provinces.' But the Borden government now claimed the right to act under section 132 of the BNA Act, which gave parliament 'all Powers necessary for performing the obligations of Canada or any Province thereof ... towards Foreign Countries, arising under Treaties between the British Empire and such Foreign Countries.' In the words of the deputy minister of labour, it was simply 'taken for granted that the Dominion had the right, if it pleased, to carry out this eight-hour law or any of these other matters under its treaty-making powers.'[1]

In view of Ontario's past record as a steadfast defender of provincial rights, it was to be expected that this federal initiative would be resisted. Yet Premier Sir William Hearst said to a deputation of strikers in June 1919:

It is difficult for me to come to the conclusion that the framers of the British North America Act intended that the Provinces should have exclusive jurisdiction in matters so vitally affecting trade and commerce and the general welfare and prosperity of the Dominion as hours of labour, rates of wages, methods of bargaining between employees and employers. In my opinion there can be no doubt of the absolute necessity, if the best results are to be obtained, that any action for the purpose of giving effect to the findings of the Peace Conference or in dealing with the matter in question, should embrace the whole Dominion and be uniform in character, subject only to whatever modifications, if any, local conditions might demand.

Hearst was convinced, of course, that most of Canada's current social and economic problems were ascribable to the war, so that Ottawa should shoulder the responsibility for dealing with them. Unilateral action by the province in the field of labour legislation would simply increase the cost of production in Ontario, leading entrepreneurs to settle in more lenient jurisdictions to the detriment of the province. The attorney-general's department even produced an official opinion to the effect that hours of work legislation would affect 'peace, order and good government' and must be handled by the federal authorities.[2] At a meeting with the prime minister and the labour minister in the fall of 1919 officials from all of the provinces agreed that unemployment and health insurance and old age pensions were federal responsibilities, and it was decided to refer the question of jurisdiction over hours of labour to the Supreme Court for an opinion.[3]

At the first meeting of the International Labour Organization in November 1919 Health minister Newton Rowell, as Canada's representative, promised that the government would support legislation to implement six draft conventions on the eight-hour day, the forty-eight-hour week, pregnancy leaves for female employees, night work for females, and child labour. On his return to Ottawa, however, Rowell found that he could not carry the cabinet with him in introducing such legislation. 'It was urged,' the deputy minister of labour reported, 'that it would be very bad and somewhat dangerous precedent to set. The provinces would object to being over-ridden in that way by the exercise in a somewhat arbitrary way of those powers by the Dominion. I do not think it was seriously proposed to do it.' The retreat was formally sounded by Rowell himself who informed the House of Commons that it might be necessary for the provinces to pass the eight-hour day legislation themselves. He was backed up by Justice

Minister C.J. Doherty, who argued that the federal parliament lacked the power to limit the civil right of contract between employers and employees by limiting hours of labour.[4]

In May 1920 the federal labour department convened a conference with representatives of the provinces, private business, and labour groups and urged that the provincial governments pass uniform legislation on these subjects.[5] In November 1920 this new stance was confirmed by an order-in-council spelling out Canada's obligations under the Treaty of Versailles. Justice Minister Doherty argued that there was no commitment by the federal government to enact the International Labour Organization conventions into law. It had agreed only to recommend them to the competent jurisdiction within Canada, so that section 132 of the BNA Act did not apply. Ottawa would simply act as a channel of communication between Geneva and the provinces. Doubtless this retreat by the Unionist cabinet reflected the deep hostility of many leading businessmen in Canada towards wages and hours legislation, and the constitution proved a handy shelter against charges of inaction.[6]

However, Ottawa was unable to escape entirely from demands for moves in the field of social policy. The trade cycle was already heading steadily downward towards its low point in the winter of 1921–22, and the growing number of unemployed could not be ignored by any level of government. By the fall of 1920 agitation began to mount steadily, but Labour Minister Gideon Robertson stood firm: 'Municipal and provincial authorities must not be permitted to continue – as in wartime – to pass every local question on to the Federal Government to find a solution. In previous periods of depression appeals were always made to the local authority first. We should, I think, guide all concerned in that direction, if Municipal and Provincial authorities are to properly function.' While 'willing and anxious' to assist, the federal government could not 'assume obligations which properly belong to a particular municipality or province.' A meeting with the Ontario labour minister, Walter Rollo, in December 1920 apparently persuaded Robertson to change his mind. If 'emergency relief measures' for the unemployed became 'necessary by reason of utterly unavoidable shortage of employment,' Robertson offered to meet one-third of the cost over and above normal expenditures, if municipalities and provinces each matched this figure. He warned Rollo, however, that in ordinary times these would be local problems, but that on this occasion he was willing to help, since unemployment had increased 'by reason of the general contraction of industrial activity following upon a period of abnormal prices during the war.' The Farmer-Labour government of E.C. Drury accepted the offer and received $172,551 over the next few months. Although the amount was trifling, this was a significant precedent upon which all subsequent aid to the unemployed was modelled in the interwar period. Like the income tax it was introduced by Ottawa rather casually to meet a crisis on the understanding that it was merely temporary.[7]

In the spring of 1921 the Labour members of the Ontario legislature persuaded Walter Rollo to introduce a resolution calling for a conference between Ottawa and the provinces to discuss the 'advisability and practicability' of legislation concerning old age pensions, unemployment insurance, and the eight-hour day; the conference also should consider which level of government ought to enact legislation on these matters. Gideon Robertson's response to this suggestion was cool; he felt it was an attempt to discredit the work of the federal labour department. Investigations of insurance and pension schemes were already under way, he advised Prime Minister Arthur Meighen, and no meeting should be held until these studies were completed. Meighen readily agreed; he thought that the division of powers fixed by the BNA Act could not be modified by a dominion-provincial conference in any case.[8]

In the fall of 1921, facing an election, the Meighen government proved a little more forthcoming. In response to a suggestion from the president of the Trades and Labour Congress that the federal government grant aid to the unemployed, the prime minister reiterated that 'unemployment relief has been, and must necessarily continue to be, primarily a municipal responsibility, and in the second instance the responsibility of the province.' But because the present situation was 'due to causes beyond the power of local or even national control,' he agreed to continue to provide matching grants to meet one-third of the cost of direct relief and municipal relief works programs over and above the amounts normally expended for such purposes during the coming winter.[9]

Mackenzie King's victory in the election signalled no new departure in the field of social policy, and the matching grants were simply continued for the next few years, although one-half the cost of a relief works programs was now paid by Ottawa. Over the next year or so Ontario received $680,000 of such aid. Like his predecessor, however, King warned that 'unemployment relief is fundamentally a municipal and provincial responsibility; the abnormal economic and industrial conditions arising in large measure out of the late war alone afford justification for action on the part of the federal authorities.'[10]

King's minister of labour, James Murdock, did call a conference in September 1922 to discuss unemployment and the implementation of the International Labour Organization conventions. In his address to the opening session of the conference the prime minister stressed that Ottawa would not take sole responsibility for social problems. Premier Drury, representing Ontario, complained that his province had the highest unemployment in Canada. Relief works programs funded by all three levels of government had cost $1.5 million, or three times as much as usual. Despite this fact and an extensive program of highway construction, the jobless had collected $700,000 in direct relief during the past winter. But the premier could suggest no remedies beyond the continuation of existing programs and a reduction in the cost of living. The conference broke up without achieving

Social Change and Constitutional Amendment 139

anything concrete, and another meeting in the fall of 1923 was no more successful.[11]

At the 1924 session of parliament Justice Minister Ernest Lapointe submitted the International Labour Organization convention on the eight-hour day to a commons committee for a report on where jurisdiction lay. The committee concluded that the law was so unclear that there should be a reference to the Supreme Court, a suggestion accepted by the government.[12] Ontario officials were convinced that Ottawa would use this pretext to try to convince the court that such matters were entirely provincial responsibilities. Attorney-General W.F. Nickle was afraid that an absence of uniform national hours-of-work legislation would create economic chaos, and he urged that Ontario take the unusual stand of calling for broader federal authority. In due course, however, the provincial cabinet reverted to the more traditional posture of arguing that civil rights should be left to the provinces. In June 1925 the Supreme Court ruled that the Treaty of Versailles committed the government only to recommending the conventions to the competent authority within Canada. As a result, section 132 of the BNA Act did not apply, and parliament had no jurisdiction in this area. Mackenzie King's government was effectively freed of the duty to see that the conventions signed with such high hopes in 1919 would become law in Canada.[13]

By 1925 federal grants-in-aid to the provinces for unemployment relief had completely ceased. Between 1921 and 1924 a total of $1,788,406 had been paid out, of which Ontario had received $856,300. At a conference with provincial officials in the fall of 1924 Labour Minister Murdock expressed anger at local officials who 'no longer ask assistance as of grace, but as a matter of constitutional right.' In future, he made plain, the provinces and municipalities themselves must be prepared to cope with these problems. Federal determination to vacate this field was redoubled early in 1925 when the Privy Council handed down a decision invalidating Mackenzie King's beloved Industrial Disputes Investigation Act as an interference with civil rights in the provinces. The Judicial Committee rejected the argument that the need for 'peace, order and good government' legitimized interference in labour disputes, except in emergencies like wartime. King seized upon this pronouncement as an excuse to declare that his government had no constitutional authority to provide unemployment relief.[14]

The Ontario government responded angrily. Attorney-General Nickle told the press: 'According to my view of the British North American Act there is absolutely nothing to prevent the Dominion from assuming a share of the unemployment relief obligation.' When irate municipal politicians and trade union leaders demanded that the province do something if Ottawa refused to, Premier Howard Ferguson passed the buck, arguing that the matter was primarily a municipal one. Beyond that, he insisted, the responsibility lay with the federal government, which controlled immigration and economic policy. Of King's refusal to grant funds he complained: 'Parliament surely is supreme and can vote public monies for any purpose it may deem proper, so that this Government is unable to see any force or substance in the position taken by the Dominion Government.' The prime minister was unmoved. Grants-in-aid for unemployment relief were not resumed, except for a minuscule $77,475 paid out by Ottawa in 1927 of which $45,000 went to Ontario.[15]

Federal initiatives in the field of social welfare policy which began in the immediate aftermath of the war thus proved short lived. Nothing concrete was done by Ottawa to see that the International Labour Organization's conventions came into force, and the provinces failed to act. Meighen did agree to grants for unemployment relief but only as a temporary remedy for the post-war recession. By the mid-1920s they, too, had ceased. Even though the provinces, in particular Ontario, seemed unusually willing to accept an expansion of federal activity in this sphere, the central government remained reluctant to move. The heavy burden of wartime debt and the innate conservatism of Mackenzie King stifled any innovative programs during the early 1920s.

II

Despite growing receipts from new taxes upon liquor and gasoline, even the well-off provinces found themselves hard pressed financially in the 1920s. By 1930 Ontario would spend almost $58 million, an increase of 80 per cent since 1920 (see Tables 1 and 3). In just three years, 1923 through 1925, the province's accumulated deficit totalled nearly $29 million or more than ordinary expenditure in 1920. Equally alarming, the gross provincial debt surged from $127,262,000 to $473,372,000 and net debt from $7.90 per capita to $62.49 per capita (see Table 4). Had it not been for the spectacular increase in returns from the sales tax on gasoline from zero in 1921 to $11,230,000 in 1930, from motor vehicle taxes which almost doubled to $5,520,000, and from liquor taxes which generated $10,285,000 in 1930 versus only $349,000 at the beginning of the decade, Ontario would have been in serious financial difficulties even before the depression. Other provinces found themselves in a similar or worse plight. While federal spending rose only 10 per cent between 1921 and 1930, provincial outlays more than doubled to $180 million annually, and provinces and municipalities borrowed $1 billion altogether in these years, while Ottawa's debt increased by only $250 million.[16]

Not surprisingly, therefore, provincial leaders began to consider ways and means of extracting more money from Ottawa. Federal subsidies now provided only a derisory amount: $1.08 for each Ontarian in 1922 – only Quebec with 98 cents per capita getting less.[17] In the fall of 1923 a number of chambers of commerce and boards of trade urged the new premier, Howard Ferguson, to seek a conference on the reallocation of tax fields between the two levels of government.

At a meeting with L.A. Taschereau of Quebec and the three maritime premiers, it was agreed that an interprovincial conference ought to be called in the near future, but nothing was done.[18] In November 1924 the acting finance minister, James Robb, responded to pressure from the Manitoba government by calling the provincial treasurers to Ottawa to discuss the delimitation of tax fields. The provincial representatives complained loudly of their problems. The treasurer of Alberta claimed: 'The Dominion income tax ... makes it extremely difficult if not altogether impossible for the provinces to enter this field at the present time. Any imposition of a provincial income tax must now be regarded as overlapping and for that reason very objectionable.' W.H. Price of Ontario supported this position, but Robb was not sympathetic. He complained that the provinces wanted Ottawa to abandon the income tax, to which it was legally entitled, and at the same time increase spending on unemployment relief. Income taxes in Canada must be cut rather than increased, he warned, or else there would be a flight of capital to the United States. He refused even to discuss the idea that all personal income taxes should be turned over to the provinces, as was done in Australia.[19]

There was little that Ontario or the other provinces could do to compel Ottawa to give them more funds or introduce new programs. During the late 1920s the only action which the King government took in the field of social welfare was the introduction of an old age pension scheme. The prime minister agreed to this move early in 1926 in order to win the support of J.S. Woodsworth and A.A. Heaps for his minority government. Defeated in the Senate it was reintroduced in 1927 and eventually became law. Howard Ferguson was not enthusiastic; he preferred to balance his budget rather than put up the province's half share of the costs. In the end, however, Ontario did join the plan.[20]

In the spring of 1926 Ferguson's interest in an interprovincial conference revived when he learned that King proposed to hand over control of their natural resources to the governments of the western provinces but permit them to keep their special subsidies in lieu of lands. The prime minister at first hoped to block any such meeting through his influence with Taschereau. King shared the fear of O.D. Skelton, a close adviser, that the only result would be 'a united raid on the Treasury' led by Ontario, 'in which the smaller provinces particularly would join with enthusiasm.'[21] However, Taschereau proved unable to persuade his fellow premiers to change their minds and the conference was fixed for June. The subsidy question was foremost in the minds of the provincial leaders, and they unanimously approved a resolution calling upon the federal government to take account of the particular grievances of the Maritimes and the west.[22]

King had no time to respond to this resolution, since he resigned from the prime ministership a few days later to avoid defeat in parliament. Once back in office, however, he persuaded his cabinet to endorse better terms for the Maritimes in the spring of 1927. In order to mollify some unhappy ministers he agreed to convene a dominion-provincial conference to ratify the new arrangements. In fact, King had been promising such a meeting since 1925 to discuss Senate reform but had been holding off for fear the provinces would gang up and demand an increase in the subsidy. Now, however, it was decided to hold the conference in November 1927. An effort by Howard Ferguson to induce the other premiers to meet beforehand and formulate a joint position was thwarted by the Liberal leaders, who had been warned by their federal counterparts to have nothing to do with the idea.[23]

When the delegates gathered in Ottawa on 3 November there were four basic issues to be discussed: the division of jurisdiction over social welfare, the redistribution of tax fields, subsidies to the provinces, and a formula for amending the constitution. Subsidies proved the least contentious. Ontario expressed none of its traditional hostility to small increases in federal transfer payments. One reason was that Howard Ferguson had other irons in the fire. He and Taschereau were eager to have the backing or at least the silent acquiescence of the other premiers in their demand for control of waterpowers on navigable rivers. A discreet payoff seemed the best way of ensuring their co-operation. Ferguson reminded the other premiers that Ontario contributed the lion's share of federal revenues but added magnanimously that 'He did not intend, however, to cavil about small things. He regarded it as supremely important to bring about a situation which would be satisfactory to all provinces.' The financial terms of the BNA Act obviously needed readjustment from time to time, and 'The big problem was to promote satisfaction and prosperity by giving fresh inspiration to those who needed it.'[24] The other provincial leaders likewise supported the special subsidies to the Maritimes and endorsed the return of the western natural resources and the continuation of the subsidy in lieu of lands. Since the federal government had already granted the Maritimes assistance, there was little difficulty in reaching a settlement. Ferguson and Taschereau also got their way on the water-power issue, which was referred to the Supreme Court for adjudication.[25]

The discussion of division of jurisdiction in the field of social policy proved abortive, however. Ontario officials were doubtful that any agreement between the two levels of government would stand up in the courts even if confirmed by enabling legislation. The province's deputy minister of labour had hoped that Ottawa could be made to acknowledge formally its responsibility to meet at least part of the cost of unemployment relief, but Ferguson evidently judged it wiser not to raise the matter at all. The conference devoted little time to this issue.[26]

Ontario was primarily interested in the allocation of fields of taxation. Ever since 1918 the province had been pressing Ottawa to abandon the income tax. Before the conference one civil servant suggested to the premier that 'If the Dominion Government finds it necessary to continue the collection of the income tax, so much of such income tax as is personal income tax should be returned to the Province, and that part of the tax collected from corporations be retained by the Dominion Government.' Otherwise there would have to be a redefinition of direct taxation if the province was to meet steadily increasing demands for assistance from the municipalities. At the very least the official wanted a federal-provincial agreement to prevent private citizens from challenging provincial taxes in the courts on the grounds that they were ultra vires; only the federal government should have this right.[27]

Attorney-General W.H. Price presented Ontario's demands to the conference, but Finance Minister Robb took the same tough line as he had in the past. He pointed out that the war debt now totalled $1 billion and that annual carrying charges were almost $163 million. Over the next several years more than $1.25 billion in debts would mature; federal taxation must therefore be maintained at the present level if this sum was to be retired or refunded. About 60 per cent of the income tax was paid by corporations of which 80 per cent had head offices in Ontario or Quebec. Robb rejected the notion that these provinces should refuse to share their wealth with the poorer areas through federal taxation. Since Ottawa was quite entitled to levy an income tax, there were no grounds for alleging that it violated the compact of Confederation. He concluded by complaining that the premiers were simply trying to have their cake and eat it too, with fewer responsibilities and more money to spend.[28]

The conference then turned to a discussion of an amending formula to permit changes in the constitution. Howard Ferguson had already made his view of the nature of Confederation clear some months earlier:

The constitution is an agreement arrived at among the provinces ... It would be essential that any amendments to it should similarly be submitted to all the provinces and receive their consent.

This is not merely a question concerning matters of local interest, it concerns the main principle underlying the Canadian constitution. Any amendments to it must have the approval not only of provincial governments but of provincial legislatures as well ...

Ontario ... would protest, and protest vigorously if it were proposed to make any change in the constitution without consulting her.

King's Private Secretary, Norman Rogers, who was in charge of devising an amending formula, disagreed; he thought that requiring unanimous consent for any changes would make the BNA Act too rigid and impossible to alter. While certain key provisions regarding linguistic or religious rights might be protected in this way, other changes should only require approval by two-thirds of the provincial legislatures. Matters affecting the federal government alone would not require agreement from the provinces at all.[29]

When Ernest Lapointe submitted this proposal to the premiers they evinced little interest, particularly in view of the fact that they were being offered no quid pro quo such as access to new revenues. Their enthusiasm for the formula arose solely from the concession of their right to be formally consulted on constitutional matters. In his address to the conference Lapointe seemed to accept that Confederation was a kind of compact: 'The BNA Act is the charter of the provinces in which powers have been fixed and determined between the Dominion and the provinces. Consequently, the provinces have a right to be consulted about establishing a new procedure to amend it.' But Ferguson declared that he felt there was no widespread demand for change, and Premier Taschereau took the same position. The matter was allowed to drop.[30]

The concrete achievements of the 1927 dominion-provincial conference were not many, although they were of a kind which pleased Mackenzie King. He had forestalled any 'united raid on the Treasury'[31] at the cost of a small increase in the federal subsidies to the west and the Maritimes. He had raised the matter of an amending formula for the constitution so that he could not be blamed for inactivity. Moreover, he had avoided taking on any new responsibilities such as unemployment relief and had even strengthened his defences against such pressure. When Howard Ferguson enquired in February 1928 whether the federal government was willing to meet one-third of the cost of relief works to provide employment that winter, Labour Minister Peter Heenan was able to point out that at the conference he and the other premiers had expressed their dislike of Ottawa's spending money on programs outside its jurisdiction. In view of that fact they must carry the burden themselves.[32]

As Canada slid towards depression in the late 1920s, however, the demand for federal funds for the relief of unemployment began to mount in intensity. Mackenzie King continued to insist that the Conservative party, federal and provincial, was exaggerating the problem for partisan purposes. There was, he told the House of Commons in April 1930, 'no evidence in Canada today of an emergency situation.' The provinces could perfectly well deal with the problem, but Tories like Howard Ferguson preferred to seek federal assistance rather than raise provincial taxes. For 'these alleged unemployment purposes, with these governments situated as they are today, with policies diametrically opposed to those of the government's,' the prime minister declared, 'I would not give a five-cent piece.' The Ontario premier, already angry at King's refusal to reach a settlement on the control of St Lawrence water-power, seized upon this unfortunate phrase. When a federal election was called for 28 July, Ferguson announced he would throw his full weight behind the federal Conservatives.[33] This action provoked King into another blunder. 'Since when,' he demanded to know, 'has the Premier of the Province dared to interject the management of the affairs of his Province into a Federal campaign? Let Mr Ferguson look after his Province's affairs. I will attend to my business.'

The premier was ready with a firm rejoinder. He represented the people of Ontario just as much as Mackenzie King, and 'When the Prime Minister of Canada makes a statement on the floor of Parliament declaring discrimination against any province, it is the bounden duty of the prime minister of that province to protest.'

King tried to insist that his government had forged an enviable record in federal-provincial relations, which were more harmonious than ever before. Ontario, he claimed, had received $16 million annually from Ottawa since 1922. Unfortunately, this total proved to be blatantly inflated by the inclusion of $97 million paid out in military pensions to Ontario residents. With just two weeks left in the campaign, the prime minister gave in and announced that his government was prepared to match any funds provided by the provinces and municipalities to relieve unemployment.[34]

The concession proved too little, too late. The Liberals were soundly defeated, losing forty seats, as the voters responded to the promises of R.B. Bennett. In Moncton on 10 July he told his audience: 'The Conservative party is going to find work for all who are willing to work or perish in the attempt. It is going to ... take such steps as will end this tragic condition of unemployment and bring prosperity to the country as a whole ... I promise to end unemployment.'[35] But once he was in office, these commitments proved mainly rhetorical, and Bennett's government merely reverted to the ad hoc remedies relied upon by Meighen and King during the post-war recession. At a special session of parliament in the fall of 1930, the Unemployment Relief Act was passed, appropriating $20 million. The money could be used for public works, for aid to the provinces and municipalities, or 'generally in any way that will assist in providing useful and suitable work for the unemployed.' The regulations drawn up by the Unemployment Relief Branch of the Department of Labour permitted one-quarter of the cost of relief works to be paid if the province matched this and the municipalities covered the other half of the cost. Where the numbers of unemployed were too great for works programs, Ottawa agreed to meet one-third of the cost of direct relief. In all, Ontario received $3,850,000 to fund projects such as highway construction plus $842,650 for direct relief.

Labour Minister Gideon Robertson, back in office again, explained the rationale behind this legislation to Ferguson in words which might have been taken from one of his letters of a decade earlier: 'The primary purpose sought to be achieved by the Federal Government is ... to assist municipalities and provinces in dealing with the situation which every one realizes is not primarily a Federal responsibility.' While prepared to assist local authorities, Robertson was determined that they should show their 'good faith' by contributing part of the cost of relief. Ontario chose J.A. Ellis of the Bureau of Municipal Affairs to administer the relief funds because of his intimate knowledge of local problems. Within a week applications for some $15 million had flooded into Toronto from all areas of the province, so that all requests had to be severely scaled down. Eventually, agreements were made with 195 municipalities to finance works and with 213 municipalities to support direct relief payments. In all, some $8 million was spent on works by the two senior levels of government, another $1 million being supplied for direct relief. Thus, by far the largest proportion of the $21 million spent for unemployment relief in Ontario in 1930–1 still came from the municipal governments of the province.[36]

When the economic crisis struck Canada, a decade or more of discussion had produced no constitutional changes which might enable government more effectively to meet the needs of an urban, industrial society. Many people believed that certain social problems and social policies, like relief of unemployment, needed to be tackled on a national basis, but jurisdiction still rested in the hands of the provinces. The provinces were far from stable financially. Consumption taxes, such as those on liquor and gasoline, were particularly vulnerable to downturns in the trade cycle, and indeed, Ontario's revenues declined by almost $3 million or 5 per cent between 1930 and 1931.[37] Municipalities, upon whom the provincial governments had in the past thrust much of the responsibility for social welfare, were even less capable of coping with mass unemployment. Blame for this failure to adapt the constitution to the social realities lay on many heads. Neither premiers nor prime ministers had shown themselves disposed to give up revenues, often preferring to try to thrust added responsibilities upon others.

III

The Ontario government, in particular, remained determined that any and all changes in the constitution should be subject to its veto. In 1927 Ernest Lapointe had conceded the need for provincial approval of any amending formula and suggested unanimous provincial consent would be needed for changes in certain key provisions and a two-thirds majority for other alterations in provincial powers. The drafting of the Statute of Westminster brought this matter to a head in 1930. The statute was intended to embody the principles of the Balfour Declaration of 1926 regarding the independence and equality of all the members of the British Commonwealth. By the Colonial Laws Validity Act any statute passed in a British possession was nullified where it conflicted with a British law; this condition would no longer apply to the self-governing dominions under the Statute. When the Canadian House of Commons debated the matter in May 1930, the Conservatives pointed out that this apparently innocuous change might have serious consequences for Canada's federal system. Since the BNA Act was a British statute, and Canada lacked any formula for constitutional amendment, might it now become possible for parliament to legislate unilaterally upon matters within provincial jurisdiction or even to alter the division of powers itself? But the Liberals rejected this idea, and the Commons approved the draft Statute of Westminster.[38]

R.B. Bennett's election victory in July determined that he, rather than Mackenzie King, would represent Canada at the Imperial Conference in the fall, called to approve the final draft of the Statute. Howard Ferguson, his influence with the new prime minister secured by his vigorous intervention in the campaign, lost no time in entering a strong protest against the proposed change. In an open letter to Bennett published on 20 September 1930 Ferguson insisted that the BNA Act was the outcome of an agreement between the provinces and argued that no alterations in it should be made without their consent.[39] Any other course, he warned, would 'not only greatly disturb the present harmonious operation of our Constitution, but I fear may seriously disrupt the whole structure of our Confederation.' A memorandum that accompanied his letter contained a classic statement of the compact theory of Confederation. 'The Dominion was ... created at the instance of the provinces,' wrote Ferguson, since 'the resolutions adopted by the Quebec Conference were in the nature of a compact or treaty between the Provinces.' The BNA Act, in turn, was 'a transcript' of those resolutions. Proof positive was that Parliament lacked the power to amend the constitution, a most sensible precaution which had prevented it from enacting legislation 'setting aside the pretensions of the provinces' whenever there was a dispute. Ontario, he pointed out, had been demanding consultation on amendments ever since 1887, and he added, '[N]o restatement of the procedure for amending the constitution of Canada can be accepted by the Province of Ontario which does not fully and frankly acknowledge the right of all provinces to be consulted and to become parties to the decision arrived at.'

Federal officials were scornful of Ferguson's protest. To them it seemed the 'high water mark' of the provincial rights movement. 'National development' would be 'absolutely blocked and Canada saddled with an absolutely rigid and stereotyped constitution,' if unanimous provincial consent were required: 'These extreme claims are all the more extraordinary in view of the fact that the present-day trend is quite in the other direction, in the direction of recognizing that economic and social changes are making it necessary to adapt old constitutions to new needs, to give the national government the wide scope necessary to deal with the nation-wide scope of present-day business and the growing insistence of international issues.' Not only was the Ontario premier denounced as a bad historian for his notion of the 'compact' of Confederation, but his objections to the proposed Statute of Westminster were dismissed as 'trivial.' The new legislation, suggested one justice department lawyer, would only 'curb provincial pretensions not provincial rights.' The government of Canada had every right to readjust its relations with Great Britain without reference to the provinces.[40]

The prime minister soon showed, however, that he was not disposed to offend a powerful ally like Ferguson, a man whom he was shortly to appoint as Canada's high commissioner in London. He persuaded the Imperial Conference to delay a decision on the Statute until the provinces had had their say. A dominion-provincial conference was summoned for 7 April 1931. The new Ontario premier, George S. Henry, fully shared the view of his predecessor that 'the British North America Act was a contract, with the original provinces at any rate, and nothing vital in it should be changed without provincial consent.' Bennett, therefore, proposed an amendment to the Statute of Westminster declaring that it conferred no new powers to alter the BNA Act on either the federal or provincial governments nor any new legislative jurisdiction. Ontario Attorney-General W.H. Price pointed out that only provincial rights covered by the BNA Act would be protected by this; the federal government might still abolish appeals to the Privy Council, for instance, without consultation. The prime minister insisted that all he wanted to do was to preserve the status quo. Eventually, under pressure from Henry and from Taschereau of Quebec, he promised that 'in the future no amendments to the British North American Act would be made by the present government until an opportunity had been given the Provinces to discuss the amendment, and the practice that has heretofore prevailed would not be relied upon.' He also promised, at Price's insistence, to call a meeting in the near future to deal with the matter of an amending formula. Having extracted these concessions, the premiers accepted the proposed amendment to the Statute of Westminster and it became law a few months later.[41]

The 1931 conference was significant because pressure from Ferguson had at last compelled the federal government to admit the need for consultation with the provinces about any amendments to the constitution. In 1906, by contrast, the premiers had simply submitted their demands to Laurier, who had agreed to accept them. Lapointe's promise in 1927 that there would be consultations had now become a reality. And the combined influence of Ontario and Quebec had persuaded the prime minister to promise that his government would not propose *any* future amendments to the BNA Act without consulting the provinces. What was left unsaid, of course, was that the victory of the Conservatives in the 1930 election had given the premier of Ontario a much more powerful voice in Canadian affairs than he had enjoyed previously. But henceforth it was assumed, at least by the provinces, that all constitutional changes would require provincial approval.

IV

The need for such constitutional change was beginning to seem imperative as economic conditions deteriorated. Early in 1931 J.A. Ellis, who had been placed in charge of unemployment relief, still remained confident. It was 'the opinion in Ottawa,' he reported to the premier, 'that the unemployment situation in Ontario has been pretty well dealt with.' But as spring approached that confidence ebbed away. Funds for relief works ran out and some projects had to be closed down before the official termination date of 31 March. By that time Ontario had appropriated more federal money than it expected to receive. The provincial share of all direct relief payments was terminated on 1 June, but it was clear that such assistance would be needed to manage through the coming winter.[42] In July Bennett introduced the Unemployment and Farm Relief Act, which gave the federal government power to make grants to alleviate unemployment, chiefly through relief works programs. When the premier of British Columbia wrote to protest at the amount allotted to his province, the prime minister brushed his complaints aside: 'Under our Constitution responsibility in connection with unemployment rests primarily with [the] Province ... The extent of unemployment, which is world-wide, has induced the Federal Government to treat the problem as national and assist [the] Provinces in the discharge of their obligations. Unless [the] Provinces relinquish [their] constitutional functions federal action must be through their governments.' Eventually, the federal government agreed to provide aid on the same basis as the previous year: matching grants to cover 25 per cent of the cost of relief works and 33 per cent of the cost of direct relief. Ontario received from Ottawa $8 million for relief works plus $2 million for direct relief.[43]

During the winter of 1931–2 relief expenditures in Ontario totalled over $38 million, each level of government putting up about one-third of the cost. Bennett and his ministers were not satisfied with the way this aid was administered by the provinces. In April 1932 the premiers were summoned to Ottawa for a meeting and it was announced that federal aid to costly relief works programs would be dropped and almost all the money would be spent on direct relief payments. Economy seems to have been the main motive, since works absorbed large sums for materials and administration. In the depths of the depression more people could be helped for less money by paying direct relief. As a result, the 440,000 people dependent on direct relief in Ontario were assisted by $6,290,967 in federal funds, while another $949,000 went to fund works' programs mostly employing single men on highway construction.[44]

In the face of this drain the prime minister decided to convene another dominion-provincial conference, but he departed on a trip to England late in 1932 leaving his private secretary, R.K. Finlayson, to draw up an agenda in consultation with O.D. Skelton, the under-secretary of state for external affairs. They concluded that unemployment insurance and the immediate relief situation must be taken up with the premiers. Finlayson noted that unemployment insurance would do nothing for the 600,000 Canadians already out of work, and that an amendment to the BNA Act would be required before Ottawa could introduce a national, compulsory scheme. He recommended that a royal commission be appointed to investigate the subject and that the provincial leaders be asked to agree in advance to a constitutional amendment once the royal commission had reported. Provided that the central government took over all responsibility for the support of single, unemployed men and moved to bring in unemployment insurance, criticism that it was doing nothing beyond providing the dole to those without jobs would be defused. Moreover, the provinces could then be made to assume all the responsibility for others still requiring direct relief. The prime minister apparently agreed with Finlayson's advice that the provinces needed to be brought into line; on his return from London he told a Vancouver audience in January 1933 that his government had 'expended $131,462,000 for the relief of the people of Canada during the depression, all as payments to the provinces, without any surrender of autonomy on their part. The time has come, however, when the Dominion, jealous of its credit, must pause before it hands over any further sums not under control.'[45]

The premiers gathered in Ottawa on 17 January. Premier Henry told the Conference that about 10 per cent of Ontario's population was then on relief. In the severely hit lumbering and pulp and paper towns in northern Ontario up to three-quarters of the population required some assistance. All the manufacturing areas were suffering, but Oshawa and the border cities, dependent on the automobile industry, were the worst hit. By and large, rural Ontario was self-supporting, although farmers had a hard time meeting debts and taxes. The only bright spots were the gold mines and the slight success of the back-to-the-land movement. Henry reported that there had been 'a good deal of feeling in his Province against the abandonment of the programme of public works, but it was generally recognized that financial considerations made a change of policy imperative.' The premiers had to endure a tongue-lashing from Bennett and his labour minister, Wesley Gordon, who denounced the wastefulness of municipal relief administration. The prime minister grumbled that his government could hardly be expected to do more when the provinces refused to hand over the constitutional authority to fight unemployment. Eventually, however, the conference resolved that the federal government should continue to assist the provinces with matching grants covering one-third of the cost of direct relief.

The delegates then turned their attention to the reallocation of fields of taxation. Having seen provincial revenues fall by almost $6 million per year from the high of 1930, Premier Henry suggested that the Dominion should surrender personal income taxes to the provinces. The hard-pressed federal authorities were most unsympathetic. Before the conference the deputy minister of finance had advised that such a move should be considered only in return for a 'substantial quid pro quo,' perhaps the abolition of all succession duties or business taxes by the provinces. Bennett took a tough line with the premiers. No move to reduce federal revenues could even be contemplated while Ottawa was spending $30 million annually on relief and another $70 million on railway deficits. The provincial governments would simply have to muddle through as they had in the past.[46]

When the first ministers turned their attention to unemployment insurance, it soon became clear that neither federal nor provincial officials were very enthusiastic. In the first place an insurance plan would do nothing for those unemployed in the present crisis, while it promised to reopen the unprofitable discussion on a constitutional amending formula. Federal officials were particularly concerned to see that relief and unemployment insurance were entirely separate to make the plan actuarially sound and avoid further drains upon revenue. The Ontario government likewise had little interest in the idea. Insurance Superintendent Leighton Foster pointed out to the cabinet before the conference that this would be the first formal change in the division of powers under the BNA Act. He recommended that 'the Ontario administration adhere to the policy of provincial rights, thus following the example of every Ontario administration since Confederation. "Hands off the BNA Act" will simplify most of the problems on the agenda. Any indication that Ontario might join with the Dominion in a petition to amend the BNA Act would probably result in a sacrifice of provincial rights and, in the result, create more problems than it solved.'[47]

The way in which the prime minister presented the matter to the 1933 dominion-provincial conference confirmed these fears. Bennett opened the discussion by demanding to know whether the provinces were prepared to surrender jurisdiction over unemployment insurance to Ottawa and how much money they would contribute to fund it. He categorically refused to consider a cost-sharing plan like the old age pension, but insisted that the premiers should announce that percentage of the costs they were prepared to meet, although he had no concrete plan to present to them. Only after agreement in principle was reached would the details be worked out. Ontario Attorney-General W.H. Price responded as his officials had advised. Reminding the delegates that unemployment insurance was no solution to their difficulties, he announced that he 'was disinclined on general grounds to amend the BNA Act. He thought it better to struggle with our difficulties than raise the highly controversial question of constitutional amendment. He thought a system of national unemployment insurance could be realized without the amendment of the BNA Act.' The provincial legislatures, he suggested, following an idea devised by his deputy attorney-general, could validate federal legislation where constitutionally necessary. Quebec and the maritime provinces shared Ontario's reservations, but the three western premiers supported Bennett. A committee was set up to try to arrive at a single provincial position but failed, because some premiers would not even say whether or not they supported the *principle* of unemployment insurance. Price, therefore, presented the conference with a resolution stating that Ottawa should study the problem and submit the results to a further meeting.

In an effort to secure some political gains Bennett severely criticized this suggestion, despite the fact that it came from an influential member of a Conservative administration. He complained that the provinces were not 'responsive.' In reality, however, this result probably suited the prime minister quite well. He had no particular enthusiasm for the idea of unemployment insurance. Indeed, he told the delegates, he 'thought all forms of social insurance were largely incompatible with the spirit of freedom.'[48] But he hoped to convince the voters that the provinces were obstructing his efforts to beat unemployment. By demanding a blank cheque from the premiers, asking them to approve in principle and agree to help fund federal unemployment insurance without any consensus on a constitutional amending formula, he ensured that the premiers of Ontario and Quebec would reject his proposal. He had promised in 1931 that there would be a discussion on constitutional amendment, but now he chose to ignore that commitment. This lapse, it should be said, did not particularly dismay Ontario, which had little interest in unemployment insurance and preferred to avoid the contentious issue of amending the constitution. As a result, the dominion-provincial conference of January 1933 achieved nothing significant.

Unfortunately, Canada's economic problems did not improve. By February 1933, 460,000 people in Ontario were dependent on relief and by April the number had passed 500,000. Although things improved with the return of warm weather, the figure hovered around 340,000 throughout the summer. J.A. Ellis had to ask the cabinet to approach Ottawa for an additional $3.5 million per month to be matched by the province to meet the costs. In July a federal-provincial agreement was signed by which each level of government met one-third of the cost of direct relief, the remainder being covered by the hard-pressed municipalities. As winter approached, the number of people on relief relentlessly rose again, reaching 410,000 by December. In an effort to hold down the numbers on direct relief Henry and Bennett announced in the fall of 1933 that some relief works programs would be revived.[49]

The western provinces were especially hard-hit. In December 1933 the four premiers called for a dominion-provincial conference to discuss a complete federal takeover of relief to homeless transients and a constitutional amendment to establish unemployment insurance. They also wanted an additional program of relief works and assistance in refunding the provincial debt at a lower rate of interest. Ottawa was unsympathetic; Bennett and his ministers believed that the provinces had brought many of their ills upon themselves by their prickly refusal to surrender jurisdiction to Ottawa, which had hampered federal efforts to cope with the crisis. Moreover, officials in the capital advised that all the economic indicators had at last turned upwards, and numbers on relief were beginning to decline. Federal aid, which had been only on a temporary, emergency basis, should not be extended further.[50]

The prime minister, therefore, decided to call another dominion-provincial conference on 17 January 1934 – not to concede the demands of the western premiers but to inform provincial leaders that his government had decided to cut off all federal contributions towards the cost of direct relief in the coming spring. A national program of public works would take up some of the slack, but responsibility for direct relief would then fall entirely on the lower levels of government. The federal ministers listened stonily to tales of woe from the western premiers during the three-day meeting. Finally, the prime minister could contain himself no longer; he launched into a diatribe against the provincial leaders for their extravagance and sloppiness. Perhaps the Maritimes and the west ought to be joined into larger units if they could not manage. As for Ontario and Quebec, they 'should not be receiving any assistance from the Dominion in connection with direct relief. They were rich and powerful enough to look after themselves.' Doubtless taken aback by this assault, the premiers obediently agreed to a resolution expressing the hope that direct relief could be discontinued altogether 'at an early date,' and the meeting adjourned.[51]

George Henry of Ontario took little part in these proceedings except to promise that his province would provide a wide-ranging program of relief works. In an election year he could hardly quarrel with the federal Conservatives if he hoped to have their assistance. 'Any work that is under way.' he pleaded with the prime minister in March 1934, 'will absorb some of those who are presently out of employment and generally sweeten the situation.' Bennett did his best to oblige. On 25 April Henry was summoned to Ottawa to meet Labour Minister Wesley Gordon for the announcement that $15 million in highway contracts would be let, providing employment for 20,000 men. However, the party ties between the two governments proved a mixed blessing. Provincial Conservatives frequently found themselves blamed for the failings of federal policies. On 19 June 1934 Mitchell Hepburn's Liberals swept into power with sixty six seats to only seventeen for the Tories.[52]

Liberal victories in Nova Scotia, British Columbia, Ontario, and Saskatchewan during 1933 and 1934 had failed to convince R.B. Bennett that radical new policies were needed to cope with the depression. Indeed, with Grits in power in five of the nine provinces there was less reason than ever for Ottawa to bail them out with financial aid. Despite the protests that poured in, Wesley Gordon informed the premiers in mid-June that federal funds for direct relief would cease on 15 July 1934. Special arrangements might be made for a few hard-pressed urban areas and the prostrate prairie governments but there would be no backing down on the principle. The flood of complaints redoubled, and the cabinet began to waver. The prime minister finally agreed to extend the deadline until the end of the month and summoned the premiers to Ottawa for another meeting on 30 July. His ministers braced themselves for a barrage of pleas, demands, and threats.[53] Wesley Gordon advised the prime minister that there was 'manifest now amongst the provinces an organized effort, which is almost Dominion-wide to cast the burden of relief upon the Federal Government.' The time had come to take drastic action: 'If the provinces continue to maintain the sanctity of their rights under the constitution, then faulty administration in connection with a problem of this character, when their monies are being augmented by contributions from the federal treasury, cannot be too vigorously criticized. The only method left to the Federal Government was to intimate to the provinces that contributions would cease in whole or in part.' In the long run, he believed, the solution was a radical change in the BNA Act to relieve the provinces of both responsibilities and fields of taxation.[54]

Mitchell Hepburn, not six weeks in office, arrived in the capital hoping that the federal government could be persuaded to continue paying one-third of the cost of direct relief. When he and the other premiers were gathered in the Railway

Committee Room, the prime minister immediately leapt to the offensive. Municipal programs of direct relief had become simply a 'racket,' he declared. Civic officials were trying to shift the entire burden of social welfare problems onto Ottawa's shoulders by packing the relief rolls with the aged, the infirm, even children. Wealthy provinces like Ontario and Quebec had attempted to 'scrap the constitution' by evading their responsibilities. In view of this the current system of matching grants would be dropped. Instead, the cabinet had decided to give each province an unconditional grant, the amount fixed by the federal government, to be spent on relief at its own discretion. Every province would have to submit to a 'means test' and the sum would cover only 'proven need,' regardless of the size of the population.[55]

Obviously disconcerted, the premiers attempted to bargain. They were bluntly informed that the matching grants would cease the next day. Take it or leave it. Each was directed to prepare an estimate of monthly relief costs for the coming winter. Then, like erring schoolboys, they were summoned one by one into the prime minister's presence and informed of the amount they could expect to receive. The premiers deeply resented this treatment. Hepburn suggested an adjournment to September to allow the provinces to decide upon the best way to spend relief funds, but the prime minister insisted that the matter had to be settled at once. Provincial officials concluded that Ontario needed at least $1 million per month from Ottawa to see it through the coming winter plus $5,408,575 for relief works. When the premier and his welfare minister were summoned into Bennett's presence, however, they were shocked to be told that the federal government considered $500,000 per month adequate. The provincial ministers stalled, claiming that in the short period since the election they had not had enough time to review existing programs or to formulate new ones. Bennett therefore offered to advance the province $1 million for the next two months while they sized up the situation, any unspent balance to be returned.

Mitchell Hepburn refused to agree to this proposal. He feared a hostile reaction from the public in Toronto, where he was scheduled to meet a group of 'hunger marchers' the following day. He left Ottawa, telling the press, 'We have not settled anything; I am coming back next week for a further conference.' Of the federal government's unilateral decision to introduce block grants without consulting the provinces, he said bitterly, 'In other words, Mr Bennett says here's your alimony, now it's up to you to bring up the children.' When told that the cabinet was sticking to its decision to end all matching grants on 31 July, he expressed surprise; Hepburn had assumed that they would continue until 15 August, so that he would have time to assess the needs of his province.[56] Three weeks later he was back in Ottawa again accompanied by Welfare Minister David Croll and Labour Minister and Attorney-General Arthur Roebuck. The Ontario contingent requested a monthly grant of $1 million, pointing out that total relief costs had averaged $3 million per month during 1934. Bennett countered with an offer of $1 million for August and September, the figure to be renegotiated in the autumn. Reluctantly, Hepburn accepted. Eventually an agreement was signed which granted the province only $600,000 per month until May 1935. Ottawa would give no further aid for relief works, and Hepburn announced that no new projects would be started, since his government now had to meet the full cost of those already authorized by the Henry administration.[57]

Thus for the third time since 1930 the administrative structure of the federal relief program had been altered. Starting with an emphasis on relief works to provide useful jobs for the unemployed, it had been shifted in April 1932 to concentrate upon matching grants for direct relief in an effort to assist more people at the lowest possible cost. Now Ottawa had concluded that sloppy administrative practices at the municipal and provincial levels made matching grants extravagant and had compelled the provinces to accept block grants for use at their own discretion. Nothing, however, had been achieved in the direction of constitutional revision to create a permanent system to cope with this kind of problem. This failure was attributable in part to R.B. Bennett's maladroitness in dealing with the premiers. He preferred to rant at them about their incompetence rather than to negotiate seriously. Moreover, lack of real desire for change in the constitution existed on both sides, but particularly among the provincial leaders. Why should they give up power to Ottawa, asked the premiers, without getting anything in return? Why, asked the federal politicians, should they take over difficult and expensive burdens when their provincial counterparts refused to make any real concessions? A stalemate resulted, leaving Canada in the depths of the depression with a system of unemployment relief little better than that which had been hastily cobbled together in 1920 to meet a temporary emergency. The prime minister professed satisfaction with this arrangement. He believed that at long last he had 'placed relief upon a proper basis. It is the constitutional responsibility of the provinces to deal with relief ... We now propose to have no division of authority but to leave it to the Provinces to carry out their duty, giving them assistance based upon necessity and means.' The provincial premiers, however, were seething with anger, reported the Ottawa correspondent of the Winnipeg *Free Press*; 'the immediate consequence of this new deal has been to stir up the deepest resentment on the part of the provincial governments. To be told that they are solely responsible for a problem that, patently, is beyond their financial capacity to cope with, to be put off like poor relations with cash handouts conceived in a niggardly, ungenerous way, has been exasperating in the extreme.'[58]

V

During his acrimonious discussions with the premiers in the summer of 1934, the prime minister had agreed to Mitchell Hepburn's suggestion that there ought to be another conference to discuss an amending formula for the constitution, the allocation of tax fields, and jurisdiction over social services. Bennett pressed ahead with this plan, despite the advice of his ministers that it seemed to constitute an admission that prosperity could be restored only through radical change, which they viewed as an invitation to disaster at the polls after four years of inaction. Civil servants also expressed doubts: O.D. Skelton warned that any discussion of an amending formula would lead only to a broader discussion of substantive changes. Did the federal government really intend 'to take the view that the consent of all the Provinces is necessary to secure an amendment giving the Dominion, for instance, control over unemployment insurance? That would be a fatal mistake for the Dominion to make and would hamper all future development and freeze our constitution forever.' What was the point, the under-secretary asked, in even considering the allocation of tax fields; the dominion could impose any taxes it wished while the provinces were limited to direct taxation. 'Any change in the situation would, therefore, mean a relative increase in provincial rights, when the duties of the Dominion, as compared with those of the provinces, are rapidly increasing.'[59]

The prime minister ignored all these objections. On 31 August 1934 he wrote to all the premiers suggesting a meeting. Ontario Attorney-General Arthur Roebuck was deeply suspicious about Bennett's intentions in light of his recent experience in dealing with Ottawa. He thought that the federal plan was 'to centralize power in the hands of the central government on the ground of greater convenience because the burden of taxation imposed is sufficiently concealed to be unknown and therefore unresisted.' Where necessary, he believed that interprovincial cooperation could create uniform, national programs. To demand agreement on an amending formula was 'no doubt good tactics, if you wish as I do, to head off a Dominion grab,' but there was little likelihood of agreement, since each province would judge the formula in the light of the changes which it believed desirable. Roebuck suggested that it made more sense to invite the other provincial leaders to come to Toronto and discuss uniform welfare legislation.[60]

Just in case Bennett decided to proceed with his conference, Roebuck set up a small committee of senior civil servants to prepare for it. The members of the 'BNA Committee' were directed to draw up a comprehensive set of briefs on each of the questions likely to be raised by the federal government, briefs which would form the basis of the provincial position.[61] By the time it held its second meeting, however, it had become clear that the federal cabinet had lost interest in pursuing this approach. Facing five by-elections in the fall of 1934, acting Prime Minister Sir George Perley announced in mid-September that the government intended to introduce unemployment insurance legislation at the next session of parliament. In view of this promise and of their recent treatment at the prime minister's hands, none of the premiers expressed any enthusiasm for another conference. Mitchell Hepburn waited for two months before even replying to the invitation. Although he expressed readiness to attend such a meeting, his tone was hostile and aggressive. What sort of redivision of tax fields was Ottawa contemplating, he asked?

Was it now ready to abandon the personal income tax altogether? Bennett must have recognized that he could expect no co-operation from the Liberal premiers who now scented victory for their party in the coming federal general election. Within forty-eight hours of receiving Hepburn's letter he informed the provincial leaders that the conference would have to be postponed.[62]

The prime minister seems to have come to the conclusion that if the provinces would not concede him the power to save the country, he must simply seize it. Few Canadians would stand upon constitutional niceties in a time of crisis, and the next election would be safely won before the courts would render an adverse verdict upon any federal interference in acknowledged areas of provincial jurisdiction. This new strategy was worked out during November and December 1934, and on 2 January 1935 the prime minister revealed his 'New Deal' to the nation in a radio address. The federal government, listeners were told, would now bring in unemployment and social insurance as well as regulations governing minimum wages and hours of labour. Asked privately how he proposed to get around constitutional limitations upon federal action in these areas, he frankly replied that 'there was no use trying to deal with the Liberal provincial governments at this time. But with a mandate he would have no hesitation to make the necessary constitutional changes.'[63]

As a pretext for action the government hastily submitted to parliament for ratification the International Labour Organization conventions covering the eight-hour day, the forty-eight hour week, a weekly day of rest, and minimum wages. Approval of the conventions might provide parliament with authority to legislate upon these subjects under the treaty-making powers contained in section 132 of the BNA Act. Bennett was convinced that recent Privy Council decisions in the *Aeronautics* and *Radio* cases, giving Ottawa jurisdiction in both areas, indicated a willingness to construe federal authority under this section more broadly. For this reason the Minimum Wage Act, the Forty-Eight Hour Week Act, and the One-Day's-Rest-in-Seven Act contained references to the relevant ILO conventions.

The other major piece of social welfare legislation was the Employment and Social Insurance Act. It was also originally intended to refer to one of the conventions, but the prime minister discovered that the International Labour Organization had linked insurance and unemployment relief together. Fearful that J.S. Woodsworth of the CCF would seize upon this connection to demand that Ottawa take full responsibility for relief, Bennett dropped the reference to the convention. In the end the preamble to this act simply referred to Canada's commitment under the Treaty of Versailles to seek and maintain fair and humane conditions of labour. Jurisdiction really depended upon an extended interpretation of the federal power over 'peace, order and good government' which Bennett now believed the Privy Council might be ready to accept.[64]

In drafting this legislation the provinces were totally ignored. Although both the Trades and Labour Congress and the Canadian Manufacturers' Association were shown the unemployment insurance bill, the deputy minister of justice dismissed the idea of consulting the provinces with the sophistical argument that any one who suggested that the bill constituted

> an invasion of provincial rights is labouring under a very evident misapprehension of the situation. The Bill is either within the competence of Parliament or not. If it is within the competence it cannot be an invasion of provincial rights or autonomy, because its validity would be based upon a judicial finding that it is enacted in the exercise of Dominion powers. If, on the other hand, it be held that the Bill is not within the competence of Parliament, it cannot affect provincial rights or autonomy, because it would be null and void.

Such a line of reasoning certainly sounded strange coming from a government which just five months earlier had proposed a conference to discuss whether the provinces were 'prepared to surrender their exclusive jurisdiction over legislation dealing with such social problems as old age pensions, unemployment and social insurance, hours and conditions for work, minimum wages, etc., to the Dominion Parliament.'[65]

Surprisingly, the Hepburn government showed little interest in the New Deal legislation. The cabinet did not discuss it and Attorney-General Roebuck was left to make whatever response he saw fit; he apparently concluded that the most effective way of challenging it was through the courts. The Conservatives in the provincial legislature did try to embarrass the government by moving a resolution calling upon the assembly to approve the principle of unemployment and social insurance as proposed by Bennett, and to declare itself ready to 'supplement, compliment [sic] or augment' such federal legislation so that a national plan could be set up without any resort to litigation. The premier simply moved a meaningless amendment, expressing the legislature's confidence that the Ontario government would co-operate with Ottawa to establish a system of unemployment insurance. This was carried on a straight party vote.[66]

Mackenzie King treated the New Deal bills in the same gingerly fashion. He was convinced that they were unconstitutional, but he did not want to oppose them openly, thus allowing Bennett to claim that he lacked sympathy for the working man. He did complain that the prime minister had 'abandoned the tried path of conference and cooperation with the provinces and set his feet upon the uncertain and perilous path of autocratic assumption by the Dominion Parliament of an authority, which he and leading members of the cabinet had declared was unconstitutional and dangerous to the unity of the Dominion.' But he kept his supporters on a tight rein and made sure that the Employment and Social Insurance Act passed second reading by a vote of 101 to 0. The opposition leader promised, however, that if he won the election he would immediately submit all the New Deal legislation to the Supreme Court for an opinion on its constitutionality.[67]

True to his word, the court heard the reference in January 1936, just three months after his victory in the election. In June of that year it rendered a decision declaring the Employment and Social Insurance Act ultra vires of the dominion.

Grouped in a separate reference were the acts concerning wages and hours of work. On these the court divided evenly, leaving the issue in doubt. Appeals to the Privy Council were promptly undertaken in both cases. Ontario chose to be represented before the Judicial Committee. Attorney-General Roebuck attacked the idea that the federal government could acquire jurisdiction over matters under provincial control by the mere act of signing a treaty. If treaties were to be signed on such matters, he suggested, taking an extreme provincial rights position, the provinces must sign them. Although the Privy Council ignored this sweeping claim, they nevertheless declared all the New Deal legislation on social welfare unconstitutional. Regarding the right of the federal government to sign treaties, Lord Atkin noted: 'While the ship of state now sails on larger ventures and into foreign waters she still retains the watertight compartments which are an essential part of her original construction.' Unemployment insurance was invalidated on the grounds that it interfered with the civil rights of employers and employees in the provinces.[68]

Thus by the mid-1930s, despite a severe economic crisis, the constitution of Canada remained unaltered. Mass unemployment was being dealt with only through a series of ad hoc arrangements first devised in the aftermath of the First World War. The burdens had rendered the prairie provinces bankrupt in all but name, and some Canadians had concluded that the only solution was to give Ottawa the power to create uniform, national programs and fund them adequately. The government of Manitoba, for instance, consistently supported the idea of broader federal powers. But other premiers, in particular Henry and Hepburn of Ontario, were less convinced. Their province could have raised sufficient revenues for its needs, but only at the cost of considerable unpopularity, as long as the federal authorities occupied the most lucrative revenue fields like income, corporation, and general sales taxes. Politically cautious and fundamentally conservative, neither the Tory Henry nor the Grit Hepburn was willing to embark on this sort of bold adventure. Hence the government of Ontario simply used its position to block all meaningful constitutional change while continuing to demand greater financial assistance from Ottawa.

R.B. Bennett showed himself little more disposed to work for constitutional change through negotiation and accommodation. Instead, he preferred to take up non-negotiable positions which the premiers could accept or reject, despite the commitment first given by Ernest Lapointe in 1927 and reiterated by Bennett in 1931 that the provinces would thereafter be entitled to consultation regarding constitutional amendments. At last, in a desperate political gamble, Bennett, who had succeeded in alienating most of the provincial leaders by his tactics, decided to take unilateral action, ignoring the constitutional division of powers. Neither the electors nor the courts were impressed by this death-bed conversion, and with Canada still mired in depression, matters in 1935 remained very much where they had stood when the First World War came to an end.

8 Water-power and the Constitution

Control of the development of water-power on the rivers forming Ontario's southern and eastern boundaries was the key economic issue in dispute between the province and the Dominion during the 1920s. By comparison, all other questions paled into insignificance. Memories of the wartime wrangle over electricity exports remained fresh. Efforts by private developers to seize the vast potential of the St Lawrence and the Ottawa rivers revived pre-war fears that Ontario Hydro might be undermined by rivals. Two wily and successful political leaders, Premier Howard Ferguson and Prime Minister Mackenzie King, did their best to secure an advantage over one another. By 1930 they had fought to a draw.

No one in Ontario underestimated the significance of cheap and abundant hydroelectricity to the future economic development of the province. During the boom of the 1920s demand for power increased steadily at the rate of 10 per cent annually, and by 1929, 69 per cent of all Canadian industry already depended upon electricity. As one astute contemporary observer pointed out: 'the development of industry is more and more resolving itself into a question of power, improved transportation facilities having made the assembling of raw materials for manufacturing progressively easier. Under modern conditions the general tendency of manufacturing is to seek the power and assemble its raw materials where the latter is most abundant.'[1] Viewed thus, Ontario's industrial future looked bright.

But there were problems. Before the vast power of the Ottawa and St Lawrence could be harnessed, agreement had to be reached on the respective roles of the province and the dominion in the development of navigable rivers. Would Ottawa simply approve the plans for powerplant construction to ensure that shipping would not be interfered with? If so, how would the costs of dams and canals be shared between the two levels? Or was the federal government entitled to take all the power developed from navigational improvements and sell it at its own discretion? Would the province have to pay rentals to use the water obtained from such rivers for power purposes?

The fact that the Ottawa was an interprovincial boundary and the St Lawrence an international one complicated matters further. On the one hand, it seemed to reinforce the federal government's claim to play the leading role in power development regardless of provincial preferences. At the very least it meant that development of the Ottawa could not proceed until Ontario and Quebec had come to terms, and the St Lawrence must wait upon an international agreement involving Canada and the United States and possibly the two provinces as well. The problem facing Ontario was to make certain that its interests were not sacrificed by the federal government in pursuit of its own objectives; for instance, by some arrangement permitting the exportation of large amounts of electricity to American customers to finance canal-building.

These complications arose because the constitution failed to provide any clear guide to the division of jurisdiction. The BNA Act granted Ottawa authority over navigation and shipping. Should the courts decide that power was 'incidental' to navigation, the province might be squeezed out altogether. Moreover, parliament had unfettered power to declare any works or undertakings for the general advantage of Canada and so secure exclusive jurisdiction over them. Yet the province claimed ownership of the bed of every navigable river to the middle of the water-course. Along with this ownership appeared to go the possession of the power developed from the flowing water. Not only had the province authorized such developments in the past, but Ontario Hydro faced a steadily growing demand for power during the 1920s which kept attention focused on the issue.

In the early years of the decade the dispute between the province and the federal government centred upon the control of the Lake of the Woods, which was managed by a joint federal-provincial board. Efforts by Ottawa to exert more authority aroused Ontario's fears of exclusion from jurisdiction over such international waters entirely. And there was also concern that the development of the lower St Lawrence River might be handed over to the American interests intending to produce for export heedless of the needs of Ontario industry. In fact, work on the international section of the St Lawrence stalled over the need to reach an agreement with the United States, which the federal authorities showed no disposition to press for prior to 1931. Eventually Hydro was able to stave off power shortages only by negotiating contracts to purchase surplus energy from power producers in the province of Quebec.

During the 1920s covetous glances were also being cast by private interests at the potential of the Ottawa River. Because the river was navigable and formed an interprovincial boundary, promoters like W.L. McDougald and the Siftons tried to outflank Ontario's opposition to their plans by applying directly to the federal government. Although the province was successful in blocking these proposals, no development could take place without some agreement on the constitutional issues. Eventually it was agreed to refer the question of jurisdiction to the Supreme Court through a reference case, but no clear answers were obtained from the judges. Not until 1930 did direct negotiations even take place between Prime Minister Mackenzie King and the premiers of Ontario and Quebec, but these efforts also proved fruitless. The election of Conservative R.B. Bennett in the summer of 1930 altered the attitude of the federal government to the provinces' case, and by 1932 an agreement had finally been reached on cost-sharing for a St Lawrence power and navigation project. At long last it appeared that Ontario would finally see its major untapped source of hydroelectricity developed.

I

Shortly after the First World War ended, Sir Adam Beck began a campaign to obtain the right to develop hydroelectricity on the St Lawrence River. In December 1919 he helped to form the Eastern Ontario Municipal Power Union, which obediently voted 'its unqualified support to the Province of Ontario in its claim for all water power in the Province of Ontario, including the St. Lawrence River and decline[d] to recognise the right of the Federal Authorities outside the requirements of navigation.' A blizzard of similar petitions and letters descended upon the newly elected government of Premier E.C. Drury. At a banquet in Toronto in the spring of 1920 Beck told the audience: 'That river shall not, if there be a revolution to prevent it, fall into the hands of the Dominion Government.'[2]

Bold words; but the Hydro chairman could not ignore the fact that under the Boundary Waters Treaty of 1909 any scheme which would affect navigation on an international river had to be referred to the International Joint Commission. Near the end of 1919 the Borden government referred a series of questions concerning the cost and technical feasibility of such a power and navigation development to the commission. More than two years would elapse before their report was received. Even the constitutional basis of Beck's claims appeared doubtful. In 1921 Ontario's deputy attorney-general advised his minister that 'The respecting [sic] rights of the Dominion and the provinces to waters for purposes of power on navigable streams has [sic] not yet been determined ... No one can possibly give an authoritative opinion on that subject because there is no very helpful decision on the matter. No matter who gives it the opinion would be more or less of a guess.'[3] Thus all of the Hydro chairman's plans were stymied for the time being.

Meanwhile, a conflict between the federal and provincial governments arose over similar issues on the Lake of the Woods in the far north-western corner of the province, a conflict which seemed to have important implications for future development on the Ottawa and the St Lawrence rivers. The water level in the lake was regulated by the Norman Dam in Kenora, Ontario, where the Winnipeg River flowed out of the lake. Repeated complaints from Minnesota residents about flooding due to high water led in 1919 to the decision to take the Norman Dam, which was owned by E.W. Backus, out of private hands. Concurrent provincial and federal orders-in-council created the Lake of the Woods Control Board to manage the dam. Each government appointed two engineers to the board, and the federally appointed chairman had a casting vote.[4]

Below the dam on the Winnipeg-English River systems were several large potential power sites, some of them beyond the provincial boundary in Manitoba and so owned by the federal government. The expectation that these powers would soon be developed apparently convinced the Meighen government in 1920 that the Lake of the Woods Control Board needed more authority. Accordingly, the prime minister approached Premier Drury, who agreed to promote concurrent legislation to widen the board's power. But when the bills were made public in the spring of 1921, the other provincial party leaders attacked the arrangement as a sell-out of provincial rights. '*The question is simply this* –' Liberal Hartley Dewart claimed, '*is the Dominion government under the guise of its superior power with reference to navigation to take control of the rights of the Province of Ontario with reference to its own waterways and to deal with them as it pleases*?' Faced with the defeat of his minority government at the hands of a united Liberal and Conservative opposition, the premier withdrew his bill.[5] But Meighen then pressed ahead with the passage of a new Lake of the Woods Regulation Act which declared all dams on the Lake of the Woods and Winnipeg-English River system to be works for the general advantage of Canada and entrusted their management to a federally appointed control board.

The angry premier protested: 'Any effort to take control of the waters and water power of this province further than is necessary for the purposes of navigation will be strongly resisted by our people, and will be considered by them to be an unwarranted invasion of the provincial domain by the federal authorities.' Former Unionist cabinet minister Newton Rowell advised the provincial cabinet that this act constituted a dangerous precedent, which might permit the Dominion to seize control of all the works erected by the HEPC on crown lands: 'If the Federal Parliament has this right, it certainly would have the right to declare the Chippawa[-Queenston plant] and other power developments for the general advantage of Canada and thus remove them from provincial jurisdiction and control.' Rowell recommended fighting the issue in the courts, all the way to the Privy Council if necessary.[6] When Mackenzie King became prime minister, however, Drury persuaded him to repeal the Lake of the Woods Regulation Act in 1922 and replace it with concurrent legislation. But Meighen drummed up enough support in the Conservative-dominated Senate to block the change.

Drury continued to complain about the 1921 legislation, arguing: 'If the Lake of the Woods Regulation Act is intra vires of the Dominion, Ontario loses not only the control of the Winnipeg and English Rivers, but also potentially loses control of every river flowing into the Great Lakes ... These waters are of tremendous importance to the Province of Ontario, and in their development we have already invested in provincially owned Hydro-Electric plants over $106,600,000 and assumed liabilities of $55,000,000, making a total of $161,000,000.'[7] More important, he refused to consent to any treaty with the United States regarding the Lake of the Woods which the International Joint Commission was proposing, unless this 'vicious' legislation was first repealed. But in 1923 another repeal effort was turned back by Conservative senators. Not until 1928, with a solid Liberal majority in the upper house, was the offending act removed, and the Lake of the Woods Control Board reconstituted under concurrent legislation.

During the dispute over the Lake of the Woods, the International Joint Commission was also proceeding with its investigation of a St Lawrence development. Sir Adam Beck appeared before the Commission to support a two-stage development of the international section of the river with dams both above and below the Long Sault Rapids. This would permit the immediate development of a smaller amount of power at lower cost than the alternative, a single dam near Morrisburg. In January 1922 the commission reported that a treaty between the two countries should be negotiated but recommended the single-stage development which would cost $252 million and generate 1.5 million horsepower of electricity. Beck, of course, was not at all enthusiastic about any development totally controlled by Ottawa, and his fears were heightened in May 1922 when Mackenzie King announced that the federal government would not proceed with the plan at present owing to the shortage of funds. But there was little that the Hydro chairman could do.[8]

In February 1923, however, it was learned that the American Super Power Company of Buffalo, New York, had applied to the United States Federal Power Commission for permission to dam the entire St Lawrence River. Two-thirds of their production, something over 1 million horsepower, would be marketed in United States. Premier Drury immediately demanded to know if the prime minister had been negotiating secretly with these interests, reputedly backed by the Vanderbilts and the Duponts. Mackenzie King hastily denied any role in the affair and promised full consultation with the province.[9]

Elected premier in the summer of 1923, Conservative Howard Ferguson promised a banquet audience soon afterwards that he would start negotiations with Ottawa on developing the St Lawrence at once. Sir Adam Beck was taken into the cabinet once more as minister without portfolio to do what he could to avert a serious power shortage expected within a couple of years. Early in 1924 the Hydro formally applied to the federal government for permission to erect the Morrisburg dam to develop 350,000 horsepower. What Ferguson wanted was to 'secure recognition, which I think is the undoubted right of the province, to make use as it may deem advisable of the waters of the St. Lawrence ... so long as the Province does not interfere with the paramount use for navigation purposes.' The premier believed that a St Lawrence waterway treaty between Canada and the United States covering power and navigation was not an essential precondition to the Hydro's plan:

I do not want to get the Province in a position that our power development would be blocked or delayed because the two Governments cannot agree to pursue the deep waterway scheme at the present time. The deepening of the canals is not essential to the power development. It is an entirely separate matter, and I am satisfied that ... if the two things are to be coupled together, Ontario must suffer from a lack of power or pay tremendous costs for steam generation while we are waiting for the International Governments to make up their minds on the navigation scheme.[10]

Mackenzie King certainly showed no enthusiasm for the waterway scheme: not only would it be enormously expensive but it was strongly opposed by powerful Liberals from Quebec. In the spring of 1924 he appointed a National Advisory Committee to assess the plans once more in the confident expectation that their report would take at least two years to prepare. As a result Howard Ferguson gradually became convinced that no power development on the St Lawrence was going to be approved in the near future. In the spring of 1925 he therefore proposed that the province divert 3,000 second-feet of water from the Albany River system into Lake Superior. If all of this water could be used by Ontario Hydro to generate current at Niagara, the threatened power shortage might be averted. But Interior Minister Charles Stewart pointed out that the Albany was also navigable; permission for the diversion must come from Ottawa and Stewart showed no disposition to approve it.[11] In the summer of 1925 the HEPC began to investigate the possibility of constructing large thermal generating stations but discovered that steam power would cost substantially more than hydroelectricity. In November C.A. Magrath, who had become Hydro chairman on Beck's death, proposed that the United States be asked to approve an additional diversion of 20,000 second-feet at Niagara to be shared equally between the two countries. Some federal ministers approved of this idea, but it quickly became entangled in the diplomatic relations between Canada and the United States, and nothing was done.[12]

Having failed to secure further supplies of power from the St Lawrence or at Niagara, Ferguson and Magrath cast about for some other means of avoiding an expensive program of constructing thermal generating plants. Providentially, the premier discovered in 1925 that his Liberal counterpart in Quebec, L.A. Taschereau, was interested in meeting him to discuss the power situation. Taschereau was well aware that private power producers in his own province would soon have surplus current available, and while he strongly opposed power exports to the United States, he had, he told Ferguson, no objection to long-term contracts between Quebec generating companies and customers in Ontario. Before long Ontario Hydro had signed an agreement to purchase 320,000 horsepower from the Gatineau Power Company over the next few years. This proved to be the first of a series of contracts signed between 1926 and 1931 by Ontario Hydro with four Quebec power producers for supplies of large quantities of energy. Only thus did the province of Ontario ensure itself of a growing supply of cheap power and avert a shortage without developing either the St Lawrence or the Ottawa systems.[13]

166 The Politics of Federalism

II

Private entrepreneurs had not ignored the huge potential of the Ottawa River. In 1921 the Meighen administration granted the National Hydro-Electric Company a water-power lease on the canal at Carillon Falls, which included the right to build a dam 120 feet high, and in 1923 the Quebec–New England Company took an interest in this undertaking with the intention of exporting most of the power developed there. Howard Ferguson promptly complained to Mackenzie King that 'Ontario does not concede that the Dominion Lease on which the present lease is founded conveys to the Lessees any right to use the surplus waters of the Ottawa River. So far as the water power is situated within the boundaries of this province we claim the right to apply such conditions and rentals as may be deemed to be in the interests of the people of Ontario.'[14] Quebec–New England did not pursue the project, but in the fall of 1924 Wilfrid Laurier McDougald, a prominent Liberal, purchased an option on National Hydro-Electric and began lobbying intensively to have the federal department of railways and canals approve a vast development at Carillon. He planned to export as much as 400,000 horsepower annually over forty years, retaining a mere 100,000 horsepower for sale in Canada. Railways Minister George Graham was uneasy: 'Candidly, I am afraid of the Carillon proposition,' he wrote to the prime minister. 'The export of power, while there are arguments in favour under any conditions, would be a powerful weapon against the government, particularly in Ontario.' McDougald, who was among King's closest confidants, did not hesitate to trade upon his influence, badgering the federal bureaucrats ceaselessly for acceptance of his proposal.[15]

Sir Adam Beck and Howard Ferguson were predictably outraged. The Hydro chairman took up his pen and prepared a pamphlet attacking McDougald's plans in typically forthright terms: 'The Provinces have their own special rights. Ontario and Quebec have their own water powers. It is inconceivable that the Dominion authorities – no matter what may be the stimulus or pretext – will be ready to take any such federal action as is proposed at Carillon, because to do so would be an aggressive usurpation of provincial rights.' The Ontario premier explained why he regarded a supply of cheap electrical energy as critical in 'the struggle for industrial supremacy': '[W]e have the advantage of our friends to the south in that respect, [and] our proper course is to require them to spend their capital on this side of the line. Unless we are able to make the best use of our natural resources we might as well make up our minds to be hewers of wood to our neighbours.' Ferguson also enlisted the aid of the premier of Quebec. Early in 1925 he held several meetings with Taschereau at which they condemned electricity exports to the United States and the presumption of the federal government in claiming jurisdiction over power developments through its control of navigation.[16]

Nonetheless, Ferguson remained concerned that Mackenzie King might yield to his importunate friend: 'I am most apprehensive that, nothwithstanding the protest made by Mr. Taschereau and myself, the Ottawa Government will grant the lease in question and with an export permit. This subject is of sufficient importance that it will be a real issue, in the Province of Ontario at any rate, when a Dominion Election comes along.' The premier's worst fears were realized in May 1925 when the government tabled in the House of Commons the proposed new lease of Carillon Falls. For an annual rental of $150,000 over 120 years National Hydro-Electric would be permitted to construct a dam to generate 400,000 horsepower of electricity, three-quarters of which could be exported to the United States. Not only that, but the federal authorities agreed to assist the company by expropriating 18,300 acres of land on the banks of the Ottawa River.[17]

Ferguson's strong protest against this lease contended that the federal government owned only the water actually required for navigation, and that no power development could be authorized without the consent of the province, which could impose its own terms and conditions. After discussion in cabinet the matter was turned over to the justice department for an opinion. Ernest Lapointe rejected the premier's claim that development at Carillon was subject to the province's consent: 'my understanding is that any power which may be developed at Carillon will result from the erection of works for the improvement of navigation ... I suggest that Mr. Ferguson be informed that as far as the improvement of navigation and the incidental development and disposal of power is concerned ... that this Government is unable to recognize any right on the part of the Province to control the Dominion in the exercise of its constitutional powers.'[18] This argument formed the basis of the federal claim to control all power development on navigable rivers during the 1920s: power was simply 'incidental' to navigation, and the BNA Act clearly gave the federal government control of 'Canals, with lands and water power connected therewith.' Unfortunately for Ferguson the interpretation of the constitution on this point remained in doubt, and since his legal advisers could not predict with any certainty the outcome of an appeal to the courts, there was little recourse in that direction.

Before the government had given final approval to McDougald's plans, however, a formidable rival for control of the Carillon development entered the field in the shape of the Shawinigan Power Company, part of Sir Herbert Holt's Montreal-based utilities empire. By June 1926 Shawinigan had not only secured control of the National Hydro-Electric Company but had opened negotiations with Ontario Hydro for the sale of a large block of power. While reluctant to deal with a private developer, Ferguson had to face the fact that Ottawa might well authorize the project despite all the province's objections. Moreover, Hydro's engineers were predicting a serious power shortage by 1928. The offer from Shawinigan was made more attractive by the inclusion of a clause permitting the Hydro to purchase one-half of the development outright after forty years. In the end, however, the price demanded by Shawinigan for Carillon power proved more than Ontario was prepared to pay, and instead the Hydro contracted with the Gatineau Power Company for 320,000 horsepower.[19]

During the summer of 1926 the King government was ousted, so that it fell to the Meighen administration to deal with Shawinigan's demands for a Carillon lease which included the right to develop large amounts of power. Hydro chairman C.A. Magrath warned the minister responsible, Sir Henry Drayton, that there would be a serious fight between the two governments if the lease was granted without Ontario's consent. The new ministry proved more susceptible to pressure from their fellow Conservatives at Queen's Park. Drayton extended National Hydro-Electric's lease temporarily but promised to approve no plans for dam construction without the agreement of Ontario Hydro, and he formally offered the province 'the ownership of one-half share and interest in the Carillon development including one-half of the stream flow.' The annual rental would be divided into three equal shares for the two provinces and Ottawa. But this arrangement was soon placed in jeopardy by Mackenzie King's victory in the fall election. He first threatened to cancel Shawinigan's lease altogether, but eventually postponed a decision on the Carillon development by extending the existing lease until 1 May 1927.[20]

By then there had emerged an additional threat to provincial control over development of the Ottawa. Near the end of 1925 Sir Clifford Sifton and his sons, Harry and Winfield, had acquired a controlling interest in a long-dormant concern called the Montreal, Ottawa and Georgian Bay Canal Company. Chartered by parliament in 1894, this company possessed the right not only to build canals on the Ottawa but to develop and sell all the water-power created by its works. What a financial coup it would be to secure control of the entire 1 million horsepower potential of the river in this way. The Siftons sounded out the great American utilities entrepreneur Samuel Insull about purchasing their power. They also approached Ontario Hydro, offering to sell 400,000 horsepower, but were rebuffed by C.A. Magrath who argued 'my understanding was that the Provincial Governments resisted the claim of the Georgian Bay Canal Company to the ownership of those power sites.' Yet the Siftons' lawyers believed that the company required only federal approval of its plans to proceed. In the spring of 1926 Harry Sifton laid siege to Mackenzie King's ministers in an effort to obtain it.[21]

Howard Ferguson feared that once the Siftons had such approval they could 'figuratively snap their fingers at us.' When King was returned to office in the fall of 1926, the premier sought the assistance of L.A. Taschereau: 'To allow a great resource like the waters of the Ottawa River to be controlled by a Corporation seeking to canalise the river as power is required, and in all probability at the expense of power users in both provinces, is something, I am sure, that should not be considered for a moment.'[22] Since the Georgian Bay Canal Company's charter would come up for renewal on 1 May 1927, the same date that National Hydro-Electric's Carillon lease would expire, Ferguson believed that the province must do its utmost to block both schemes and gain control over the development of the Ottawa.

With this goal in mind he had a lengthy brief prepared entitled 'Federal and Provincial Rights in Waterways, Georgian Bay Canal Charter and Dominion Lease of Carillon Rapids to National Hydro-Electric Company,' which set forth the provincial case in full.[23] This memorandum argued that authority over canals and navigation had been used by Ottawa 'to expand the jurisdiction of federal authority to the most extreme conceivable.' The result had been 'considerable invasions' of provincial rights and a repudiation of the compact of Confederation. Over the next twenty years Ontario and Quebec could be expected to develop another 8 million horsepower of hydroelectricity, and to permit Ottawa to gain control of that vast resource would be to condone 'a concealed assault upon the federal system. In effect, if admitted, it would mean that federal action could completely oust the provinces from all benefits whenever a stream was or could be made navigable.' The result would be to 'slowly convert Canada from a federal union into a legislative union under the supreme control of the Parliament at Ottawa.'

The Ontario brief strongly criticized the Georgian Bay canal scheme as a highly speculative venture designed solely for private profit. Exorbitant power rates would be needed to finance the canal works, while Ontario would suffer from being deprived of 500,000 horsepower of cheap electricity from the Ottawa: 'The federal parliament should not stand in the way of the development of power so much needed by provincial industries which otherwise are largely dependent on foreign fuel. It should give no appearance of assuming to exercise the functions of the Ontario legislature or of standing in the way of Ontario's exercise of them.' It was quite possible to make the distinction between power and navigation. Direct federal-provincial negotiations were required as 'a clean cut line must be drawn between the two uses of water so as to recognize unequivocally that water power belongs to the sphere of the provinces, and can be developed independently of navigation, though of course with due regard for the interest of navigation.'

Publicly, Ferguson attacked the Siftons for 'trying to pick off some plum to which they are not entitled.' In March 1927 he moved a resolution in the legislature condemning the renewal of the Georgian Bay Canal charter as an 'attempt ... to alienate valuable water powers from the control and ownership of this province, and thereby deprive the people of Ontario of the advantage of one of our greatest natural resources for the benefit and advantage of private promoters.' This motion passed unanimously. The federal Conservative party also joined in the opposition to the renewal of the charter.[24]

Mackenzie King became increasingly uneasy in the face of this barrage of criticism. He still firmly believed, like Ernest Lapointe, that the federal government alone had the right to authorize power projects on navigable rivers, and he could see the importance of any precedent when the St Lawrence came to be developed. Should the Dominion control all of these energy supplies it would be in a position to impose a national electricity policy. But by resisting the claims of Ontario, now endorsed by Quebec, he risked driving the two most powerful premiers into an alliance against him. A provincial rights' campaign based on the refusal to permit the provinces to develop badly needed energy supplies would surely damage Liberal party fortunes, especially in Quebec. As a result, King decided that the game was not worth the candle.[25]

When the Georgian Bay Canal Company's charter renewal bill reached the Commons in March 1927, it was referred to the railway committee. The pros and cons of the matter were fully aired in deference to the Siftons' influence within the Liberal party and the business community. Harry and Winfield Sifton appeared for the company, W.N. Tilley and Aimé Geoffrion for Ontario and Quebec. On orders from the cabinet the committee then voted not to report the bill and the charter lapsed. At the same time the National Hydro-Electric Company got its lease renewed, but was permitted to develop only 250 horsepower of electricity to work the existing canal at Carillon.[26]

The provinces thus succeeded in blocking these two efforts to obtain control of large power developments on the Ottawa River. Had the Quebec government not thrown its support behind Howard Ferguson, it seems much less certain that this would have been the outcome. Premier Taschereau shared with the Ontario leader a hostility to federal control over major water-power projects on the Ottawa River as well as to massive power exports to the United States. Their joint opposition proved sufficient to convince Mackenzie King that the political cost of approving either the Carillon scheme or the Georgian Bay Canal charter would be too high.

III

Simply blocking undesirable projects did nothing to solve Ontario's long-term energy supply problems. Although the contracts between the private Quebec producers and the Hydro provided temporary breathing space, the steady growth of power demand seemed to require the development of both the Ottawa and the St Lawrence rivers within the next decade. But every move in this direction ran into stubborn resistance on the part of the federal government.

Once the Sifton and Holt interests had been denied the right to develop the Ottawa, Howard Ferguson suggested an immediate effort to settle the matter of jurisdiction by intergovernmental negotiation. But Mackenzie King would have none of it; he insisted that 'the Dominion Government holds, if not all, practically all, the rights at the Carillon rapids controlling water power development.' He was prepared to go no further than the suggestion that Ottawa might undertake to develop the power itself and sell it to the province. During the summer of 1927 the railways and canals department became embroiled in another dispute over the control of the St Mary's River at the Sault. The departmental position was that the 'ownership of the water power lies in the Federal Crown ... and that the province has no right to develop power here except under lease from the Federal Crown.'[27]

Ferguson complained bitterly to Taschereau of the 'aggressive anti-provincial course that the federal government is pursuing,' and urged Quebec to join in 'resistance to Ottawa's invasion of provincial rights.' But what was the best means? Should the federal government refuse to negotiate, the province's only recourse was to the courts. Eminent legal counsel retained by Ontario advised that all water powers belonged to the province, subject only to the federal right to prevent interference with navigation.[28] 'Ontario and Quebec stand together upon this opinion,' declared Ferguson in releasing it to the press, 'and we are prepared, if necessary, to carry the matter to the highest court in the empire.' But in fact, the attorney-general's department thought it 'unwise to risk placing the matter in litigation.' If the federal government lost in the courts, it might simply declare all water-power works for the general advantage of Canada, thus destroying provincial jurisdiction altogether.[29]

For his part, Mackenzie King remained convinced that the dominion had a strong case in law and he saw no need to enter into negotiations. But he could not prevent Ferguson and Taschereau from raising the issue at the dominion-provincial conference in November 1927. By this time the Ontario premier had evidently concluded that it was wisest to risk a contest in the courts, and he suggested to the conference that the matter should immediately be submitted to the Supreme Court as a reference case. Although the prime minister temporized, he eventually agreed to this proposal, although with a good deal of reluctance. In January 1928 the cabinet announced a series of seven questions which the court would be asked to answer.[30]

Ferguson was angered that the province had not been consulted about the form of the questions. W.N. Tilley, Ontario's counsel, thought them 'so vague and general' that the courts would be unable to answer them satisfactorily. Taschereau was equally discontented, and as a result King was forced to agree to consultation. After much wrangling, the province's legal adviser remained unhappy but concluded that little could be done to improve matters in the face of federal resistance. The hearing before the Supreme Court was scheduled for October 1928.[31]

The federal government was represented by Newton Rowell. He argued that jurisdiction over navigation and international relations entitled the federal government to control waterpower development on boundary waters. W.N. Tilley for Ontario put forward the familiar arguments for provincial control developed over the past few years. But as Tilley had predicted, the judges found the questions too general and too abstract to be answered precisely. The decision handed down in February 1929 noted at one point, for instance, that, 'In the absence of information as to such facts, it is impracticable to give an intelligible answer to the questions propounded.' Mackenzie King admitted that he 'could not make head or tail' of the decision. Only an explanatory statement by Mr Justice Lyman Duff seemed to dispel the murk somewhat. Duff noted that the courts had always held that the dominion could not exercise its powers in such a way as to obliterate the provincial sphere of authority. Thus Ottawa might authorize construction of a canal, but this did 'not involve the right to appropriate the whole beneficial interest of the site of the work ... The Dominion could not constitutionally assume the administration or control of water powers so acquired for purposes not connected with the canal.'[32] King confessed that he found this opinion chastening: 'Out of it I seem to glean that the Dominion has no right to go into the navigation business for power purposes as such. Power belongs primarily to the provinces and such power as the federal government gets out of navigation works must be used in connection with the works.' But he was by no means prepared to give in to Ferguson's demands entirely. '[W]e might be willing to give the provinces power,' he told the United States Minister, 'if they did the developing – if they would help us with the St. Lawrence we would help them with the power. If not, we would not.' Since the courts had failed to settle the dispute, further negotiation would obviously be necessary.[33]

Aware of the prime minister's unwillingness to make concessions, the government of Ontario was already exploring other means to secure increased electricity supplies which did not necessitate an intergovernmental agreement. Late in 1928, at the suggestion of Hydro officials, discussions were begun again with the Americans about increasing the amount of water diverted at Niagara under the Boundary Waters Treaty of 1909.[34] To the HEPC this seemed likely to be the quickest means of acquiring additional supplies of cheap power without becoming embroiled in the complications which beset the development of the Ottawa and the St Lawrence rivers.[35] The negotiations proceeded smoothly and in January 1929 a convention was signed between the two countries authorizing the diversion of an additional 10,000 second-feet of water on each side of the falls. Unfortunately, this agreement fell afoul of hostile interests in the Foreign Relations Committee of the United States Senate, and the idea had to be dropped.[36]

In the search for additional power supplies Howard Ferguson and Ontario Hydro also became intensely interested in the Beauharnois project. In 1927 Montreal financier R.O. Sweezey had formed a syndicate to develop power on the St Lawrence just west of Montreal, where the river lay entirely in Quebec. Sweezey proposed to divert 40,000 second-feet of water through a fourteen-mile canal, thus generating 500,000 horsepower as well as creating a thirty-foot-deep shipping channel. The government of Quebec gave its approval to the plan in June 1928. By 1929 Ontario Hydro engineers were predicting that the province would need at least another 100,000 horsepower of electricity by 1932 and a total of 900,000 more by 1940. Premier Taschereau had promised to permit the exportation of large quantities of power from the Beauharnois plant to Ontario, and the

HEPC was eager to contract for as large a quantity as possible. Chairman C.A. Magrath even suggested that the commission might assist with the company's financing in return for an option on additional current.[37]

Diverting water from a navigable river, as Beauharnois wished to do, required the approval of the federal government. Company executives hoped that the ministers would be won over by their offer to hand over the navigation facilities to Ottawa for nothing. The cabinet, however, became deeply divided about the proposition. The Quebec ministers insisted that approval be given at once, since it had the province's endorsement, while the Ontario ministers disliked the idea of granting control over such a big project to a private firm. Eventually, however, the company received the necessary permission in March 1929. In the fall Howard Ferguson and C.A. Magrath travelled to Montreal to sign a contract for the delivery of 250,000 horsepower to the HEPC. At the same time negotiations were begun with the Ottawa Valley Power Company and the Maclaren-Quebec Power Company which ultimately resulted in agreements, signed in 1930 and 1931, to purchase a total of 221,000 horsepower.[38] Ferguson was very conscious of the need for careful planning. As he wrote to the Hydro chairman in the spring of 1930: 'I am intensely interested in seeing that we have ample power to take care of the future expanding needs of the Province. I think the public generally want to be assured that our development will not be delayed or retarded by the shortage of power.'[39] Thus he was still eager to see the federal-provincial conflict over water-power development ironed out.

Mackenzie King suggested a meeting with the two premiers in the fall of 1929, but Ferguson was occupied with an election campaign. Not until January 1930 did the first ministers gather in Ottawa. Four days before the conference O.D. Skelton, a close adviser to the prime minister, admitted that he did not know what line the government proposed to take. On the eve of the meeting King warned Taschereau that he thought the constitutional position of the federal government 'unassailable, particularly in the International Section, where the Dominion, in addition to its navigation and treaty powers, is in large measure the riparian owner.' Nonetheless, he expressed the hope that 'it would be possible to work out a practical basis for the further development in each specific case which would be consistent with the policy of each government and not involve any sacrifice of its constitutional rights.'[40]

Certainly his legal and technical advisers in the federal civil service were urging him to take a tough line with the provinces. The justice department was still convinced that the federal government not only had exclusive legislative jurisdiction over navigable waters but actually owned the water-power:

The works for the improvement of navigation are national undertakings constructed, operated and maintained at the expense of the whole nation, and the Dominion has the right to develop any water power which has been, or can be, incidentally created or made available by such works for all purposes of operation thereof, and also has the right, as a legitimate means of helping to meet and recoup such expense, to dispose of, for compensation, any surplus power that may be so created or made available by such improvements of navigation and as an incident of their main purpose.[41]

At their meeting King refused to concede the premiers' claim to the ownership of the power, but he suggested that the federal authorities 'might agree as a matter of policy to treat with the provinces as if they had the right to the power.' Ferguson and Taschereau apparently concluded that this was simply a formula, of customary King-like vagueness, by which the prime minister was accepting their demands. But they soon discovered they were mistaken. They drafted a letter embodying the conclusions of the conference and forwarded it to King to sign. The letter declared that 'the federal government recognizes the full proprietary rights of the provinces in the beds and banks and water powers of all navigable rivers subject, of course, to the right of control of navigation by the federal authority.' King promptly replied that this was 'a position that we could not possibly take, as it amounts to a renunciation of the Dominion's legal position, which we have no authority to make.'[42]

The prime minister also countered with a wordy and diffuse ('expanded' was his term) proposal drafted by the justice department and personally approved by him and by Lapointe. This paper opened by noting that the federal government had not in the past required 'any payment to the Dominion or other recognition of Dominion rights in respect of the water power thereby developed.' Having implicitly rejected the provincial case, three pages were filled up with suggestions about a modus vivendi which, in substance, amounted to the federal government paying only for navigation works while the provinces met the cost not only of power works but of all dual-purpose works.[43]

Any such suggestion was bound to be strenuously resisted by Howard Ferguson. Throughout the 1920s he had laboured to prevent the enthusiasts in the Canadian Deep Waterways and Power Association from publicizing the notion that the power sales would provide enough revenue to build a waterway for 'free,' since this would ultimately load onto Ontario's electricity consumers the huge cost of the canal project. In 1926 he had advised F.H. Keefer, MPP, that 'no matter how important it may be, it will be many years before a proper ship channel can be constructed down to the sea. In the meantime this province would be the subject of intense suffering for want of power. For this reason I am pushing the power project, and I do not propose, if I can help it, to allow it to be hitched up with navigation so the waterways development will become a condition of the power development.' Hence his hostile response to Mackenzie King's proposal: 'This province has always held the view ... that water power is one of the natural resources which is the property of the province, and representing the people of Ontario it is the bounden duty of the government to urge upon the federal authority the full recognition of this fundamental right of the province.'[44]

The prime minister might have ignored this protest altogether had it not been for Taschereau's vociferous support for Ferguson. The Quebec premier even implied that King was guilty of bad faith. He, therefore, invited the provincial leaders to come to Ottawa again in March 1930 and submitted a brief for them to study. This second offer was basically similar to the first: the issue of ownership was evaded, but the federal government agreed to permit the provinces to develop power on navigable rivers. Where Ottawa constructed navigation works it would make available all surplus water to generate electricity upon payment of the sum which it would have cost to develop the power alone.[45] Faced with this offer Ferguson apparently decided to seek a compromise by trying to make only minor changes in the federal proposal to preserve the legal rights of the province without embarrassing Ottawa. He and Taschereau wanted it clearly established that the provinces could develop power wherever navigation was not affected. But when canals and electricity were to be developed together, the federal government must pay for all works not required for power. In return the provinces would agree to undertake a power development whenever Ottawa wanted to improve navigation. After lengthy consultation these suggestions were submitted to King in April 1930, but by that time he seemed to have lost interest. Either he felt that enough had been done to conciliate the premiers, or, more likely, his attention was now focused on the forthcoming federal election.[46]

During the campaign, however, the water-power issue did surface. Mackenzie King was extremely proud of his record in federal-provincial relations, believing that there had been 'a virtual reconstruction of Confederation' since he took office in 1926. In a speech at Peterborough, Ontario, he blamed the province for holding up development of the St Lawrence. The angry Ferguson denied this, then both men released all the correspondence they had exchanged and issued verbose justifications of their actions. King was sufficiently upset by this row to describe Ferguson as a 'skunk' in his diary, but it is hard to see that this dispute affected the outcome of the election.[47]

R.B. Bennett's victory in 1930 was looked upon by the provincial government as a guarantee that Ontario would get a fairer hearing in Ottawa. Since it would take six to eight years to bring the St Lawrence into power production, and demand for power seemed to be rising steadily, there was still interest on the part of the Hydro in such a development. This interest increased in the spring of 1931 when the Beauharnois syndicate applied to the government to have the whole flow of the St Lawrence diverted through its power canal. The provincial government, headed by George S. Henry after Ferguson's appointment as high commissioner in London, became alarmed. Attorney-General W.H. Price advised Bennett:

If ... we are going to consent to a further diversion of water at Beauharnois enabling them to produce 2,000,000 horsepower, we are going to postpone for at least ten years our own development in Ontario.

... [T]his would be a great political error. It might raise a situation in Ontario which might lose you a great many seats and would be a very great thing for us to overcome in a general election. I think, therefore, there is still time to leave the Beauharnois development at 500,000 horsepower until we have developed that amount on the St Lawrence.[48]

The company's application was refused by the federal cabinet.

At the same time the Canadian embassy in Washington, DC, reported that Herbert Hoover's electoral prospects for 1932 looked poor. Since he was an ardent advocate of a St Lawrence deep waterway, Canada seemed likely to get a better bargain in a treaty signed now than at any time in the foreseeable future. In September 1931 Bennett notified Washington that he was ready to begin negotiations.[49] Both George Henry and the new Hydro chairman, J.R. Cooke, were determined to see that the interests of the province were protected, but the premier advised Bennett that Ontario might be prepared to overlook the constitutional niceties in order to get control of the power. In addition, the HEPC must be satisfied with all the technical and financial aspects of the project before the treaty was signed. With the costs of thermal generation steadily declining, the commission felt it was essential to obtain hydroelectricity at the lowest possible cost. Some works would be required for navigation alone, some for power alone, and some would be dual-purpose. The crucial issue was thus the formula for sharing the cost of construction of the latter.[50]

At the end of October Hydro's chief engineer was sent to Ottawa to meet with officials of the external affairs department. W.D. Herridge, the minister to Washington, informed commission officials that there was no intention on Ottawa's part to load an undue part of the cost onto the province, but that political considerations required Ontario to pay its full share. After this meeting Bennett formally advised the premier that he accepted the province's position in principle and suggested a meeting with representatives of the two federal governments at which Ontario might make its stand clear. On 13 January 1932 George Henry and J.R. Cooke met with Bennett, Herridge, and the American minister to Canada to outline Ontario's point of view.[51]

The federal and provincial governments had reached agreement on the development of waterpower on the St Lawrence. This consensus was achieved because both sides had dropped their insistence upon a general settlement applicable to all situations. Neither insisted that the other concede that the constitution gave it complete authority. Because of their party ties the two governments trusted one another to fulfill their obligations, as Howard Ferguson and Mackenzie King had never done. The means to a settlement had been suggested by federal officials in the fall of 1930. J.T. Johnston of the water power branch of the department of the interior proposed that instead of a general agreement, which might arouse provincial fears, Ottawa should discuss particular developments. When the costs were known, some formula for apportioning them might be arrived at, and the province could undertake the development and sale of power leaving the question of ownership aside.[52]

When negotiations over cost-sharing on the international section of the St Lawrence got under way early in 1932, the federal government proposed to pay only one-quarter òf the cost of the joint works. The province argued that the cost of joint works should be divided equally, but federal negotiators rejected this offer.[53] It was finally agreed that the costs should be apportioned so that the savings on account of the joint venture (as against a scheme solely for power or solely for navigation) should be equal for each party. Premier Henry approved this idea, but a final settlement proved difficult to reach owing to differing cost estimates. In the end the cost of the joint works had to be split on a flat percentage basis: 70 per cent to the province, 30 per cent to the dominion. As a result, it was expected that power from the St Lawrence could be delivered at about $14 per horsepower annually.[54]

On 3 May 1932 Premier George Henry visited Ottawa to initial the final agreement, and the treaty with the United States was signed a few weeks later.[55] At last it seemed that the decade-long struggle by Ontario to secure control of the vast energy supplies in its boundary waters had been successful. It was not to be, however. A coalition of enemies blocked the treaty in the United States congress, and the collapse of the Canadian economy destroyed all vestiges of enthusiasm for the huge expenditures which the St Lawrence waterway would require. From the provincial point of view the fight had nonetheless proved well worthwhile. The phenomenal success of Ontario Hydro had convinced political leaders of all parties that the future development of the province depended upon cheap hydroelectricity. Conversely, a power shortage could mean political ruin. Once this relationship became clear, the province's strategy unfolded naturally: opposition to power exports to the United States, the demand for provincial control of boundary waters, and the refusal to permit power rates to subsidize navigation schemes. Whether the danger came from private interests like the Siftons, Sir Herbert Holt, and W.L. McDougald or from the refusal of Mackenzie King to make concessions, the provincial government stood firm, until the Bennett administration conceded most of what it sought.

9 The Battle of the St Lawrence

Electrical energy policy continued to disrupt relations between Ontario and the federal government during the later 1930s. Once the economy of the province began to recover from the depression, Ontario Hydro came to fear a renewed shortage of power. Cheap electricity was still the basis of Ontario's industrial strength, but having been caught with a surplus of energy in the early 1930s the government subtly altered its power policy. After 1934 Mitchell Hepburn's administration was determined to secure for itself a maximum of manoeuvrability. The huge investment required to harness the power of the St Lawrence River not only seemed beyond Ontario's means, but it involved the danger that the Hydro would once more find itself with great quantites of unneeded current on its hands should economic recovery not proceed satisfactorily. Thus Hepburn displayed none of the enthusiasm shown by his Conservative predecessors, Ferguson and Henry, for St Lawrence development. Instead he sought to undertake less costly and ambitious schemes which would permit the gradual increase of power supplies without risking heavy capital investment. Unfortunately, his efforts embroiled him in as much controversy with Mackenzie King as Howard Ferguson had experienced with the prime minister during the 1920s.

What Hepburn and his advisers wanted was to raise power production in the existing plants at Niagara Falls by increasing the amount of water diverted from the river there. Not only would this strategy permit more efficient use of installed generating equipment, but additional machinery could be brought into production at a relatively low cost. The resulting current would be available right in the industrial heart of Ontario, there to spur the long-awaited recovery of the province, without the need to build long and expensive transmission lines from the Cornwall area. The federal government had no objection to these plans in principle; indeed a convention with the United States to permit this arrangement had been negotiated in 1929 and had been blocked by American interests. In practice, however, serious difficulties cropped up. The United States was still interested in the St Lawrence deep waterway and saw no reason to deal with power and navigation projects on the Great Lakes–St Lawrence system in a piecemeal fashion. The Americans wanted a comprehensive settlement which would include the Niagara diversion. Mackenzie King was eager to please president Franklin Roosevelt but Mitchell Hepburn responded with loud denunciations of Ottawa as a mere cat's-paw for Washington, unconcerned about Ontario's needs. Thus the two governments became engaged in a war of words, and the development of additional power was stalled for several years until the outbreak of war in 1939 brought a new urgency to the negotiations.

I

In 1933 and 1934 few citizens of Ontario were concerned about the development of additional electrical energy. At the nadir of the depression it hardly seemed to matter that the United States Congress had refused to ratify the 1932 St Lawrence deep waterway treaty with Canada. The contracts with private power producers in Quebec, signed between 1926 and 1931, had committed Ontario Hydro to purchase a total of 791,000 horsepower annually. Now the problem was not a power shortage, but a surplus, as commercial and industrial customers curtailed their demand in the economic crisis. Mitchell Hepburn, who became leader of the provincial Liberal party in 1930, soon began to make an issue of the profligacy of the Conservative government in undertaking these commitments. With a general election due in 1934, Hepburn stepped up his charges, claiming that the HEPC had 1 million unsaleable horsepower on hand.

The government of George Henry tried to fight back. Conservative power policy from the time of Sir James Whitney and Sir Adam Beck was recalled as an unending triumph for the rights of the province. Conservative candidates were advised to 'state with emphasis the opinion that in the Federal-Ontario compact re the Waterways, Conservative leadership has at last won a signal victory for provincial rights.' But the voters remained unimpressed, and the impact of the depression helped to sweep Hepburn into office with a large majority in the summer of 1934. He promptly dismissed all three Hydro commissioners and installed Stewart Lyon as chairman along with his attorney-general, Arthur Roebuck, and his highways minister, T.B. McQuesten.[1] Within a few days the new commissioners had met and concluded that the HEPC should try to produce more power at Niagara, the most convenient and economical source for additional energy. When approached by Hepburn, Prime Minister Bennett promised that he would sound out the Americans on the possibility of reopening negotiations on the Niagara Convention of 1929, which would have permitted each country to divert an additional 10,000 cubic feet per second from the Niagara River for power purposes during the winter months.[2]

The Niagara Convention had been turned down by the United States Senate in 1931, and when the Canadian minister to Washington raised the matter with the state department he was told that there was no chance that it could pass. The only hope that he could hold out was that the Roosevelt administration might resubmit the 1932 waterway treaty to the Senate. This was not at all to Hepburn's liking: 'I am opposed to the St. Lawrence Waterways project because, in my opinion, it is unpractical [sic] and cannot be justified on economic grounds at the present time ... We have in Ontario a huge surplus of electrical energy and we could not utilize any more electricity for some years to come. Coupled with that both the Province of Ontario and the Dominion of Canada are heavily in debt, and not in a position to borrow the monies required to finance any scheme which would not provide additional revenue.'[3] In October 1934 the premier publicly repudiated the Canada-Ontario agreement of 1932 which granted the province control of the waterpower on the international section of the St Lawrence. The HEPC now claimed that construction would cost too much, and that power users would be paying as much as $8 per horsepower for navigational works. As a result, the provincial government allowed the three-year term for ratification of the agreement to expire in July 1935 without taking any action.[4]

Once again it seemed that Ontario's plans to secure cheap energy supplies were being blocked by international complications. In March 1934 President Roosevelt himself suggested that there should be no further diversions of water at Niagara for power purposes because of the deterioration of the scenic beauty of the falls. In the face of this American resistance there was little that the Canadian government could do. Nonetheless, Mitchell Hepburn found it politically advantageous to blame Ottawa, just as Sir Adam Beck had done over power exports during the First World War. The premier repeatedly requested that Ottawa raise the issue with Washington; the external affairs department, knowing the American position, did so only in a perfunctory manner, thus providing further ammunition for Hepburn.[5]

Prior to the 1934 election the Liberals had been loud in their criticism of Conservative power purchases from Quebec, which they insisted had been tainted with graft. Although he had failed to secure additional power at Niagara, Hepburn apparently felt that he must carry out his threats to cancel these deals once he attained office, if only to compel the Quebec companies to lower their prices. Early in 1935 Hydro Commissioner Arthur Roebuck denounced the contracts in a series of radio addresses and insisted they were not binding on the HEPC. In April Hepburn introduced a Power Commission Act which declared the agreements 'illegal, void and unenforceable,' while barring any legal action against the Hydro for non-performance. Despite charges that this repudiation would completely destroy the financial reputation of the province, the Liberal government quickly pushed the bill through, although provision was made that it should not come into force until proclaimed by order-in-council. This provision would strengthen the position of the Hydro in bargaining with the companies for better terms.[6]

At the outset, Hepburn really may have intended to cancel the contracts if he could not force the Quebec companies to stretch out the schedule of deliveries over a few more years and to lower their prices. No doubt he also wished to demonstrate to the citizens of Ontario that he was a forceful and vigorous leader, unafraid to live up to his election promises. Very soon, however, he learned that Ontario could really not do without the power that the companies supplied, especially if the diversion at Niagara was not increased. In July 1935 the well-known Boston engineering firm of Stone and Webster reported to the Hydro that if the contracts were cancelled completely, funds would have to be appropriated at once to build a $14 million steam generating plant, and a site would have to be purchased for an additional thermal generating plant near Windsor, whose power would be required by the end of 1937. Thus the premier was well aware that the outright cancellation of the contracts would simply create a power shortage for the province within a couple of years.[7]

The Canadian financial community was predictably outraged by Hepburn's high-handed legislation. Many people demanded that the federal government intervene to protect the interests of the security-holders of the Beauharnois, Gatineau, Ottawa Valley, and Maclaren-Quebec companies. Finance Minister E.N. Rhodes explained to the president of the Royal Bank why he would give no assistance, even though Hepburn's actions had damaged the credit of all levels of government: 'We are on the eve of an election when the political atmosphere is surcharged [sic], and if the Dominion were to wield the verbal club immediately, we would have the old cry raised not only of provincial rights but it would be said that this administration was showing hostility from political motives.'[8] During the election campaign in the fall of 1935 Bennett challenged Mackenzie King to say whether or not he would intervene to block the cancellation of the contracts. King made the politically adept reply that the legislation had not been proclaimed and no contracts had yet been cancelled.[9] The Liberal campaign which returned King to office, with Hepburn's energetic assistance, ensured that there would be no interference by Ottawa.

Negotiations between the companies and the Hydro on the modification of the contracts achieved nothing, and in October 1935 the commission unanimously recommended that the cancellation legislation be proclaimed. After further efforts to reach a settlement this advice was accepted and the act came into force on 6 December 1935. Soon after the Gatineau and Maclaren companies accepted new contracts, but Beauharnois petitioned the federal government for disallowance of the Power Commission Act. No serious consideration was given to this request; King ordered Justice Minister Ernest Lapointe to prepare his refusal to disallow as quickly as possible. The prime minister hoped to have the whole matter disposed of before parliament met in February 1936, since the opposition was likely to try to embarrass the government over this issue. Lapointe, however, did not report until 30 March 1936. He refused disallowance on the grounds that the courts could properly deal with any provincial legislation which was ultra vires. Quoting Justice Minister Aylesworth's report on the Florence Mining Company's 1909 application for disallowance, Lapointe made it clear that provincial legislation of this sort, however unjust it might seem, would no longer be nullified by Ottawa. As a result, both the Beauharnois and the Ottawa Valley companies took their cases to the courts.[10]

By that time the Hydro commissioners were growing increasingly eager to obtain a larger diversion at Niagara. During the winter of 1935–6 water levels on the Great Lakes fell to unprecedented lows. The equipment in Hydro's generating stations at Niagara which had a rated capacity of 830,000 horsepower could produce no more than 745,000, so that almost 10 per cent of the capital equipment was standing idle. Accordingly, Hydro Chairman Stewart Lyon again suggested to Undersecretary of State O.D. Skelton in November 1935 that negotiations on increasing the diversion at Niagara should be reopened. Aware of Roosevelt's hostility to this idea, Lyon then took up an idea first suggested to Mackenzie King by Howard Ferguson back in 1925. Why not divert the flow of the Ogoki River over the height of land separating Hudson Bay from the Great Lakes system? An investment of $3 million would produce a flow of 4,000 second-feet, water which could generate 100,000 horsepower if used at Niagara.[11]

The difficulty was that under the Boundary Waters Treaty of 1909 the two countries were to share the flow equally. Lyon naturally thought that Ontario should have the exclusive benefit of the diversion, which required the consent of the United States. Early in 1936 Skelton reported that the outlook seemed grim. Not only did the Roosevelt administration prefer to deal with all the boundary waters in a single treaty including the St Lawrence waterway, but the Senate would probably not ratify a convention covering the diversions alone. The Hydro chairman chose to regard this reply as 'evasive,' complaining that Ottawa was trying to force the province to agree to the waterway scheme on the terms of the 1932 agreement as a condition of consenting to the Ogoki diversion. 'This whole issue of who owns the water that originates in Ontario and reaches the sea must be settled as speedily as possible,' he wrote to the premier, 'and I have been trusting that you would take as firm and decisive action in regard to this question as Sir Oliver Mowat took a generation ago, when he fought Sir John Macdonald on the question of who owned the bed of the streams.' Lyon had no difficulty in convincing Hepburn in the spring of 1936 that continued pressure for a larger diversion at Niagara was 'both good economics and good politics.' Still smarting from a rebuff administered by Mackenzie King when he had proffered advice on cabinet-making in the fall of 1935, Mitchell Hepburn was quite content to blame his difficulties on Ottawa. Skelton hoped, however, that the premier would eventually recognize that it was the United States, not Canada, which was blocking him: 'The Provincial Government of Ontario is slowly, but only slowly, being converted to see that unless it participates in the development of the St. Lawrence, its desire to secure further power at Niagara and Ogoki is not feasible.'[12]

Further negotiations with Washington were held in abeyance during the presidential election year, but with Roosevelt safely re-elected, an American delegation came to Ottawa for discussions in December 1936. They informed the Canadians that Roosevelt was now eager to see the St Lawrence waterway proceed but were told that Ontario's continuing opposition to any power development on the international section effectively barred any progress towards a treaty. In an effort to break this impasse Mackenzie King made arrangements for a meeting between the two levels of government; in January 1937 Hydro Commissioner Arthur Roebuck came to Ottawa for discussions with O.D. Skelton. Pressed for immediate approval of the Ogoki diversion, Skelton pointed out that nothing could be done without a general treaty. Once a treaty was signed, the Ogoki works could be commmenced immediately, while St Lawrence power would not become available for at least six or seven years. Hepburn was not satisfied with Roebuck's report. He would have nothing to do with the deep waterway, which he considered just 'another beautiful dream' to soak up vast amounts of money.[13]

With the threat of a power shortage looming, however, Hepburn apparently underwent a quick change of heart. In February he sent Hydro Chairman Stewart Lyon to see Skelton in Ottawa. If the province were permitted to complete the Ogoki diversion and to use an additional 5,000 second-feet of water at Niagara, Hepburn was now prepared to support a general treaty including the waterway. The only proviso was that Ontario should not be required to take or pay for any power from the St Lawrence for at least ten years. Since the 1932 treaty already provided for such a delay, both federal and provincial officials agreed that this document, taken in conjunction with the 1929 Niagara Convention to increase the diversions at the Falls, should form the basis for a new approach to the Americans. Prospects for an early settlement seemed particularly favourable when the United States forwarded a draft treaty proposal to Ottawa which seemed to meet all the conditions fixed by the province. The end of the wrangling between the two levels of government over power developments on the boundary water appeared imminent.[14]

At the last minute, however, Mitchell Hepburn drew back. In reality, he found himself in a tight spot. In January 1937 the Supreme Court of Ontario had upheld the 1929 contract between Beauharnois and the Hydro and awarded damages to the company. Roebuck and Hepburn hastily drew up new legislation to exempt the HEPC retroactively from all damage claims. Beauharnois still refused to be intimidated into renegotiating its agreement. If the courts struck down this new act, which seemed quite likely to happen, the Hydro would owe Beauharnois $7 million in damages as well as another $8 million to the other three Quebec companies. To complicate matters further, the Hydro engineers were now warning that far from having a power surplus, the province was likely to face a shortage during the coming winter as economic recovery proceeded. Hepburn decided to gamble. He would call a provincial election in the late summer or early fall before the likelihood of a shortage became common knowledge, knowledge which could be politically fatal in Ontario. This was no moment to consent to a St Lawrence waterway treaty, against which the Premier had been fulminating for the past three years. In March 1937, therefore, Hepburn informed Mackenzie King that he wanted the negotiations shelved until after the vote, a tactic which suited the prime minister.[15]

What Mitchell Hepburn needed was a good election issue. What could be better than a ringing call for Ontario to go 'Back to Niagara' to secure the power needed to promote its future industrial growth. Not only could the shades of Adam Beck and James P. Whitney be invoked in support of this stand, but the blame for blocking the move could be directed at Washington and Ottawa. They would not be in a position to answer for themselves during the campaign, although the premier had been told repeatedly that the United States would not agree to any increase in the diversion except as part of a general treaty. By refusing to discuss the treaty, Hepburn made certain that there could be no going 'Back to Niagara' and guaranteed himself a live issue in the coming months.

In order to heighten interest in the 'Back to Niagara' proposal and keep attention focused on the conflict with the federal government, the Hepburn cabinet made a new suggestion. In February 1937 the Hydro had devised another diversion scheme by which 1,200 second-feet of water from Long Lac in the Hudson Bay watershed would be channelled into Lake Superior. This flow could be used to generate more power at Niagara, and it would permit the driving of large quantities of pulpwood from previously inaccessible areas. Plans were also prepared to use this water at the Decew Falls power plant near St Catharines. Not only did the diversion from a navigable river require permission from Ottawa, but the United States had to approve any new diversion from the boundary waters. In July 1937 the province suggested that Ottawa and Washington should exchange diplomatic notes authorizing the plan. Without waiting for approval from Ottawa the Hydro set about constructing the diversion works.[16]

Mackenzie King had to point out to the province that all diversions from the boundary waters were regulated by the 1909 treaty and only a formal agreement with Washington could alter that situation. He predicted that the Roosevelt administration would not accept a treaty covering the Ogoki or Long Lac diversions alone. And he concluded with a gentle reminder that the Long Lac works had not yet been approved by the federal government. By then the province was in the midst of the election campaign. Speaking at Thorold on 27 September, Hepburn declared he was not going to be persuaded to support the 'folly' of the Seaway by 'a lot of ballyhoo.' 'Our policy,' he declared 'is back to Niagara to keep Ontario more and more dependent on her [own] power production. That was the policy of the great Sir Adam Beck, and I feel that we have fulfilled the Beck dreams by cancelling the Quebec power contracts which were nefarious contracts ... I'm not in favour of the deepening of the St. Lawrence, at present at least, for either transportation or power. My policy is the Beck policy of "Back to Niagara."'[17]

Mackenzie King was too canny to be drawn into a squabble with Hepburn.[18] The premier had been angered by what he considered inadequate support from the federal government during the Oshawa strike of the CIO at General Motors. And in June he had openly attacked King in a speech, announcing, 'I am a Reformer – but I am not a Mackenzie King Liberal any longer.' The prime minister responded by cancelling all his political engagements in the province, owing, as he put it, 'to Mr. Hepburn's intention to hold an election and my desire not to be drawn into controversy, directly or indirectly, with him, or to have Federal and Provincial issues intermixed any more than in necessary.' He issued only a single statement on St Lawrence development during the summer of 1937, criticizing the United States Senate for not ratifying the 1932 treaty and promising not to enter into further negotiations without full consulation with both Ontario and Quebec.[19]

Hepburn's political strategy of running against supposed interference by American unions and federal politicians in Ontario affairs proved successful. On 6 October 1937 he was re-elected easily and immediately set about altering his policies to meet realities. First priority went to a settlement with Beauharnois. During the campaign the Liberal leader had repeatedly insisted that he would make no such deal, yet he was afraid not only of the company's winning substantial damages for the nullification of its contract but of a serious power shortage during the coming winter. When Hydro Chairman Stewart Lyon objected to a new agreement with the company, he was dismissed and replaced by the more compliant Dr T.H. Hogg, Hydro's chief engineer. By late Novermber a tentative agreement with Beauharnois had been reached, which Hepburn claimed would meet the province's power needs 'for many, many years to come.'[20]

In his first three and a half years in power Mitchell Hepburn had succeeded in doing little to alter provincial energy supply policy. He had simply stretched out the delivery schedule for power purchased by his Conservative predecessors from the four Quebec companies and obtained a reduction in the price from about $15 per horsepower annually to $12.50.[21] In the changed economic circumstances of the 1930s he had become convinced that the St Lawrence was too big and too expensive for Ontario Hydro to develop, but clearly another power shortage was not many years in the future. Hepburn had been no more successful than Howard Ferguson or George Henry in obtaining the right to use more water at Niagara to develop additional power there.

II

With the Ontario election over, the American minister in Ottawa once more approached Mackenzie King to enquire if Ontario might now be prepared to resume discussion of a St Lawrence waterway treaty. The prime minister invited Mitchell Hepburn to a conference in Ottawa on 29 November 1937; he and ten of his most prominent and powerful ministers received the premier.[22] Hepburn quickly made it clear that for the time being Ontario had no interest in developing the St Lawrence. After the renegotiation of the contracts with all the Quebec power companies, the Hydro once more found itself with a temporary power surplus on hand in eastern Ontario. As a result, the Ontario leader made a most surprising counter-proposal: the federal government should license the exportation of 120,000 horsepower of electricity by the HEPC at Cornwall. This proposal ran directly contrary to one of the most sacred tenets of provincial electricity policy since 1905: steadfast opposition to exports. But Hepburn had twice presented himself to the electorate as a man who would take a tough line with the Quebec power producers. That he had been unsuccessful in this strategy was now clear, and in an effort to conceal the extent of his failure he wanted Mackenzie King and his ministers to bail him out by authorizing the exports until the power was needed at home in Ontario.[23]

The cabinet proved unsympathetic. The prime minister even suspected that the

Real purpose is to enable Mr. Hepburn to cover a power shortage in Ontario by buying from Quebec a much larger amount of power than he intends to export ... and retain the balance for domestic consumption. It looks as if he desires to have it appear that the whole amount is being exported and to use this as a blind to cover the difficulty in which he finds himself ... See no reason why Ontario should not get whatever power it wants from Quebec without going through the export device. Does not think the Federal Government should be made scapegoat.[24]

After Hepburn left the cabinet room the ministers speedily decided to reject his application. Only if parliament approved would the exports be permitted. In an effort to placate the premier, King followed him to his hotel to deliver the news personally. But Hepburn was infuriated at the 'snub' from the cabinet, and it reinforced his determination to carry on his feud with the prime minister. In announcing the terms of the new contracts between Hydro and the Quebec companies on 11 December the premier complained that the federal government was still claiming control over all navigable water regardless of provincial riparian rights. He criticized Ottawa's refusal to permit power exports 'on the rather amazing and wholly ridiculous premise' that the power could not be withdrawn when needed in Canada. The dominion, he charged, was ignoring the welfare of Ontario and its people.[25]

Hepburn clearly hoped to arouse public opinion and change King's mind. After meeting with Premier Maurice Duplessis in Montreal and receiving his support, Hepburn told the press, 'I don't see how the federal government can reasonably deny our request to export a surplus product derived from the natural resources of this province. In fact, I question the validity of Dominion legislation under the provision of which they exercised the power of refusing permission.' He suggested that exports would mean lower electricity rates in Ontario. After meeting with his cabinet King issued a statement to the press explaining his government's position: parliament must decide the issue. Apparently still hoping to force the prime minister's hand, Hepburn summoned reporters and stepped up the war of words. Federal policy, he charged, was 'made in Washington.' Why had Ottawa never consulted the Americans over Ontario's request for the Long Lac diversion? 'Now let me tell the people this,' he continued. 'Until such time as we weaken under the pressure of Ottawa and Washington for the St. Lawrence project, we'll secure no further rights for development at Niagara.' Having suffered two personal electoral defeats in the province, he added, 'Mr. King was never friendly to Ontario. I happen to know that, because I was with him and watched him at Ottawa.' King could not afford to ignore the 'made in Washington' barb; it had 'no foundation in fact.' he told the press, insisting that his government had always done its best to co-operate with Ontario.[26]

Hepburn kept up his scattershot attacks by demanding that the prime minister publish their entire correspondence on this subject. Several letters had been 'improperly' marked confidential by King so that they could not be used against him. The documents, the premier insisted, would show that in the spring of 1937 the federal government had tried to force him to back the St Lawrence waterway or face economic retaliation by the Americans. A few days later he released a selection of the correspondence to the press. Mackenzie King laboriously denied these charges, pointing out that he had willingly shelved discussions of the waterway in the spring of 1937 at Hepburn's request and that the correspondence over the Long Lac diversion had made it quite clear why the Americans would not agree to a piecemeal settlement. He promised to table all the letters on this subject in the House of Commons, provided that the United States consented.[27] Hepburn was not deterred. On 20 January 1938 he formally applied to the minister of trade and commerce for permission to export 110,000 horsepower at Cornwall. Copies of the application went to all members of parliament, and Hepburn suggested to Maurice Duplessis that both provincial legislatures should be asked to approve the exports. 'We could project into the discussion,' Hepburn pointed out, 'the principle of the Provinces having sole control of their own natural resources.' Duplessis put through an order-in-council approving the deal and offered his support.[28]

Publicly at least, Mackenzie King remained conciliatory. He spoke highly of Hepburn to the federal Liberal caucus. Pointing out that in 1929 the House of Commons had unanimously approved the principle that all future power exports should be approved by parliament, he promised that when the matter came up for discussion a free vote would be permitted. But privately he was extremely annoyed at both Hepburn and Duplessis. To a friend in England he complained: 'We are having an interesting time in Canada at present. Some of our provincial Premiers seem to have caught the contagion of Old World dictators.' And to one of his secretaries he wrote: 'Please note the unpatriotic attitude of Duplessis and Hepburn. Sir Wilfrid Laurier devoted his whole political life to the consolidation of English and French and a united nation. This work these two men now seek to destroy.'²⁹

Yet Hepburn's new application had to be handled carefully. He had astutely referred to the current to be sold as 'surplus interruptible' power which was 'immediately withdrawable.' These words were designed to make the deal seem quite innocuous, and many Liberals feared that the people of Ontario would be angered if the federal government blocked the sale of unneeded power which might otherwise be earning over $1 million per year for Ontario Hydro. However, federal engineers warned the prime minister that the proposed five-year contract for the sale of firm power made it neither 'interruptible,' or 'withdrawable.' Now it fell to Ottawa to marshal the arguments so often reiterated by Sir Adam Beck: the great comparative advantage enjoyed by Canadian industry over American competition was cheap electricity. To export power might mean short-term gains but it involved large long-term disadvantages. Demand for electricity in Ontario and Quebec was now rising at a rate of 200,000 horespower annually, which meant that all the best sources would be fully utilized within Canada in a generation.³⁰

Mackenzie King found these arguments convincing. He decided to deal with Hepburn by introducing changes in the Electricity and Fluid Exportation Act to require anyone without an existing licence wishing to sell power in the United States to secure approval from parliament by a private member's bill setting forth the terms and conditions of the contract. Such legislation would force Ontario to submit a bill, but a private bill on which the government would not be required to take a position. As part of this strategy the prime minister refused to give any hint of his personal views regarding the Ontario application, despite pressure from within his own caucus.³¹ While the debate on the amendments to the Electricity Exportation Act was continuing in March 1938, the discussion suddenly was rendered academic. Washington announced that it would not consent to any further power imports from Canada even on a temporary basis until a comprehensive treaty on St Lawrence development had been negotiated. The Roosevelt administration had become convinced that private power interests in Quebec and New York were blocking the waterway scheme and that further imports from Canada would simply keep the United States dependent on foreign power. By refusing to condone this state of affairs the Americans hoped to persuade the Ontario government to show more enthusiasm for a treaty. Premier Hepburn, his plans thwarted, declared angrily that this action proved conclusively that Ontario would get no concessions from Washington until it agreed to support the St Lawrence waterway. Nonetheless, he insisted that he would not give in.³²

The tactical skill of Mackenzie King, supported by the intervention of the United States, had thwarted Mitchell Hepburn's plans for the export of power from eastern Ontario. To a considerable degree, however, his gamble suceeded. By raising an outcry against Ottawa and Washington, he had distracted attention from his failure to secure significant modifications in the Quebec power contracts, despite his boasts to the electorate. By representing the current to be sold as 'surplus' to Ontario's needs, he avoided any criticism for abandoning one of the most time-honoured principles of Ontario energy policy: opposition to exports. Like many another politician he had saved his skin at the cost of his principles.

III

Cosmetic proposals for power exports did nothing to meet the real problems of Ontario Hydro. The central part of the province still faced an imminent power shortage, a shortage which could best be met by increasing the amount of water available to the generating stations at Niagara Falls. Even while continuing to demand the right to export 'surplus' power in February 1938, Mitchell Hepburn renewed his request to Ottawa for an agreement which would permit increased diversions. He repeated his charge that the federal government had failed to take up the matter with the Americans in the fall of 1937 and implied that this irresponsibility was what had led him to settle with the Quebec power companies. The prime minister responded angrily. He had never tried 'to impose a general scheme upon Ontario against her will. None of the correspondence or consultations with Ontario representatives affords any foundation for such suggestions.' Mackenzie King had simply advised the province that he did not believe that the Americans would consider the diversions separately from a general agreement on St Lawrence development. Triumphantly, he concluded by pointing out that despite 'public misrepresentation' his government had already dispatched a note to the Americans in January 1938 asking if they would consent to Ontario using the 1,200 second-feet of water from the Long Lac diversion.[33] Hepburn could only respond lamely that he was glad that the external affairs department had finally got around to putting this proposition to Washington. As King had predicted, Secretary of State Cordell Hull rejected any notion of a settlement of diversions alone.[34]

At the end of May 1938 Hull presented the Canadians with a new and comprehensive agreement. Similar to the abortive 1932 treaty, the draft also proposed an immediate increase in the diversion at Niagara of 5,000 cubic feet per second, and offered Canada the exclusive use of another 5,000 second-feet drawn from the Ogoki and Long Lac diversions. Together these resources would generate an additional 150,000 horsepower for Ontario Hydro at Niagara Falls. Under the terms of the agreement Ontario would also be required to pay Ottawa $70 million for dual-purpose power and navigation works on the international section and to put up another $40 million to build and equip the powerhouses. But Secretary Hull pointed out that construction of the latter could wait until Ontario Hydro required additional power.[35]

When Mackenzie King referred the draft to Toronto, Premier Hepburn again informed the press that he was immune to all 'propaganda or ballyhoo,' but he made no immediate response. By mid-August O.D. Skelton was mildly optimistic: 'Aside from the political factors involved in the decision much will depend on the estimate that is reached of Ontario's future power needs and the question of how far they can be met from the Ottawa River in cooperation with Quebec. At least there has been no definite objection to the scheme.'[36] But the very next day produced one of those explosions from Mitchell Hepburn which had by then come to characterize his relations with the federal government. At the opening of the Ivy Lea Bridge in the Thousand Islands, President Roosevelt rhapsodized about the potential of the St Lawrence waterway: 'When a resource of this kind is placed at our very doors, I think the plain people of both countries agree that it is ordinary common sense to make use of it. Yet, up to now, the liquid wealth which flowing water is, has run in large part unused to the sea. I really think that this situation suggests that we can agree upon some better arrangement than merely letting it contribute a microscopic fraction to the level of the North Atlantic Ocean.' 'The moment I saw the press report,' Skelton recorded gloomily, 'I felt certain that he had pressed a button that would automatically result in Mr. Hepburn coming out with a blast against it in 24 hours.'[37]

Skelton knew his man; the premier immediately summoned reporters and told them: 'There can be no development of power on the St. Lawrence River without the consent of the governments concerned. There will be no consent from this government.' In a letter to Mackenzie King he repeated all of his objections to the waterway scheme, concluding fiercely: 'Irrespective of any propaganda or squeeze play which might be concocted by you, you may rest assured that this Government will resist any effort to force us to expend funds in such an unwarranted manner or to foist upon the people of Ontario an additional burden of debts or taxation.'[38]

Any chance that the provincial government would accept the draft treaty seemed to have disappeared. King was infuriated with the premier. 'I have not the least doubt,' he told the governor-general, 'that Hepburn has become the instrument of the privately owned power companies in the United States and Canada to help them maintain their monopoly.' Unfortunately, there is no evidence to show whether or not King was correct. Elsewhere he described the Ontario leader as 'a menace to national as well as party unity.' But publicly he was still conciliatory, suggesting further meetings with Hydro officials 'to clear away the obstacles to the Province's freedom to develop its resources at its own discretion, however long and complicated the task may be.'[39]

Hepburn thought further conferences useless. To repeat the technical work would be a waste of time. 'This Province is simply not interested in the production of any more power,' he told King. 'To take any part in any negotiations which may lead to this end would be unwise and misleading.' Cordell Hull's draft treaty, he charged, was designed simply to ensure that there would be large quantities of St Lawrence power available for export when the United States required it. All he wanted was approval for the Ogoki and Long Lac diversions which would meet Ontario's immediate requirements.[40]

When Cordell Hull began to press the Canadian minister in Washington for a reply to his treaty proposals, he had to be told that Hepburn had effectively vetoed them.[41] Meanwhile, the Ontario government pressed ahead with the diversion works at Long Lac. By December 1938 the channel was completed and ready for use, despite the lack of federal approval. But as long as the diversion was used only for floating pulpwood into Lake Superior, the federal authorities apparently preferred to ignore the matter rather than be drawn into a renewed controversy.[42] In February 1939 the American minister to Canada reported that Ottawa opinion was that the premier was so deeply involved with private power interests on both sides of the border that he could not relax his opposition to the St Lawrence waterway even if he wished to do so. King and Skelton had informed the minister that any settlement was impossible while Hepburn persisted in his 'implacable opposition.' The only positive sign for Washington came in March when Hydro Chairman Hogg mentioned to the American consul in Toronto that Ontario would need more power 'within a few years.'[43]

The outbreak of war in September 1939 swiftly transformed the situation. An Ontario resources committee was set up, consisting of the premier, Opposition Leader George Drew, and Lieutenant-Governor Albert Matthews. The committee requested a meeting with the cabinet and was received by King and most of his ministers on 3 October 1939. Hepburn informed the gathering that he now 'visualized Ontario as the arsenal of the British Empire during the war, which he anticipated would be of long duration. In order to make effective use of Ontario industrial capacity increased power must be made available.' The provincial government was

> prepared to reverse completely its former policy, and in order that the St. Lawrence system might be developed further, to give the necessary additional horsepower, it would withdraw all opposition to the undertaking of the St. Lawrence Waterway scheme. While still of the opinion that from a navigation standpoint the St. Lawrence Waterway scheme was impractical, the Ontario government was prepared to agree to its undertaking, in order to obtain the additional power supply which it felt was essential in war conditions.[44]

Hepburn stipulated that the talks should be secret, however, and that there should be no final settlement with Washington until a federal-provincial agreement had been reached. King privately regarded the premier's change of heart as a personal triumph:

> By taking the firm stand that I did when we came into office we have succeeded not only in making Hepburn and his government ... reverse the position they had taken on the St.

Lawrence Waterway, which has been made the excuse of all the controversy between the two governments since, but have, what is more important, made them request the making of a treaty on lines practically agreed upon before ...

Altogether the St. Lawrence Waterway promises to be another great progressive stroke, added to the already splendid record of the present administration.[45]

Hydro Chairman T.H. Hogg and Transport Minister C.D. Howe began discussions in mid-October. Hogg admitted that all surplus power was expected to be absorbed by 1941. Either the Ottawa or the St Lawrence would then have to be developed further to meet the expected flood of war orders. With difficulty the premier had been persuaded that the St Lawrence project was preferable, and the provincial cabinet was now prepared to withdraw its objections to a treaty with the United States, provided a satisfactory new Canada-Ontario agreement could be negotiated. The critical issue was cost-sharing on the dual-purpose works for both navigation and power. The seventy–thirty division provided for in the 1932 agreement was not acceptable, and the province hoped to persuade Ottawa to accept a fifty–fifty split, pointing out that New York state had been offered liberal treatment by Washington.[46]

Negotiations continued during the next few months, while the premier and the prime minister exchanged cordial letters on the subject. Nonetheless, Hogg pointed out to O.D. Skelton 'the precariousness of the present truce between Ottawa and Toronto and the necessity of trying to get an agreement at an early date.'[47] And on 18 January 1940 the unpredictable Hepburn fully confirmed the fears of the Hydro chairman by moving a resolution in the legislature condemning the federal government for failing to prosecute the war effort more vigorously. This motion passed by a vote of forty-four to ten. Although he professed unconcern, Mackenzie King was convinced that this move presaged a campaign by Hepburn and George Drew to oust him and install a wartime 'national' government. He responded by calling an immediate federal election to seek a new mandate in the face of their challenge.[48]

Despite the outbreak of new hostilities between King and Hepburn, discussions on the development of the St Lawrence went ahead. O.D. Skelton pointed out to the prime minister that since the province had reopened the negotiations 'and had taken up a fair position on the details of the project, our alibi to Mr. Roosevelt against action was gone.' To delay was to risk further attacks by the provincial government: 'Granted it could not be more hostile in intent than it is at present, it might, however, very easily find in a rejection or indefinite stalling of the project very effective political weapons.' Some people in Ottawa had long believed that in blocking the waterway project, Mitchell Hepburn was being used as a cat's-paw by private power interests in Quebec, but 'It is very easy to see how this argument could now be reversed and how it could be alleged that Ottawa had rejected the scheme because of the influence of its friends, the power barons of Montreal.'

Aside from all these political considerations, the fact remained that a power shortage still loomed ahead.⁴⁹

On 26 March 1940 Mackenzie King was triumphantly re-elected with a huge majority. Meanwhile, federal and provincial officials continued to hold talks on cost-sharing, but obstacles now arose in a different quarter. At the end of April President Roosevelt informed the prime minister that it was politically impossible for him to proceed with a waterway treaty in an election year; he asked that all negotiations be shelved for the time being. King was content, not solely because of his annoyance with Hepburn but because of the continued hostility to the project of his Quebec ministers.⁵⁰ All that Hydro Chairman Hogg could do was suggest that there should be an immediate increase in the diversion at Niagara. He visited Washington in May to press the case in person with American officials, and in mid-July the state department let it be known that once the Democratic convention had renominated Franklin Roosevelt, 'something will be done for Tommy Hogg.'⁵¹ In September the Americans agreed that Ontario could use the entire 5,000 second-feet of water from the Ogoki and Long Lac diversions in its existing plants once the necessary works were completed. In addition, the two countries would set up a temporary Great Lakes–St Lawrence basin committee to plan the development of the international section and to draw up a treaty when 'convenient.'⁵²

The American idea created problems for Mackenzie King. His Quebec ministers, who had never favoured the waterway project, were acutely unhappy. P.J.A. Cardin grumbled: 'Are we to dance to Ontario's tune, throw the whole project aside when Ontario proposes and jump at it when she wants it? We were told a year ago that we would not be asked to agree to any piecemeal scheme – it would be the whole scheme or nothing. Now we are asked to accept a piecemeal scheme.' Skelton quickly pointed out to the prime minister that he could hardly go back on his word at this stage. Hydro Chairman Hogg had been told repeatedly over the past year that the source of the holdup lay not in Ottawa but in Washington. If he now discovered that it was the Quebec ministers who were blocking additional power supplies there would be a 'real explosion' from the Ontario government. King agreed. Skelton was told to see Cardin and inform him that if the understanding between Roosevelt and King were questioned by the cabinet he would resign as prime minister: 'He was not personally concerned or enthusiastic about the St. Lawrence, but it had all been settled and could not be reopened.' This threat proved effective.⁵³

Near the end of September 1940 Hogg pointed out that even the new arrangement might not be adequate to meet the expected power shortage. The Long Lac diversion was finished and ready to flow, but completion of the Ogoki works would require another year and a half, and the Ogoki would provide four-fifths of the total flow of 5,000 cubic feet per second. In view of the wartime emergency, would the Americans permit the whole 5,000 second-feet to be taken at Niagara immediately? The state department agreed to allow the larger diversion as soon as Ontario began construction on the Ogoki.[54] This arrangement was entirely satisfactory to the province and by early November Ontario Hydro had opened the Long Lac diversion and was drawing an additional 1,200 cubic feet per second at Niagara. Premier Hepburn remained adamant, however, that his government considered the St Lawrence waterway unnecessary and had consented to discuss it only in order to secure more water at the Falls.[55]

By December 1940 President Roosevelt was safely re-elected and pressing for swift agreement on a waterway treaty. In January 1941 the Great Lakes–St Lawrence basin committee (which included Hogg as Ontario's representative) reported in favour of damming the international section at Cornwall to produce 2 million horsepower of electricity at a cost of $266 million and a draft treaty to embody this proposal was drawn up.[56] Meanwhile, Ontario and the federal government resumed their negotiations on cost-sharing. Delays occurred because Hogg became ill, but eventually Hepburn consented to go ahead without the Hydro chairman. By the end of February the province had agreed to pay 62.5 per cent of the cost of the joint works, a substantially smaller proportion than the 1932 agreement stipulated. In addition, the federal government promised to pay the entire cost of both the Ogoki and the Long Lac diversion works, or $5 million in all. Once the province paid the first instalment of the $164,125,000 it owed Ottawa (one year after the first power was delivered), ownership of the lands and powerhouses in Ontario would formally pass to the Hydro.[57]

By early 1941, then, over two decades of squabbling between the province of Ontario and the federal government over the development of the vast power of the St Lawrence seemed to be at an end. But still Mackenzie King procrastinated, as his Quebec supporters continued to complain about the unnecessary expense of the canal project and the damage to the port of Montreal. Perhaps, he suggested, the Americans could be persuaded to undertake alone the power development on the international section. After sounding out the Roosevelt administration, King discovered that the president was prepared to let the navigation project wait until peacetime, but for political reasons the president was insistent that a formal agreement covering all aspects of the scheme should be signed at once.[58] The state department was prepared to help the prime minister to overcome domestic opposition. A personal message from the president was sent to Ottawa declaring the waterway project 'a vital necessity,' making it 'imperative that we undertake it immediately.' Armed with this declaration, King signed the Great Lakes–St Lawrence Basin Agreement and the revised Canada–Ontario Agreement on 19 March 1941.[59] The twenty-year struggle over the development of the power of the St Lawrence had apparently ended.

Mitchell Hepburn's twistings and turnings on the issue of St Lawrence development arose from his desire to extract the maximum political advantage from it, however inconsistent he might have to be. The new premier took office in 1934 convinced of two things: that the contracts signed by his Conservative predecessors with private Quebec power producers were too extravagant for Ontario Hydro to fulfil, and that the St Lawrence Waterway was too grandiose and expensive a project for the taxpayers to finance during the depression. Once in power, however, he was confronted with the fact that Ontario's electricity surplus was largely illusory. In view of the time which it took to bring major hydroelectric developments into production, the Hydro would have barely adequate reserve capacity in a few years' time when economic recovery began. For political reasons the premier could not admit this fact, so he quickly cast about for some means to increase power production at Niagara Falls, where the shortages were likely to be most acute. In 1937 he sought re-election on a 'Back to Niagara' plank in the hopes of concealing an imminent power shortage.

However, Hepburn's efforts collided with the hard facts of international relations. President Franklin Roosevelt would not consent to a larger diversion except as part of a broader St Lawrence waterway treaty. Efforts by Ontario to increase production at Niagara by diverting water from the watershed of Hudson Bay into Lake Superior also required amendments to the Boundary Waters Treaty of 1909. The Americans would have demanded some sort of quid pro quo in exchange for this concession.

Repudiation of the Quebec power contracts embroiled the premier in a lengthy legal battle, a battle which the producers won. Forced to settle with the Quebec companies, Hepburn found himself with a temporary power surplus in eastern Ontario in 1937, a predicament from which he tried to escape by securing permission to export power to the United States. The federal government refused and in any case, such action was prohibited by the Americans in 1938. The outbreak of war in 1939 finally destroyed the notion of a power shortage. With economic recovery now well under way, Hepburn at last agreed to sign a new St Lawrence waterway agreement, provided that a cost-sharing arrangement could be negotiated. Meanwhile, in view of the exceptional circumstances, the United States consented to a temporary increase in the diversion of water at Niagara.

So erratic was Hepburn's behaviour that some people believed he was blocking the development of the St Lawrence in the interest of the existing private power producers in Quebec, who feared low-cost competition. No clear evidence for this allegation seems to exist. More likely, Hepburn's behaviour can be explained by the immediate political imperatives. Having adopted a certain public stance, he had to retreat from it in the face of an imminent power shortage, but he hoped to lay down a smoke-screen which might permit him to shift his ground undetected. He never lost sight of the critical importance of an ample supply of low-cost power for Ontario's industrial development, even when political exigencies might force him temporarily to advocate exports. His federal counterpart, Mackenzie King, was in the fortunate position of being able to wait as long as necessary for the Ontario premier to come around. In the end, the outbreak of war solved problems for both of them.

Settlement of this federal-provincial conflict did not lead to the speedy completion of the St Lawrence waterway. Powerful sectional and economic forces within the United States proved able to use their influence upon congress to delay the project for more than a decade. Not until the early 1950s, when Canada threatened to proceed independently with the building of an all-Canadian waterway, did the Americans finally approve the project. In 1954 an exchange of notes cleared the way for construction to begin and the St Lawrence Seaway opened for business in 1959. During the delay the question of provincial control of water-power developed on the Canadian side of the boundary did not arise again. The concessions offered by the federal government to Ontario in 1932, confirmed by the 1941 agreements, had effectively put an end to the federal-provincial friction generated by this issue.

10 Revising the Constitution

Prospects for constitutional reform in Canada had never seemed better than they did in late 1935. A severe depression had clearly demonstrated that the existing system of government was ill-equipped to deal with mass unemployment. Only the central government could fund and manage a national relief system, but it was the provinces who possessed jurisdiction, and the municipalities alone had the machinery to administer relief. By the mid-1930s both provinces and municipalities were staggering under the financial burden of caring for the jobless, although they were assisted to some extent by grants-in-aid from Ottawa. Many people were convinced that a modern industrial state could no longer carry on in such makeshift fashion. The constitution seemed to need a thorough overhaul to redistribute duties and responsibilities and the sources of tax revenue which would meet the costs. And if the constitution was to be refashioned, was it not also time to agree upon a formula for future amendments and to 'patriate' the BNA Act to take it out of the hands of the British parliament once and for all?

Fortunately, the political portents for such a change looked equally promising. Mackenzie King had just taken power with an overwhelming majority, and the Liberals also controlled seven of the nine provincial governments. The prime minister summoned a dominion-provincial conference in December to set the wheels in motion. Yet the results of this meeting were paltry. Premier Mitchell Hepburn of Ontario proved to be unenthusiastic about federal plans to refund provincial debts at a lower rate of interest, and after further discussions the idea was dropped. Agreement was reached upon the need for an amending formula for the BNA Act, but here, too, no final settlement was arrived at, owing to objections raised by New Brunswick. By the end of 1936 the attempt to secure wide-ranging constitutional change had been abandoned.

By 1937 relations between Hepburn and King had begun to deteriorate, as the Ontario leader sniped away at federal policies. When the prime minister announced the appointment of a royal commission on dominion-provincial relations, Hepburn soon became a strident critic of the commission. In the spring of

1938 Ontario's submission to the commissioners criticized any move in the direction of greater centralization of power in Ottawa's hands. The outbreak of war in 1939 created more cordial feelings between the provincial government and King's administration, but this entente proved only temporary: early in 1940 Hepburn openly attacked Ottawa for failing to prosecute the war effort strenuously enough. The prime minister promptly called an election on the issue and was sustained in office.

The royal commission's report was finally delivered in mid-1940, and eventually Mackenzie King was persuaded to call another dominion-provincial conference to discuss its recommendations. Hepburn's hostility to the proposed constitutional changes prevented the meeting in January 1941 from reaching any agreement. As a result, the federal government proceeded to make changes in the taxation system unilaterally, to ease the problems of financing the war effort. Despite the Ontario premier's reluctance, he was eventually manoeuvred into consenting to the arrangement for the duration of the fighting. Nonetheless, Hepburn's persistent opposition to wide-ranging constitutional change, his insistence upon the province's right to veto any proposed amendments, left the constitution of Canada fundamentally unchanged, falsifying the expectations of the mid-1930s.

I

During the Bennett regime the Liberals wrested control of six provincial governments from the Conservatives under the impact of the depression. In October 1935 Mackenzie King was swept back into office with an overwhelming majority as the voters were asked to choose 'King or Chaos.' The prime minister was a noted conciliator, who had often argued that negotiation was the only route to federal-provincial co-operation: 'The provinces cannot be extinguished by any act of the Dominion parliament. To attempt to do so would split Confederation asunder ... To ignore the provinces or deliberately invade their constitutional rights is a dangerous assault upon the very foundations of our national life.' With this spirit and the ability to appeal to the party loyalties of seven of the nine premiers could King succeed in achieving consensus on constutitional change where others had failed?[1]

Mitchell Hepburn of Ontario seemed to be one of the prime minister's strongest backers; he had travelled 10,000 miles in six weeks during the federal campaign to make sixty-five speeches on Mackenzie King's behalf. When a dominion-provincial conference was summoned for 9 December 1935, it appeared that a new age of harmony in Ontario-federal relations might be dawning. Almost at once, however, friction had begun to develop between Ottawa and Queen's Park. The premier had suggested that his close friend Arthur Slaght, member of parliament for Parry Sound, should be taken into the cabinet. King rebuffed Hepburn with the pointed reminder that *he* had made no such suggestions about the composition of the cabinet after Hepburn's victory in 1934. Hepburn started to sulk. Before the election he had been the second most prominent Liberal in the country; now it seemed that his advice was unwelcome. This wound to his self-esteem, which was at least as massive as Mackenzie King's, began to fester, and Hepburn became abnormally sensitive to slights, both real and imaginary. From time to time over the next seven years the premier would burst out in sudden tirades against the federal leader, disrupting the negotiations about the development of the St Lawrence and even helping to bring on the federal election of 1940. Thus personal friendship and party ties would prove less a mediating factor than might have been expected once the discussion of constitutional reform was under way.[2]

The agenda for the 1935 dominion-provincial conference covered three main areas: the immediate problems of unemployment and relief, the search for an amending formula for the constitution, and the financial condition of the provinces. Since 1930 the provinces and municipalities had borrowed over $500 million, and now some were faced with default. Federal officials were deeply concerned that Canada's credit rating might be seriously impaired if this occurred. W.C. Clark, the deputy minister of finance, believed that the nation needed some sort of loan council on the Australian model which would supervise government borrowing; loans approved by the council would receive a guarantee. He hoped that the provinces might be induced to submit to these controls because of the promise of lower interest rates, since debt charges were gobbling up much of provincial revenues. Mitchell Hepburn was certainly interested in refunding the Ontario debt, which by 1935 stood at about $700 million, borrowed at an average rate of 5 per cent. The province's debt charges were consuming over a quarter of its revenues, while unemployment relief accounted for an additional 25 per cent (see Table 5). If the rate of interest on the debt could be reduced to 3 per cent, the provincial treasury might save as much as $15 million annually.[3]

On his return from negotiating a new trade agreement with the United States, Mackenzie King lost little time in summoning the premiers to Ottawa. After the obligatory opening addresses the conference broke up into specialized committees to deal with detailed proposals.[4] When Finance Minister Charles Dunning explained to the committee on financial questions what he and his officials had in mind in the way of a loan council, the enthusiasm of the Ontario delegation for the idea diminished rapidly.[5] Half the votes in the council would be held by the finance minister, the other half by the participating provinces. Hepburn listened with growing unease as it was explained that Ottawa would cover only half the loss in the case of any default; the rest of the guarantee would be shared among the provinces in proportion to their outstanding debts. 'I am not very enamoured of that proposal,' Hepburn told the delegates. 'We pay over 40% of all federal taxation, and a lion's share of the other 60%. I do not like the idea.' But what

TABLE 5
Per cent of supply bill expenditures by item, province of Ontario, 1925-40

Item	1925	1930	1936	1940
agriculture	4.4	4.7	1.9	2.3
attorney-general	4.9	5.4	2.8	3.6
education	18.0	19.9	12.4	14.0
game & fisheries	0.7	1.0	0.6	0.6
health	1.2	1.5	7.8	12.1
highways	6.9	8.6	5.4	10.9
insurance	0.1	0.1	0.1	0.1
labour	4.5	6.8	0.3	0.7
lands & forests	5.9	4.2	1.6	2.3
legislation	0.7	0.6	0.3	0.3
lieutenant-governor	0.01	0.01	0.01	0.01
mines	0.5	0.8	0.3	0.4
municipal affairs	–	–	0.1	5.1
northern development	–	3.6	2.9	–
prime minister	0.6	0.4	0.2	0.2
provincial auditor	0.2	0.2	0.1	0.1
provincial secretary	12.1	14.6	0.9	1.8
provincial treasurer	4.1	3.3	1.0	1.4
public welfare	–	0.003	5.7	9.8
public works	1.6	1.6	0.7	0.9
miscellaneous	0.2	2.0	0.1	0.01
public debt	33.5	20.7	26.9	23.3
unemployment: direct relief & administration	–	–	27.6	9.9

SOURCE: Table 3; the calculations are mine.

disturbed the premier most was that Dunning made it clear that he had no plans to include federal securities in the refunding scheme. To Hepburn it made no sense to convert the debt of Canada on a piecemeal basis; it should be all or nothing.

Dunning refused to accept Ontario's objections. Most people outside of Ontario, he reminded Hepburn, saw the province not as the source of half the nation's tax revenues but as a greedy collector of wealth generated elsewhere in the country. To the inclusion of federal securities in the refunding scheme, he was adamantly opposed. Too much of Canada's debt was held abroad. Even a hint of compulsory refunding would destroy the nation's financial reputation in London and New York. He told the committee that despite Ontario's opposition, Ottawa would hold open the offer to form a loan council. Any province might join if it would pledge its subsidy payments to cover a default. Should the losses exceed that amount the other members of the council, including the federal government, would meet them jointly. But at the outset Hepburn's objections had seriously damaged the prospects for a successful debt conversion scheme.

In an effort to salvage something the committee turned to a discussion of the reallocation of tax fields. Hepburn warned the committee that 'If a complete refunding programme was not instituted it would be necessary for the Dominion to abandon direct taxation or at least share part of direct taxation.' He complained repeatedly that the federal governnment had invaded the provincial sphere by imposing an income tax; he demanded that Ottawa should relinquish it or at least alter the regulations to permit the provinces to enter the field more easily. He also wanted Ottawa to drop all succession duties. Not surprisingly Charles Dunning refused to agree to any of these proposals. W.C. Clark had pointed out to his minister that the notion of 'double' taxation, about which the provinces complained so much, was really specious.[6] If taxes on income raised the largest revenues in the most equitable fashion, then both levels of government ought to utilize them, regardless of protests. Dunning would not commit the newly elected federal ministry to any significant fiscal changes. As a result, the committee on financial questions achieved nothing concrete except an agreement to set up a continuing committee to examine such problems as debt refunding and taxation and to try to reach some compromise. This agreement, at least, bolstered the illusion that progress had been made.[7]

A similar conflict developed in another committee of the conference set up to discuss mining development and taxation. Hepburn personally represented Ontario on this committee too, and he immediately proposed that all federal taxes on mines should cease. Minerals were non-renewable resources, entirely lost to the provinces once extracted. If the federal tax load of $6,600,000 per year were reduced, then his province would receive more revenue from mining, in which it had invested $100 million over the past twenty-five years, while only $12 million had been recovered. The Ontario premier demanded that at least half the income taxes on mining companies be turned over to the provinces. Mines Minister T.A.

Crerar, backed up by Dunning, refused to pledge the government to this scheme. On his return to Toronto the premier complained bitterly to the press that the federal ministers had been unwilling to make any commitments yet had insisted that the provinces be prepared to do so. He blamed the failure to reach an agreement on mining taxation on the 'total lack of guidance and spirit of cooperation shown by the Dominion government.'[8]

The deliberations of the conference committee on unemployment and relief were more productive. The seven Liberal premiers had travelled to Ottawa with the confident expectation that Mackenzie King's government would be prepared to give them more financial assistance. Since the acrimonious dominion-provincial conference of July 1934, Ontario had been receiving a block grant of only $600,000 monthly (out of a total of $1.750 million). In July 1935 Premier Hepburn had announced that his government could not continue to spend such a high percentage of its budget on the 400,000 people on relief. To protect the solvency of the province Ontario would no longer cover two-thirds of the cost of direct relief but would substitute per capita grants of $7.50 per month to municipalities which could not meet their share and $5.00 to those that could, at a saving of $750,000 per month. With the federal election imminent, however, this change was not to be implemented until 1 January 1936. Obviously the provincial authorities hoped that a new King government would prove more munificent than the Bennett government had been.

Their hopes were not disappointed. Deputy Finance Minister W.C. Clark suggested to Charles Dunning before the conference that matching grants should be resumed with the federal government meeting between 40 and 50 per cent of the cost of direct relief, the provinces and municipalities putting up the rest. At the same time a National Employment Commission should be set up to register and classify all relief recipients into 'employables' and 'unemployables,' to set standards for federally assisted programs, and to supervise spending by the provinces and municipalities.[9] Labour Minister Norman Rogers was enthusiastic about the idea of a national employment commission but opposed to matching grants, since he believed that they encouraged wastefulness and inefficiency. Nevertheless, he agreed that the provinces were entitled to a hefty increase in federal block grants for relief.

Ontario's welfare minister, David Croll, went to the conference with hopes of persuading Ottawa to take over three-quarters of the cost of direct relief to 'employables,' provided that the province and its municipalities took over care of the 'unemployables.' Rogers refused to agree to this proposal, because he and Dunning feared that it would raise federal relief costs by as much as $30,000,000 per year. After lengthy discussions the delegates agreed to accept Rogers's plan for a large increase in block grants for relief and the formation of a National Employment Commission. Within a few weeks the cabinet had approved substantial increases, Ontario's grant rising from $600,000 monthly to $1.050 million.[10]

The third important item on the conference agenda was the matter of constitutional amendment. If an amending formula could be worked out, then changes might be made in the BNA Act to eliminate some long-standing causes of friction. When R.B. Bennett introduced his "New Deal" legislation in the spring of 1935, J.S. Woodsworth of the CCF had moved for a select committee to study the subject. The government had permitted his motion to pass, and the committee invited the provinces to submit their views. None had responded, however, since they agreed that this was not the proper method of dealing with the question. Although a number of civil servants and legal scholars did testify, about all they had agreed upon was the dubious historical validity of the compact theory of Confederation. The committee had suggested, therefore, that only a dominion-provincial conference could cope with the task of devising an amending formula.[11]

Ontario's attorney-general, Arthur Roebuck, received the invitation with none of the scepticism with which he had treated R.B. Bennett's proposed discussions in the fall of 1934. Obviously he had more confidence in his fellow Liberal Mackenzie King than in the domineering Bennett. King had made it clear that he hoped to return 'as regards our revenues and expenditures ... to responsible government in the fullest meaning of that term, whereby the governments that spend public monies must be the governments which, through the agency of taxation, raise what is to be spent.'[12] This attitude was certainly in keeping with the views of the Ontario government on the federal system. Even Premier Taschereau of Quebec expressed a new willingness to discuss the issue, although his primary concern was with the patriation of the constitution. In this promising atmosphere Roebuck met with Attorney-General W.J. Major of Manitoba and drew up a detailed proposal for an amending formula, dividing the constitution into several sections, each with a different method of amendment. The discussions in the constitutional committee of the dominion-provincial conference were most amicable, and it was agreed that there was a sound basis on which to continue talks. Ernest Lapointe was given authority by the conference to convene a meeting of provincial officials for further negotiations within a few months.[13]

By the time the dominion-provincial conference held its final plenary session to approve the reports of the committees, Hepburn, ill with bronchitis, had returned to Toronto. Arthur Roebuck remained as leader of the Ontario delegation to sound a few sour notes amid the general self-congratulation. He pointed out, for instance, that on the vital matter of refunding the public debt nothing had actually been accomplished, even though interest charges continued to eat up half of provincial revenues in some cases. He also complained of lack of action on the larger problem of creating jobs for the unemployed. Mackenzie King professed himself extremely pleased with the conference, but some of his ministers were less enthusiastic. T.A. Crerar thought that 'nothing of a very tangible kind resulted from it.' He was also worried about the future of relations between Ottawa and Queen's Park; for he saw that Mitchell Hepburn had come to the gathering 'trailing his coat and daring anyone to tread on it.'[14]

Nevertheless, the conference had opened the way for further discussions.

Charles Dunning called another meeting of provincial representatives in Ottawa on 13 January 1936 to discuss financial matters. The provinces were eager to secure an amendment to the BNA Act authorizing them to collect sales taxes. The federal government had no objection to this change. Finance department officials were really interested in creating some sort of loan council to prevent a default by one of the prairie provinces which might seriously damage Canadian credit. The difficulty lay in persuading the provinces to agree to surrender their independent borrowing authority in return for a federal guarantee of their debts: 'The *only* real object of the guarantee is to get control. *If*, therefore, control can be obtained in any other way there should be no guarantee ... Control must extend to legal attachment of provincial revenues ... The alternative to control is default; therefore there must be control.'[15] Dunning proposed to the provincial delegates a constitutional amendment legalizing both the sales tax and the loan council plan in an effort to win the support of the provinces. A separate loan council could be set up for each province, and all subsidies and grants-in-aid from Ottawa would have to be pledged to the council to cover any defaults.

Since Hepburn was holidaying in the southern United States, Ontario was represented at this gathering by Deputy Provincial Treasurer Chester Walters. Walters made it clear that while the province would like to levy a retail sales tax, it had no intention of participating in any such loan council scheme. For one thing, the province was now able to borrow at 3 per cent, the rate at which the guaranteed securities were supposed to be issued. But as long as the loan council scheme was not compulsory, Ontario had no opposition to such an amendment to the constitution.[16]

Having obtained provincial consent, Dunning proceeded to draft the necessary amendment. When Hepburn returned to Canada he made it clear that he would have nothing to do with any refunding scheme which did not include federal securities, but he raised no objection to the amendment. Only William Aberhart of Alberta expressed reservations, but he was finally coerced into agreeing by Ottawa's refusal to advance him further funds to meet maturing obligations. On 1 May 1936 Dunning announced that the government would proceed with the amendment; the motion was quickly approved by the House of Commons. However, strong opposition developed in the Senate. Arthur Meighen believed that the changes would upset the balance of power between the two levels of government. Like many business leaders he was also apprehensive that these sales taxes would become a kind of interprovincial tariff. The banking and commerce committee refused to approve the amendment, and despite a Liberal amendment to outlaw the use of the sales tax to interfere with trade the Senate turned down the proposed change.[17]

Dunning went ahead, nonetheless, and set up a National Finance Committee. Although membership was voluntary, finance department officials hoped that it would have enough weight with the public that any province which ignored its advice would lose credibility not only with lenders but with the public. In fact, this committee appears to have held only one meeting, in December 1936, with Chester Walters, Provincial Secretary Harry Nixon, and Mines Minister Paul Leduc representing Ontario.[18] The proceedings opened with a review of the financial position of the nine provinces and the federal government, followed by a statement from the governor of the Bank of Canada. Walters promptly attacked the Bank claiming that it had promised to buy $10,000,000 worth of Ontario treasury bills in the spring of 1935, then reneged on the offer. The province, he argued, would put itself in a dangerous financial position if it placed itself in the hands of the governor of the Bank of Canada, who could not even be overruled by the minister of finance. He called for closer control of the Bank by the government. Graham Towers, the governor of the Bank, insisted that there had been a misunderstanding, but it was clear that prospects for financial co-operation by Ontario were not at all good.

Paul Leduc also complained at length about the federal income tax, pointing out that Premier Hepburn had objected to Ottawa's occupation of this field of direct taxation at the dominion-provincial conference a year earlier. Since then, Ontario had been forced to impose its own income tax, but had found the public unhappy with the additional impost. Charles Dunning responded that that federal government could not even consider giving up the income tax at such a time since it generated $100 million annually for Ottawa. Harry Nixon added his protests about overlapping services in the fields of health, agriculture, and labour, and the meeting broke up. About the only concrete achievement of this committee was to initiate discussion of a royal commission to study federal-provincial relations and the reallocation of revenues and responsibilities, the genesis of the idea which led to the creation of the Royal Commission on Dominion-Provincial Relations in 1937.

Despite the failure of these efforts to create a national loan council with real powers, the dominion-provincial conference of 1935 did seem to improve the prospects for agreement on a formula for amending the constitution to permit a more rational distribution of jurisdiction. The premiers concluded that Canada should have the right to amend its own constitution, and a consensus seemed to be emerging about a formula. A memorandum drawn up by officials of the justice department showed a remarkable similarity to one prepared by Arthur Roebuck and W.J. Major of Manitoba. Constitutional provisions were to be divided into four categories. Those clauses affecting the dominion alone could be amended simply by act of parliament, while those matters affecting the dominion and some but not all the provinces could be changed by the consent of parliament and the provinces involved. Certain fundamental rights such as the existence of civil law in Quebec and linguistic and educational provisions would be changed only with the unanimous consent of parliament and the nine provincial legislatures. All other matters would require the approval of six of the nine provinces, and those six must contain 55 per cent of the total population. The advantages of such an arrangement from Ontario's point of view were succinctly summed up by the province's deputy attorney-general: 'This method definitely recognizes the compact or contract theory. Changes cannot be made without the consent of the provinces affected, and this settles for all time the question as to whether the provinces should be consulted or not.'[19]

This formula was referred by the dominion-provincial conference to a continuing committee of federal and provincial officials which held a series of meetings in Ottawa between 28 January and 11 February 1936. A new section of the BNA Act was drafted embodying the amending formula. When the draft was submitted to the provincial governments, only New Brunswick dissented, pointing out that the other six provinces might gang up on the maritime provinces and impose changes against their will. To counter this criticism the committee held another meeting in March and proposed that a dissenting province might retain exclusive legislative jurisdiction over matters affected by an amendment, should it wish to do so. But this 'opting-out' clause did not please several of the provinces, and the committee adjourned without reaching any decision. The meetings were never reconvened, and the King government, apparently tiring of the effort, decided to press ahead instead with the amendment concerning taxation and the loan council already approved by the provinces, without waiting for agreement on a formula, an amendment which the Senate ultimately blocked.[20]

As a result, the dominion-provincial conference of 1935, convened with such high hopes, failed to make any substantial progress towards constitutional reform. Even though eight of the nine first ministers were Liberals they failed to agree. The Dysart government of New Brunswick helped derail the amending formula for the constitution, while Hepburn's refusal to participate in a loan council blocked the scheme to refund provincial debts. The Conservative majority in the Senate turned back the only concrete change agreed to by the provinces.

Meanwhile, there were still 430,000 people out of work at the beginning of 1936, and the relief system continued to operate on the old, ramshackle basis. Faced with a rapidly increasing budget deficit the federal cabinet decided to reduce grants-in-aid for relief by 15 per cent on 1 April, dropping Ontario's payment from $1.05 million to $892,500. Premier Hepburn protested that the cuts imposed by the Bennett government in the summer of 1934 had already forced the province to shoulder three-quarters of the cost of relief in the past year. Now the increases granted in the past December were to be largely taken away. Despite pleas from the Ontario cabinet on behalf of the hard-pressed municipalities, the provincial grant was reduced again in June 1936 to $803,250. So heavy were the demands upon the provincial treasury, Hepburn announced, that he would be forced to bring in an income tax which it was hoped would produce more than $5 million annually.[21]

II

Relations between Mackenzie King and Mitchell Hepburn remained correct, if not amicable, prior to 1937, but during that year a whole series of events occurred which roused the hostility of the Ontario premier. First there was the nagging problem of securing more hydroelectricity at Niagara Falls, blocked by the refusal of the United States to discuss it in isolation from the development of the St Lawrence. Hepburn felt King had failed to act decisively enough on Ontario's behalf. Then in the spring of 1937 came the strike at General Motors of Canada. Hepburn rallied to the support of the company and demanded that Ottawa should expel the American union organizers. The cabinet refused. Then he requested Justice Minister Lapointe to send the RCMP to Oshawa to keep the peace. Over 100 men were dispatched to Toronto in case of need, but the federal government refused a request for a further detachment. Accusing the ministers of vacillating, Hepburn insisted that all the men be withdrawn. When Labour Minister Norman Rogers offered to mediate in the strike if the parties desired, the premier complained to King of his 'unwarranted interference': 'This action is quite in common with the treatment that this Government has received from most of your ministers, and in my opinion constitutes an overt act.'[22]

At the end of May the federal government requested the province to pay for the services of the RCMP. Hepburn repeated his attacks upon the federal ministers, alleging that they had failed to support him at a critical time. A few days later in an address to the Canadian Life Insurance Officers' Association, he reiterated his complaints, declaring, 'I want to say there will be no lawlessness in Ontario. I cannot speak for Canada because we have a vacillating Canadian government in Ottawa ... I am a Reformer – but I am not a Mackenzie King Liberal any longer. I'll tell the whole world that and I hope he hears me.'[23] In an effort to limit the federal budget deficit Ontario's grant-in-aid for relief purposes was further reduced in March 1937 to $600,000 and cut again in July to $480,000 per month. Hepburn complained to Premier T.D. Pattullo of British Columbia that there had been no consultation, no chance for the province to put forward its case: 'The whole attitude of the Dominion Government on this problem had been an arbitrary one and never at any time has the province been consulted with regard to this or any other problem. In general, the attitude of King and his associates has been to treat the Ontario Government or anyone known to be friendly with our administration as so many burglars. Their whole policy has been one of studied insults, one heaped upon another.' Efforts to mediate by Defence Minister Ian Mackenzie, an old friend of the premier, were unsuccessful. 'The whole impression he gave me,' the minister reported to Mackenzie King, 'was one of instability and wounded pride.'[24] Hepburn had by then decided upon an election in the autumn of 1937 to capitalize on the popularity of his stand on the General Motors strike, and he wanted no interference in his campaign by federal politicians. This suited Mackenzie King well enough. He stayed out of the provincial campaign until the very last minute, when he told the press that he hoped that the Liberals would be re-elected.

Hepburn was triumphantly returned with sixty-six Liberals versus only twenty-three Conservatives, and King allowed himself to hope that relations between the two governments might improve, but within a few weeks the two men were embroiled in a foolish dispute over who should be appointed lieutenant-governor of Ontario.[25] No sooner was that settled than an even more bitter public quarrel broke out over the premier's demand to be allowed to export electricity to the United States. Mackenzie King tried his best to remain above the wrangling, but he had to respond to some of Hepburn's more outrageous allegations. By the beginning of 1938 relations between Ontario and the federal government seemed to have reached a new low, owing to Hepburn's disruptive influence.

Mackenzie King was concerned not only with Ontario. He and his advisers were deeply worried about the shaky financial condition of the western provinces; Alberta had already defaulted on an interest payment on 1 April 1936. By the fall of that year both the governor of the Bank of Canada, Graham Towers, and the deputy minister of finance, W.C. Clark, had concluded that a royal commission ought to be set up to examine the balance of revenues and responsibilities within the federal system in the light of recent experience.[26] At the National Finance Committee's only meeting in December 1936 Premier John Bracken of Manitoba made the same suggestion. The other premiers expressed approval, although Provincial Secretary Harry Nixon of Ontario was non-committal in the absence of instructions from Mitchell Hepburn. The prime minister did not show much enthusiasm for the suggestion at first, but he soon changed his mind and informed the House of Commons in mid-February 1937 that he intended to appoint such a body. The cabinet decided that the commission should be a fact-finding group which would examine the financial position of the provinces in the light of their responsibilities and report back by the end of the parliamentary session of 1938.[27] Choosing the members of the commission proved more difficult. Ontario Highways Minister T.B. McQuesten suggested 'as the Ontario representative' the province's deputy treasurer, Chester Walters, the 'foremost authority on public finance in the Dominion' and a man of good political sense who would leave no troubles at the prime minister's door. The idea was unappealing to King in view of Walters's close association with Mitchell Hepburn. The chief justice of Ontario, Newton Rowell, was appointed chairman in July 1937 along with Mr Justice Thibaudeau Rinfret of the Supreme Court and J.W. Dafoe, editor of the Winnipeg *Free Press*. Strong protests from the Maritimes and British Columbia led to the addition of Professors R.A. MacKay of Dalhousie University and H.F. Angus of the University of British Columbia.[28] Within a few months Rinfret's poor health forced his retirement; he was replaced by Dr Joseph Sirois, a Quebec notary and law teacher.

The order-in-council establishing the Royal Commission on Dominion-Provincial Relations noted that the range and cost of governmental services had increased in a way quite unforeseen by the Fathers of Confederation. Lack of clarity in the division of powers had adversely affected the quality of services to the public, and the shortage of provincial and municipal revenues made some reallocation of responsibilities or revenue sources imperative. The commissioners were directed to consider what would 'best effect a balanced relationship between the financial powers and obligations of each governing body and conduce to a more efficient, independent and economical discharge of governmental responsibilities in Canada.' Although feuding with Mackenzie King over the Oshawa strike and the St Lawrence waterway, Premier Hepburn expressed his approval of the commission in 1937: 'This government will co-operate in every possible way. We are entirely satisfied with the personnel of the Federal commission and we feel that an amendment of the BNA Act is long overdue. The Act was made for the people, not the people for Act, and it is generally recognized that the Act is now out of date.'[29]

His views changed once the commissioners got to work. By late 1937 they were hearing testimony from the governments of Manitoba and Saskatchewan. Hepburn, after a meeting with Maurice Duplessis, claimed that it was 'clear from the demands emanating from the western provinces and being submitted to the Rowell Commission that Ontario and Quebec will have to stand together.' The premier reminded reporters that since 47.5 per cent of federal tax revenues came from Ontario, additional transfer payments for the prairie provinces would come mainly from the pockets of Quebeckers and Ontarians.[30] At that time he also began to voice doubts about the wisdom of a constitutional amendment to permit the introduction of a national unemployment insurance scheme. Mackenzie King had decided to press ahead with this change without waiting for the commission's report, provided all of the provinces approved. When the matter was first raised by King in November 1937, Hepburn had expressed enthusiasm and announced that he was 'prepared to waive any constitutional objections and to give the fullest measure of co-operation and support to the proposed amendments to the British North America Act.' Then the acrimonious dispute with Mackenzie King over power exports arose. The Ontario premier now complained that the prime minister refused to give him any details about the plan he proposed to implement. 'It is clear to me,' he wrote Maurice Duplessis, 'that with the Western provinces hopelessly bankrupt any national scheme of unemployment insurance will have to be borne by the two central provinces, and if unemployment insurance is necessary it probably will be better to run our own show.'[31] In January 1938 King forwarded a draft amendment to the BNA Act to each of the premiers, and Hepburn protested to reporters: 'Mr. King has asked us for a blank cheque. He wants us to consent to the revision of the B.N.A. Act without telling us exactly what he proposes to do. We agree in principle but we want the details, and if we consider the measure does not meet the needs of Ontario we reserve the right to object. Our consent to a revision of the B.N.A. Act is predicated on the condition that we will be able to study the bill which the Federal Government proposes.'³² What the premier apparently feared was a narrowly drawn scheme, which would exclude a large percentage of the labour force such as seasonal workers from the insurance plan. If so, the province would still find itself bearing a heavy relief burden from the employable unemployed without financial assistance from Ottawa. Nonetheless, since Hepburn knew that unemployment insurance was a popular notion in his province, he included in the 1938 throne speech a reference to the 'keen interest' which Ontario had in the proposed plan. But when some of the provinces failed to agree to the constitutional amendment, the federal cabinet decided in April 1938 to drop the matter for the time being. Thus the second effort by the government since its return to office to amend the constitution was abandoned.³³

By the spring of 1938 nothing had occurred to temper the antagonism which Mitchell Hepburn felt towards Mackenzie King. The debate over power exports dragged on in parliament until the Americans put an end to it by banning all additional imports from Canada. The premier frequently complained about periodic reductions in the grant-in-aid for unemployment relief. In March he claimed that Labour Minister Norman Rogers had reneged on a promise to match provincial spending for relief. Ottawa, he declared, was 'trying to shelve the jobless on us entirely.' The federal government ought to recognize 'the prior right of the provinces in the field of income tax,' by making provincial tax payments a deduction from taxable income. A resolution calling for this received unanimous support in the legislature.³⁴ Even Mackenzie King found himself tested to the limit by this barrage of criticisms from Queen's Park: '[W]e have all tried to avoid giving "offence," and much that we would like to do we have refrained from doing for that reason. Just how long it will be wise to continue this policy is a matter, I think, which will require immediate consideration. I have been trying to keep things on an even keel, but I confess that at times one's patience becomes sorely tried.'³⁵

In this charged atmosphere, the Royal Commission on Dominion-Provincial Relations opened its hearings in Toronto. Hepburn was ready; he and Duplessis had consulted fully on the position the two provinces should adopt towards the enquiry. 'The more I read of the representations made by the other provinces,' wrote Hepburn, 'the more convinced I am of the necessity of Ontario and Quebec resisting together, and in no uncertain way, the ever-increasing, unreasonable and impossible demands ... I can readily understand the advantage it would be to the other provinces for them to raid the Federal Treasury, particularly when Ontario and Quebec contribute 80% of the revenue.' With the help of W.H. Moore, a Liberal member of parliament, the premier drafted a personal brief, while Chester Walters and Professor Kenneth Taylor of McMaster University worked on a detailed statement of the Ontario government's position. Both documents were discussed by the two premiers at a meeting on 20 April. To show his displeasure with the proceedings the premier refused to return from his farm to welcome the commissioners when they opened their hearings on 25 April.[36] Attorney-General Gordon Conant greeted them, then left them to hear private briefs in the legislative chamber. During the next week or so, one observer reported, 'public interest in the Commission reached an all-time low.'[37] That situation changed dramatically, however, when Hepburn finally appeared on 2 May, flanked by seventeen ministers and civil servants, to deliver his views to the commission.

The premier left no doubt about his distaste for the whole proceeding.[38] For a start he now objected to entrusting the revision of the constitution to a royal commission: 'I have always regarded Confederation as the outcome of a conference ... If there is to be a change in Confederation, in my opinion, it can be brought about only by renewed conference of the representatives of the people and with unanimity of approval.' He charged that in addition to ignoring the compact of Confederation, the western provinces had been given advance notice of the appointment of the commission; they had gathered in Regina in June 1937 and agreed to demand $58 million per year in additional grants. Although Ontario would have to supply half of this money, the province had not even been consulted by Ottawa, an omission that 'went deeper than discourtesy.' If a dominion-provincial conference were not going to be held, the commission should at least have been chosen by parliament, not the cabinet, in view of its importance. All in all, the Ontario government had so many doubts about the legitimacy of the proceedings that it would not appear before the commission 'either as an applicant or as a defendant.'

Hepburn also made it clear that he believed that the job of the commission was simply to provide an elaborate justification for an increase in the powers of the federal government. He served notice that he and his ministers were 'not here to bargain away functions with which we have been charged, not here to trade off the resources we are sworn to preserve.' Indeed, he deplored the whole trend towards centralization. While the division of powers was not inviolable and there was clearly a demand for services unheard of in 1867, he reminded the commissioners that 'our grandfathers were definitely and bitterly opposed to the concentration of political power.' More authority for Ottawa might set Canada on the same road down which some European nations had travelled towards fascism: 'The accumulation of power leads to autocracy; its distribution is the safety zone of democracy ... Canadians ought to strengthen the hands of the government closest to the people or get ready to look back on the past seventy-five years as merely an interlude of freedom.'

The Ontario premier claimed that 'by rearranging the public services we may eliminate waste, increase efficiency and at the same time bring the government closer to the people – all without changing the Constitution.' What was needed was to transfer services in areas where jurisdiction overlapped, like agriculture and health, exclusively to the provinces. The federal government would still have plenty of new responsibilities of its own, such as central banking, aeronautics, and broadcasting. Hepburn rejected the arguments of the poorer provinces that the provision of a uniform standard of social services for Canadians required federal programs: 'It may be in a country with Canada's economic diversities "federal codes" are impracticable.' The cost of social programs ought to be charged against the incomes arising in each area; for 'Equity between the provinces is impossible. Prince Edward Island can never be like Manitoba; Ontario may not have the coal and petroleum with which Alberta is so richly endowed; and yet, somehow, we must get along together.'

If the provinces were to have even wider responsibilities, Hepburn was convinced that they needed larger revenues. Increased federal subsidies he rejected as a bone of contention between the provinces. A reallocation of tax fields would be preferable. If the provinces had first crack at income taxes they could finance services on any scale their citizens wanted. The obvious rejoinder to this suggestion was that the prairie provinces had been unable to cope with even their present duties during the depression. But Hepburn insisted that the westerners were 'the makers of their own (and other people's) misfortunes'; the farmers had probably suffered less than unemployed industrial workers in the cities. Over-specialization had caused over-production of wheat, and 'if the millions of state funds (provincial and federal), expended on wheat seed that blew away, had been put into mills and factories the west would have been able to clothe itself and provide most of the goods of life.' After all, some 99,000 farm operators received over 50 per cent of the income generated by wheat, and the premier did not feel it was 'necessary to upset Confederation on their behalf.' Western politicians were given a stern reminder of the virtues of thrift: 'Provinces are fiscal entities; and governments like individuals must learn to manage within their means.' Hepburn insisted that Ontario was presenting no counter-claim against the other provinces. Instead of rendering accounts to one another, all political leaders should be working for a better Canada, he declared sententiously, and proceeded at once to ignore his own advice by concluding brutally that if the western provinces could not finance an adequate level of social services out of their own resources, they would have to amalgamate.

The commission members, who had been given Hepburn's statement in advance, listened in glum silence. Chairman Newton Rowell did make an effort to soothe the umbrageous premier by noting that the commissioners 'were not appointed and we do not understand our functions to revise the constitution ... We are a fact-finding body ... If on the facts as we find them it appears that there should be some change in the financial relations between the Dominion and the provinces, it is our duty to recommend what those changes should be, but our recommendations must be within the strict limits of a federal constitution.' Their report, he added, would have to be considered by a dominion-provincial conference. Others were less restrained. Western outrage at the Ontario premier knew no bounds; J.B. McGeachy denounced him in the Winnipeg *Free Press* as 'the Great Hepburn, defender of hard-pressed Ontario against the idle rich of Saskatchewan and Manitoba,' while condemning his statement as 'full of half-baked economics, appeals to prejudice, jumbled logic and parish politics.' Even the eastern press regarded this performance by the premier as an incitement to national disunity.[39]

Perhaps fortunately for the reputation of the Ontario government the 'general statement' prepared by Chester Walters and Professor Taylor was more restrained.[40] Canada, they argued, required a federal constitution; a central government was needed for control of the natural unity of the St Lawrence system (as extended by the railways), while 'economic diversity, differences of race and culture and sheer size' made local self-government essential. This fact had been recognized in 1867 when Confederation came about as a result of agreement between the separate colonies. Greater centralization was not the solution to present-day problems; for they had different origins and distinct remedies in each region. Reducing the provinces to glorified municipalities would accomplish nothing. Manitoba had suggested, for instance, that the federal government should meet half the cost of mothers' allowances, hospitals, and the care of the insane, and assume all payments for old age pensions, unemployment insurance, succession duty collection, and the management of the provincial debt. The result would be, in the words of Ontario's legal counsel, D.W. Lang, 'rigid control and central authority not consistent with the federal principle as we know it in Canada.'[41] If some redistribution of powers were necessary, it could come about only through the 'time-honoured British custom of conference' between the provinces and the dominion.

According to the 'general statement' the problems facing Canada in 1938 were not constitutional at all but were simply financial. Provincial subsidies combined with the income from the public domain had been expected to meet the basic financial needs of the provinces forever. In the nineteenth century this expectation had proved true, but 'changes in the functions of government, dictated by changing technical conditions, have altered the whole base of provincial public finance and completely destroyed the balance of revenues and responsibilities set up by the framers of our Constitution.' Since 1900, federal outlays had quadrupled, but Ontario spent thirteen times as much in 1937 as it had at the turn of the century. Even the wealthy provinces were feeling the pinch, and the natural result was a demand in some quarters for increased federal transfer payments. Such payments were natural and proper within a federal system, and the citizens of Ontario had always met their share, and more than their share, of such costs. But Professor Taylor produced figures to show that while industrial development might have made some regions richer than others, progressive taxation bore most heavily on the well-off. Between 1927 and 1937 the percentage of federal taxes collected in Ontario had increased from 40.4 to 45 per cent, while the share of the prairie provinces declined from 21.5 to 15.3 per cent. The net result of the existing federal financial system, therefore, was to transfer between $75 million and $80 million annually from Ontario to the west and the Maritimes. Moreover, a large number of federal loans and guarantees granted to the prairie governments would clearly have to be written off, and Ontarians would have to cover about half the cost of that as well.⁴²

As Chester Walters admitted privately, this 'general statement' was intended to 'Show that part Ontario has played in building up Canada and demonstrate, if possible, that with our share of the national income and with the financial burden that we have undertaken, the taxpaying capacity of the people of Ontario has been burdened almost to its limit.'⁴³ From this one obvious conclusion flowed: giving the federal government wider authority was not the answer to Canada's problems. Ontarians would still be called upon to meet the lion's share of the cost of new programs, and Ottawa would almost certainly insist on taking over the most lucrative tax sources. But, faced with the rising demand for provincial services, Ontario could not afford to surrender any more revenue. Nor were larger subsidies the answer. In 1880, 60 per cent of Ontario's revenues had come from federal grants, in 1937 only 3 per cent. Now it was imperative that the province should have more tax sources because Ontario was 'convinced that the development of agricultural policies, roads, education, health, mothers' allowances and other public welfare activities can be more efficiently entrusted to the province than to the Dominion.' The province 'must, in fact, insist on a more strict recognition of its clearly established legal and moral rights in the field of direct taxation and natural resources.'⁴⁴ Between 1867 and 1913, for instance, resources had netted Ontario about $40 million and between 1913 and 1920 revenues and expenditures in that field had roughly balanced one another. Since that time, however, the province had invested almost $250 million in resource development and had received only $150 million in revenues in return, leaving a huge deficit to be covered. To the annoyance of the provincial authorities, 'The Dominion Government by its corporation tax on the profits of mining and lumbering has levied a tax that belongs to the provinces, and, therefore, disregards the intention of Confederation that the natural resources should be the particular property of the provinces and that any benefit that should be derived therefrom should flow to the provinces.' Nearly three-quarters of the taxes paid by the mining industry went not to Queen's Park but to Ottawa.

Even more irritating to the Ontario government was the federal income tax. The 'general statement' rehearsed this long-standing grievance fully: how the tax had been introduced in a wartime emergency; how Ontario had protested against it ever since 1918; how the federal government had not only continued it, but assumed a prior right to it 'contrary to the spirit of the B.N.A. Act and not in accordance with the conventions of the Constitution.' In 1936 Mitchell Hepburn had been forced to impose a provincial income tax in an effort to balance the budget. While the tax raised over $6 million, $3 million had been paid out in municipal subsidies and another $3.3 million had been required to cover old age pension and mothers' allowance contributions formerly met by the municipalities. The net result of abolishing all civic income taxes was thus a $300,000 deficit to be met from general revenues. 'So the income tax grab of the province of Ontario,' as Chester Walters quaintly put it, 'is like a man leading with his left eye into a man's right fist';[45] a situation all the more unjust because the federal debt would stabilize if military pensions and railway deficits levelled off. Any national scheme of social insurance should be contributory and self-supporting, while the province would face ever-increasing demands for funds for education, housing, health, and welfare. If the federal government would simply acknowledge the province's 'moral and equitable right to priority in income taxes and all other direct taxes,' then Ontario would take over total responsibility for aid to the unemployed and for municipal tax relief.

The 'general statement' maintained that such an arrangement would be in keeping with the federal nature of Canadian society: 'The proper role of the state in relation to social services is still a matter of controversy ... There are wide differences of opinion in Canada as to how far government should go in these matters ... Under these circumstances the provinces should be free to follow their own lines of historical development.' Thus, it was claimed, 'A desire for local control does not denote any dissatisfaction with Confederation but rather serves to cement it,' and the statement went on, 'We submit that each province, if it is to enjoy that measure of political self-government which is the essence of Canadian federalism, must have the right to impose its own standards of fiscal morality in its own fields of taxation. After the provinces have established their policies the Dominion may impose its conception of fiscal justice in relation to Confederation as a whole.'

This Ontario brief represented a fundamental challenge to the notion that the federal government had a duty to provide a minimum standard of social services to all Canadians. Commissioner H.F. Angus asked Chester Walters whether he believed that there should be a transfer of wealth from the richer to the poorer parts of the federation. Walters insisted that the Hepburn government supported this principle but complained that the federal government had used the income tax without regard for the 'crying need of the provinces as well as the province's desire to help the distressed municipalities.' This injustice would be remedied if the province controlled the income tax. When Chief Justice Rowell suggested that the dominion had to raise its revenues wherever it could, Walters retorted: 'It is not for the people of Czechoslovakia to tell Herr Hitler where he is to get a further outlet.' Rowell could only remark sadly that he hoped the relations between Ontario and the federal government were not similar to those of Hitler and the Czechs. When

Angus asked Walters how fiscal redistribution from rich to poor areas could take place without the income tax, he replied lamely that federal corporation taxes might do the job.[46]

Rowell pointed out to the Ontario representatives that what suited them might not be a universal solution: '[T]here are some provinces that cannot handle unemployment relief even if they have full priority on income tax ... particularly the western provinces.' Walters was unyielding: 'I have understood from conversations and items that I have read in the press ... that these provinces are able to meet debts and carry the load ... If they are to carry on ... as Provinces they should be able to find ways and means to look after their local affairs.' If the federal government wanted to give higher subsidies to some provinces on an interim basis it could do so.[47] When R.A. MacKay pressed him to admit that this was hardly a sound foundation for a federal system, Walters was evasive: 'I do not think I should attempt to outline a new scheme of Confederation with respect to transference by way of subsidies from the central cash box to the Provinces.' That could be left to the commission.[48]

Once Walters's testimony was completed, Professor Taylor submitted a detailed refutation of the claims of the prairie provinces concerning the disadvantageous effects of the tariff. He supplied figures to bolster Hepburn's claim that over $75 million per year was transferred from Ontario to the west and the Maritimes through federal taxation.[49] Welfare Minister E.W. Cross and a number of other departmental officials were also heard from before the province's counsel, D.W. Lang, wound up after five days the formal presentation of Ontario's view. By that time relations between the premier and the commissioners had been improved somewhat by an informal dinner, at which Hepburn entertained them with a skit about an English gentleman and an Arab, using a napkin as a prop.[50] Yet for all the goodwill, Attorney-General Gordon Conant stoutly reiterated the views of his colleagues in his closing address to the commission.[51] He was critical of 'the thought ... that the Federal Government should take over the griefs, worries and responsibilities that are confronting some of the provinces in the Dominion, and should extend the taxation which has been commenced ... We in this province look upon that with very great alarm.' Somewhat incoherently he invoked the shades of the Fathers of Confederation: they had done 'all they could foresee evidently to bring about a just distribution of the burden of nationhood upon which they were emerging. I submit again that they had not thought that their handiwork might conceivably be entirely destroyed by the basis on which they left the power of taxation.'

Conant defended his province's stand; Ontario was no 'Midas, as it were, the villain in the piece sitting back without obligations but with unbounded wealth.' The government had its own scale of priorities, and the loss of taxation on incomes and natural resources could seriously jeopardize its financial stability. After all, 'the word "transfer" ... [is] a refinement on the good old-fashioned idea of taking from one person or body and giving ... to somebody else ... And the matter of alarm so far as this province is concerned is in the present tendency to apply that to our present day condition.' While admitting that the root of the problem was that 'all the provinces are not in the same economic condition,' he nevertheless insisted that 'Ontario ... is not the one primarily responsible for this economic status, whatever may have been the cause.'

The attorney-general had already suggested to the commissioners at the dinner that their proceedings might be set to music, and the theme song of the other provinces, he said, should be 'I Want What I Want When I Want It.'[52] A good many people might have added that this would have seemed an entirely accurate title for the Ontario brief. Yet those who criticized the province's submission as harmful to national unity often ignored the fact that it came not solely out of Mitchell Hepburn's antagonism for Mackenzie King or some anti-western bias of the premier. Rather it represented a typical, if somewhat flamboyantly phrased, statement of the Ontario's government's traditional view of the federal system and the province's role within it. The emphasis, as always, was squarely on autonomy rather than on equalization. Shorn of its statistical stage sets and rhetorical flourishes it might have been prepared in similar circumstances by any government of the province after the First World War. Hepburn simply felt that Ontario had already been asked to give too much to Ottawa to be passed on to the poorer regions. He rejected the notion of federal minimum standards and argued that in a democratic federation each province ought to fix and finance its own level of services. Having the highest level of such services already, Ontario naturally preferred to keep its tax revenues and continue to improve standards. There is some evidence that the commissioners were impressed by the force of the arguments in the 'general statement' even if they did not entirely accept them. The province had been expected to take a firm line, and the staff work by Walters and Taylor was taken seriously by the commission's officials. Indeed, Taylor was later approached to join the commission staff.[53]

'The long deep note of discontent' sounded by Mitchell Hepburn before the commission by no means exhausted his list of grievances about Mackenzie King's handling of federal-provincial relations during 1938. In mid-June he complained to Finance Minister Dunning about federal efforts to stimulate employment through self-liquidating municipal works projects. Hepburn warned that his province would refuse to guarantee loans for such purposes: 'The way to stimulate the building trade is not this foolish housing scheme which exists only on borrowed money. There is certainly nothing creditable or even clever about this boasted plan. The only way to stimulate building is by the reduction of taxes.'[54] At the end of that month he also protested strongly against an increase in federal gift taxes. King insisted that these taxes, first imposed by the Bennett administration, were not intended to raise large revenues but to prevent income tax evasion by the wealthy through the giving of large income-producing gifts. Nonetheless, the premier seized the occasion for a diatribe against federal tax policy:

Ever since the introduction of the Business War Profits Tax and the Income War Tax Act the invasion by the Dominion authorities of the Provincial field of taxation has been the subject of protests by practically every provincial government regardless of political stripe ...

Various Provinces made strong representations before the Rowell Commission, complaining bitterly against the impoverishment of their own revenues by reason of the Dominion's invasion of the field of direct taxation, which, according to the implicit understanding at Confederation, was to be left to the Provinces ...

I desire to protest against the further invasion of Provincial fields of taxation, which invasion seriously menaces the budgetary position of some of the very Provinces you claim to be attempting to assist.[55]

When King refused to drop the amendments to the gift tax, Hepburn publicly denounced him for violating the understanding 'that there would be no tax changes while the [Rowell] Commission was sitting.' The federal government's action was, he declared, 'little short of effrontery to the Provinces that entered protests, if not a snub to the Commission itself.' In view of this attitude, Ontario would cease to co-operate with the commission in future. The prime minister, however, insisted that the province's change of heart was of no importance, since its views had already been heard. The commission would go ahead and report as planned. He rejected the premier's claim that its value had been destroyed: 'It is not the business of the Commission to change the constitution. Its business is to find facts that will be of value to a Conference later.'[56] Privately, however, federal officials were concerned that Hepburn might try to arrange a conference of the premiers without inviting representation from Ottawa, 'to try to line them all up for increased federal subsidies and relief responsibility and decreased federal powers otherwise.'[57]

Mitchell Hepburn took no steps in this direction, but his persistent complaints made the commissioners wonder about the wisdom of their plan to hold further hearings in Ottawa during September 1938 at which the provinces could comment upon the briefs already submitted, followed by a round table discussion with all the premiers. If Ontario refused to attend and Quebec and Alberta followed suit, only one-third of the Canadian population would be represented. The commission's secretary, Alex Skelton, sought Mackenzie King's advice on what ought to be done but he got no help. Having appointed this body to draw the fire of angry provincial leaders, the prime minister refused to get involved in its activities beyond constantly urging that its report be completed. Despite a strong protest from British Columbia the commissioners decided to cancel the round table, and the research studies prepared for the commission were submitted to the provinces by mail. Further hearings were scheduled at which the premiers could be heard individually.[58]

Newton Rowell fell ill in the summer of 1938, and once it became clear that he could not resume the chairmanship, Dr Joseph Sirois was appointed to replace him.[59] By the beginning of October the prime minister had become most impatient because the commission had failed to complete its report. When Sirois informed him that it could not be ready before the spring of 1939, King directed Ernest Lapointe to try to hurry the commissioners along.[60] Lapointe could do little, however, because the commission had already scheduled the final series of hearings for the end of November. Only then could the commissioners settle down to drafting their report based upon the millions of words of briefs, testimony, and staff studies.

Mitchell Hepburn, meanwhile, kept up a volley of complaints about the federal government and the commission. Canadian unity, he declared, would by achieved only 'when Ontario is no longer being made the milch cow of the rest of the country.' He reiterated his charges that changes in the federal Income War Tax Act violated the understanding upon which the commission had been appointed. Henceforth, his government would have nothing to do with the commission or its findings. In a speech to the Empire Club in Toronto in mid-December 1938, he repeated all these allegations, going out of his way to deny the charge, 'continually levelled against Ontario, to the effect that we are an exploiting province. If it were not for the riches of Ontario, I don't know what would happen to the rest of the Dominion. ... We submit to these drains upon us because we want to maintain Confederation ... It doesn't necessarily follow that we should be the goats of everybody.' On his return from a trip to Australia in February 1939 he remarked jauntily that the federal government now seemed 'worse than he thought it before he left.'[61]

III

During 1939 the Ontario premier continued to snipe away at Ottawa. What particularly alarmed Mackenzie King were his veiled threats to back the Conservatives in the forthcoming federal election. The prime minister blamed the whole row on 'wounded vanity on Hepburn's part and an unwillingness on my part to submit to dictatorship of any kind.'[62] Only the outbreak of war in September brought a temporary *rapprochement* as negotiations over the development of the St Lawrence were revived. Taking advantage of this more cordial atmosphere, and of the election of a Liberal government in Quebec, King decided to renew his efforts to secure provincial approval for a constitutional amendment to permit a national unemployment insurance scheme. He approached the four provinces which seemed likely to object, New Brunswick, Alberta, Quebec, and Ontario. If they agreed, the change could be made without waiting for the Rowell-Sirois

Commission's report, and this move might also offset pressure for immediate action on the commission's other recommendations.[63]

Labour Minister Norman McLarty was dispatched to Toronto to sound out the provincial cabinet and found them willing to co-operate. Despite his reservations about King's method of proceeding, Hepburn had never withdrawn the consent he had given in 1937. Unemployment insurance clearly had wide popular appeal in a highly industrialized province like Ontario. An actuarially sound plan would require no contributions by the province and would lessen the cost of unemployment relief. Once the reluctant assent of Alberta and Quebec had been obtained, the change was quickly made. It was fortunate that King had acted swiftly once he decided to proceed with the constitutional amendment; for the brief *détente* between Ottawa and Toronto came to an abrupt end within a week. On 18 January 1940 Premier Hepburn moved a resolution in the provincial legislature 'regretting that the Federal Government has made so little effort to prosecute Canada's duty in the war in the vigorous manner the people of Canada desire to see.' This passed with the support of all but ten Liberals. Mackenzie King immediately seized upon this as the pretext for calling the election he had been contemplating for some time, and to Hepburn's chagrin his government was easily re-elected.[64]

Despite the prime minister's impatience, the Rowell-Sirois Commission did not complete its report until February 1940, in the middle of the campaign. King then had to ask the chairman to hold it back so that the recommendations would not become an issue in the election. Not until 10 May did the provinces receive advance copies of the report which was made public when parliament met one week later.[65]

After three years of deliberations the commissioners had concluded that developments since 1867, particularly the economic collapse after 1930, had destroyed any 'logical relationship ... between the local income of any province and the constitutional powers and responsibilities of that province.' By 1937 over $250 million per year was being spent on social services, and relief costs had 'seriously strained' the financial stability of eight of the nine provinces. It was doubtful whether the hard-pressed provincial governments would be able to carry even their present share of the cost of public services in future. Federal grants-in-aid had proved a 'thoroughly unsuitable' means of financing new programs. As long as the primary responsibility for relief rested with the provinces and municipalities, federal assistance could be handed out 'only as a matter of grace.' Over the past decade this system had produced 'large inter-governmental debts, arbitrary transfers and difficult problems of administration which have seriously disrupted the harmony of Dominion-Provincial relations.' Moreover, regional disparities had actually increased.

Such a situation cried out for radical reform, because Canadian unity was likely be seriously endangered, 'if the citizens of distressed provinces come to feel that their interests are completely disregarded by those of their more prosperous neighbours, and that those who have been their full partners in better times now tell them they must get along as best they can and accept inferior education and social services.' Therefore, the commissioners had sought to find some way 'in which the financial position of the provinces could be improved and assured without disastrous financial consequences to the Federal Government on whose efficient functioning all the provinces are dependent.' To this end they devised 'Plan I,' which provided that Ottawa should take complete responsibility for the 'employable unemployed.' The provinces would withdraw from the field of income taxes, succession duties, and corporation taxes, and all existing subsidies would cease. In return the federal authorities would assume the entire burden of provincial debt and pay over to the poorer provinces 'national adjustment grants.' These grants would permit provincial governments to provide services equal to the Canadian average without imposing above-average taxes. From time to time the amount would be adjusted as necessary, and emergency grants could also be awarded to meet unexpected situations. Thus a new principle would underlie Canadian federalism in future: '[P]rovincial need has not hitherto been expressly recognized as a principle of federal assistance, but we think it should be. Our recommendations for adjustment and emergency grants are based on this principle ... [T]hey aim to make possible for every province, social and educational services on the standards set by the provinces in the "peak" years, 1923-31.' For provincial governments which might wish to provide a different level of services the federal government would promise to respect those tax fields left to the provinces and to allow them to set their own priorities.

The commissioners recognized that their proposals would not be acceptable to some provinces. In an obvious reference to their experiences in Toronto they remarked sourly that 'Some provincial governments explained to the Commission that they could pay their own way and perform their functions to their own complete satisfaction, if the Dominion were to assume this or that onerous service, or were to withdraw from this or that field of taxation, or were to increase their subsidies.' The report declared firmly that 'on examination it was found that a solution on these lines could not be generalized and that, while it might meet the needs of one or more of the provinces, it would do so at the cost of impairing the Dominion's finances, or of prejudicing the position of the other provinces. The Commissioners were, therefore, compelled to dismiss any such solution as inadequate.' They insisted, however, that they had been careful 'to safeguard the autonomy of the provinces, and to ensure each province the ability to decide issues of particular importance to itself. We emphasize throughout ... the importance of limiting transfer of jurisdiction to what is strictly necessary.'

Plan I, it was pointed out, had much to offer Ontario, Canada's industrial and commercial centre: 'Anything which stabilizes conditions in Canada and which makes it possible for other provincial governments to maintain the level of their services will be of great benefit to the people of Ontario and the financial stability of that province.' Since Ontario residents paid half the federal taxes, they had a deep interest in placing the finances of other provinces on a 'rational and businesslike basis.' Admittedly Ontario was too well-off to qualify for a national adjustment grant, but the commission's figures showed that the implementation of plan I in 1937 would have produced a net improvement in the province's finances of $5,326,000 and provided an additional $2,388,000 for its municipalities.

In case plan I was too radical, the commissioners presented 'plan II' as an alternative. It involved, in the words of the report, 'simply a continuation of the present system of financial arrangements between the Dominion and the provinces with the exception of the Dominion assumption of responsibility for ... unemployed employables.[5]. The commission was careful to point out that while plan II might appear to provide substantial surpluses for Ontario, British Columbia, Manitoba, and Alberta, they were largely illusory in the first two instances. Plan II would actually cost the federal government an additional $13 million per year, which would have to come from taxes levied on the most prosperous provinces. The Commissioners concluded that plan II would not really be a satisfactory alternative, especially since the war had already led the federal government to increase its competition with the provinces for the most lucrative tax fields: 'Palliatives of this sort, however attractive superficially, are damaging and dangerous.' In summing up their recommendations the commissioners took a final poke at the likes of Mitchell Hepburn: 'National unity and provincial autonomy must not be thought of as competitors for the citizen's allegiance, for in Canada at least, they are but two facets of the same thing. National unity must be based on provincial autonomy, and provincial autonomy cannot be assured unless a strong feeling of national unity exists throughout Canada.'

What use the politicians would make of the Rowell-Sirois report remained to be seen. As a keen student of Mackenzie King's political methods, Commissioner J.W. Dafoe recognized that 'The chief danger to the Report was that the Dominion Government would, after saying that it was a grand piece of work, put it on the highest and most remote shelf and then forget about it.' Even though Maurice Duplessis was out of office and Mitchell Hepburn, it was to be hoped, was chastened by the recent federal election, Dafoe admitted that 'It will take a good deal of pressure to get action either during the war, or even in the period immediately following, unless all the interests who think the recommendations should be carried out can support one another in their pressure upon the Government.'[66] Dafoe proved entirely correct. When Premier John Bracken of Manitoba suggested an immediate conference to discuss the report, he received a temporizing reply from the prime minister: 'With the war in progress, it would certainly be felt by many that the government should await developments before seeking to bring the provinces as a whole into conference with the Dominion on matters so all-important as those dealt with in the Commission's report.'[67]

Yet other more powerful influences were working on getting action on the report. In July the federal finance minister, J.L. Ilsley, met with representatives of Canadian banks and insurance and investment companies, who 'pointed out that they had put up substantial amounts of money in recent years to avoid provincial defaults during the time that the Royal Commission on Dominion-Provincial Relations was studying the situation ... If no action was going to be taken to implement the recommendations, the institutions did not feel that they would be justified in becoming further involved.' Finance department officials were also convinced that changes in the system of taxation suggested in the report would make it easier to finance the war, and 'in addition to being a necessary step to make the maximum possible war effort, it has constructive and lasting value for post-war difficulties. It need not be presented as war legislation, but it should have a very wide appeal to the many Canadians who are eager to see Canada brush aside petty sectional differences and selfish local interests which weaken her in the present emergency.'[68]

In August 1940 the prime minister received an alarming report from the governor of the Bank of Canada.[69] Graham Towers pointed out that the four western provinces had been experiencing great difficulty in meeting interest payments on their debts and that Alberta had actually defaulted. He reiterated that the country's financial institutions would endanger their own stability if they had to carry these provinces any longer by taking up their unsaleable new issues. There was a strong possibility that Saskatchewan and New Brunswick would default in the next few months unless the fiscal changes recommended in the report were introduced. If New Brunswick defaulted, Nova Scotia would probably be unable to refund its debts and would also have to default. Towers concluded: 'It is hard to say how far the trouble would spread, but I think it is safe to say that the repercussion would be very serious, and likely to have a bad effect on Dominion credit and the Dominion's war financing.'

Towers also emphasized the need for a reallocation of tax fields. Not only had federal taxes risen since the war began but five provinces had increased their income or corporation taxes as well. Future tax increases would mean greater pressure on taxpayers, and the need for an efficient system of taxation to lessen the strain was becoming more and more acute. Finally, Towers painted a gloomy picture of the post-war era. Mass unemployment was certain and 'on such a scale in some areas as to make it quite impossible to contemplate local responsibility for financing, planning or administration.' Only one-quarter of the unemployed would be protected by the new insurance plan, and national relief programs would still be required. If Ottawa tried to push the responsibility onto the provinces and municipalities with their inadequate resources, 'Is it not likely that workers will face unemployment in the post-war period with much greater resentment – to put it mildly – than displayed during the depression years? In the interests of peace, order and good government the Dominion may well have to assume full responsibility. But if it does so without having made other arrangements along the lines contemplated in the Sirois report, the financial situation will be chaotic.' Towers was convinced that the implementation of the report could not be left until peacetime: 'In fact ... the necessity for solving the problems under discussion is rendered more acute by reasons of the war and inevitable post-war readjustments.'

The Prime Minister created a special cabinet committee headed by the finance minister, and on 19 September 1940 the committee held an all-day meeting with officials of the finance department and the Bank of Canada. It was decided that Ilsley should approach each of the provinces and sound them out on their willingness to implement the changes recommended by the commission. He was authorized to take a tough line with recalcitrant provinces, warning them that the cost of mobilization would soon make it necessary to increase succession duties and corporation taxes. The introduction of gas and liquor rationing would also severely affect provinces like Ontario which depended heavily upon consumption taxes.[70]

When the Rowell-Sirois report had first appeared, acting Premier Harry Nixon told a reporter: 'My advice at this time is to concentrate all our energies on winning the war. We will debate these matters afterwards.' An unidentified treasury official was more direct: 'There isn't a chance in the world of the Ontario government accepting the recommendations ... The Federal Government is trying to sell us a bill of goods and take plenty of return for little.' A study of the report by the provincial department of health was also highly critical. Health services were to remain a provincial responsibility, but the provinces were asked to give up their prime tax sources and the right to independent capital borrowing. How then could Ontario continue to provide services at the existing level? The study concluded that Ontario should 'argue the point of reasonable standard in public health against national average,' since the commissioners admitted the existing average was highly inadequate.[71]

Finance Minister Ilsley's hopes were not high when he set off for Toronto in late October. He met with the premier and a number of his colleagues, Nixon, Highway Minister T.B. McQuesten, and Chester Walters. Although the premier was friendly, he stated frankly that he remained 'irreconcilably opposed' to the changes. Although he proved poorly informed about the details of plan 1, he complained about the proposal to lump together provincial and municipal debts, because he argued that Ontario municipalities had been much thriftier than their Quebec counterparts during the depression. Now Ottawa proposed to take over the entire burden and make the taxpayers of Ontario carry the largest share of it. When Ilsley reported this response to the cabinet, the prime minister persuaded his colleagues that Hepburn's opposition ruled out any possibility of holding a dominion-provincial conference to discuss the proposed changes. King and Ernest Lapointe believed that there was no point in forcing another open clash with Hepburn on the issue, and they preferred to try to muddle through somehow. But Ilsley's cabinet committee disagreed. They believed that properly presented, the proposed fiscal changes would be well received as war measures, even in Ontario.

They preferred to risk a confrontation with Mitchell Hepburn, and in view of the dire warnings of the financial experts about the need for speedy action, their views eventually carried the day. The cabinet agreed to call a conference, because the ministers recognized that this was a necessary preliminary to the introduction of tax reform, even if no agreement could be reached.[72] 'It will serve the advantage of enabling our government to state clearly the financial problem as it presents itself to the government at this time of war,' wrote King. 'It will lay the ground for such action as may shortly become imperative, and it should help to advance the necessary reforms by at least a step.'[73]

Since the prime minister believed that the dominion-provincial conference would accomplish little, he resisted the idea of committing his government by endorsing the recommendations of the Rowell-Sirois Commission. In a draft of his invitation to the premiers he pencilled out the declaration that his administration was 'wholly in favour of the Report' and substituted the more ambiguous phrase: 'The Report commends itself strongly to our judgement.' Despite the stubborn efforts of Mines Minister T.A. Crerar to commit the government to endorse the report, he refused to go further, telling his colleagues that 'if we take the "take it or leave it" attitude, that attitude would be blamed for the failure of the Conference ... Hepburn and Aberhart would like [nothing] better than for the Federal Government and myself in particular to take an arbitrary and dictatorial position. Hepburn would run his provincial [election] campaign on the effort of Ottawa to take from Ontario all its power, privileges, rights, to sacrifice them to Quebec or to the Prairies.'[74]

The Ontario premier agreed to attend the conference. His formal reply noted that he had hoped to postpone this discussion until the war was over, so that the controversy might not 'impair national unity and the effective prosecution of the war,' but he promised to be present. For the next two and a half months he maintained an uncharacteristic silence on the subject of federal-provincial relations, although this did not indicate any change of heart. One federal official reported that Chester Walters had complained to him about the 'extensive propaganda' in favour of the Rowell-Sirois report: 'Members of Parliament and Senators were being button-holed in the streets urging that the report be adopted.'[75] When R.M. Fowler, a former staff member of the royal commission, made a public speech advocating the adoption of the report, the premier promptly dismissed him from a position with the Ontario government. In his usual colourful style, Mitch Hepburn advised a friendly Liberal that he was coming to Ottawa 'with blood in my eye and dandruff in my mustache – but of course that's the way you expect me.'[76]

As the premiers gathered in the capital for the opening of the conference on 14 January 1941, King could count upon support for the commission's recommendations from Bracken of Manitoba, W.J. Patterson of Saskatchewan, A.S. Macmillan of Nova Scotia, and Thane Campbell of Prince Edward Island. Adélard

Godbout of Quebec and J.B. McNair of New Brunswick remained non-committal. Alberta's William Aberhart had now reversed his earlier approval of the report and joined the opposition. While T.D. Pattullo of British Columbia might be prepared to consider financial changes for the duration of the war, he would not agree to any permanent changes in the constitution. On their arrival in Ottawa, Aberhart and Pattullo were reported to have lunched with Mitchell Hepburn to discuss strategy.

King's opening address to the conference defended the decision to call the meeting in wartime because of the urgent need to readjust the financial relations between the two levels of government. The prime minister was careful to repeat that the Rowell-Sirois Commission's recommendations were not the only solution, but the sooner the pressing financial problems were settled the better for fighting the war and coping with post-war problems. He insisted that the proposed changes would not endanger provincial autonomy. While some regions might appear to suffer in the short run, the benefits to the Canadian economy would enrich everybody in the long term.[77]

Hepburn followed with a speech which left the delegates in no doubt about where he stood.[78] Ontario was as unalterably opposed to the commission's recommendations as ever. After Rowell's departure the province had not even been represented on that body. The report was the product of 'the minds of three professors and a Winnipeg newspaper man, none of whom had any governmental administrative experience.' It was a mere propaganda exercise to claim that the proposed changes 'would make the provinces richer and, at the same time, make the dominion richer by the simple process of transferring debts and revenues to the central government.' Much of the pressure to implement the changes, he charged, arose from 'a well-cooked, nefarious deal to make good the losses in depreciation of certain bonds held largely by financial houses, to collect unpaid interest on Alberta bonds and to cause a sharp appreciation in the bonds of certain provinces.' The premier was just as critical of the notion that the war required such constitutional changes. Ontario had certainly done its best to co-operate with Ottawa; federal income taxes had been allowed as a deduction from the provincial levy so that every increase by Ottawa reduced the local tax base; capital spending had been postponed; great efforts had been made to earn foreign exchange by attracting American tourists. '[I]f the propagandists believe for a moment,' he warned, 'that ... we will remain silent while insinuations are broadcast deliberately for the purpose of branding us as unpatriotic, unneighbourly with our sister provinces, or guilty of doing anything to block Canada in achieving our maximum war effort, then I say to them, "We shall defend ourselves from that kind of attack here, on the floor of the legislature and on the public platform."'

The Ontario premier insisted that the war had actually rendered the commission's proposals irrelevant. All those who wanted work would soon have jobs, so it was 'unadulterated "humbug"' to say that Ottawa was doing the provinces a favour by taking full responsibility for the employable unemployed. The federal authorities would simply escape from their present duty to provide 40 per cent of the cost of food, clothing, and shelter for those on relief. To meet its financial needs Ontario would have only the receipts from the Liquor Control Board, vehicle licence fees, and gasoline taxes. Wartime prohibition and gasoline rationing would soon drastically reduce even those funds and force the province 'to go to the Dominion authorities with a tin cup in our hands saying "either contribute to the extent of our loss of revenue or pay for the social services of Ontario."' As a result, Hepburn declared his government would have nothing to do with the suggested changes in the constitution. Under the War Measures Act Ottawa already had 'extreme, even dictatorial power,' and the province would gladly pass any additional enabling legislation required by the fighting. With the Allied cause in danger, this constitutional 'fiddling while London is burning' was shameful; worse, it was a threat to Canadian unity, an act of 'national vandalism.' Insultingly, Hepburn added that 'so long as my colleagues and I have any say at directing public policy for Ontario, and so long as there is a British North America Act in its present form, which cannot be amended at will by a mushroom government that may in future take office in Ottawa, we shall, as a sister province, stand solidly beside Quebec if at any time her minority rights are threatened.'

The prime minister was embarrassed by this demagoguery. The *Globe and Mail*'s reporter noticed that 'When he is upset, Mr King has a mannerism of tapping his fingers; sometimes he twiddles his glasses or his thumbs. He did all three today while the Ontario Premier spoke.' Perhaps it was just as well that Mitchell Hepburn omitted the vindictive comment (contained in one draft of his speech) that the country should get on with the war effort by getting rid of a prime minister who seemed 'determined to spill the last drop of printer's ink in prosecuting this war to the very last page of Hansard.'[79] The rest of the session was occupied with statements by the other premiers along predictable lines.[80] Pattullo and Aberhart joined in expressing opposition to the Rowell-Sirois Commission's plan. Mackenzie King had planned to split the conference into committees on labour and unemployment, finance, and the constitution to discuss the commission's recommendations and report back. In view of the opposition, however, the prime minister proposed that the nine premiers meet with Ernest Lapointe and T.A. Crerar the next morning to decide how to proceed.

This gathering, like the first session, was dominated by Mitchell Hepburn. One observer called it 'the god damnedest exhibition and circus you can imagine.' The Ontario leader repeated his sneers at the royal commissioners and referred to a growing feeling in his province that the recommendations were 'a nice bribe for the province of Quebec.' He denounced the prime minister for trying to foist on Canadians these changes 'dressed ... up with the garments of patriotism and cloaked ... with the exigencies of war.' The federal government was accused of saying to the premier: 'We want you to accept the findings of this report as a war measure in perpetuity.' If they agreed, it 'might well wreck Confederation.' As a result, Hepburn categorically refused to take part in any committee discussions, particularly in private, as this would be tantamount to accepting the report in principle. He did, however, express readiness to continue public sessions on how the provinces might aid in the war effort.[81]

Despite the collective urgings of the six other premiers, Aberhart and Pattullo supported Hepburn. After two hours of wrangling, which forced the postponement of the scheduled morning meeting, one of the three dissenters suggested that the federal finance minister be invited to make a statement to the conference on the problems posed by the war. Lapointe and Crerar hastily conferred with King at midday, and he agreed to this proposal, since it would help lay the groundwork for any future tax changes. When the first ministers gathered again in the afternoon, Hepburn lost no time in insisting that he should have the right to reply to any points raised by the minister of finance. King grimly agreed that everyone who wished could have their say. Ilsley began rather timidly, asking whether he was supposed to avoid any controversial topics, to which the prime mininster abruptly replied: 'Oh no, go ahead.' The minister then read the submission which his officials had prepared for presentation to the conference committee on financial matters.[82]

First, Ilsley dealt with one of the claims made by Mitchell Hepburn: that support for the Rowell-Sirois recommendations came from bond speculators. The commissioners, he noted, had been careful to call for a capital gains tax on the sale of depreciated bonds to eliminate speculative profits. He denied that plan I would destroy provincial fiscal autonomy. The finance minister then set forth four arguments for adoption of the report. It would make the Canadian tax system more equitable and would permit Ottawa to deal with the economic distortions caused by mobilization. The provinces would be able to meet their own financial needs, and their improved credit would benefit everyone, including the dominion. Once the new system was in place, national minimum levels of social services could be established, which in turn would place Canada in a much better position to restore its economy to a peacetime footing.

Although denying any intention of a threat, Ilsley bluntly told the premiers that unless the report or some variant of it were adopted, the federal government would certainly take action which would reduce provincial revenues, such as raising the income tax or bringing in succession duties. Ottawa would no longer meet 40 per cent of the cost of unemployment relief, and there would be no more advances to help the provinces meet bond maturities or cover declining revenues from liquor and gas taxes. In closing, the finance minister defended the federal government's method of proceeding: it had power to impose the new taxes unilaterally but preferred to seek an agreement with the provinces. Not surprisingly, Mitchell Hepburn did not let this statement pass unchallenged. Highways Minister T.B. McQuesten read a statement prepared by the province for use in the finance committee. He pointed out that Ontario had steadily improved its level of social services since 1934 and had balanced its budget since 1936. Yet under plan I the province would have to give up $40 million in revenues and its municipalities $5 million, for which it would receive in return only $23 million. This loss of income was only the beginning, since the cost of services left to the provinces was certain to rise in future. McQuesten contended that 'in taking the attitude he has Hon. Mr. Hepburn has been but living up to the tradition of [George] Brown, and has defended and upheld all that Brown stood for, and is safeguarding the rights and responsibilities vested in the separate provinces by confederation ... [P]rovincial autonomy without adequate revenues for discharging the functions of government for which provinces are responsible is but little more than a farce.' He then announced that Ontario was withdrawing from the conference, leaving 'the rest of the members to continue their efforts to do what we are bound to say would result in wrecking confederation, as we understand it, and in destroying provincial autonomy and rights.'[83]

Immediately, however, Mitchell Hepburn leapt to his feet to amplify these criticisms in an impassioned speech. Ilsley's arguments were simply 'ridiculous'; one moment he claimed that provincial revenues would not be affected and the next he threatened to impose gasoline rationing and destroy an important source of funds. For a third time he repeated his accusation that the Rowell-Sirois report was 'the product of the minds of a few college professors and a Winnipeg newspaperman, who has had his knife into Ontario ever since he was able to write editorial articles.' To accept their recommendations would be fatal: 'I myself will not sell my province down the river for all time to come and allow our social services to remain a victim of dictatorial methods of a bureaucracy to be set up in Ottawa.' Pounding the table, he challenged Mackenzie King: '[I]f you want to do something as a war measure, go ahead and do it. But don't smash this confederation and stir up possible racial feuds in your effort.'[84]

For all practical purposes the conference was at an end, yet Mackenzie King did not want Hepburn's statements to stand uncontradicted. He called on several of his ministers to answer the charges. Ilsley questioned the accuracy of McQuesten's figures and Agriculture Minister James Gardiner praised the commissioners. Hepburn listened, then demanded a further say. He repeated his charge that those who supported the Rowell-Sirois report were 'wreckers of Confederation,' although he again added that he was willing to stay and discuss the war effort as long as necessary.[85] Some of the other provincial delegates seized upon this concession in the hope of salvaging something from the conference, but the prime minister's mind was made up. During a ten-minute adjournment he met privately with his ministers who approved a statement he had brought along declaring the conference at an end. He had no intention of offering Hepburn a platform to continue his criticisms of the federal government. In his closing address to the conference King admitted the differences of opinion within his cabinet over proceeding with fundamental constitutional changes in wartime, but he argued that a conference had been necessary, particularly if changes in the financial system of the federation should be required.[86] Privately, the prime minister felt satisfied: 'Far from being a failure, the conference has resulted in achieving beyond expectation the principal aim for which it was called, namely the avoidance of any excuse for protest on the part of provincial governments once the Dominion government begins, as it will be obliged very soon to do, to invade fields of taxation which up to the present have been monopolized in whole or in part by some of the provinces.'[87]

Mitchell Hepburn also went home pleased that he had blocked the Rowell-Sirois recommendations, apparently indefinitely. Despite criticism from the press at his boorish behaviour, the premier was confident that he had expressed the views of a majority of Ontarians. A few days after the conference he issued a statement calling for the federal government 'to make available sufficient new currency in order to take care of expanding requirements of wartime.' The Bank of Canada could issue as much as $480 million in new bills without any risk of inflation, he argued. Such inflationary ideas were anathema to J.L. Ilsley and his officials, who feared that Canadians might take seriously the premier's claim that the war could be financed by 'rubber money' without more borrowing or increased taxation. If such a notion took hold, it might provoke a serious financial crisis.[88] The finance minister abruptly rejected Hepburn's suggestion and pressed ahead with his plans to offer a new financial relationship to the provinces in his 1941 budget. Some ministers wanted another conference with the provinces before Ottawa further invaded their fields of taxation, but King was strongly opposed, arguing that the federal government had been given a free hand to do whatever was necessary for the effort at the meeting in January. The time for negotiation was past; now his government would simply go ahead and act.[89] The ministers finally agreed that Ottawa should take over personal and corporate income taxes completely and offer to give back to the provinces only what these taxes has netted them during 1940. Any province which refused such an arrangement would subject its taxpayers not only to the new federal taxes but to existing levies. The federal cabinet was confident that angry citizens would soon force all the provinces to toe the line. If they did, Ottawa would receive an additional $90 million in revenues, while aid to the provinces would be frozen for the duration of the war.[90]

Ilsley brought down his budget on 29 April 1941, and eight provinces speedily agreed to the Wartime Tax Agreements.[91] The lone dissenter was, of course, Ontario, where Provincial Treasurer Hepburn had recently announced a surplus of $12 million, the largest in provincial history. The premier made no direct comment on Ilsley's proposals at first but he did complain violently about a new 15 per cent tax imposed on interest from provincial bonds paid to non-residents. Mackenzie King, he complained, was 'discriminating against the provinces and undermining their credit at the very time when you have submitted for the consideration of the provincial governments proposals whereby they are called upon to surrender for the duration of the war certain fields of direct taxation authorized by the British North America Act.' The prime minister rejected these criticisms, and Hepburn then attacked those 'bent on building up a new despotism in Ottawa.' Until the interest tax, 'your latest provocative act,' was withdrawn, his province would have nothing to do with any tax sharing agreement: 'In no other way does the Government of Ontario believe that its revenues and credit may be kept on the present levels, and you have given this Province the very best reasons in the world for retaining full control of its own fiscal machinery.'[92] This situation was worrisome to Mackenzie King. Whoever was to blame, Ontario taxpayers would not take kindly to new income taxes on top of existing levies, and Ontario was the largest source of federal revenues. Perhaps if the interest tax on foreign bondholders were dropped Hepburn might be pressured into agreeing to tax sharing. In what he called an effort to avoid 'serious controversy' between the two governments the prime minister released to the press an offer to drop the interest tax. Still Hepburn stalled. Now he wanted another dominion-provincial conference to discuss the problems of war finance. No, said King, the premiers had given him full authority to manage the war effort last January, and nobody except Hepburn had expressed any dissatisfaction since then. To have such a meeting would 'only serve to accentuate differences raised at the last Conference.'[93]

Hepburn was in a difficult position. With a large surplus, he could not avoid making concessions to prosecute the war without opening himself to severe criticism. Outmanoeuvred by that master politician Mackenzie King, he finally gave way in the summer of 1941 and agreed to the drawing up of a Wartime Tax Agreement.[94] Nevertheless, the negotiations proved lengthy and complex, lasting over six months. Ontario officials claimed that Ottawa was trying to pare down the amount to be paid over to the province in various ways, so that existing levels of service could not be maintained. Attorney General Gordon Conant summed up the provincial government's complaints: 'We are asking for nothing. We would prefer to be left alone. We simply say ... that we feel, having plotted our course for the year, having trimmed our sails as we expected the weather to prevail to the end of our fiscal year, that it is unfair to blow up a storm in the midst of a charted course and ask us to change the whole trim of our ship.'[95] By January 1942 Finance Minister Ilsley had become so exasperated at the province's procrastination that he prepared to release a statement to the press in which he came near to charging that Ontario was obstructing the war effort: 'I think it is a great pity that the province of Ontario is not prepared, like the other provinces, to place in the hands of the Dominion Government for the duration of the war the exclusive use of the most powerful and efficient taxing instrument known – I mean the income tax on corporations and individuals.'[96] Negotiations dragged on through January and February, until the Ontario premier adjourned the legislature to show his disgust at the failure to reach a settlement. Even Pensions and National Health Minister Ian Mackenzie, one of Hepburn's few friends in the cabinet, was dismayed at his behaviour: 'It seems to me that Ontario is getting the same treatment as the other provinces, and that their attitude is very disloyal in the middle of a Victory Loan.' At long last, however, the Ontario government gave way, and a Wartime Tax Agreement was signed and ratified by the legislature in the spring of 1942.[97]

The great quantity of energy devoted to constitutional reform in Canada after 1935 produced minimal results. One by one the efforts were abandoned with the sole exception of the amendment to legalize a national unemployment insurance plan. Despite the depression crisis, the nation's political leaders failed to arrive at a consensus on the kind of restructuring necessary to enable the country to deal with its problems. And it must be said that a good deal of the credit or the blame for the failure was borne by the premier of Ontario, Mitchell Hepburn. He proved a vocal and pugnacious defender of provincial autonomy, who resisted all changes in the direction of greater concentration of power at Ottawa. His greatest positive achievement was to reinforce the principle that the provinces must be consulted before any drastic changes in the constitution could be made, to secure formal acceptance, in fact, for the much-maligned compact theory of Confederation which he and his predecessors had argued for almost from the beginning of Canada's existence.

True, Hepburn was crude, displaying few of the airs and graces which other statesmen put on, but he left little doubt as to where he stood. He rejected the conventional wisdom of the 1930s that the problems of the modern, industrial state could be solved only through the centralization of power. He preferred to take the position that given sufficient funds Ontario could cope quite well with the problems it faced. He suspected, correctly enough, that the Royal Commission on Dominion-Provincial Relations was really created to ward off criticism of the federal government for its inactivity and to provide an elaborate justification for strengthening Ottawa at the expense of the provinces. While economy and efficiency in government were laudable objectives, Hepburn was correct in pointing out that local self-government had always been an equally valued concept in Canada and that some balance between the two needed to be struck.

Mackenzie King did make genuine efforts to secure agreement on consitutional change in this period, but too often when he encountered opposition from Hepburn or anyone else, he preferred to try to muddle through with the status quo rather than persevere in pursuit of change. Too rarely was his government ready to make real concessions to the provinces, preferring simply to offer to take over and run things more efficiently if only the premiers would permit it. The western provinces, in dire financial straits, were prepared to co-operate, but other provincial leaders frequently objected to one or another of King's plans. Mitchell Hepburn, of course, was his most persistent and steadfast opponent. In the end, under the pressure of a military emergency, King achieved part of what he sought by the Wartime Tax Agreements, but the constitution was not formally altered; the balance of power in the federal system was not shifted. In the end, Mackenzie King's passivity held Mitchell Hepburn's aggressiveness to a draw.

Conclusion

From Confederation to the Second World War (and beyond) the strategy for the conduct of relations between the province of Ontario and the federal government, which had first been mapped out by Sir Oliver Mowat in the late nineteenth century, continued to be followed by his successors as premier. All of them sought the widest possible sphere of independence in shaping policies designed to promote the economic growth of the province, particularly through the development of natural resources, where ownership of lands, forests, and minerals gave the provincial government great authority. Beginning with the dispute with Ottawa during the 1870s and 1880s over the north-western boundary, the province demonstrated its continued determination to manage its own growth. At the turn of the century it imposed a manufacturing condition on sawlogs, pulpwood, and ore. Ultimately, federal-provincial conflict over resource development focused on the related problems of waterpower on navigable rivers like the St Lawrence and the exportation of electricity to the United States. Ontario doggedly pursued its goal of cheap energy for domestic industrialization and resisted all efforts by Ottawa to use its jurisdiction over navigation and international relations to dominate the formulation of policy.

Relations between the two levels of government were frequently complicated by the activities of private interest groups. They attempted to secure their own ends by playing off the jurisdictions against one another in a kind of federal-provincial game. Abstract considerations about the virtues of local autonomy versus centralization did not govern the conduct of these players. In a recent study of the economic development of Alberta and Saskatchewan, the authors correctly note that

There is no evidence that big business in Canada has typically resisted centralization and supported local autonomy. The only things that capital consistently supports are its own interests, and when these have been threatened by aggressive provincial governments, business has unhesitatingly pushed for a stronger central government ... About all that can be concluded is that big business understands that a federal system provides interest groups with a number of potential sources of leverage and veto points, and that capital, like perfidious Albion, has no permanent allies or enemies, only permanent interests.[1]

Ontario's experience with the insurance industry during the 1920s and 1930s and its efforts around the turn of the century to prevent local businessmen from securing federal charters demonstrate the accuracy of these assertions. Private interests, therefore, have helped to provoke federal-provincial friction from time to time, as one level of government was enlisted to protect its clients against the activities of the other. This complexity, in turn, has made the resolution of conflicts more difficult, not to be achieved solely by direct intergovernmental negotiations.

The second principle which Mowat established for the conduct of Ontario's relations with Ottawa was the need to maintain a sceptical attitude towards increased federal transfer payments as a solution to the problems of the province. Financially stronger than the other provinces, Ontario could afford to look with disfavour upon increased federal grants to other provinces. Although nearly half the federal revenues were raised in Ontario, it was unlikely that the province would receive a proportionate share of any increased largesse from Ottawa. On occasion, of course, Ontario's premiers might yield to temptation and seek federal funds. The subsidy arrangements in the BNA Act which permanently tied the level of payments to the size of the population in 1861 became a source of irritation as time went on, and it did not escape the notice of Ontario politicians that their province would net the largest amount from any across-the-board increase. Thus Mowat gave his support to a subsidy tied to current population at the abortive 1887 interprovincial conference, and James Whitney followed suit at the conference in 1906, after which the subsidy was finally adjusted. At other times Ontario leaders found it politic to agree to better terms for the other provinces in order to rally support for some cause of their own. In 1927, for instance, Howard Ferguson endorsed additional funds for the Maritimes to silence any possible criticism from the other premiers during his fight with Mackenzie King over power development on the St Lawrence. In general, however, the premiers of Ontario continued to look with suspicion upon offers of financial aid from Ottawa.

The danger in accepting federal funds lay in the likelihood that they would come with strings attached. Hard-pressed financially, Sir James Whitney supported the introduction of conditional grants for agricultural education and highway construction in 1912. But he made it plain that he would not tolerate interference even from the friendly Conservative administration of Robert Borden in the administration of these programs. Similarly, during the depression there was constant friction between Ottawa and the provinces because of the conviction that local authorities were misusing federal grants-in-aid for the relief of unemployment. As a result, the Bennett government frequently altered the terms and conditions of these grants to the irritation of the provincial ministers. Such experiences seemed only to confirm the correctness of Mowat's coolness towards transfer payments and to demonstrate the virtues of raising and spending provincial revenues independently.

The First World War had a significant impact upon the financial relations between the province and the federal government. In 1917 the Borden government decided to impose personal and corporate income taxes for the first time. The provinces, including Ontario, registered no protests, owing to the wartime emergency. As soon the fighting ended, however, they mounted a campaign to have Ottawa withdraw entirely from this field, because they were limited to such direct taxes for the raising of provincial revenues. The federal government steadfastly resisted, claiming that the burden of war debts and post-war expenditures made withdrawal financially impossible. Although this issue was raised from time to time during the 1920s, the fiscal relations of the two levels of government remained fundamentally unaltered when the crisis of the 1930s occurred. Ottawa responded with temporary grants-in-aid for the relief of unemployment but refused to agree to any further alterations in the financial structure of the federation. In 1936, therefore, Mitchell Hepburn introduced a provincial income tax and stepped up his demands that Ottawa vacate at least part of this field to the provinces. But all to no avail.

When the Second World War broke out, federal officials soon reached the conclusion that total mobilization required a rationalization of the Canadian system of taxation. Having failed to persuade Hepburn to agree to the changes recommended by the Royal Commission on Dominion-Provincial Relations, the King government eventually cornered the province into signing a Wartime Tax Agreement under which Ottawa would collect all income taxes and remit a fixed sum to Ontario. Nonetheless, Hepburn's rejection of the Rowell-Sirois Commission's proposals in 1941 left the provinces with their fiscal powers formally intact once the war ended. In 1947 Ontario (along with Quebec) was able to decline to enter a new Tax Rental Agreement designed to continue the wartime arrangements. While never averse to taking Ontario's share (and more) of federal transfer payments, the province's premiers always remained wary of this means of correcting regional disparities. The government of Ontario preferred to defend its sphere of autonomous authority, and no right was more prized than the right to levy taxes and spend without reference to Ottawa's wishes.

In addition, Ontario politicians remained faithful to the compact theory of Confederation. If the union of 1867 resulted from an agreement among the provinces, no constitutional changes were possible without provincial consent. However historically unsound the theory was, it had obvious utility as a justification for Ontario's claim to a veto over amendments to the BNA Act. When Mowat and Honoré Mercier tried to represent the interprovincial conference of 1887 as a reconvening of the 1864 Quebec conference which had drafted the terms of Confederation, Sir John A. Macdonald simply ignored them. Although Sir Wilfrid Laurier consented to the premiers' holding a meeting in 1906 to discuss the revision of the subsidies, other constitutional amendments continued to be made at the behest of the federal parliament alone. Not until 1927 did Justice Minister Ernest Lapointe formally concede that the provinces had the right to be consulted about a formula for amending the BNA Act. This commitment to consultation was reiterated by R.B. Bennett after he took office in 1930, owing to strong pressure from Howard Ferguson of Ontario, who presented an elaborate defence of the compact theory. Although no changes in the constitution were made during Bennett's term of office, when Mackenzie King returned to power in 1935 it seems to have been accepted without question that the premiers must be consulted. The formula devised in 1936 would have granted Ontario the veto it sought over key amendments, but it never became law, owing to the opposition of the New Brunswick government.

After 1936 the search for agreement on an amending formula was abandoned. Instead, King sought the approval of the premiers for specific changes, like the one authorizing a national unemployment insurance scheme, which was passed in 1940. Meanwhile, the Royal Commission on Dominion-Provincial Relations was deliberating, and in the same year recommended far-reaching changes in the division of powers. By that date there was no question that the approval of the premiers would be required, which set the stage for Mitchell Hepburn's antics at the dominion-provincial conference in January 1941. His rejection of the Rowell-Sirois Commission's proposals effectively ended any hope of thoroughgoing reform for the time being. Within the space of some seventy years, therefore, the implications of the compact theory of Confederation regarding consultation with the provinces had come to be accepted dogma. Even those who rejected the theory conceded the provinces' veto powers over constitutional change. Throughout that period Mowat and his successors had stood in the front line in the fight to secure this objective.

Many Canadian historians have dealt harshly with the activities of Mowat and his successors. This attitude seems to reflect a reluctance to accept the legitimacy of federalism, to concede that a real division of powers will inevitably create friction and conflict. Mowat has been criticized for misleading the Judicial Committee of the Privy Council into making decisions which subverted the clear intentions of the Fathers of Confederation that Canada should be a highly centralized state. The provincial rights movement, usually headed by Ontario, has been blamed for the emergence of a weak and decentralized union of co-ordinate sovereignties, when the Fathers had planned that the provinces should possess little more power than large municipalities.[2]

As early as 1889 D'Alton McCarthy warned the House of Commons that 'The worship of local autonomy, which some gentlemen have become addicted to, is fraught ... with great evils to this Dominion. Our separation into provinces, the rights of self-government which we possess, is not to make us less anxious for the promotion of the welfare of the Dominion.'[3] For many Canadians the state's uncertain response to the economic crisis of the 1930s seemed to confirm that the legal and political manoeuvring of the province's leaders had reduced the Dominion to a collection of semi-autonomous and sorely enfeebled principalities, scarcely capable of providing even a minimum level of social services to the citizenry and resistant to the development of a strong and cohesive national will. The rise of aggressive Québécois nationalism since the Second World War might be seen as another bitter fruit of the provincial rights movement.

Certainly many English-Canadians have assumed, like D'Alton McCarthy, that local and regional loyalties pose a bar to the development of a strong national feeling. Yet as Edmund Burke wrote: 'To be attached to the subdivision, to love the little platoon we belong to, is the first principle (the germ as it were) of public affections. It is the first link in the series by which we proceed towards a love of our country and to mankind.'[4] The distinguished American historian, David Potter, has pointed out 'the general similarity between nationalism and other forms of group loyalty.'[5] While nationalism and local feeling may sometimes stand opposed to one another they need not necessarily be antithetical. The editor of the *Globe* grasped this point when he declared in 1883: 'Only upon condition that Provincial rights are respected is there any hope of building up a Canadian nationality.'[6] He recognized that national loyalties flourish not by overpowering the citizen's other attachments but by reinforcing them and maintaining them in a mutually supportive relationship.

Too ready acceptance of the notion that Canada's past is a saga of 'nation-building' by the central government has predisposed historians to conclude that those who have voiced local interests or provincial demands contrary to national policies are to be condemned. Yet a federal system would not have been necessary, in 1867 or later, but for the existence of real and persistent differences between one region of the country and another. In a federation with a genuine division of powers conflict between the two levels of government was certain to be unavoidable and persistent. Despite the wishes of the Fathers of Confederation, Canada has developed as it has not merely because of Mowat's actions or the decisions of the Judicial Committee of the Privy Council, but because a decentralized federalism suits Canadian society.[7]

Moreover, it should be noted that the federal government retains wide-ranging powers and not merely in emergencies. Provincial activities can still be controlled by disallowance or the right to declare undertakings for the general advantage of Canada, although these are blunt instruments which can be used only in extraordinary circumstances without provoking violent protests from provincial governments. More subtle is the arsenal of financial weapons which Ottawa began to develop even before the First World War, which depends fundamentally upon the spending of federal funds for purposes which fall under provincial jurisdiction. Particularly when combined with the requirement that the provinces put up matching contributions in order to qualify, the spending power has proved to be a powerful instrument for shaping provincial priorities, since local policy-makers are reluctant to forgo federal money. During the 1930s conditional grants for the relief of unemployment became a permanent fixture of national fiscal policy, and after the Second World War the same methods permitted the extension of federal power into fields as diverse as health care and higher education.

Yet the provinces have failed to wither away. Ownership of lands and natural resources has proved to be as significant a source of provincial power as jurisdiction over 'property and civil rights.'[8] Provincial finances stabilized after the Second World War through sharing in taxes on income and the levying of general sales taxes. Provincial bureaucracies have been created which can formulate and execute policies as expertly as their counterparts in Ottawa. Intergovernmental relations have become increasingly extensive and complex.

Instead of lamenting the strength of the provincial rights movement and criticizing its leaders, it would seem more fruitful simply to analyse how the federal system has actually worked in the past. Big, rich, and powerful, the province of Ontario has rarely hesitated to express its views, and this outspokenness has made its premiers among the leading crusaders for provincial rights throughout most of the country's history. The people of Ontario, moreover, have always considered themselves to be 'real' Canadians and assumed that their wishes are the wishes of the national collectivity. Any apparent conflict between national and provincial objectives may be dissolved by the conviction that the interests of Ontario are the interests of Canada. That people in other parts of the country might not share this view has not prevented Ontarians from trying to impose their vision of Canada upon the rest of the nation.

Appendix

PREMIERS OF ONTARIO

John Sandfield Macdonald
(16 July 1867 to 19 December 1871)

Edward Blake
(20 December 1871 to 25 October 1872)

Sir Oliver Mowat
(25 October 1872 to 14 July 1896)

Arthur S. Hardy
(14 July 1896 to 21 October 1899)

George W. Ross
(21 October 1899 to 8 February 1905)

Sir James P. Whitney
(8 February 1905 to 25 September 1914)

Sir William H. Hearst
(2 October 1914 to 14 November 1919)

Ernest C. Drury
(14 November 1919 to 16 July 1923)

G. Howard Ferguson
(16 July 1923 to 15 December 1930)

George S. Henry
(15 December 1930 to 10 July 1934)

Mitchell F. Hepburn
(10 July 1934 to 21 October 1942)

PRIME MINISTERS OF CANADA

Sir John A. Macdonald
(1 July 1867 to 5 November 1873,
17 October 1878 to 6 June 1891)

Alexander Mackenzie
(7 November 1873 to 9 October 1878)

Sir John J.C. Abbott
(16 June 1891 to 24 November 1892)

Sir John S.D. Thompson
(5 December 1892 to 12 December 1894)

Sir Mackenzie Bowell
(21 December 1894 to 27 April 1896)

Sir Charles Tupper
(1 May 1896 to 8 July 1896)

Sir Wilfrid Laurier
(11 July 1896 to 6 October 1911)

Sir Robert Borden
(10 October 1911 to 10 July 1920)

Arthur Meighen
(10 July 1920 to 29 December 1921,
29 June 1926 to 25 September 1926)

W.L. Mackenzie King
(29 December 1921 to 28 June 1926,
25 September 1926 to 6 August 1930,
23 October 1935 to 15 November 1948)

R.B. Bennett
(7 August 1930 to 23 October 1935)

SOURCES: *Centennial Edition of a History of the Electoral Districts and Ministries of the Province of Ontario 1867–1968*, Roderick Lewis, comp. (Toronto: Queen's Printer, n.d.); Canada, *Guide to Canadian Ministries since Confederation, July 1, 1867–January 1, 1957* (Ottawa: Public Archives of Canada, 1957)

Note on Sources

This study is based mainly upon the papers of the first ministers, federal and provincial, and the records of those government departments which were intimately involved in intergovernmental relations. The papers of all the premiers are at the Provincial Archives of Ontario with the (huge) exception of Sir Oliver Mowat's and Arthur S. Hardy's papers, which have not been preserved. Similarly, the papers of all the prime ministers are at the Public Archives of Canada in Ottawa. I have also consulted the papers of certain cabinet ministers, who seemed particularly influential on certain issues or because the first minister's papers seemed to lack much material on a given subject.

Among the publications which proved particularly valuable were the official records of the dominion-provincial conferences and the two compilations of correspondence and orders-in-council regarding provincial statutes considered for disallowance, covering the years 1867–95 and 1896–1920. In addition, there were several volumes of documents issued by the King's Printer dealing with the negotiations with the United States regarding St Lawrence development from 1925 to 1941. J.C. Morrison's 'Oliver Mowat and the development of provincial rights in Ontario: a study in dominion provincial relations, 1867–1896,' in *Three History Theses* (Toronto: Ontario Department of Public Records and Archives, 1961) was invaluable for the early years of this study.

Notes

INTRODUCTION

1 Canada, *Dominion-Provincial Conferences, November 3–10, 1927, December 9–13, 1935, January 14–15, 1941/Conférences Fédérales-Provinciales, du 3 au 10 novembre 1927, du 9 au 13 décembre, 1935, les 14 et 15 janvier, 1941* (Ottawa: King's Printer, 1951) [hereafter *Dominion-Provincial Conferences, 1927, 1935, 1941*]; *Dominion-Provincial Conference, 1941*, 101
2 For a more extended discussion of this point see Christopher Armstrong, 'The Mowat Heritage in Federal-Provincial Relations,' in Donald Swainson, ed., *Oliver Mowat's Ontario* (Toronto: Macmillan, 1972), 93–118.
3 See H.V. Nelles, 'Empire Ontario: Problems of Resource Development,' in Swainson, ed., *Oliver Mowat's Ontario*, 189–210.

CHAPTER 1: *Remoulding the Constitution*

1 I have benefited greatly from J.C. Morrison's study 'Oliver Mowat and the Development of Provincial Rights in Ontario: A Study in Dominion-Provincial Relations, 1867–1896,' in *Three History Theses* (Toronto: Ontario Department of Public Records and Archives, 1961), on which I have depended for much of the material contained in this chapter.
2 The 'ministerial explanations' made upon the formation of the coalition are quoted in ibid., 28. Macdonald's statement in the Canadian Assembly on 19 April 1861 is quoted in Joseph Pope, *Memoirs of the Right Honourable Sir John Alexander Macdonald, G.C.B.* (Toronto: Musson, n.d.), 242–3.
3 *Parliamentary Debates on the Subject of Confederation of the British North American Provinces, 3rd Session, 8th Provincial Parliament of Canada* (Quebec: Hunter, Rose and Co., 1865) [hereafter *Confederation Debates*], 108 (Brown's speech); G.P. Browne, comp., *Documents on the Confederation of British North America, A Compilation based on Sir Joseph Pope's Confederation Documents Supplemented by Other Official Material* (Toronto: McClelland and Stewart, 1969), 122–3
4 Browne, *Documents on Confederation*, 142–3
5 Sir John A. Macdonald to Brown Chamberlin, 26 Oct. 1868, in Joseph Pope, *Correspondence of Sir John Macdonald* (Toronto: Doubleday, 1921), 75; George Brown to Anne Brown, 27 October 1864, quoted in J.M.S. Careless, *Brown of the Globe*, vol. 2, *Statesman of Confederation 1860–1880* (Toronto: Macmillan, 1963), 171; *Confederation Debates*, 108
6 J.M.S. Careless, 'The Toronto *Globe* and Agrarian Radicalism, 1850–1867,' *Canadian Historical Review*, 29 (1948), 14–39; *Confederation Debates*, 88
7 M.C. Urquhart and K.A.H. Buckley, eds, *Historical Statistics of Canada* (Toronto: Macmillan, 1965), 14, 614; E.V. Jackson, 'The Organization of the Canadian Liberal Party 1867–1896 with Particular Reference to Ontario,' unpublished MA thesis, University of Toronto, 1962, 95

8 Morrison, 'Mowat and Provincial Rights,' 250–5 quoting *Globe*, 24 Nov. 1869; Bruce W. Hodgins, *John Sandfield Macdonald 1812–1872* (Toronto: University of Toronto Press, 1971), 103–4
9 Morrison, 'Mowat and Provincial Rights,' 40, quoting *Globe*, 23 Dec. 1871; Joseph Schull, *Edward Blake, the Man of the Other Way (1833–1881)* (Toronto: Macmillan, 1975), 84–5
10 Morrison, 'Mowat and Provincial Rights,' 42–5; G. Ramsay Cook, *Provincial Autonomy, Minority Rights and the Compact Theory* (Ottawa: Queen's Printer, 1969), 12–3, 19–20; Jackson, 'Organization of the Liberal Party,' 89–104; Bruce Hodgins, 'Disagreement at the Commencement: Divergent Ontarian Views of Federalism, 1867–1871,' in Swainson, *Oliver Mowat's Ontario*, 56
11 See Morrison, 'Mowat and Provincial Rights,' 95–176 for an extended account of this dispute and Ontario, *Sessional Papers*, 1882, no. 69, *Correspondence, Papers and Documents of Dates from 1856 to 1882 Inclusive, Relating to the Northerly and Westerly Boundaries of the Province of Ontario, Printed by Order of the Legislative Assembly* (Toronto: C. Blackett Robinson, 1882).
12 Ibid., 1873, no. 44, William McDougall to provincial secretary, 9 March 1872
13 Ibid., Ontario order-in-council, 25 March 1872
14 Ibid., Joseph Howe to W.P. Howland, 16 May 1872, enclosing Macdonald's report; Howland to Howe, 31 May 1872; Howe to Howland, 12 Nov. 1872
15 Morrison, 'Mowat and Provincial Rights,' 114–7; Ontario, *Sessional Papers*, 1882, no. 69, memorandum of agreement for provisional boundary in respect of patents of lands between David Laird and T.B. Pardee, 26 June 1874
16 Morrison, 'Mowat and Provincial Rights,' 118–26; Mackenzie quoted at 123
17 Ibid., 126–7
18 Ontario, *Sessional Papers*, 1879, no. 13, statement of the Ontario case re westerly and northerly boundaries prepared for the arbitrators, 7 Feb. 1879; ibid., 1882, no. 69, statement of the case of the government of the dominion of Canada regarding the boundaries of the province of Ontario, prepared by Hugh MacMahon, QC, counsel for the dominion, 1878; report of the proceedings before the arbitrators in the matter of the boundaries of the province of Ontario, at Ottawa, 1, 2, 3 Aug. 1878; ibid., 1879, no. 22; *North Western Ontario: Its Boundaries, Resources and Communications, Prepared under Instructions from the Ontario Government* (Toronto: Hunter, Rose and Co., 1879)
19 Ibid., 1879, no. 80, A.S. Hardy to secretary of state, 31 Dec. 1878; ibid., 1880, no. 46, I.R. Eckhart to secretary of state, 23 Sept. 1879; Hardy to J.C. Aikins, 19 Dec. 1879; the quotations are from Eckhart's letter. Morrison, 'Mowat and Provincial Rights,' 133, cites the Conservative Toronto *Mail*'s view that the arbitration was a 'farce.'
20 Ontario, *Sessional Papers*, 1881, no. 30, report of Justice Minister James McDonald, 20 Jan. 1880; report of Attorney-General Oliver Mowat, 18 March 1880; report of Justice Minister James McDonald, 17 March 1880; report of Justice Minister James McDonald, 23 April 1880; ibid., 1882, no. 23, Ontario order-in-council, 28 May 1880; Morrison, 'Mowat and Provincial Rights,' 134–5
21 Ontario, *Sessional Papers*, 1882, no. 23, Mowat to James McDonald, 1 Feb. 1881; Morrison, 'Mowat and Provincial Rights,' Macdonald quoted at 137–9
22 Ontario, *Sessional Papers*, 1882, no. 23, Lieutenant-Governor John Beverley Robinson to secretary of state, 15 March 1881; Provincial Archives of Ontario [hereafter PAO], provincial secretary's records, series I-I-D, 1881, no. 1785, Robinson to secretary of state, 30 Sept. 1881
23 Ontario, *Sessional Papers*, 1882, no. 23, report by Attorney-General Oliver Mowat, 1 Nov. 1881
24 Morrison, 'Oliver Mowat and Provincial Rights,' 140–51; Macdonald quoted at 145, Mowat at 147–8
25 See P.B. Waite, *Canada 1874–1896, Arduous Destiny* (Toronto: McClelland and Stewart, 1971), 117–18, for a brief account of the Rat Portage affair; A. Margaret Evans, 'Oliver Mowat and Ontario, 1872–1896; A Study in Political Success,' unpublished PH D thesis, University of Toronto, 1967, 508–20; John Wilson and David Hoffman, 'Ontario, a three-Party System in Transition,' in Martin Robin, ed., *Canadian Provincial Politics* (Scarborough, Ont.: Prentice-Hall, 1972), 204.
26 Ontario, *Sessional Papers*, 1884, no. 3, Memorandum of Agreement between governments of Ontario and Manitoba, 18 Dec. 1883; ibid., 1885, no. 8, Lieutenant-Governor John Beverley Robinson to secretary of state, 29 April 1884; Morrison, 'Oliver Mowat and Provincial Rights,' 151–60

Notes pages 21-31 245

27 Ibid., 160-73; Macdonald is quoted at 171.
28 Ibid., 46-94, contains a full discussion of this dispute. On the powers and responsibilities of the lieutenant-governor, see John T. Saywell, *The Office of the Lieutenant-Governor, a Study in Canadian Government and Politics* (Toronto: University of Toronto Press, 1957) passim, and James McL. Hendry, *Memorandum on the Office of Lieutenant-Governor of a Province: Its Constitutional Character and Functions (with Appendices)* (Ottawa: Department of Justice, 1955).
29 Ontario, *Sessional Papers*, 1888, no. 37, Lieutenant-Governor John Beverley Robinson to secretary of state, 22 Jan. 1886
30 Canada, Senate, *Report Pursuant to Resolution of the Senate to the Honourable Speaker by the Parliamentary Counsel [W.F. O'Connor] Relating to the Enactment of the British North America Act, 1867, Any Lack of Consonance between Its Terms and Judicial Construction of Them and Cognate Matters* (Ottawa: Queen's Printer, 1961) [hereafter *O'Connor Report*], annex 3, case no. 10; C.R.W. Biggar, *Sir Oliver Mowat* (Toronto: Warwick Bros and Rutter, 1905), vol. 2, 518
31 G.V. LaForest, *Disallowance and Reservation of Provincial Legislation* (Ottawa: Queen's Printer, 1955), 24-5, reprints Macdonald's report to council of 8 June 1868.
32 LaForest, *Disallowance and Reservation*, 36-43; Blake quoted at 41
33 Morrison, 'Mowat and Provincial Rights,' 177-233, discusses the dispute over disallowance. The disagreement between the two Macdonalds is described at 186-9 and Mowat is quoted at 194.
34 Ibid., 199-203, 206-10; LaForest, *Disallowance and Reservation*, 53-4; Canada, Justice Department, *Correspondence, Reports of the Ministers of Justice and Orders-in-Council upon the Subject of Dominion and Provincial Legislation, 1867-1895* (Ottawa: Government Printing Bureau, 1896), W.E. Hodgins, comp. [hereafter *Provincial Legislation, 1867-1895*], 177, report of minister of justice, James McDonald per J.A.M., 17 May 1881.
35 Ibid., 179, report of acting Attorney-General Adam Crooks, 14 Oct. 1881; Morrison, 'Mowat and Provincial Rights,' 210-13
36 LaForest, *Disallowance and Reservation*, 54-6; Macdonald quoted at 55; Morrison, 'Mowat and Provincial Rights,' 213-14
37 Ibid., 223-8; Macdonald quoted at 225
38 LaForest, *Disallowance and Reservation*, 56-8; John P. Heisler, 'Sir John Thompson, 1844-1894' unpublished PH D thesis, University of Toronto, 1955, 223-4
39 See Morrison, 'Mowat and Provincial Rights,' 235-85
40 Ontario, *Sessional Papers*, 1887, no. 51, Mercier to Mowat, 8 March 1887
41 Ibid., Mowat to Mercier, 15 March 1887; Fraser quoted in Morrison, 'Mowat and Provincial Rights,' 260-1
42 'Minutes of the Interprovincial Conference held at the City of Quebec from the 20th to the 28th October, 1887, inclusively,' in *Dominion Provincial and Interprovincial Conferences from 1887 to 1926/Conférences Fédérales-Provinciales et Conférences Interprovinciales de 1887 à 1926* (Ottawa: King's Printer, 1951) [hereafter *Dominion Provincial Conferences 1887-1926*]
43 Ibid., 20-1
44 Ibid., 21-4
45 Ibid., 24-7
46 Donald Creighton, *John A. Macdonald, the Old Chieftain* (Toronto: Macmillan, 1955), 472-3, 498-500; Pope, *Correspondence of Macdonald*, 431-3, Mowat to Macdonald, 17 Nov. 1888; Macdonald to Mowat, 3 Dec. 1888
47 See above n. 38 and Public Archives of Canada [hereafter PAC], justice department records, series A2, vol. 65, Mowat to Thompson, 29 June 1886; J.R. Miller, '"As a Politician He Is a Great Enigma": The Social and Political Ideas of D'Alton McCarthy,' *Canadian Historical Review*, 58 (1977), 403-4.
48 Gerald Rubin, 'The Nature, Use and Effect of Reference Cases in Canadian Constitutional Law,' in W.R. Lederman, ed., *The Courts and the Canadian Constitution* (Toronto: McClelland and Stewart, 1964), 223-7; Canada, House of Commons, *Debates* [hereafter Can., H. of C., *Deb.*], 1891, 3586-7
49 On 29 June 1891, Mowat wrote to Thompson: 'If we are to have a Conservative government, I have great pleasure in saying that there is no Conservative from whom in the common interest I should expect so much good and so little of the contrary as the present Minister of Justice'; quoted in Heisler, 'Thompson,' 274.

50 PAC, justice department records, series A2, vol. 83, Mowat to Thompson 1 April 1891, private. The seemingly interminable negotiations preceding the fisheries reference can be followed in PAO, Aemilius Irving papers, and the decisions may be found in *O'Connor Report*, annex 3, cases no. 13, 16.
51 Cook, *Provincial Autonomy and the Compact Theory*, 44; *Brophy v. Attorney General for Manitoba* (1895) quoted in W.P.M. Kennedy, *The Constitution of Canada* (London: Oxford University Press, 1922), 421, and *Attorney General for Canada v. Attorney General for Ontario (Fisheries Reference)* (1898) in *O'Connor Report*, annex 3, case no. 16
52 See Armstrong, 'The Mowat Heritage in Federal-Provincial Relations,' in Swainson, ed., *Oliver Mowat's Ontario*, 93–118.
53 *Globe*, 12 Feb. 1897

CHAPTER 2. *Federalism and Economic Development*

1 Simon Kuznets, 'Underdeveloped Countries and the Pre-industrial Phase in Advanced Countries,' in A.N. Agarwala and S.P. Singh, eds, *The Economics of Underdevelopment* (New York: Oxford University Press, 1963), 135–7
2 H.V. Nelles, *The Politics of Development, Forests, Mines and Hydro-electric Power in Ontario, 1849–1941* (Toronto: Macmillan, 1974), 48–107, contains an excellent analysis of the background and implementation of the manufacturing condition; see also Nelles, 'Empire Ontario: The Problems of Resource Development,' in Swainson, *Oliver Mowat's Ontario*, 189–210.
3 Nelles, *Politics of Development*, 63–7; the phrase 'hewers of wood' recurs frequently in anti-American literature of the period. The quotation is from *Industrial Canada*, October 1903, 102, cited in Michael Bliss, *A Living Profit, Studies in the Social History of Canadian Business, 1883–1911* (Toronto: McClelland and Stewart, 1974), 104. Bliss shows that a belief in this crude version of mercantilism was common among businessmen who assumed 'that economic progress was a straight line growth from lower through higher stages of manufacture. If wealth was created primarily by labour, by working on raw materials, then the more labour that was added in the manufacturing process the more wealth would be created in the community' (103).
4 Nelles, *Politics of Development*, 64–6; PAC, Laurier papers, John Bertram to Laurier, 26 March 1897 enclosing memorial of John Waldie, George J. Leask, H.H. Cook, n.d., 224457–9
5 Nelles, *Politics of Development*, 67–8; University of Toronto Archives, John Charlton diary, 28 July 1897
6 Nelles, *Politics of Development*, 69–71; *Globe*, 7 Aug. 1897
7 *Mail and Empire*, 4 Sept. 1901; *Globe*, 5 Nov. 1897; [Liberal Party of Ontario], pamphlet no. 10, 'Export of Saw Logs to the United States.' *Ontario General Election* (Toronto 1894)
8 Ontario, *Sessional Papers*, 1898, no. 58, resolution passed at a special meeting of Ontario lumbermen at Toronto, 19 Aug. 1897, and presented to the Ontario Executive Council by Messrs Scott, Rathbun, and Waldie; University of Toronto Archives, John Charlton diary, 19 Aug. 1897 records Gibson's view, and Whitney is quoted in the *Globe*, 3 Dec. 1897, Rathbun in *Globe*, 11 Dec. 1897
9 University of Toronto Archives, John Charlton diary, 27 Dec. 1897; [Liberal Party of Ontario] 'The Export of Sawlogs,' *Ontario General Elections* (Toronto, 1898)
10 R.C. Brown, *Canada's National Policy, 1883–1900* (Princeton: Princeton University Press, 1964), 333–7; PAC, Laurier papers, Laurier to G.A. Copeland, 25 May 1898, 23871–2; PAO, attorney-general of Ontario's records [herafter AGO Records], 1898, no. 997, Dickenson and Lansing to William R. Day, 11 June 1898
11 Ibid., Day to Pauncefote, 13 June 1898; Davies to Dickenson, 28 June 1898, personal and confidential. Dickenson did persuade Davies to suggest to the premier that the embargo be suspended; there was no reply.
12 PAC, Laurier papers, Joseph Chamberlain to Lord Aberdeen, 16 July 1898, 215023; ibid., Sir Richard Scott papers, vol. 4, Scott to Laurier, 23 July 1898; Hardy to Scott, 1 Aug. 1898, private.
13 Ibid., Hardy to Scott, 22 July 1898, private; ibid., Laurier papers, Laurier to Scott, 26 July 1898, 25245; Ontario, legislative assembly, *Journals*, 1898, 6; *Globe*, 23 Aug. 1898
14 PAO, AGO records, 1898, no. 997, memorandum of Attorney-General Hardy, n.d.
15 PAC, Laurier papers, Hardy to Laurier, 26, 29 Aug. (private), 1898; Chamberlain to Lord Aberdeen, 9 Sept. 1898; 26014–15, 26067–9, 26285; *Globe*, 21 Sept. 1898

Notes pages 40–5   247

16   University of Toronto Archives, John Charlton diary, 1, 14 April 1899; PAC, Laurier papers, petition of Michigan lumbermen to Lyman J. Gage, n.d.; Lord Minto to Sir Julian Pauncefote, 18 April 1898; Pauncefote to Minto, 22 April 1899; Laurier to Charlton, 6 March 1899, 29183g-i, 215033, 215036, 30939–40
17   Ibid., Farrer to Rodolphe Boudreau, 5, 23 May [1899], confidential; Laurier to Hardy, 16 May, private and confidential; Hardy to Laurier, 17 May 1899, confidential, 124999–5002, 125522–3, 33561 and 33515, 33679–80
18   Ibid., J.R. Cartwright to Messrs Scott and Houston, 27 June 1899; H.J. Scott to John Charlton, 29 June 1899; Cartwright to Scott, 6 July 1899; W.A. Charlton to Laurier, 14, 20 June 1899, private and confidential; Laurier to W.A. Charlton, 19 June 1899, 34953, 34955, 35273, 34566, 34568, 34567. Laurier was much annoyed by Hardy's refusal to grant the fiat and told Sir Richard Cartwright: 'The situation will become serious and very acute, and it seems to me that our friends at Toronto care very little for the consequences. I submit to you that we ought to make a strong effort upon Hardy to induce him to reconsider his determination'; ibid., Laurier to Cartwright, 15 May 1899, 33610.
19   Ibid., John Charlton to Reginald Tower, 26 June 1899; Lord Minto to Joseph Chamberlain, Sept. 1899; W.A. Charlton to Laurier, 28 July 1899, private; 37021–2, 19285–7, 35964; University of Toronto Archives, John Charlton diary, 10, 15, 17, 18, 19 July 1899; the Charlton brothers believed that Gibson and Hardy, never enthusiastic about the embargo, were attracted to the bonding scheme, but nothing came of it.
20   Nelles, *Politics of Development*, 79–80; E.J. Davis, *Speech in the Budget Debate* (Toronto, 1902), 9–10, 19–20
21   The background of the pulpwood manufacturing condition is sketched in Nelles, *Politics of Development*, 81–7.
22   O.W. Main, *The Canadian Nickel Industry, a Study in Market Control and Public Policy* (Toronto: University of Toronto Press, 1955), 19–32.
23   Nelles, *Politics of Development*, 90–2; PAC, Laurier papers, Stevenson Burke to Laurier, 22 Feb. 1898; Laurier to J.M. Gibson, 28 June 1898; R.M. Thompson to Laurier, 5 May, 22 Nov. 1898; 20847–52, 24547, 23070–5, 27734–5. For protests from British nickel producer Ludwig Mond, see ibid., trade and commerce department records, series A1, vol. 1206, Mond to Lord Strathcona, 6 May, 20 Dec. 1899.
24   *Papers, Orders-in-Council and Correspondence on the Mining and Treatment of Nickel and Copper Ore in the Province of Ontario* (Toronto: Queen's Printer, 1899); *Statutes of Ontario, 1900*, c. 13
25   PAC, Laurier papers, Stevenson Burke to E.J. Davis, 26 Jan. 1900; Ross to Laurier, 1, 23 Feb. personal, 13 March 1900; Laurier to Ross, 1 March 1900; 225461–5, 42718–21, 42723, 42724; those interested in how such things are arranged might note Thompson's letter to Laurier dated 18 Oct. 1906 (Laurier papers, 114779), enclosing a cheque for $5,000 of profit on an unnamed stock transaction.
26   PAO, James P. Whitney papers, Wallace Nesbitt to Arthur F. Wallis, 11 April 1900, private; PAC, Laurier papers, Ross to Laurier, 4 May 1900, personal; Laurier to Ross, 7 May 1900, private and confidential; 45254–5, 45257–8; petition of W.R.P. Parker et al. to the governor-general in council, 13 Sept. 1900, in Canada, department of justice, *Correspondence, Reports of the Minister of Justice and Orders-in-Council upon the Subject of Provincial Legislation, 1896–1920*, F.H. Gisbourne and A.A. Fraser, comps (Ottawa: King's Printer, 1922) [hereafter *Provincial Legislation, 1896–1920*], 5–9. For similar protests from Britain see PAC, trade and commerce department records, series A1, vol. 1206, Ludwig Mond to Lord Strathcona, 11 April 1900, and from the CPR see ibid., T.G. Shaughnessy to W.G. Parmelee, 31 March 1900.
27   Report of Attorney-General Gibson, 20 Dec. 1900; memorandum as to disallowance of 63 Vic. (Ont.), chap. 13, submitted by J.M. Clark, n.d.; *Provincial Legislation, 1896–1920*, 20–2, 32–4; H.H. Vivian's petition is contained in PAC, Laurier papers, R.W. Sinclair to Laurier, 10 May 1901, 56072–3.
28   Ibid., Parker to Laurier, 19 March 1901; E.S. Clouston to Laurier, 6 May 1901, private; Burke to Cartwright, 20 Jan. 1900; Bertram to Laurier, 11 April, 15 May, confidential, 1901; 54486–7, 55947, 225455–60, 55278–9, 56232. But not all federal officials were convinced; Richard Cartwright's deputy, W.G. Parmelee, added a note to a letter from Bertram to Cartwright: 'I am not particularly impressed by Mr. Bertram's statements ... The whole situation is, of course

controlled by the "Canada Copper Company," whose interests are in New Jersey; and as long as they can keep up the bluff they will make no effort to do any refining in Canada'; see ibid., trade and commerce department records, series A1, vol. 1221, personal memo to the minister from W.G.P. attached to Bertram to Cartwright, 9 April 1901.
29 *Canadian Annual Review* [herafter *CAR*], 1901 (Toronto: Canadian Annual Review, 1902), 42–5; the value of output was up almost 50 per cent over 1898; Ontario, legislative assembly, *Journals*, 1901, 165–7
30 Ross had been negotiating with Canadian Copper over the smelter throughout 1900; see PAC, J.S. Willison papers, Ross to Willison, 14 May 1900, 26126, and PAC, Laurier papers, Ross to Laurier, 19 Nov. 1900, confidential, 50872–3; PAO, George W. Ross papers, special series, Mills to Ross, 11 April 1901; Ross to Mills, 27 April 1901; Mills to Ross, 25 April 1921 [sic, 1901] in *Provincial Legislation, 1896–1920*, 34–5. The excuse that the legislature had adjourned was feeble, since Mills's first warning had arrived the very day, 12 April, on which the Conservative motion calling for the implementation of the nickel tax was debated.
31 PAC, Laurier papers, Ross to Laurier, 27 April 1901, private; Gibson to Laurier, 27 April 1901, private and confidential; 55769–70, 55760–1
32 Ibid., Laurier to John Bertram, 16 April 1901, private and confidential; Laurier to Ross, 29 April 1901; Laurier to Gibson, 29 April 1901; 55280, 55278–9, 55763, 55762.
33 Mills to Ross, 7 May 1901; report of Justice Minister Mills, 10 May 1901, *Provincial Legislation, 1896–1920*; PAC, Laurier papers, Laurier to E.S. Clouston, 7 May 1901; Ross to Laurier, 14 May 1901, private; Laurier to Ross, 15 May 1901; 55951, 56180–1, 56182–3
34 Ibid., Laurier to Ross, 16 May, private, 17, 31 May, private, 1901; Ross to Laurier, 17 May, 4 June, personal, 1901; 56281, 56284, 56280a, 56282, 56280, 56681; *Provincial Legislation, 1896–1920*, report of Premier George Ross, 14 May 1901, 50–1
35 For a description of the later efforts to establish a nickel refinery see Royal Ontario Nickel Commission, *Report* (Toronto: King's Printer, 1917); Main, *Canadian Nickel Industry*, 82–9; Nelles, *Politics of Development*, 326–35, 349–61.
36 An excellent history of the T&NO is Albert Tucker, *Steam into Wilderness, Ontario Northland Railway, 1902–1962* (Toronto: Fitzhenry and Whiteside, 1978).
37 Nelles, *Politics of Development*, 157–73; *Provincial Legislation, 1896–1920*, 73–80, contains petition of J.M. Clark and James Baird to the lieutenant-governor in council of Ontario, 8 June 1906; petition of the Florence Mining Co., Limited, to the governor-general in council, 1906; C.A. Masten to A.B. Aylesworth, 11 Dec. 1906; report of Justice Minister Aylesworth, 21 May 1907.
38 *Statutes of Ontario*, 1907, c. 15; PAO, Whitney papers, Maw to Whitney, 12 Feb. 1907; PAC, Laurier papers, Reverend C.W. Gordon to Laurier, 10 Sept. 1907, 129010–19; Connor's brother, Col. J.R. Gordon, had a large interest in the Florence Mining Company.
39 Laurier's descriptions of the act are contained in ibid., Laurier to J.M. Clark, 20 Nov. 1908, 17 Feb. 1909, private; Laurier to C.W. Gordon, 14 Sept. 1907; 147916–17, 151845, 129021–2; *Globe*, 29 Jan. 1907; Ontario, legislative assembly, *Journals*, 1907, 302–5.
40 PAC, Laurier Papers, petition of F.R. Latchford 'To the Honourable the Minister of Justice, Ottawa, in the Matter of an Act Respecting Cobalt Lake and Kerr Lake ...,' n.d. [25 Oct. 1907]; Latchford to Laurier, 18, 20 (Private) Nov. 1907; Laurier to Latchford, 19 Nov. 1907; 135744–52, 132332, 132333, 132334.
41 Ibid., J.M. Clark to Laurier, 15 April 1908, private; Laurier to J.M. Gibson, 5 Jan. 1909; 139084–7, 134636–7; PAO, AGO records, 1907, no. 1498, 'Rough sketch of matters to be considered in reply to Petition for disallowance,' attached to Thomas Gibson to J.R. Cartwright, 28 Oct. 1907; draft of Ontario reply to petition for disallowance, 13 Dec. 1907. This last has been added to in Whitney's own hand.
42 *CAR*, 1908, 285–7; PAC, Laurier papers, Clark to Laurier, 30 Jan. 1908, private; Laurier to Clark, 3 Feb. 1908, private; 135739–42c, 135743
43 *Provincial Legislation, 1896–1920*, report of Justice Minister Aylesworth, 29 April 1908, 80–5
44 PAO, Whitney Papers, special series, judgment of Mr Justice Riddell in *Florence Mining Co. v. Cobalt Lake Mining Co.*, 15 June 1908
45 PAC, Laurier papers, Laurier to Clark, 17 Feb. 1909, private, 151845; Can., H. of C., *Deb.*, 1909, 1751–8
46 *Globe*, 3 March 1909

47 *The Florence Mining Company v. the Cobalt Lake Mining Company, Judgment of the Court of Appeal of Ontario* (Toronto: King's Printer, 1909); PAO, Whitney papers, Whitney to E.C. Whitney, 7 April 1909; Whitney to R.L. Borden, 7, 12 (private) April 1909; A.C. Boyce to Whitney, 7, 15 April 1909; Whitney to Boyce, 8, 16 April 1909, private; Borden to Whitney, 17 April 1909; Britton Osler to Whitney, 30 March 1910 enclosing copy of the Privy Council decision; Aylesworth to Whitney, 31 March 1910
48 Laurier used this adjective in his letter of 20 Nov. 1908 to J.M. Clark; see PAC, Laurier papers, 147916–17.
49 *Globe*, 6 Aug. 1897

CHAPTER 3: *Public Power and Disallowance*

1 Royal Ontario Nickel Commission, *Report*, 19
2 Nelles, *Politics of Development*, 215–23
3 Whitney is quoted in W.R. Plewman, *Adam Beck and The Ontario Hydro* (Toronto: Ryerson, 1947), 47.
4 For an analysis of the way in which private interests tried to play off the two levels of government in the case of the manufacturing condition, Cobalt Lake and Hydro, see Christopher Armstrong and H.V. Nelles, 'Private Property in Peril: Ontario Businessmen and the Federal System, 1898–1911.' *Business History Review* XLVII (1973), 158–76.
5 The origins of the public power movement are discussed in Nelles, *Politics of Development*, 237–55, and Plewman, *Adam Beck*, 28–42.
6 PAO, Whitney papers, letters re water power development, 1901–1906, T.W.H. Leavitt to Kaiser, 10 Aug. 1901, 29 Jan. 1902 strictly private and confidential; Whitney to Kaiser, 9 Feb., 3 March 1903; copy of 'Resolution Drafted by Dr. Kaiser, Alex Wright, Leavitt and Dr. B. Nesbitt,' n.d.; Ontario, legislative assembly, *Journals*, 1902, 85, 105
7 PAO, Whitney papers, 'Memorandum upon the Policy of the Government in Regard to the Draft Agreement of the 9th January, 1905, Between the Commissioners of the Queen Victoria Niagara Falls Park of the First Part and the Electrical Development Company of the Second Part, and upon the General Policy to be pursued with reference to the Development of Hydraulic and Electrical Power at Niagara Falls and Other Parts of Ontario'; the agreement referred to granted all the remaining water rights to the EDC after the Ross administration had been defeated at the polls and was promptly repudiated by the incoming Conservatives.
8 Whitney's remarks on public ownership are quoted in the *CAR*, 1906, 179; PAO, Whitney papers, Sir Henry Pellat to Whitney, 9 Feb. 1906; PAC, Laurier papers, Whitney to Laurier, 26 May 1906, private; enclosing copy of Whitney to H. Evans Gordon, 23 May 1906, 11591–6.
9 PAO, Whitney papers, Whitney to J.V. Lyon, 13 Sept. 1906, private; Whitney to E.C. Whitney, 4 Dec. 1907, private; 18 March 1908
10 Nelles, *Politics of Development*, chap. 7, 'Power Politics,' 256–306 gives a first-rate account of the fight over public power from 1905 to 1910; see also Plewman, *Adam Beck*, 51–4. The enabling legislation was *Statutes of Ontario*, 1908 c. 22.
11 Plewman, *Adam Beck*, 89–90; PAO, Whitney papers, memorandum 'Re: Amendment of Section 8, Chapter 19, Hydro Electric Power Act of 1909,' n.d.; J.S. Hendrie to Whitney, 4 March 1909; *Statutes of Ontario*, 1909, c. 19
12 *CAR*, 1909, 374; PAO, Whitney papers, Whitney to F.W. Taylor, 9 Aug. (private and confidential), 13 Dec. (confidential) 1909
13 PAC, Laurier papers, E.R. Wood to Laurier, 17 June 1909, personal; 157957–60; PAO, Whitney papers, F.W. Taylor to Whitney, 18 May 1909 enclosing clipping from the London *Financial Times*
14 PAO, AGO records, 1909, no. 1210, petition of members of Toronto Stock Exchange; PAC, Laurier papers, Col. James Mason to Laurier, 1 Dec. 1909; Reverend Dr Macklem to Laurier, 25 Nov. 1909, 163066–7, 162741–2; *The Credit of Canada* (Toronto, 1909).
15 *CAR*, 1909, 374–7; PAO, Whitney papers, Whitney to E.C. Whitney, 21 June 1909, private; Whitney to Edward Farrer, 3 Aug. 1909, private; clipping from the *Economist*, 28 Aug. 1909; F.W. Taylor to Whitney, 12 May 1909, confidential; Whitney to Taylor, 9 Aug. 1909, private and confidential

250 Notes pages 60-7

16 Ibid., Whitney to Aylesworth, 9 Oct. 1909; one copy of *A Question of Disallowance* (n.p., n.d.) may be found in ibid., special series.
17 Ibid., Whitney to Aylesworth, 13, 20 (2 letters), 24 Nov. 1909; Aylesworth to Whitney, 15, 22 Nov. 1909; at some time in early November the two men met to discuss the matter; see ibid., Aylesworth to Whitney, 10 Nov. 1909, personal; Whitney to Aylesworth, 11 Nov. 1909, private; Whitney to E.C. Whitney, 11 Nov. 1909.
18 Ibid., Whitney to Beck, 9 Oct. 1909; Whitney to Aylesworth, 7 Dec. 1909, confidential; ibid., special series, report of attorney-general J.J. Foy, 7 Dec. 1909; PAO, AGO records, 1909, no. 1210, memorandum, unsigned, n.d.
19 PAO, Whitney papers, Whitney to F.W. Taylor, 13 Dec. 1909, confidential; Whitney to Borden 15 Dec. 1909
20 Ibid., Whitney to Andrew Broder, 17 Dec. 1909; Broder to Whitney, Dec. 24, 1909; Whitney to E.C. Whitney, 20 Dec. 1909; Borden to Whitney 14 Dec. 1909
21 PAC, Laurier papers, Laurier to Aylesworth, 3 Sept. 1909, private; Aylesworth to Laurier, 15 Sept. 1909; 159828-30, 159814-25. The justice minister was absent in England much of the summer, but even there he did not escape the furore raised by opponents of the legislation: 'I have been flooded all summer with marked copies of newspapers attacking the legislation, and Mr Asquith here talked to me about it.'
22 Ibid., Laurier to W.M. German, MP, 24 Sept. 1909; Laurier to J.L. Blaikie, 14 June 1909; 160120-1, 156871
23 Ibid., Laurier to B.E. Walker, 5 June 1909; Laurier to F.A. Vanderlip, 24 Nov. 1909; 156482-3, 162564
24 Ibid., Laurier to Hugh Blain, 23 Nov. 1909; Laurier to C.W. Kerr, 25 Nov. 1909; 162331-2, 162632
25 Ibid., Henry O'Brien to Laurier 25 Nov., 3 Dec. 1909; Laurier to B.E. Walker, 5 June 1909; 162735-6, 162738-40, 156482-3
26 Ibid., R.C. Smith to Laurier, 15 Jan. 1910; Laurier to Aylesworth, 17 Jan. 1910; 165215, 159413; *Mail and Empire*, 25 April 1910
27 PAO, Whitney papers, Whitney to A.J. Dawson, 18 April 1910, confidential; PAC, Laurier papers, Whitney to Laurier, 30 March 1910; Laurier to Whitney, 31 March 1910; 168695, 168966
28 *Provincial Legislation, 1896-1920*, report of Justice Minister Aylesworth, 15 April 1910, 92-7
29 PAO, Whitney papers, Whitney to A.J. Dawson, 18 April 1910, confidential; *Mail and Empire* 25 April 1910
30 PAC, Laurier papers, Wallace Nesbitt to Laurier, 1 Nov. 1909; Laurier to Nesbitt, 3 Nov. 1909; 161564-7
31 PAO, Whitney papers, Whitney to Grey, 14 Dec. 1910, 9 Jan. 1911 private; University of Toronto Archives, B.E. Walker papers, Walker to Grey 30 Jan. 1911, private.
32 Report of the Minister of Justice, 17 May 1881, in *Provincial Legislation, 1867-1895*, 177
33 *Attorney-General for Canada v. Attorney-General for Ontario (Fisheries Reference)* (1898) *O'Connor Report*, annex, 3, case no. 16
34 *CAR*, 1909, 381-3
35 PAC, Laurier papers, Laurier to Reverend Dr Macklem 26 Nov. 1909, 162743
36 Nelles, *Politics of Development*, 175
37 PAC, Laurier papers, Laurier to Wallace Nesbitt, 3 Nov. 1909, 161567
38 Ibid., David Mills to Laurier, 5 July 1898; Laurier to Joseph Chamberlain, 11 Feb. 1899; Chamberlain to Laurier, 10 March 1899, private; Sir Louis Davies to Laurier, 20 Oct. 1899, private and confidential; 24760-2, 31226-33, 31219-25, 224399-400
39 PAO, Whitney papers, Whitney to R.L. Borden, 11 Sept. 1907
40 Ibid., special series, memorandum for the Hon. the prime minister with respect to the Petawawa camp site from Aubrey White, 28 March 1907; report of Premier Whitney to the lieutenant-governor, 2 April 1907
41 Ibid., Whitney to Sir Frederick Borden, 26 March 1907; Borden to Whitney, 26 March 1907, private; *Documents and Correspondence Regarding Petawawa Camp and Proceedings in the Legislature, Printed by Order of the Legislative Assembly of Ontario* (Toronto: King's Printer, 1907), 12; Ontario, legislative assembly, *Journals*, 1907, 326; Can., H. of C., *Deb.*, 1907, 7620-8
42 LaForest, *Disallowance and Reservation*, Appendix A, table of disallowed statutes, 1867-1954

Notes pages 68-75   251

CHAPTER 4: *Exporting Electricity*

1   See Nelles, *Politics of Development*, 310-26, 362-375
2   Can., H. of C., *Deb.*, 1906, pp. 3078-9, 3091, 3095, 3097
3   Ibid., 3094; PAO, Whitney papers, Fitzpatrick to Whitney, 11 May 1906; to which are attached memorandum from J.R. Cartwright to Attorney-General J.J. Foy, 'Re Dominion Bill No. 145,' 14 May 1906, and memorandum from Cartwright, 'Memo re Dominion Bill No. 145,' 17 May 1906; Whitney to Fitzpatrick, 17 May 1906; Fitzpatrick to Whitney, 18 May 1906
4   PAC, Laurier papers, Gibbons to Laurier, 29 Nov. 10 Dec. (strictly private) 1906, 7, 22 (confidential) Jan. 1907; Laurier to Gibbons, 24 Jan. 1907; 116166-70, 116504-6, 117937-44, 118550-3, 118554; ibid., J.S. Willison papers, Gibbons to Willison, 8 Jan. 1907, confidential, 11626-7
5   Ibid., Gibbons to Willison, 2 May 1906, 11621-3, enclosing 'Second Interim Report of the Canadian Section of the International Waterways Commission,' 15 March 1906; quotation from ibid., Laurier papers, E.W. Thomson to Laurier, n.d., 100212-13
6   Ibid., Gibbons to Laurier, 10 Dec. 1906, strictly private, 7 Jan. 1907; Laurier to Gibbons, 9 Jan. 1907; 116504-6, 117937-44, 117945; PAO, Whitney papers, Whitney to Adam Beck, 7 Dec. 1906, private; memorandum for the Honourable J.P. Whitney, 12 Dec. 1906
7   PAC, George C. Gibbons papers, vol. 5, Aylesworth to Gibbons, 29 Dec. 1906; PAO, Whitney papers, Aylesworth to Whitney, 30 Jan. 25 Feb. 1907; Whitney to Aylesworth, 28 Feb. 1907; Borden to Whitney, 31 Jan. 1907; Whitney to Borden 28 Feb. 1907, private; Can., H. of C., *Deb.*, 1907, 4967-8
8   PAC, Laurier papers, Gibbons to Laurier, 24 Sept. 1907 (2 letters); 'Summary of Memorandum Prepared by Mr. Bryce, 23rd February, 1908, of his Conversation with Sir W.L. during his visit to Ottawa'; 129636, 129648-51, 136223-4; PAO, Whitney papers, Beck to Whitney, 14 Feb. 1908; Whitney to Laurier, 15, 18 Feb. 1908; *CAR*, 1908, 309
9   PAC, Gibbons papers, vol. 6, Whitney to Gibbons, 6 March 1908
10 PAO, Whitney papers, Whitney to A.C. Macdonnell, 14 May 1909, Private; 'Memorandum of Minister of Justice on proposed treaty between Great Britain and United States regarding waters between United States and Canada,' 27 May 1909, reprinted in *Documents on Canadian External Relations, 1909-1918*, vol. 1 (Ottawa: Queen's Printer, 1967), 388-95
11 PAO, George W. Ross papers, memorandum re 'Province vs. Dominion re Water Powers, Three Principles to be Agreed Upon,' n.d.
12 Ibid., Whitney papers, Whitney to J.W. Allison, 27 Dec. 1907; PAC, Gibbons papers, vol. 8, Gibbons to Laurier, 14 Oct. 1907. Gibbons later changed his mind and complained that opponents of the development were taking a 'dog-in-the-mangerish' attitude in refusing even to examine a scheme which promised to produce power and improve navigation; ibid., Laurier papers, Gibbons to Laurier, 2 Nov. 1908, 147044-5.
13 PAO, AGO records, 1912, no. 187, memorandum from George Lynch-Staunton, n.d., attached to Whitney to Lynch-Staunton, 21 March 1911; 'Memorandum for the Honourable J.J. Foy re bed of Navigable Rivers,' attached to Lynch-Staunton to Foy, 16 March 1912
14 Can., H. of C., *Deb.*, 1909, 1052
15 PAC, Laurier papers, transcript of hearings of International Waterways Commission on the application of the Long Sault Development Company and the St Lawrence Power Company to dam the St Lawrence, 9-10 Feb. 1910, 166394a-628; Hilliard's statement, 108 of transcript; J.W. Dafoe, *Clifford Sifton in Relation to His Times* (Toronto: Macmillan, 1931), 349-50, 446-7
16 Can., H. of C., *Deb.*, 1910, 5317-5495; Pugsley's speech at 5377-8; PAO, Whitney papers, Whitney to J.G. Steacey, 14 Feb. 1910. Laurier complained to George Gibbons that 'The matter was brought up as private bill, [and] we paid no attention to it, but we were placed in a somewhat false position by what occurred in the House Wednesday'; PAC, Gibbons papers, vol. 7, Laurier to Gibbons, 18 March 1910
17 Can., H, of C., *Deb.*, 1910, 6227-9; *CAR*, 1910, 248-9
18 PAC, Gibbons papers, vol. 3, Laurier to Gibbons, 1 March 1910, private; ibid., vol. 7, same to same, 18 March 1910 (quoted)
19 Ibid., Laurier papers, Laurier to Gibbons, 7 April 1910; Laurier to H.M. Mowat, 26 Dec. 1910; 169465, 178754
20 Despite this the promoters kept the scheme alive and tried to revive it in both 1911 and 1912

252   Notes pages 75-81

21 *Statutes of Ontario*, 1911, c., 6; PAO, Whitney papers, Whitney to George Lynch-Staunton, 21 March 1911
22 Report of Justice Minister C.J. Doherty, 12 Feb. 1912; report of Attorney-General J.J. Foy, 16 March 1912; report of Justice Minister Doherty, 19 April 1912, in *Provincial Legislation, 1896-1920*, 103-4, 107-12, 104-7
23 PAC, George P. Graham papers, A.B. Aylesworth to Graham, 4 July 1911, confidential, 769-70
24 PAC, Robert L. Borden papers, memorandum of *Attorney-General of Ontario v. Attorney General of Canada, Trent River and Welland Canal cases*, from E.L. Newcombe, n.d. [4 Oct. 1915], confidential; George-Lynch Staunton to Borden, 5 Jan. 1913 [sic, 1914]; Arthur Meighen to Borden, 3 Feb. 1914; Newcombe to Borden, 9 May 1914; Hearst to Borden, 17 Sept. 1915; Newcombe to Borden, 2 Nov. 1915; Cochrane to Borden, 4 Nov. 1915, private; 99021-39, 98936-44, 98948, 98957-9, 98964-5, 98982-5, 93992
25 Ibid., Beck to Perley, 23 April 1914; Perley to Borden, 28 May 1914, 98362-5, 98392-3
26 PAO, E.C. Drury papers, special series, Ontario order-in-council, 18 June 1914; Plewman, *Adam Beck*, 176-80; *Statutes of Ontario*, 1916, c. 20
27 PAC, Borden papers, Robert Lansing to Sir C. Spring-Rice, 6 April 1916, 98407-9; PAO, AGO records, 1916, no. 818, Lucas to Borden, 11 May 1916, personal, enclosing report of the attorney-general, 11 May 1916
28 *CAR*, 1916, 511; 'Petition for Disallowance ... of the Electrical Development Company ... 'n.d. [21 April 1917], in *Provincial Legislation, 1896-1920*, 142-7
29 I.B. Lucas to E.L. Newcombe, 30 April 1917; report of Justice Minister C.J. Doherty, 4 May 1917; in *Provincial Legislation, 1896-1920*, 138-42, 136-8
30 PAO, William H. Hearst papers, special series, Sir Adam Beck to Hearst, 16 March 1916; ibid., Drury papers, special series, 'Memorandum to Sir Adam Beck, KB, re Conference with Cabinet, at Parliament Buildings, May 23rd, re Supply of Power at Niagara' [from F.A. Gaby], 27 May 1916; memorandum from W.W. Pope to Beck, 25 May 1916
31 Ibid., Hearst papers, special series, Hearst to E.L. Patenaude, 2 June 1916; *CAR*, 1916, 509-12. On the shortage in the autumn of 1916 see PAC, J.W. Flavelle Papers, vol. 7, folder 82, R.H. Brand to Flavelle 26 Oct. 1916 and other letters in this folder.
32 *CAR*, 1917, 651-2; Plewman, *Adam Beck*, 201-2; PAC, George E. Foster Papers, vol. 36, folder 28, memorandum by Foster re Niagara Power, n.d. [1917], shows that a federal order-in-council dated 29 March 1917 fixed the annual exports for 1916-17 of the three power companies at Niagara as follows: Ontario Power, 52,000 horsepower; Canadian Niagara, 45,500 horsepower; Electrical Development, 45,500 horsepower.
33 *Statutes of Ontario*, 1916, c. 20, 21; 1917, c. 21, 22; Plewman, *Adam Beck*, 206-9; 'Memorandum Concerning Recent Provincial Legislation and Executive Action in Canada with Special Reference to the Niagara Question,' in *Provincial Legislation, 1896-1920*, 147-63
34 Lucas to E.L. Newcombe, April 30, 1917; Report of Justice Minister C.J. Doherty, 4 May 1917, in *Provincial Legislation, 1896-1920*, 136-42; PAO, AGO records, 1917, no. 2741, Ontario order-in-council, 25 July 1917
35 Petition of the Electrical Development Company, n.d. [9 Nov. 1917]; report of Attorney-General I.B. Lucas, 19 March 1918, in *Provincial Legislation, 1896-1920*, 176-84; PAO, AGO records, 1917, no. 785, Kilmer to Edward Bayly, 13 April 1918
36 Report of Justice Minister C.J. Doherty, 24 April 1918, in *Provincial Legislation, 1896-1920*, 174-6; PAO, AGO records, 1917, no. 2741, report of the commissioners re the Electrical Development Company, 25 April 1918
37 PAC, Flavelle papers, vol. 7, folder 82, Imperial Munitions Board to London representative, 20 June 1917; ibid., Foster papers, vol. 70, folder 179, Flavelle to Sir Joseph Pope, 5 July 1917
38 Ibid., Borden papers, Flavelle to Borden, 5 July 1917; Borden to Hearst, 12 July 1917; Hearst to Borden, 18 July 1917, confidential, 124631-3, 124637, 124640-3
39 Protests from munitions makers in ibid., Flavelle papers, vol. 7, folder 82; quotation from ibid., Borden papers, R.H. Brand to Flavelle, 8 Oct. 1917. Ibid., Sir Cecil Spring-Rice to governor-general, 18 Sept. 1917; Frank Cochrane to Borden, 8 Sept. 1917; 124674, 124667, 124660-1
40 See, Canada, Royal Commission on the Export of Electricity, *Report on the Export of Electricity from Canada and Report of the Power Controller* (Ottawa: King's Printer, 1919) [hereafter, Power Controller, *Report*], 11-23

41 PAC, Borden papers, Beck to Borden, 25 Oct. 1917, 124685–6; Plewman, *Adam Beck*, 204–6; order-in-council, 6 Nov. 1917, in Power Controller, *Report*, 4–5, 25–7
42 Ibid., 26–34; PAC, Borden papers, Flavelle to Borden, 6 March 1918, 124698–703
43 Ibid., L.L. Summers to Flavelle, 18 Jan. 1918; Lloyd harris to Flavelle, 31 Jan. 1918; Flavelle to Borden, 1 Feb. 1918; Hearst to Borden, 4 Feb. 1918; 124507, 124509–10, 124512–13, 124693, and Borden diary, 16, 19 Feb. 1918
44 Ibid., diary, 22–4, 28 Feb. 1918; R.J. Bulkley to Borden, 2 March 1918; N.W. Rowell to Drayton, 8 March 1918, 124694–5, 124704–5
45 Ibid., Lloyd Harris to Borden, 3 April 1918, Confidential; Borden to Harris, 9 April 1918, 124708–9, 124712; Borden diary, 6 April 1918; ibid., G.E. Foster papers, vol. 70, folder 28, order-in-council, 17 April 1918
46 Ibid., vol. 36, folder 28, transcript of meeting of Toronto Branch, Canadian Manufacturers' Association, with power controller, 18 Oct. 1918
47 Ibid., Flavelle to Rowell, 22 Oct. 1918; John Murphy to Arthur Meighen, 21 Oct. 1918
48 Ibid., Flavelle to Rowell, 22 Oct. 1918; Power Controller, *Report*, 58
49 *CAR*, 1920, 572–3
50 Nelles, *Politics of Development*, 375

CHAPTER 5: *Playing the Federal-Provincial Game*

1 s. 92 (11)
2 s. 92 (10); Andrée Lajoie, *Le Pouvoir Déclaratoire du Parlement, Augmentation Discrétionnaire de la Compétence Fédérale au Canada* (Montreal: Presses de l'Université de Montréal, 1969), gives a full account of the subject and list of declarations, 1867–1961.
3 *Citizens Insurance Co. v. Parsons, O'Connor Report*, annex 3, case no. 5
4 PAO, provincial secretary's records, series 1-1-D, 1882, no. 599, lieutenant-governor of Ontario to secretary of state, 10 March 1882; *Dominion-Provincial Conferences, 1887–1926*, 21
5 PAC, E.H. Bronson Papers, vol. 702, Bronson to A. G. Blair, 12 Feb. 1897
6 Can., H. of C., *Deb.*, 1896, 2010–18, 2060–79; Fitzpatrick quoted at 2017
7 See n. 5 above
8 Can., H. of C., *Deb.*, 1902, 3131–50; Borden quoted at 3141, Laurier at 3143
9 Ibid., 3628–35
10 PAO, AGO records, 1903, no. 710, Gibson to Fitzpatrick, 5 March 1903
11 Ibid., Fitzpatrick to Gibson, 11 March 1903; Gibson to Blair, 11 May 1903; Blair to Gibson, 12, 18 May 1903
12 Ibid., Irving to J.R. Cartwright, 28 May 1903, enclosing draft letters from Gibson to Blair and to Fitzpatrick; Blair to Gibson, 2 June 1903; Ontario, legislative assembly, *Journals*, 1903, 329
13 Can., H. of C., *Deb.*, 1903, pp. 6080–6108
14 Ibid., 6110–30, 6173
15 Ibid., 6116–7, 6092–3
16 Ibid., 6198; PAC, Laurier papers, memorandum submitted in support of the Toronto and Hamilton Railway Bill by H.H. Dewart, 22 July 1903; Markey to Laurier, 15 July 1903, 76096–103, 75093–8; ibid., J.S. Willison papers, Frederick Hamilton to Willison, 12 Aug. 1903, 13140–1
17 Ibid., Laurier papers, petition of W.D. Lighthall et al. in reply to H.H. Dewart's memorandum on the Toronto and Hamilton Railway Bill, 27 July 1903, 76076–85; Can. H. of C., *Deb.*, 1903, 7813–14; PAC, Willison papers, Frederick Hamilton to Willison, 14, 15 (telegram and letter) Aug. 1903, 13142–3, 13144, 13147–56; quotation from Hamilton's telegram
18 Can. H. of C., *Deb.*, 1903, 9424–5, 9431
19 PAC, Laurier papers, Laurier to Senator J.K. Kerr, 5 Sept. 1903; Ross to Laurier, Oct. 1903; 76815, 77387–8
20 Report of Attorney-General J.M. Gibson, 25 June 1904, in *Provincial Legislation, 1896–1920*, 69–72
21 See Armstrong and Nelles, 'Private Property in Peril: Ontario Businessmen and the Federal System, 1898–1911,' 158–76
22 PAC, Laurier papers, vol. 630, Ontario order-in-council, 13 Jan 1905
23 Can., H. of C., *Deb.*, 1905, 2715–22

254 Notes pages 93-100

24 PAC, Laurier papers, J.P. Whitney to Laurier, 1 April 1905, 96218-19; PAO, Whitney papers, R.G. Code to Whitney, 17 May 1905; Can., H. of C., *Deb.*, 1905, 9817-19
25 Matheson quoted in *CAR*, 1905, 407; PAO, Whitney papers, Whitney to R.G. Code, 11 May 1905, personal; Code to Whitney, 12, 17 May 1905; Code to Whitney, 31 Oct. 1905; Whitney to Code, 1 Nov. 1905
26 PAO, William H. Hearst papers, special series, memorandum from the Ontario Railway and Municipal Board, 29 Sept. 1906; Code to Whitney, 25, Sept. 1906; Can. H. of C., *Deb.*, 1906, 3153-4; 'Minutes of the Proceedings in Conference of the Representatives of Canada and of the Provinces, October, 1906,' *Dominion-Provincial Conferences, 1887-1926*, 59, 63
27 In 1906, for instance, the Canadian Niagara Power Company, applied for legislation confirming its provincial charter because a recent court decision (*Hewson v. Ontario Power Company* [1905]) seemed to cast doubt upon the authority of the province to authorize companies to transmit electricity across the international boundary. The provincial government protested and the bill eventually was allowed to drop. See PAO, AGO records, 1905, no. 2265; 1906, no. 632
28 *CAR*, 1907, 495-6; PAO, Whitney papers, R.G. Code to Whitney, 7 Feb. 1908 enclosing Gibson to Whitney, 9, 22 March 1907
29 Whitney quoted in *CAR*, 1907, 494-5
30 Ibid.; PAC, Laurier papers, Graham to Laurier, 18 Nov. 1907, confidential, 132283-4
31 *CAR*, 1907, 495-6 quotes Whitney; Can., H. of C., *Deb.*, 1907, 7314-7407, 7485-91, 7915-17; the last of these contains a defence of Gibson by the bill's chief promoter, Archibald Campbell, Liberal MP for York Centre, who attacked the *Globe* for its criticisms.
32 PAC, Laurier papers Graham to Laurier, 18 Nov. 1907, confidential, 132283-4
33 *CAR*, 1908, 283; PAC, Laurier papers, George P. Graham to Laurier, 31 Jan. 1908, confidential, 135802-4; Can., H. of C., *Deb.*, 1908, 3724 (speech of Edmund Bristol, Toronto Centre)
34 PAC, Laurier papers, Gibson to Laurier, 27 Jan. 1908, private; Laurier to Gibson, 30 Jan. 1908; 135613-15, 135616; Can., H. of C., *Deb.*, 1908, 3721-30, 4368-70, 4543-4
35 See n. 20 above
36 Can., H. of C., *Deb*, 1910, 6792-3 (Sproule), 6787-91 (Graham), 6796-7 (Crothers). The debates concerned applications from the Hamilton, Waterloo and Guelph Railway (rumoured to be linked to the Hamilton Radial group) and the Toronto and Eastern Railway.
37 PAO, Whitney papers, Whitney to Robert Borden, 19 April 1907, private. This interpretation of Conmee's plans is drawn from his parliamentary critics; he, of course, repeatedly denied any such intent.
38 Ibid., Whitney to Graham, 18 Dec. 1907, private; Ontario, legislative assembly, *Journals*, 1908, 215-18; PAC, Laurier papers, MacKay to Laurier, 30 March 1908 (2 telegrams); Laurier to MacKay, 30, 31 March 1908; C.M. Bowman to Laurier, 31 March 1908, personal; Laurier to Bowman, 31 March 1908, 138454, 138456, 138457, 138455, 138505, 138506
39 Ibid., Conmee to Laurier, 1 April 1908, private; Laurier to Conmee, 2 April 1908; A.G. MacKay to H.H. Miller, 7 April 1908, 138533-6, 138537-8, 138747-50
40 *CAR*, 1909, 220-1; R.L. Borden, *Robert Laird Borden: His Memoirs* (Toronto: Macmillan, 1938), 243-4; Can., H. of C., *Deb*, 1909, 1026-53; PAO, Whitney papers, Andrew Broder to Whitney, 15 Feb. 1909; Whitney to E.C. Whitney, 17 Feb. 1909, private
41 Ibid., Whitney to Broder, 16 Feb. 1909, private; Broder to Whitney, 17 Feb. 1909, confidential; R.G. Code to Whitney, 4 March 1909; Can., H. of C., *Deb.*, 1909, 4476-4538; Aylesworth's speech at 4476, Boyce's at 4520-1, Lennox's at 4522
42 Ibid., 4536-8; PAO, Whitney papers, Code to Whitney, 20 April 1909; Boyce to Whitney, 20 April 1909
43 PAC, Laurier papers, Conmee to Laurier, n.d. [April 1909], 27 April 1909; Laurier to Conmee, 26, 28 April 1909; 155252-71, 155273, 155272, 155275
44 PAO, Whitney papers, R.G. Code to Whitney 3, 4 May 1909; Can., H. of C., *Deb.*, 1909, 5352-5430, 5561-4; Laurier's statement at 5405
45 Ibid., 5958-60; *CAR*, 1909, 221
46 Ibid., Can., H. of C., *Deb.*, 1909, 6001-6; PAO, Whitney papers, R.G. Code to Whitney, 8, 14 (2 letters), 15 May 1909; A.C. Macdonell to Whitney, 9 May 1909; Bowell to Whitney, 17 May 1909
47 Ibid., A.C. Boyce to Whitney, 4 March 1910; PAC, Laurier papers, Sifton to Laurier, 7 March 1910, 167906-8; Dafoe, *Clifford Sifton*, 351-2

Notes pages 100-7   255

48 Report of speech at Halifax, 20 Aug. 1907, reprinted in *The Liberal-Conservative Platform as Laid Down by R.L. Borden, M.P., Opposition Leader, at Halifax, August 28, 1907* (n.p., n.d.), 22
49 Report of Justice Minister Thompson, 28 Jan. 1889, *Provincial Legislation, 1867-1895*, 583; report of Justice Minister Mowat, 15 Nov. 1897, *Provincial Legislation, 1896-1920*, 452-3
50 Canada, Senate, *Debates*, 1898, 841-2; PAO, AGO records, 1899, no. 677, observations upon the Bill entitled 'An Act Respecting Loan Companies,' by J.H. Hunter, 28 Feb. 1899
51 Ibid., Hardy to Mills, 21 March 1899; PAC, Laurier papers, Hardy to Mills, 22 March 1899, private; Laurier to Hardy, 27 March 1899; 31581-2, 31579; Hardy's private letter quoted
52 PAO, AGO records, 1899, no. 677, J.W. Longley to Hardy, 28 March 1899; H.R. Emmerson to Hardy, 28 March 1899; F.G. Marchand to Hardy, 1 April 1899; Joseph Martin to Hardy, 11 April 1899
53 Ibid., Mills to Hardy, 9 May 1899; Hardy to Mills, 10 May 1899; Canada, Senate, *Debates*, 1899, 317; Toronto *Evening Star*, 6 June 1899, reprinted the full text of Hardy's official letter to Mills of 21 March cited in n. 51 above
54 Ontario, *Statutes*, 1900, c. 24; PAC, trade and commerce department records, series A1, vol. 1214, Geoge Hately, secretary, Brantford Board of Trade, to Sir Richard Cartwright, 1 Dec. 1900; T.A. Russell, secretary, Canadian Manufacturers' Association, to secretary of state, 29 Oct. 1900, *Provincial Legislation, 1896-1920*, 13; PAC, Laurier papers, Pope to Laurier, 22 Nov. 1900, 51004-8
55 Copy of a proposed report of the minister of justice submitted as a statement of objections to the premier of Ontario by David Mills, 22 Nov. 1900; Ross to Mills, 8 Feb. 1901; Mills to Ross, 14 March 1901; Ross to Mills, 18 March 1901; Mills to Ross, 19 March 1901; *Provincial Legislation, 1896-1920*, 15-20, 23-7
56 Report of Justice Minister Mills, 3 May 1901, ibid., 39-44, 51; PAC, Laurier papers, Ross to Laurier, 14 May 1901, private, 56180-1
57 Report of Justice Minister Fitzpatrick, 20 June 1904; report of Attorney-General Gibson, 4 Aug. 1904; *Provincial Legislation, 1896-1920*, 69-72
58 Aylesworth to Fred J. Fulton, attorney-general of B.C., 19 April 1907, ibid., 689; 39, *S.C.R.*, 405; PAO, AGO records, 1907, no. 308, Angus MacMurchy to J.J. Foy, 23 Feb. 1907
59 Ibid., *Factum of the Attorney-General of the Province of Ontario in Canadian Pacific Railway v. Ottawa Fire Insurance Co.* (Toronto, 1907); ibid., 1908, no. 873, E.L. Newcombe to J.J. Foy, 4 Feb. 1908; memorandum from W.J. Hanna to J.J. Foy, 21 Feb. 1908
60 Ibid., D.L. McCarthy to Foy, 30 March 1908; opinion of Sir Robert Finlay re provincial powers of incorporation, 24 March 1908; E.L. Newcombe to J.R. Cartwright, 23 March, 11 Nov. 1908
61 PAC, Laurier papers, Laurier to Aylesworth, 3 Sept. 1909, private; Aylesworth to Laurier, 15 Sept. 1909; Murphy to Laurier, 5 Sept. 22 Oct. 1909; 159828-30, 159814-25, 159560-1, 161209-25
62 *CAR*, 1910, 546-7; PAO, Whitney papers, special series, file re inter-provincial conference, 27 Oct. 1913; ibid., AGO records, 1910, no. 518, resolution of the interprovincial conference, 29 March 1910, re incorporation of companies.
63 Ibid., 1910, no. 1024, memorandum from Edward Bayly, 13 Aug. 1910; ibid., no. 1041, Bayly to J.J. Foy, 8 Sept. 1910; ibid., 1916, no. 415A, memorandum from Edward Bayly, n.d.
64 *CAR*, 1910, 547-50; PAO, AGO records, 1910, no. 518, minutes of meeting of Attorney's General at Toronto, 22 Oct. 1910
65 Report of Justice Minister Aylesworth, 14 March 1911, *Provincial Legislation, 1896-1920*, 99-102
66 *CAR*, 1912, 125; PAO, AGO Records, 1910, no. 518, memorandum from Edward Bayly, 10 June 1912; PAC, Borden papers, Borden diary, 6 Nov. 1912
67 PAO, AGO records, 1910, no. 518, Factum of the Attorney General of Ontario in the Corporations Reference to the Supreme Court, n.d.; ibid., Whitney papers, memorandum from Edward Bayly to Horace Wallis, 23 Oct. 1913; W.J. Hanna to Whitney, 15 July 1914
68 PAC, Borden papers, Frank Cochrane to Borden, 6 Oct. 1914; C.J. Doherty to Borden, 8 Oct. 1914; 109812, 109810-11.
69 *O'Connor Report*, annex 3, case no. 34
70 Ibid., cases no. 36, 37
71 PAO, AGO records, 1916, no. 415A, memorandum from Edward Bayly, n.d.

72 For a more detailed account of this wrangling see Christopher Armstrong, 'Federalism and Government Regulation: The Case of the Canadian Insurance Industry, 1927–1934,' *Canadian Public Administration/Administration Publique du Canada* (1976), 88–101.
73 PAC, W.L.M. King papers, F.W. Weganast to King, 3 July 1924, personal, 94256–65, E.L. Newcombe quoted
74 'Proceedings of the Interprovincial Conference held at Ottawa, June, 1926,' *Dominion-Provincial Conferences, 1887–1926*, 112
75 PAO, AGO records, 1927, no. 527, memorandum from Edward Bayly to W.H. Price, 28 Feb. 1927; ibid., no. 2981, memorandum from Foster to the solicitor to the attorney-general, 18 Oct. 1927; Ontario, superintendent of insurance, *Annual Report*, 1927, xi
76 PAC, King papers, memorandum from G.D. Finlayson to J.A. Robb, 10 Oct. 1927, c69144–9
77 'Precis of Discussion, Dominion-Provincial Conference, November 3 to 10, 1927,' *Dominion-Provincial Conferences, 1927, 1935, 1941*, 13, 37; PAO, AGO records, 1927, no. 2981, draft minutes of subcommittee meeting of deputies of committee of the dominion-provincial conference of companies, 7 Nov. 1927 by R.L. Foster, note by Price attached. Finlayson's words are quoted from a memorandum to J.A. Robb, 5 Nov. 1927 in PAC, King Papers, C69 150–2.
78 Ibid., 1929, no. 1387, oral argument of counsel in Quebec insurance reference, 16 Nov. 1929; PAC, Arthur Meighen papers, W.H. Price to R.B. Bennett, 8 Dec. 1931, 103354c-d
79 Provincial Archives of Nova Scotia [hereafter PANS], E.N. Rhodes papers, memorandum on the constitutionality of the accompanying bill entitled 'A Bill Respecting the Status and Powers of Dominion Insurance Companies,' n.d., 75321; PAO, AGO records, 1932, no. 161, W.H. Price to R.B. Bennett, 18 Jan. 1932
80 PAC, Meighen papers, A.N. Mitchell to Meighen, 10 Feb. 1932; G.C. Moore to G.D. Finlayson, 25 Feb. 1932; W.S. Edwards to Meighen, 27 Feb. 1932; 102081–3, 102101, 102111
81 Ibid., W.H. Price to Meighen, 2 April 1932; A.H. Hinds to R.B. Bennett, 7 April 1932; 103354i-k, 102193; PANS, Rhodes papers, Price to Rhodes 8 April 1932, 48535
82 PAC, Meighen papers, Meighen to Rhodes, 23 April 1932, personal and confidential, 102554–6; PAO, AGO records, 1932, no. 539, memorandum from R.L. Foster to Edward Bayly, 17 June 1932
83 PANS, Rhodes papers, Rhodes to Meighen, 30 July 1932; Price to Meighen, 28 Sept. 1932; Meighen to Rhodes, 30 Sept. 1932, personal; 48799, 49016, 49012
84 PAO, AGO Records, 1932, no. 539, minutes of proceedings, Ontario-Quebec conference, Ritz-Carlton Hotel, Tuesday, 12 Oct. 1932, secret; scheme no. 2, exclusive provincial regulation with federal assistance, private and confidential, presented to Senator Meighen, 7 Nov. 1932
85 Ibid., Meighen to Price, 12 Nov. 1932; Price to Meighen, 21 Nov. 1932; PAC, Bennett papers, dominion-provincial conference, 1933, memoranda regarding questions on the agenda, 17 Jan. 1933, no. 5-A, memorandum by the department of justice on jurisdiction over insurance companies, 116457–582
86 Ibid., minutes of the dominion-provincial conference, 17–19 Jan. 1933, 346894–955; ibid., Meighen papers, R.L. Foster to A.E. Fisher, 11 Feb. 1933, 103354b
87 Ibid., Rowell to J.A. Mann, 8 Feb. 1934; Meighen to E.N. Rhodes, 24 April 1934; 103066–71, 103128; ibid., W.L.M. King papers, memorandum re insurance legislation, confidential, n.d. [1934], C128959–70
88 PANS, Rhodes papers, memorandum from G.D. Finlayson to Rhodes, 16 May 1934, 66313–14; PAC, Meighen Papers, Rowell to Bennett, 4 June 1934, personal and confidential, 103225–9
89 PANS, Rhodes papers, Bennett to Rhodes, 31 Jan. 1934, 561462; Rhodes had come (at least temporarily) to a similar point of view over two years earlier; he wrote to the general manager of Sun Life, 'I do not see how the Dominion can continue to maintain a Department of Insurance and at the same time retain its self-respect, and we are very rapidly reaching the point where I propose to advise my colleagues to abandon the insurance field to the provinces'; see ibid., Rhodes to A.B. Wood, 16 Dec. 1932, 49074. That the federal government failed to follow this course was explained to the prime minister by Rhodes in October 1933, when he wrote that the life insurance 'companies do not desire to challenge Dominion jurisdiction and are most anxious that the jurisdiction of the Dominion should be maintained'; see ibid., Rhodes to Bennett, 2 Oct. 1933, 55925.
90 Gabriel Kolko, *The Triumph of Conservatism, a Reinterpretation of American History, 1900–1916* (Chicago: Quadrangle, 1967), 5–6.
91 James Willard Hurst, *The Legitimacy of the Business Corporation in the Law of the United States, 1780–1970* (Charlottesville: University of Virginia Press, 1970), 147

92 Harry N. Scheiber, 'Federalism and the American Economic Order, 1789-1910,' *Law and Society Review* x (1975), 114, 115-6
93 PAO, AGO records, 1916, no. 415A, memorandum re the Judicial Committee of the Privy Council's decisions in *Bonanza v. the King* and in *Companies and Insurance References*, n.d.

CHAPTER 6: *Financing the Federation in Peace and War*

1 Tucker, *Steam into Wilderness*, appendix C, 209
2 Can., H. of C., *Deb.*, 1899, 1981; PAC, Laurier papers, Ross to Laurier, 14 May 1901, private, 56180-1
3 Tucker, *Steam into Wilderness*, 1-10; PAC, Laurier papers, Ross to Laurier, 7 (private), 20 (personal) Nov. 1901, 16 Jan. (personal) 1902; Laurier to Ross, 9, 21 Nov. 1901, 22 (personal) Jan. 1902; 59799, 59801-2, 61595-6, 59800, 60123; quotation from Laurier's letter of 9 Nov.
4 Ibid., Ross to Laurier, 13 (private), 17 (private), 25 (2 letters), 26 (private) Feb. 1904; Laurier to Ross, 15 (private), 19 (private and confidential), 20, 23 Feb. 1904; 82391-2, 82606, 82613, 82891, 82905, 82393-4, 82614-15, 82607-12, 82616; Ontario, legislative assembly, *Journals*, 1904, 134-5; quotations from Ross's letter of 13 Feb. and Laurier's of 20 Feb.
5 Ontario, legislative assembly, *Journals*, 1905, 42; PAO, Whitney papers, special series, memorial of the Ontario government to the federal government, 10 July 1905; memorandum '*Re: Railway Aid*' from H[orace] W[allis], n.d.; PAC, Laurier papers, Whitney to Laurier, 12 (private), 24 (personal) Jan. 1906; Laurier to Whitney, 17 Jan. 1906, private; 105903, 105905, 105904; quotation from Whitney papers, Whitney to E.C. Whitney, 6 July 1906, private
6 *CAR*, 1902, 42-5; 'Minutes of the proceedings of the Interprovincial Conference held at the City of Quebec, from the 18th to the 20th of December, 1902, inclusively,' *Dominion-Provincial Conferences, 1887-1926*, 31, 38-44
7 *CAR*, 1903, 109-10; Ontario, *Sessional Papers*, 1903, no. 4, proceedings of the interprovincial conference of 1902; *Globe*, 28, 29 Jan. 1903
8 PAC, Laurier papers, Laurier to Ross, 1 April 1903, private and confidential; Ross to Laurier, 27 April 1903, private; 71677-8, 72565-6; Ontario, legislative assembly, *Journals*, 1903, 322-7
9 PAC, Laurier papers, Ross to Laurier, 2 Feb. (private), 16 May 1904; Laurier to Ross, 3 Feb. (private), 17 May 1904; 82854, 82855, 85761, 85762-3
10 PAO, AGO records, 1905, no. 745, J.W. Longley to Whitney, 31 March 1905, personal; Whitney to Longley, 8 May 1905, personal.
11 Ibid., Whitney papers, Gouin to Whitney, 8, 23 Sept. 1905; Whitney to Gouin, 18 Sept. 1905; Whitney to Laurier, 7 Oct. 1905; PAC, Laurier papers, memorandum from R.J. Cartwright, n.d.; Gouin to Laurier, 22 Nov., 16 Dec. confidential, 1905; Laurier to Gouin, 19 Dec. 1905; 117610-15, 103540-2, 104372-3, 104374
12 *CAR*, 1906, 512-17; PAO, Whitney papers, memorandum respecting proposed increase of subsidy, etc., presented to the interprovincial conference at Ottawa, on 8 Oct. 1906, on behalf of the province of Ontario, by J.P. Whitney, J.J. Foy, and A.J. Matheson, 6 Oct. 1906
13 'Minutes of the Proceedings in Conference of the Representatives of Canada and of the Provinces, October, 1906,' in *Dominion-Provincial Conferences, 1887-1926*, 53-63; *CAR*, 1906, 517-23; J.A. Maxwell, *Federal Subsidies to Provincial Governments in Canada* (Cambridge, Mass.: Harvard University Press, 1938), 110-11; PAC, J.S. Willison papers, Frederick Hamilton to Willison, 18 Oct. 1906, 13605-8
14 Maxwell, *Federal Subsidies*, 114-15; PAC, Laurier papers, Hamar Greenwood to Laurier, 5 June 1907, private; Laurier to Lord Elgin, 11 June 1907, private; Elgin to Laurier, 14 June 1907; 125737-8, 125739-40, 125741-2
15 Ibid., Borden papers, Borden to W.B.A. Ritchie, 15 June 1909, 6646-7; *The Liberal-Conservative Platform, 1907*, 5. See above, chapter 5.
16 Robert D. Cuff, 'The Conservative Party Machine and Election of 1911 in Ontario,' *Ontario History* (1965), 149-56. For a full analysis of the relations between Whitney and Borden see Catharine L. Warner, 'Sir James P. Whitney and Sir Robert Borden: Relations between a Conservative Provincial Premier and His Federal Party Leader,' unpublished M PHIL thesis, University of Toronto, 1967.
17 *Memorandum Submitted on Behalf of the Province of Ontario with Reference to the Claim of the Province of Manitoba for an Extension of Boundaries and with Reference to the Question of*

258 Notes pages 123–30

Extending the Limits of the Other Provinces (Toronto, 9 Nov. 1906); G.R. Cook, 'Church, Schools and Politics in Manitoba, 1903–1912,' *Canadian Historical Review*, 39 (1958), 1–23
18 PAC, Laurier papers, Whitney to Laurier, 11 Nov. 1909, 162022–4; Whitney papers, text of speech in the Ontario legislature by Whitney, 8 Feb. 1912; Whitney to Dr T.E. Kaiser, 6 Oct. 1911, confidential
19 Ibid., Whitney to Cochrane, 14 Dec. 1911, private; Whitney to Borden, 18 Jan. 1912, private; order-in-council, 20 Feb. 1912
20 Ibid., Whitney to Cochrane, 2 Jan. 1912; Cochrane to Whitney, 4 Jan. 1912, private; Can., H. of C., *Deb.*, 1912, 6425
21 Ibid., Cochrane to Whitney, 7 June 1913, private and confidential; Ontario, legislative assembly, *Journals*, 1915, 136
22 Ibid., Whitney to Cochrane, 17 Nov. 1911, private; Cochrane to Whitney, 20 Nov. 1911
23 PAC, J.S. Willison papers, F.D.L. Smith to Willison, 1 Feb. 1912, 27933–40; PAO, Whitney papers, Whitney to Cochrane, 2 Jan. 1912; Cochrane to Whitney, 4 Jan. 1912, private
24 PAC, Borden papers, C.C. James to Martin Burrell, 7 Nov. 1912, strictly confidential, 71413–38; PAO, Whitney papers, Whitney to Borden, 13 Nov. 1912, private
25 Ibid., Whitney to Cochrane, 13 Nov. 1912, private; PAC, Borden Papers, Whitney to Borden, 18 Jan. 1913, 7889; Maxwell, *Federal Subsidies*, 200–5; Luella Gettys, *The Administration of Canadian Conditional Grants, a study in Dominion Provincial Relationships* (Chicago: Committee on Public Administration of the Social Science Research Council, 1938), 21–36
26 Robert Craig Brown, *Robert Laird Borden, a Biography*, vol. 1, *1854–1914* (Toronto: Macmillan, 1975), 220–1
27 PAO, Whitney papers, special series, Cochrane to William H. Hearst, 4 Dec. 1912, private and confidential; PAC, Borden papers, Thomas White to Borden, 27 Dec. 1913, personal, 2443
28 PAO, Whitney papers, Gouin to Whitney, 17 June 1913; Whitney to Gouin, 20 June 1913; Whitney to Cochrane, 23 Oct. 1913, confidential; PAC, Meighen papers, Whitney to Borden, 21 Oct. 1913, confidential, 17835–6
29 PAO, Whitney Papers, special series, memorandum re federal subsidies, n.d. [1913]; first draft of resolution re financial arrangements within Confederation, n.d.
30 Maxwell, *Federal Subsidies*, 133–6; 'Minutes of the Proceedings in Conference of the Representatives of the Provinces, October, 1913,' *Dominion-Provincial Conferences, 1887–1926*, 73
31 Ibid., 76; PAC, Borden papers, Borden diary, 28 Oct. 1913
32 Ibid., Meighen papers, memorandum from Whitney, 5 Dec. 1913, 17861–3; ibid., Thomas White to Borden, 11 Oct. 1913, personal, 2424
33 Sir Thomas White, *The Story of Canada's War Finance* (Montreal, 1921), 12–18; PAC, Borden papers, Borden diary, 21 Jan. 1915; Can., H. of C., *Deb.*, 1915, 86, 855–6
34 White, *War Finance*, 22–6; PAC, W.T. White papers, White to W.H. Hearst, 30 Oct., confidential, 10 Nov. 1915; Hearst to White, 3 Nov. 1915, private; 1637, 1690, 1661–2
35 White, *War Finance*, 32–4, 53–4; Can., H. of C., *Deb.*, 1916, 2630–1
36 Ibid., 1917, 719, 1424–5, 3760–3, 3766–7, 3770–1; White, *War Finance*, 54–5; see PAC, Borden papers, White to Borden, 13 July 1917, 2549–50: 'If during my absence you find it necessary ... to make a statement as to further taxation, I suggest that you announce that I shall later in the session make a supplementary financial statement and bring down a measure of income taxation ... If you announce income taxation please say that further revenue will be required by reason of the immediate increase in our forces due to operation of the Military Service Bill. This is consistent with our position throughout respecting taxation.'
37 White, *War Finance*, 59–61; *CAR*, 1918, 477–8; PAC, Borden papers, Charles Stewart to Borden, 17 Jan. 1918; White to Borden, 22 Jan. 1918; 130596, 130601–2; Can. H. of C., *Deb.*, 1918, 115–28; PAC, justice department records, series A2, vol. 218, memorandum, 30 June 1917; draft order-in-council, 3 July 1917; White to E.L. Newcombe, 5 July 1917; I.B. Lucas to C.J. Doherty, 15 Feb. 1918
38 *CAR*, 1918, 426; *Conference, Dominion and Provincial Governments, Canada, February, 1918, Agenda, Conference Papers, Minutes* (n.p., n.d.); PAO, W.H. Hearst Papers, special series, George Murray to Hearst, 1 March 1918
39 Ibid., Hearst to Murray, 11 March 1918; PAC, White papers, memorandum from White per B.J. Roberts to R.W. Breadner, 5 Feb. 1918, 4264

Notes pages 130-8 259

40 'Proceedings of the Conference between the Government of Canada and the Provincial Governments at Ottawa, November, 1918,' *Dominion-Provincial Conferences, 1887-1926*, 95-103; PAC, Borden papers, Borden to F.B. Carvell, 9 Nov. 1918, confidential, 84273; PAO, W.H. Hearst papers, speeches, draft of speech on address in reply to the throne speech, Ontario legislature, 1919; PAC, White papers, Hearst to White, 31 Dec. 1918, 5901-4
41 Ibid., White to A.E. Arsenault, 3, 11 Feb. 1919, 6181-2, 6186; 'Proceedings of the Conference ... November, 1918,' *Dominion-Provincial Conferences, 1887-1926*, 101
42 Ibid., 99; Can., H. of C., *Deb.*, 1919, 730-42; Maxwell, *Federal Subsidies*, 214-21; Gettys, *Conditional Grants*, 64-78.
43 PAO, W.H. Hearst papers, Hearst to Willison, 29 May 1918, personal; *Letter from Sir William Hearst to Sir John Willison, Chairman of the Ontario Housing Committee, containing the plan of finance proposed by the Ontario Government to meet the present urgent need for increased house accommodation* (n.p., n.d.)
44 PAO, Hearst papers, Willison to Hearst, 8 Nov. 1918; Hearst to Willison, 23 Nov. 1919, private and confidential; PAC, Willison papers, White to Willison, 9 Nov. 1918, 35275-6
45 See PAO, Hearst papers, correspondence between Hearst and J.A. Ellis and Hearst and N.W. Rowell, Dec. 1918 to Feb. 1919; Hearts to Ellis, 13 Jan. 1919 quoted
46 Ibid., Hearst to Rowell, 8 Feb. 1919; Rowell to Hearst, 19 Feb. 1919; *CAR*, 1921, 319

CHAPTER 7: *Social Change and Constitutional Amendment*

1 Margaret Prang, *N.W. Rowell, Ontario Nationalist* (Toronto: University of Toronto Press, 1975), 328-31; PAC, Rowell papers, Rowell to Thomas White, 24 May 1919, confidential, 3160; F.A. Acland's statement at 267 of the 'Report of the Proceedings of the Unemployment Conference, held at Ottawa, September 5-6-7, 1922,' in PAC, R.B. Bennett papers, 12531-825
2 PAO, Hearst papers, speeches, reply to deputation re Toronto strikers, 6 June 1919; ibid., AGO records, 1919, no. 2169, Edward Bayly to Hearst, 17 Sept. 1919. Premier Hearst had been invited to go to the founding convention of the ILO as an adviser to the Canadian delegation, but he nominated Ontario's superintendent of labour, W.A. Riddell, to go in his place; see PAC, labour department records, vol. 109, Gideon Robertson to Hearst, 26 Aug. 1919, and Hearst to Robertson, 27 Sept. 1919
3 Ibid., vol. 249, Robertson to J.W. Farris, 28 Oct. 1919; PAO, E.C. Drury papers, special series, Robertson to W.H. Hearst, 14 Oct. 1919
4 See Acland's statement referred to in n. 1 above; *CAR*, 1920, 473.
5 PAC, Borden papers, summary report, proceedings and discussions of the dominion-provincial commission appointed to consider the subject of uniformity of labour laws, 26 April 1920, 144958b; the federal labour minister explained what he hoped this conference would achieve: 'The Provincial Conference ... will, I think, be useful and will definitely cause some of the workingmen's complaints to be diverted from the federal arena to where they belong if they are not satisfactorily adjusted,' ibid., Gideon Robertson to Borden, 16 April 1920, 3906-10.
6 *CAR*, 1920, 473; PAC, labour department records, vol. 249, Robertson to Newton Rowell, 10 March 1921; PAC, King papers, re draft conventions of the International Labour Organization, C43387, contains Doherty's statement to the Commons on the subject, 28 May 1921.
7 PAC, Meighen papers, Robertson to Meighen, 5 Dec. 1920; Robertson to Rollo, 14 Dec. 1920; 18511-13, 29699-700. For the sums paid out see ibid., King papers, comparative statement of amounts paid under unemployment relief by the provinces during the fiscal years 1920-1, 1921-2, and 1922-3, enclosed in James Murdock to King, 31 July 1925, 102818. See also James Struthers, 'Prelude to Depression: The Federal Government and Unemployment, 1918-29,' *Canadian Historical Review*, 58 (1977), 277-93.
8 Ontario, legislative assembly, *Journals*, 1921, 380-1; PAC, Meighen papers, memorandum from Robertson to Meighen, 26 May 1921; Meighen to Tom Moore, 11 May 1921; 18609-10, 18605
9 Ibid., Moore to Meighen, 26 Sept. 1921; Meighen to Moore, 5 Nov. 1921; 18629-40, 18652-4; ibid., labour department records, vol. 208, J.H.H. Ballantyne to F.A. Acland, 3 Dec. 1921
10 PAC, King papers, Murdock to King, 18 July 1922, 66508-10; order-in-council, 25 Jan. 1922, quoted in H.M. Cassidy, *Unemployment and Relief in Ontario, 1929-1932, a Survey and Report* (Toronto: J.M. Dent, n.d. [1932]), 73-4

11 PAC, Bennett papers, report of proceedings of unemployment conference, held at Ottawa, 5-6-7 Sept. 1922, 12531-825; PAO, Drury papers, G.H. Brown to Drury, 21 Sept. 1922
12 Ibid., AGO records, 1925, no. 57, order-in-council, 12 Jan. 1925; the reference was discussed with the provinces and agreed to at a meeting in Sept. 1923; see ibid., J.H.H. Ballantyne to Edward Bayly, 17 Feb. 1925.
13 Ibid., Bayly to Charles Lanctot, 12 Feb. 1925; Bayly to W.F. Nickle, 12 March 1925; Bayly to Lanctot, 25 April 1925; copy of the judgment of the Supreme Court of Canada in hours of labour reference delivered by Duff, J., June 1925
14 Murdock's statement is reprinted in Ottawa *Citizen*, 24 Sept. 1924; *O'Connor Report*, annex 3, case no. 47, *Toronto Electric Commissioners v. Snider* (1925)
15 Nickle quoted in Toronto *Daily Star*, 2 Feb. 1925; PAO, G.H. Ferguson papers, press release re unemployment relief, n.d. [8 Feb. 1925]
16 Ontario, *Budget Statement, 1963*, 65-7; Canada, Royal Commission on Dominion-Provincial Relations [hereafter RCDPR], *Report*, book III, *Documentation* (Ottawa, 1940), 20, 34-5, 42-3; ibid., book I, *Canada 1867-1939*, 127
17 PAO, AGO records, 1927, no. 2981, minutes of conference on taxation between representatives of the dominion and the provinces, held at Ottawa, 11 Nov. 1924; Provincial Treasurer W.H. Price discussed Ontario's financial situation at 61-8.
18 Ibid., Ferguson papers, correspondence, 1923, file re 'taxation'; ibid., J.D. Stewart to Ferguson, 27 Dec. 1923; Ferguson to Taschereau, 3 Jan. 1924
19 Ibid., AGO records, 1927, no. 2981, minutes of conference on taxation between representatives of the dominion and the provinces, held at Ottawa, 11 Nov. 1924
20 Kenneth Bryden, *Old Age Pensions and Policy-Making in Canada* (Montreal: McGill-Queen's, 1974), 66-74; Ferguson quoted in Hamilton *Spectator*, 24 March 1926
21 PAO, Ferguson papers, J.D. Stewart to Ferguson, 13 March 1926; Ferguson to Stewart, 17 March 1926; PAC, King papers, memorandum [from O.D. Skelton?] to King, 26 March 1926, 118756-7
22 Ibid., Taschereau to King, 2 April 1926, personal, 118759; *CAR*, 1926-7, 619-21; 'Proceedings of the Interprovincial Conference held at Ottawa, June 1926,' *Dominion-Provincial Conferences, 1887-1926*, 110
23 Neatby, *King, 1924-32*, 127, 221-3; Maxwell, *Federal Subsidies*, 137-44; PAC, King papers, G.H. Ferguson to J.G. Gardiner, 23 Sept. 1927; King to Gardiner, 4 Oct. 1927; 121740-1, 121759
24 Neatby, *King, 1924-32*, 232-43; Peter Oliver, *G. Howard Ferguson, Ontario Tory* (Toronto: University of Toronto Press, 1977), 299-307 discusses the premier's role in the Conference; 'Precis of Discussions, Dominion-Provincial Conference, November 3 to 10, 1927,' *Dominion-Provincial Conferences, 1927, 1935, 1941*, 25.
25 Ibid., 25-7, 35
26 Ibid., 18-23, 31-2; PAO, AGO records, 1927 no. 2981, memorandum re unemployment relief from department of health and labour of Ontario, 8 Nov. 1927
27 Ibid., memorandum from J.T. White to G.H. Ferguson, brief re delimitation of fields of taxation and amendments to British North America Act, n.d. [1927]
28 'Precis of Discussions ... 1927,' *Dominion-Provincial Conferences, 1927, 1935, 1941*, 28, 33-6; PAC, King papers, text of opening statement by Finance Minister J.A. Robb to dominion-provincial conference, 1927, C52658-70. A memorandum prepared by the Finance Department argued that 'the Dominion would seem to be practising economy that is not reflected in the provincial accounts, inasmuch as the Dominion accounts show reductions in net debt while the accounts of the provinces are showing increases apart from investments which have been made in revenue-bearing utilities'; see PAC, finance department records, series E1, vol. 2670, subsidies to provinces, 1927.
29 Toronto *Daily Star*, 26 Jan. 1927; PAC, external affairs department records, series D1, vol. 760, memorandum from N. McL. Rogers on amendment of the British North America Act, 11 Oct. 1927
30 'Precis of Discussions ... 1927,' *Dominion-Provincial Conferences, 1927, 1935, 1941*, 11-12; PAC, Bennett papers, precis of discussions, dominion-provincial conferences, 1927, 16298-312, a verbatim transcript of the meeting
31 See n. 21 above.

32 PAC, labour department records, vol. 208, Peter Heenan to Ferguson, 10 Feb. 1928; Heenan also noted that in January Ferguson had informed the municipalities of Ontario that they would have to bear the entire burden in the coming year.
33 Neatby, *King, 1924–32*, 316–19; Oliver, *Howard Ferguson*, 315–17, 365–8
34 PAO, Ferguson papers, text of speech, 19 [?] June 1930; PAC, King papers, memorandum re grants to Ontario by Liberal administration, 1922–30; M.A. MacPherson to King, 17 July 1930; King to MacPherson, 23 July 1930; C53159, 145293–5, 145296
35 PAC, King papers, C108920–30 contains a collection of Bennett's 1930 campaign promises.
36 Cassidy, *Unemployment and Relief in Ontario*, 55–61, 82–92; PAO, George S. Henry papers, Gideon Robertson to Howard Ferguson, 27 Sept. 1930; Ontario order-in-council, 14 Oct. 1930
37 Ontario, *Budget Statement, 1963*, 65
38 Paul Gérin-Lajoie, *Constitutional Amendment in Canada* (Toronto: University of Toronto Press, 1950), 98–102, 228–31
39 *Amendment of the Canadian Constitution, Statement and Protest by the Prime Minister of the Province of Ontario* (Toronto: King's Printer, 1930)
40 PAC, external affairs department records, series D1, vol. 759, representations of the Ontario government on the conference of 1929 on the operation of dominion legislation, n.d.; ibid., Bennett papers, memorandum re conference with the provinces, n.d., 115746–50. Similar criticisms were made by King's former secretary, Norman McLeod Rogers, in a scholarly article, 'The Compact Theory of Confederation,' in Canadian Political Science Association, *Papers and Proceedings* (1931), 205–30.
41 PAC, Bennett papers, Bennett to George S. Henry, 23 Feb. 1931; report of the dominion-provincial conference, 1931; 115774–7, 115899–923.
42 PAO, Henry papers, memorandum from J.A. Ellis to Henry, 3 Feb., 23 March 1931; memorandum from Ellis to J.D. Monteith, 13 May 1931
43 PAC, Bennett papers, Bennett to S.F. Tolmie, 23 Oct. 1931, 447413–4; Cassidy, *Unemployment and Relief in Ontario*, 69–71, 98–105; PAO, Henry papers, memorandum from J.A. Ellis, n.d. [May 1934]
44 *CAR*, 1932, 106; Cassidy, *Unemployment and Relief in Ontario*, 70–1
45 PAC, Bennett papers, memorandum for the prime minister, n.d. [1932–3]; dominion-provincial conference 1933, memoranda regarding questions on the agenda, Ottawa, 17 Jan. 1933, no. 1-B; 505027–40, 116457–582; PAC, King's papers, report of speech by Bennett in Vancouver, 9 Jan. 1933, C151839
46 PAC, Bennett papers, minutes of meetings of dominion-provincial conference, 17–19 Jan. 1933, Ottawa; dominion-provincial conference 1933, memoranda regarding questions on the agenda, Ottawa, 17 Jan. 1933, no. 3-D; 346894–955, 116457–582
47 Ibid., minutes of the meetings of the dominion-provincial conference, 17–19 Jan. 1933, Ottawa; W. Clifford Clark to Bennett, 18 Jan. 1933; 346894–955, 501802–3; PAO, AGO records, 1933, no. 31, memorandum from R.L. Foster to W.H. Price, 7 Jan. 1933
48 PAC, Bennett papers, minutes of the meetings of the dominion-provincial conference, 17–19 Jan. 1933, 346894–955; Price is quoted at 19 and Bennett at 22 of the transcript; PAO, AGO records, 1933, no. 31, memorandum from Edward Bayly to Price, 9 Jan. 1933
49 Ibid., Henry papers, memorandum from J.A. Ellis, 24 Feb. 1933; Ellis to Henry, 12 May 1933; *CAR*, 1934, 141–2
50 PAC, Bennett papers, J.T.M. Anderson, J.E. Brownlee, J. Bracken, and T.D. Pattullo to Bennett, 4 Dec. 1933, 501830–1; ibid., J.W. Dafoe papers, vol. 7, Grant Dexter to Dafoe, 17 Jan. 1934; PANS, E.N. Rhodes papers, Dominion Bureau of Statistics, memorandum on employment, employment at 1 Dec. 1933, compared with that at the low point, at 1 Dec. 1932, and at the high point of the present cycle, n.d. 69264
51 PAC, Bennett papers, minutes of the dominion-provincial conference, 1934, 121484–512; *Report of the Dominion-Provincial Conference, 1934* (Ottawa: King's Printer, 1934)
52 PAO, Henry papers, Henry to Bennett, 22 March 1934; *CAR*, 1934, 142
53 PAC, Bennett papers, W.A. Gordon to provincial premiers, 12 June 1934; Sir George Perley to Bennett, 12 July 1934; 486454, 121642; PAO, Mitchell Hepburn papers, Perley to Hepburn, 13 July 1934
54 PANS, E.N. Rhodes papers, Gordon to Bennett, 26 July 1934, 71419

262   Notes pages 154–65

55   *CAR*, 1934, 31; PAC, Bennett papers, dominion-provincial meeting on relief, 30–31 July 1934, notes by Dominion Commissioner of Unemployment Relief Harry Hereford, 121763–82
56   PAO, Hepburn papers, memorandum of the province of Ontario, 31 July 1934; *Globe*, 1 Aug. 1934; Toronto *Daily Star*, 1 Aug. 1934
57   Otawa *Citizen*, 21 Aug. 1934; PAC, labour department records, vol. 200, memorandum from W.M. Dickson to the minister of labour, 24 Aug. 1934; ibid., Bennett papers, Dickson to Bennett, 25 May 1935, 349596–70
58   Ibid., Bennett to W.J. McCully, 6 Aug. 1934, personal, 486476; Grant Dexter in the Winnipeg *Free Press*, 4 Sept. 1934
59   PAC, Bennett papers, draft letter to provincial premiers with comments by O.D. Skelton, 31 Aug. 1934, 121800–4
60   PAO, Hepburn papers, Bennett to Hepburn, 31 Aug. 1934; PAC, J.W. Dafoe papers, vol. 8, Roebuck to Dafoe, 7 Jan. 1935
61   PAO, provincial secretary's records, series 1-7-E, vol. 1, Blue Sky report, 1922 [sic], contains R.L. Foster to F.V. Johns, 31 Oct. 1934 enclosing the minutes of the two meetings of the 'BNA committee.'
62   PAC, Bennett papers, George Perley to Bennett, 7 Sept. 1934; Hepburn to Bennett, 30 Oct. 1934; 501840, 121913–14
63   For a collection of material on this subject see J.R.H. Wilbur, ed., *The Bennett New Deal: Fraud or Portent?* (Toronto: Copp Clark, 1968); *The Premier Speaks to the People, the Prime Minister's January Radio Broadcasts Issued in Book Form* (Ottawa: Dominion Conservative Headquarters, 1935); PAC, J.W. Dafoe papers, vol. 8, Grant Dexter to Dafoe, n.d. [Jan. 1935].
64   *CAR*, 1935–6, 29–34; W.H. McConnell, 'Judicial Review of Prime Minister Bennett's New Deal Legislation,' unpublished PH D thesis, University of Toronto, 1968, 83–5
65   PAC, King papers, memorandum from W.S. Edwards to Maurice Dupré, 1 March 1935, 176049–50; PAO, Hepburn papers, Bennett to Hepburn, 31 Aug. 1934
66   Ontario, Legislative Assembly, *Journals*, 1935, 224–5
67   H. Blair Neatby, *William Lyon Mackenzie King, 1932–1939: The Prism of Unity* (Toronto: University of Toronto Press, 1976), 90–7
68   McConnell, 'Bennett's New Deal,' 154–7, 204–8, 274–5; *O'Connor Report*, annex 3, cases no. 62, 64 both called *A.G. for Canada v. A.G. for Ontario and Others* (1937)

CHAPTER 8: *Water-power and the Constitution*

1   PAC, King papers, memorandum from R.H. Coats re probable line of future Canadian progress-industry and the tariff-immigration, confidential, n.d. [1929], C44543–50
2   PAO, E.C. Drury papers, J.A. Johnston to Drury, 9 Dec. 1919; PAC, Borden papers, G.W. Yates to Borden, 19 April 1920, private and confidential, 64531–7
3   PAO, AGO records, 1921, no. 1367, memorandum from Edward Bayly to W.E. Raney, 15 April 1921
4   Ibid., Drury papers, special series, brief re Lake of the Woods control, n.d.; order-in-council, 21 Jan. 1919; Ontario order-in-council, 13 Feb. 1919
5   *CAR*, 1921, 363–4, 630–4; PAC, Meighen papers, memorandum from J.B. Challies to G.F. Buskard, 18 Dec. 1920, 18728; PAC, King papers, Dewart to King, 7 March 1922 enclosing text of speech of 23 June 1921, 61415–45; Toronto *Mail and Empire*, 28 April 1921
6   PAC, Meighen papers, Drury to Meighen, 25 May 1921, 19073; PAO, Drury papers, special series, Rowell to W.E. Raney, 30 June 1921
7   *CAR*, 1922, 646; PAC, King papers, Drury to King, 4 May 1922, 61581–4; PAO, Drury papers, Drury to J.G. Turiff, 5 Feb. 1923
8   *CAR*, 1921, 157–8; PAC, King papers, Charles E. Hughes, to Sir Auckland Geddes, 17 May 1922; order-in-council, 29 May 1922; C69733–4, C95807
9   *CAR*, 1923, 56–7; PAO, Drury papers, Drury to King, 14 Feb. 1923; King to Drury, 15 Feb. 1923
10   For an account of the negotiations from 1923 to 1926 see Oliver, *Howard Ferguson*, 174–88; see PAO, Ferguson papers, Ferguson to A.G. Chisholm, 28 July 1924; Ferguson to F.H. Keefer, 4 Feb. 1924, personal.
11   *CAR*, 1924–5, 83–4; Ferguson to Charles Stewart, 9 Feb. 1925, and Stewart to Ferguson, 4 May 1925, reprinted in Canada, external affairs department, *Correspondence and Documents Relating*

Notes pages 165-72   263

to the St. Lawrence Deep Waterway Treaty 1932, Niagara Convention 1929 and Ogoki River and Kenogami River (Long Lake) Projects and Export of Electrical Power (Ottawa: King's Printer, 1938) [hereafter *Correspondence re St Lawrence, 1925-38*], 17-19

12   PAO, unprinted sessional papers, 1935, no. 53, Clarkson, Gordon, and Dilworth to Ferguson, 17 July 1925; ibid., Ferguson papers, Ferguson to Charles Stewart, 30 Nov. 1925; Stewart to Ferguson, 11 Jan., 17 April 1926

13   Ontario Hydro Archives [hereafter OHA], L.A. Taschereau to G.H. Ferguson, 18 Dec. 1925; J.H. Dales, *Hydroelectricity and Industrial Development, Quebec, 1898-1940* (Cambridge, Mass.: Harvard University Press, 1957), 151-3; Oliver, *Howard Ferguson*, 181-2, suggests that Taschereau insisted on alteration of Ontario's regulation 17 concerning bilingual schools as a quid pro quo for the power deal.

14   PAO, AGO records, 1925, no. 2955, Ferguson to King, 7 Sept. 1923.

15   PAC, King papers, Graham to King, 26 Nov. 1924, strictly confidential, 85215

16   *A Statement by Sir Adam Beck Protesting against Exportation of Electric Power with Special Reference to the Proposed Lease of the 'Carillon' Power Site* (Toronto, 1925), 11; PAO, Ferguson papers, Ferguson to the Editor, *La Presse*, 19 May 1925; Ferguson to H.G. Acres, 5 Feb. 1925

17   Ibid., Ferguson to R.W. Shannon, 16 May 1925

18   PAC, justice department records, series A2, vol. 318, King to Ernest Lapointe, 17 April 1925; ibid., King papers, Lapointe to King, 1 June 1925, 99360-1

19   Neatby, *King, 1924-32*, 224; PAO, Ferguson papers, memorandum from F.A. Gaby to H.E.P. commissioners, 10 March 1926; C.A. Magrath to Ferguson, 13 Aug. 1926

20   Ibid., Magrath to Drayton, 18 Aug. 1926; Drayton to Ferguson, 24 Aug. 1926; PAC, King papers, R.O. Campney to King, 15 Nov. 1926, 111244

21   Dafoe, *Clifford Sifton*, 515-21; PAO, George S. Henry papers, Magrath to Ferguson, 25 Jan. 1929; PAC, King papers, Harry Sifton to King, 22 April 1926, private, 118078-80

22   Oliver, *Howard Ferguson*, 293-9, discusses the Ferguson-Taschereau alliance; see PAO, Ferguson papers, Ferguson to Taschereau, 29 Sept. 1926

23   Oliver, *Howard Ferguson*, 295-6, argues convincingly that this brief was prepared by Loring C. Christie, who had been hired by Magrath to assist with the preparation of the legal-constitutional side of the Ontario case. Copies of the brief, dated 24 Feb. 1927, are to be found in both the Ferguson papers and the Christie papers at the PAC.

24   *Globe*, 18 Feb. 1927; Ontario, legislative assembly, *Journals*, 1927, 91-2; PAC, Bennett papers, Arthur Meighen to Hugh Guthrie, 25 Feb. 1927, personal, 49060-1

25   Neatby, *King, 1924-32*, 225-8

26   PAC, King papers, Text of statement by Harry Sifton before parliamentary committee considering Georgian Bay Canal charter, April 1927, C58922-31; J.W. Dafoe to Clifford Sifton, 13 April 1927, in Ramsay Cook, ed., *The Dafoe-Sifton Correspondence 1919-1927*, vol. II, Manitoba Record Society Publications (Altona, Man.: D.W. Friesen and Sons, 1966), 272-6.

27   PAC, King papers, Ferguson to King, 13 April 1927; King to Ferguson, 23 April 1927; 121435-8, 121439-43; PAO, Ferguson papers, A.H. McKee to W.W. Pope, 26 July 1927

28   Ibid., Ferguson to Taschereau, 9 Aug. 1927; AGO records, 1928, no. 332, opinion re waterpower at the Carillon Rapids in the Ottawa River by E. Lafleur, A. Geoffrion, and W.N. Tilley, 13 Sept. 1927

29   Toronto *Mail and Empire*, 25 Oct. 1927; PAO, AGO records, 1927, no. 2310, memorandum from A.W. Rogers to W.H. Price, 26 Aug. 1927

30   See above, chapter 7 for an account of the 1927 dominion-provincial conference; PAC, King papers, order-in-council, 18 Jan. 1928, C105849-51.

31   PAO, Ferguson papers, Ferguson to Ernest Lapointe, 2 Feb. 1928; PAC, King papers, W.N. Tilley to Charles Lanctot, 11 Feb. 1928; Taschereau to King, 2 Feb. 1928; King to Taschereau, 20 Feb. 1928, personal and confidential; 134867, 134854-5, 134856-60; PAO, AGO records, 1928, no. 332, Edward Bayly to W.N. Tilley, 25 May 1928

32   *CAR*, 1928-9, 136-42; PAO, AGO records, 1928, no. 332, factum of the attorney-general of Canada in the water power reference, 1928; factum of the attorney-general of Ontario in the water power reference, 1928; PAC, King papers, typescript of questions and answers in the water power reference, 1929, with opinion of Smith and Duff, JJ., attached, 5 Feb. 1929, C105871-907; PAC, King papers, King diary, 5 Feb. 1929

33   PAC, King papers, memorandum re diary entries on Beauharnois, 5, 26 Feb. 1929, C42277-93

34 The idea of a greater diversion at Niagara Falls was first suggested by Ferguson in November 1925; see PAO, Ferguson papers, Ferguson to Charles Stewart, 30 Nov. 1925. Preliminary discussions with the Americans led to the creation of a Niagara Board of Control to consider whether larger diversions would harm the scenic beauty of the falls, and the board reported in May 1928 that with some minor remedial works another 20,000 cubic feet per second could be diverted without adverse aesthetic effects.
35 PAC, external affairs department records, series D1, vol. 741, Hydro-Electric Power Commission of Ontario, report on Niagara power situation in respect of diversions from Niagara River by T.H. Hogg and L.C. Christie, 29 Oct. 1928, confidential.
36 Ibid., memorandum re Niagara convention, 28 Jan. 1931; ibid., Bennett papers, memorandum re Niagara convention of 2 Jan. 1929, with notes by O.D. Skelton, 27-8 Jan. 1931, 508074-8
37 Neatby, *King, 1924-32*, 261-3; OHA, C.A. Magrath to Ferguson, 11 March 1929
38 Neatby, *King, 1924-32*, 273-7; Oliver, *Howard Ferguson*, 352-6
39 OHA, Ferguson to Magrath, 3 May 1930
40 Neatby, *King, 1924-32*, 312-13; Oliver, *Howard Ferguson*, 363-4; PAC, King papers, King to Ferguson, 21 Sept. 1929, confidential; King to Taschereau, 20 Jan. 1930, confidential; 137497, 155708-12.
41 Ibid., memorandum from G.W. Yates, 23 Jan. 1930, c96816-40
42 Ibid., King diary, 24 Jan. 1930; Taschereau to King, 4 Feb. 1930; King to Taschereau, 15 Feb. 1930; 155725-33, 155734-7
43 Ibid., King to Ferguson and to Taschereau, 15 Feb. 1930, 148023-6, 155725-33
44 PAO, Ferguson papers, Ferguson to Keefer, 23 July 1926; Ferguson to King, 24 Feb. 1930
45 PAC, King papers, Raoul Dandurand to King, 6 March 1930, 147295-6; PAO, Ferguson papers, King to Ferguson, 8 March 1930
46 Ibid., Ferguson to King, 28 April 1930
47 PAC, King papers, King to Norman Rogers, 25 Jan. 1930, personal and confidential, 153886-8; King diary, 17 June 1930; Ottawa *Citizen*, 2 July 1930
48 PAO, George S. Henry papers, Henry to R.B. Bennett, 7 March 1931; PAC, Bennett papers, W.H. Price to Bennett, 22 April 1931, private and confidential, 510667-9
49 Ibid., H.H. Wrong to Bennett, 18 April 1931, 508168-71; *CAR*, 1932, 371
50 PAO, Henry papers, J.R. Cooke to Henry, 17 Sept. 1931; Henry to Bennett, 15 Oct. 1931
51 Ibid, memorandum from F.A. Gaby to J.R. Cooke, 4 Nov. 1931; Bennett to Henry, 10 Nov. 1931, confidential; *CAR*, 1932, 374
52 PAC, Bennett papers, international problems on the Great Lakes, St. Lawrence deep waterway, Chicago diversion, Niagara, with suggested action, by J.T. Johnston, 16 Sept. 1930, confidential; memorandum re basis of agreement between the dominion and Ontario re St Lawrence development, international rapids section, 25 Jan. 1932; 508216-304, 508340
53 Ibid., external affairs department records, series D1, vol. 733, suggested basis of agreement with Ontario covering international reach of the St Lawrence, 19 Jan. 1932; points to be raised with Ontario in support of Dominion's proposals 22 Jan. 1932; ibid., Bennett papers, St Lawrence Waterway, memorandum re Ontario's share of the cost of the improvement of the international section for navigation and power by Guy A. Lindsay, May 1932, 508575-636
54 Ibid., notes re dominion, Ontario, and St Lawrence agreement, 8 March 1932; draft agreement between dominion and Ontario re St Lawrence Waterway, May 1932; 508368, 509973-80.
55 Although the province clearly grained control of power development, the issue of provincial ownership of power rights was not specifically dealt with. Ontario's deputy attorney-general later noted that he had consulted the negotiators and 'that there was never any agreement to this effect, verbally or otherwise. Mr. [J.E.] Read [of external affairs] said that he thought Parliament would be very loath to make a declaration of this kind in the Statute, and I agree with him in this because the Dominion generally has been very tenacious, not only of its authority, but even of its encroachments of Provincial jurisdiction'; see PAO, AGO records, 1932, no. 2478, Edward Bayly to Henry, 22 Jan. 1934. Nonetheless, the issue was effectively settled after 1932.

CHAPTER 9: *The Battle of the St Lawrence*

1 Neil McKenty, *Mitch Hepburn* (Toronto: McClelland and Stewart, 1967), 42-5, 61; PAO, George S. Henry papers, memorandum from George H. Challies to Henry, 23 Jan. 1934

Notes pages 179-86   265

2 OHA, Hydro-Electric Power Commission of Ontario to Hepburn, 10 Aug. 1934; Hepburn to Bennett, 13 Aug. 1934; Bennett to Hepburn, 29 Aug. 1934, *Correspondence re St Lawrence, 1925-38*, 23-8
3 PAC, Bennett papers, W.D. Herridge to O.D. Skelton, 20 Aug. 1934, personal, 509186; PAO, Mitchell Hepburn papers, Hepburn to Thomas Wayling, 9 Nov. 1934
4 PAC, Bennett papers, Hepburn to Henry Timmis, 9 Nov. 1934, 510382; PAO, Hepburn papers, Stewart Lyon to Hepburn, 16 Sept. 1935
5 OHA, HEPC minutes, 19 March 1935; Hepburn to Bennett, 30 March 1935, *Correspondence re St. Lawrence, 1925-38*, 29-30
6 Richard M. Alway, 'Mitchell F. Hepburn and the Liberal Party in the Province of Ontario, 1937-1943,' unpublished MA thesis, University of Toronto, 1965, 70-89; McKenty, *Mitch Hepburn*, 64-9
7 OHA, report on power supply in southern Ontario for the Hydro-Electric Power Commission of Ontario, Toronto, Canada, by Stone and Webster Engineering Corporation, Boston, 29 July 1935
8 PAC, Bennett papers, Wood, Gundy and Co. to clients, 30 March 1935, 349679-80; PANS, E.N. Rhodes papers, Rhodes to M.W. Wilson, 5 April 1935, 71779
9 PAC, King papers, memorandum from Percy Parker to King, n.d. [1935], C116393. Privately, however, King thought 'Hepburn's action is unnecessarily extreme, and most unsettling from the point of view of confidence in governments-a bad precedent for the future'; ibid., King diary, 3 April 1935
10 *CAR*, 1935-6, 197-200; PAO, Hepburn papers, press releases, 23 Oct., 6 Dec. 1935; PAC, King papers, memorandum from E.A. Pickering to King. 31 Jan. 1936, C114182
11 OHA, T.S. Lyon to Hepburn, 14 April 1936; Lyon to Skelton, 16 Nov. 1935, *Correspondence re St. Lawerence, 1925-38*, 32-4
12 Lyon to Skelton, 15 Feb. 1936, confidential, *Correspondence re St. Lawrence, 1925-38*, 40-1; PAO, Hepburn papers, Lyon to Hepburn, 14 April, 21 May 1936; PAC, King papers, Skelton to King, 30 July 1936, private, 196234-40
13 King to Hepburn, 8 Jan. 1937, confidential; Hepburn to King, 16 Jan. 1937, confidential; *Correspondence re St. Lawrence, 1925-38*, 41-4; PAC, King papers, memorandum from O.D. Skelton, 30 Nov. 1936; memorandum from J.T. Johnston re St. Lawrence, Niagara, and Long Lac, 9 Nov. 1937; secret; C153484-93, C144238-45.
14 OHA, T.H. Hogg to Hepburn, 21 Jan. 1937; PAC, external affairs department records, series D1, vol. 734, 24 Feb. 1937, conference in Ottawa between Candian government officials and Ontario Hydro-Electric Power Commission representatives, 25 Feb. 1937; suggested consolidation and revision of St Lawrence Waterway and Niagara treaty, Feb. 1937, most secret
15 McKenty, *Mitch Hepburn*, 91-4; Neatby, *King, 1932-9*, 201-2; OHA, T.S. Lyon to William F. Ryan, 17 April 1937, personal and confidential
16 PAO, Hepburn papers, T.S. Lyon to Hepburn, 17 Feb. 1937; H.C. Nixon to Fernand Rinfret, 21 July 1937; Lyon to Hepburn, 6 Aug. 1937
17 King to H.C. Nixon, 7 Sept. 1937, in *Correspondence re St Lawrence, 1925-38*, 46-8; Memorandum re Hepburn's campaign statements on power policy, n.d., C153939-41
18 For a further account of the squabbling between Mitchell Hepburn and Mackenzie King, see Reginald Whitaker, *The Government Party: Organizing and Financing the Liberal Party of Canada 1930-58* (Toronto: University of Toronto Press, 1977), 314-40, and Alway, 'Mitchell Hepburn,' 200-16
19 Neatby, *King, 1932-9*, 204-9; PAC, King papers, King to Sir William Mulock, 16 Aug. 1937, personal; statement issued by Mr King re St Lawrence Waterway on 31 Aug. 1937, 205709-10, C153943.
20 PAO, Hepburn papers, T.S. Lyon to Hepburn, 28 Oct. 1937; Hepburn to King, 25, 1937, confidential, *Correspondence re St. Lawrence 1925-38*, 49-50
21 PAO, Hepburn papers, press release re Hydro contracts, 11 Dec. 1937
22 King to Hepburn, 12 Nov. 1937, confidential, *Correspondence re St. Lawrence, 1925-38*, 49; PAC, King papers, memorandum from E.A. Pickering, 29 Nov. 1937, C114596.
23 Nelles, *Politics of Development*, 480-7, discusses the friction between Hepburn and King created by the issue of power exports.
24 PAC, King papers, memorandum re export of power [from E.A. Pickering?], 25 Nov. 1938, strictly confidential, C153532

25 Neatby, *King, 1932-9*, 239-42; PAO, Hepburn papers, press release re power exports, n.d. [Dec. 1937]
26 Montreal *Gazette*, 16, 18 Dec. 1937; PAC, King papers, text of press release, 17 Dec. 1937, C153579-80
27 Ibid., Hepburn to King, 18 Dec. 1937; King to Hepburn, 19 Dec. 1937, 202099-101
28 Hepburn to W.D. Euler, 21 Jan, 1938, *Correspondence re St. Lawrence, 1925-38*, 72-84; PAO, Hepburn papers, Hepburn to Duplessis, 24 Jan. 1938; Duplessis to Hepburn, 14 Feb. 1938
29 Ibid., Thomas Vien to Hepburn, 9 Feb. 1938; PAC, King papers, King to L.S. Amery, 20 Dec. 1937; memorandum from King to E.A. Pickering, 29 Dec. 1937; 198314-15, C138071
30 Ibid., memorandum from J.T. Johnston and M.F. Cochrane to King, 27 Dec. 1937, confidential; memorandum re Mr Hepburn's arguments and possible replies, n.d. [1938], C153583-611, C153690-3
31 Ibid., memorandum from E.A. Pickering to King 31 Jan., 28 Feb. confidential, 1938, C153726-7, C154088
32 Cordell Hull to Sir Herbert Marler, 17 March 1938 enclosing memorandum from the department of state, 17 March 1938, reprinted in Canada, external affairs department, *Correspondence relating to Kenogami River (Long Lake) Project and Export of Electrical Power, (Supplement to publication tabled in the House of Commons, February 28, 1938, entitled "Correspondence and Documents relating to the St. Lawrence Deep Waterway Treaty 1932, Niagara Convention 1929, and Ogoki River and Kenogami (Long Lake) Projects and export of Electrical Power"*) (Ottawa: King's Printer, 1938) [hereafter cited as *Correspondence re St. Lawrence, 1925-38, Supplement*], 9-16; William R. Willoughby, *The St. Lawrence Waterway, a Study in Politics and Diplomacy* (Madison, Wis.: University of Wisconsin Press, 1961), 173
33 Hepburn to King, 14 Feb. 1938; King to Hepburn, 22 Feb. 1938; W.A. Riddell to Cordell Hull, 27 Jan. 1938; *Correspondence re St. Lawrence, 1925-38*, 51-6, 15-16
34 Hepburn to King, 25 Feb. 1938; King to Hepburn, 1, 21 March 1938; Cordell Hull to Sir Herbert Marler, 17 March 1938; in *Correspondence re St. Lawrence, 1925-38, Supplement*, 57-8, 9-16
35 Cordell Hull to Sir Herbert Marler, 28 May 1938, reprinted in Canada, external affairs department, *Correspondence and Documents Relating to the Great Lakes-St. Lawrence Basin Development, 1938-41* (Ottawa: King's Printer, 1941) [hereafter *Correspondence re St. Lawrence, 1938-41*], 20-32
36 Willoughby, *St. Lawrence Waterway*, 175; PAC, King papers, memorandum from Skelton to King, 17 Aug. 1938, C144077-9
37 *Globe and Mail*, 19 Aug. 1938; PAC, King papers, memorandum from Skelton to King, 19 Aug. 1938, C144081-2
38 Willoughby, *St. Lawrence Waterway*, 176, Hepburn quoted; Hepburn to King, 19 Aug. 1938, *Correspondence re St. Lawrence, 1938-41*, 43-4
39 PAC, King papers, King to Lord Tweedsmuir, 25 Aug. 1938; King to W.A. Buchanan, 29 Aug. 1938; 222496-74, unnumbered but after 211237; King to Hepburn, 30 Aug. 1938, *Correspondence re St. Lawrence, 1938-41*, 45-7
40 Hepburn to King, 21 Sept. 1938, in ibid., pp 48-50
41 Willoughby, *St. Lawrence Waterway*, 177-8
42 PAC, King papers, memorandum from J.T. Johnston to O.D. Skelton, 13 Dec. 1938, confidential, C144438-53
43 Willoughby, *St. Lawrence Waterway*, 179-80
44 PAC, King papers, memorandum from Arnold Heeney to King, 29 Sept. 1939; memorandum from Heeney for file, 3 Oct. 1939, strictly confidential, C114599, C114601-9
45 PAC, King papers, King diary, 21 Dec. 1939
46 Ibid., memorandum from Skelton to King, 12 Oct. 1939, C144133-40; ibid., external affairs department records, series D1, vol. 735, memorandum from O.D. Skelton, 31 Oct. 1939, confidential.
47 Ibid., memorandum from O.D. Skelton, 29 Nov. 1939
48 Ontario, legislative assembly, *Journals*, 1940, 20-1; J.L. Granatstein, *Canada's War, the Politics of the Mackenzie King Government, 1939-1945* (Toronto: Oxford University Press, 1975), 76-7
49 PAC, external affaris department records, series D1, vol. 739, memorandum from O.D. Skelton, 3 Feb 1940, secret and personal

Notes pages 193–202   267

50 Ibid., vol. 736, memorandum from Skelton, 2 May 1940; Skelton to L.C. Christie, 18 May 1940, private and personal
51 Ibid., M.M. Mahoney to Skelton, 29 May 1940, private and confidential; memorandum from Skelton, 12 July 1940
52 Ibid., memorandum from Skelton to King, 19 Sept. 1940
53 Ibid., memorandum from Skelton to King, 20 Sept. 1940; memorandum from Skelton, 20, 21 Sept. 1940
54 Ibid., memorandum from Skelton, 24 Sept. 1940; L.C. Christie to Skelton, 10 Oct. 1940, confidential
55 Ibid., memorandum from Skelton, 1 Nov. 1940; PAO, Hepburn papers, Hepburn to Gordon Challies, 6 Feb. 1941
56 Canada, external affairs department, *St. Lawrence Deep Waterway, International Rapids Section, Reports Submitted to the President of the United States of America and the Prime Minister of Canada by the Canadian Temporary Great Lakes–St. Lawrence Basin Committee and the United States St. Lawrence Advisory Committee, Ottawa, Canada, January 3, 1941* (Ottawa: King's Printer, 1941) [hereafter *St. Lawrence Waterway, 1941*]
57 See the King-Hepburn correspondence Jan.-Feb. 1941, reprinted in *Correspondence re St. Lawrence, 1938–41*, 57–65; *St. Lawrence Waterway, 1941*, part II, summary of outstanding features
58 Willoughby, *St. Lawrence Waterway*, 186–7; J.W. Pickersgill, ed., *The Mackenzie King Record*, vol. I, *1939–44* (Toronto: University of Toronto Press, 1960), 162–5; PAC, King papers, J.P. Moffatt to H.R.L. Henry, 29 Jan. 1941, 55412–14
59 King to Moffatt, 5 March 1941; Moffatt to King, 10 March 1941; *Correspondence re St. Lawrence, 1938–41*, 38–42; Canada, external affairs department, *Agreement between Canada and the United States of America Relating to the Great Lakes – St. Lawrence Basin Development, Signed at Ottawa, March 19, 1941* (Ottawa: King's Printer, 1941)

CHAPTER 10: *Revising the Constitution*

1 PAC, King papers, text of speech, n.d. [1935], C115572–90; Quebec remained Liberal until 1936; Manitoba was controlled by John Bracken's Progressive government, Alberta by William Aberhart's Social Credit administration
2 Neatby, *King, 1932–9*; other analyses of the ill-will between the two men are cited in n. 18, chapter 9.
3 PAC, dominion-provincial conference records, vol. 62, W.C. Clark to Charles Dunning, 7 Dec. 1935; ibid., vol. 64, dominion-provincial conference 1935–6, provincial statistics, chart 7–3
4 Neatby, *King, 1932–9*, 148–52; 'Dominion-Provincial Conference, 1935, Record of Proceedings Ottawa, December 9–13, 1935,' *Dominion-Provincial Conferences, 1927, 1935, 1941*, appendix A1, report of the proceedings of the opening plenary session, 8–28
5 The account of these meetings is taken from PAC, dominion-provincial conference records, vol. 65, transcript of proceedings of sub-conference on financial questions, 10–11–12, Dec. 1935
6 Ibid., vol. 62, Clark to Dunning, 7 Dec. 1935
7 Ibid., draft minutes of first meeting of continuing committee appointed by sub-conference on financial questions, 13 Dec. 1935, confidential; 'Record of Proceedings, 1935,' *Dominion-Provincial Conferences, 1927, 1935, 1941*, 44–5
8 Nelles, *Politics of Development*, 662–3; PAC, dominion-provincial conference records, vol. 60, dominion-provincial conference, 1935, confidential record of proceedings of conference and of sub-conferences, Ottawa, 9 Dec. to 13 Dec. 1935, draft minutes of Committee on Mining Development and Taxation, 10–12–13 Dec. 1935, confidential; PAO, Hepburn papers, press statement, 18 Dec. 1935
9 PAC, dominion-provincial conference records, vol. 62, Clark to Dunning, 5 Dec. 1935
10 Ibid., vol. 60, dominion-provincial conference, 1935, confidential record of proceedings of conference and sub-conferences, Ottawa, 9–13 Dec. 1935, minutes of the Committee on Unemployment and Relief, 9–10–11–12 Dec. 1935; 'Record of Proceedings, 1935,' *Dominion-Provincial Conferences, 1927, 1935, 1941*, 38–44

11 Gérin-Lajoie, *Constitutional Amendment in Canada*, 235–7; Canada, House of Commons, Special Committee on the British North America Act, 1935, *Proceedings and Evidence and Report* (Ottawa: King's Printer, 1938)
12 'Record of Proceedings, 1935,' *Dominion-Provincial Conferences, 1927, 1935, 1941*, 64
13 PAC, dominion-provincial conference records, vol. 60, dominion-provincial conference, 1935, confidential record of proceedings of conference and sub-conferences, Ottawa, 9–13, Dec. 1935, draft minutes of Committee on Constitutional Questions, 10 Dec. 1935, confidential; 'Record of Proceedings, 1935,' *Dominion-Provincial Conferences, 1927, 1935, 1941*, 37–8
14 Ibid., 49–51; PAC, J.W. Dafoe papers, vol. 8, Crerar to Dafoe, 17 Dec. 1935, personal
15 PAC, dominion-provincial conference records, vol. 74, memorandum re dominion government guarantee of provincial loans, 13 Jan. 1936
16 Ibid., proceedings of the Permanent Committee on Financial Questions of the dominion-provincial conference, Ottawa, 13, 14 Jan. 1936
17 *CAR*, 1935–6, 125–7, 193–4; PAO, Hepburn papers, Dunning to Hepburn, 1 May 1936; PAC, Meighen papers, Meighen to Sir Thomas White, 18 May 1936, 92105–6; ibid., King papers, memorandum from W.S. Edwards to King, 16 Sept. 1936, C109862–6
18 Ibid., report on the meetings of the National Finance Committee held on 9–10–11 Dec. 1936, attached to Dunning to King, 16 Dec. 1936, 186209–13; ibid., dominion-provincial conference records, vol. 73, transcript of the meeting of the Permanent Committee on Financial Questions of the dominion-provincial conference, Ottawa, 9–10–11 Dec. 1936, 3 vols
19 Gérin-Lajoie, *Constitutional Amendment in Canada*, 244–9, 301–5; PAC, external affairs department records, series D1, vol. 759, dominion-provincial conference, 1935, constitutional documents for submission to Continuing Committee on Constitutional Questions, Ottawa, 3 Jan. 1936; I.A. Humphries, *Observations on a Proposed Method of Amending the British North America Act* (n.p., n.d.), 18
20 T.C. Davis, *The Canadian Constitution and Its Amendment* (Regina, 1936), 13–16; PAC, external affairs department records, series D1, vol. 759, W.S. Edwards to O.D. Skelton, 15 Feb. 1936; ibid., J.W. Dafoe papers, vol. 10, Dafoe to G.V. Ferguson, 14 Oct. 1938
21 *CAR*, 1935–6, 236–7; PAC, King papers, Norman M. Rogers to Hepburn, 1 April 1936; Hepburn to Rogers, 2 April 1936, 185066–7
22 On the conflict over hydroelectric policy see chapter 9 and for the Oshawa strike, I.M. Abella, 'Oshawa 1937,' In Abella, ed., *On Strike, Six Key Labour Struggles in Canada 1919–1949* (Toronto: James Lewis and Samuel, 1974), 93–125. PAC, King papers, Hepburn to King, 13 April 1937; King to Hepburn, 13 April 1937, 202073–5
23 McKenty, *Mitch Hepburn*, 125–6; Toronto *Daily Star*, 4 June 1937
24 PAO, Hepburn papers, Hepburn to Pattullo, 27 July 1937; PAC, King papers, Mackenzie to King, 28 July 1937, personal and confidential, 203801–4
25 McKenty, *Mitch Hepburn*, 139–44; see also PAC, King papers, index of events re lieutenant-governorship of Ontario, 29 Sept., 29 Oct. 1937, C135934–6.
26 Ibid., dominion-provincial conference records, vol. 74, Towers to Clark, 20 Oct. 1936, personal and confidential; memorandum from Clark re Royal Commission on Economic Basis of Confederation, 7 Dec. 1936, confidential
27 Neatby, *King, 1932–39*, 199–200; PAC, dominion-provincial conference records, 47, vol. 73, transcript of the meeting of the Permanent Committee on Financial Questions of the dominion-provincial conference, Ottawa, 9-10-11 Dec. 1936; ibid., J.W. Dafoe Papers, vol. 10, T.A. Crerar to Dafoe, 11 Jan. 1937, personal
28 PAC, King papers, McQuesten to King, 27 March 1937; memorandum from O.D. Skelton to King, 24 July 1937, secret and personal; King to Ian Mackenzie, 9 Aug. 1937; 204084, C142593–6, 203805
29 RCDPR, *Report*, book 1, 9–10; Toronto *Telegram*, 17 Aug. 1937. In October he promised Rowell the 'hearty cooperation' of his government; see PAC, Royal Commission on Dominion-Provincial Relations Records [hereafter RCDPR], vol. 56, Rowell to Alexander Skelton, 30 Oct. 1937
30 Ibid., King papers, vol. 225, copy of wire to King in Lake Wales, Florida
31 Ibid., King to Hepburn, 5 Nov. 1937; Hepburn to King, 25 Nov. 1937; 202083–4, 202095; PAO, Hepburn papers, Hepburn to Duplessis, 14 Feb. 1938

Notes pages 210-20   269

32 PAC, King papers, King to Hepburn, 20 Jan. 1938, 214196; Toronto *Telegram*, 31 Jan. 1938
33 Ontario, legislative assembly, *Journals*, 1938, 2-3; PAC, King papers, memorandum from E.A. Pickering to King, 20 June 1938, C151270-5
34 Ibid., memorandum from J.W. Pickersgill to King re Mr Hepburn and the federal government, 23 Sept. 1938, C121438-53; Ontario, legislative assembly, *Journals*, 1938, 38-40
35 PAC, King papers, King to Arthur Roebuck, 23 April 1938, personal, 219392-3
36 PAO, Hepburn papers, Hepburn to Duplessis, 14 Feb. 1938; G.D. Conant to Hepburn, 22 April 1938. Mr Taylor described the preparation of the Ontario brief in an interview with H.V. Nelles; see Nelles, 'Premier Hepburn and the Ontario Objection to the Rowell-Sirois Report,' graduate seminar paper, University of Toronto, 1966, 19
37 RCDPR, *Report of Hearings, Ontario*, 5 vols. (n.p., n.d. [1938]), [hereafter cited as *Ontario Hearings*], vol. 3, 6629; J.B. M[cGeachy], 'Confederation Clinic, 1867-1937,' Winnipeg *Free Press*, 28 April 1938; subsequent references to the *Free Press* are to this regular feature on the commission's activities by McGeachy.
38 See RCDPR, *Statement by the Government of Ontario*, 3 vols. in 1 (n.p., n.d.) [hereafter *Ontario Statement*], book I, statement by M.F. Hepburn, 1-29, from which the following paragraphs are taken.
39 RCDPR, *Ontario Hearings*, vol. 3, 7452b-c; Winnipeg *Free Press*, 3 May 1938
40 RCDPR, *Ontario Statement*, book II, general statement, 1-80
41 Ibid., *Ontario Hearings*, vol. 5, 7945
42 Ibid., vol. 3, 7472-507
43 PAO, Hepburn papers, memorandum from Walters to H.J. Chater, 30 March 1938
44 RCDPR, *Ontario Hearings*, vol. 3, 7545-6
45 Ibid., 7564-6
46 Ibid., vol. 4, 7608-14
47 Ibid., 7622-3
48 Ibid., 7624-5
49 Ibid., 7767-98
50 R.M. Fowler of the Commission staff recalled this in an interview with H.V. Nelles; see Nelles, 'Ontario's Objection to Rowell-Sirois,' 20
51 RCDPR, *Ontario Hearings*, vol. 5, 7964a-69
52 Ottawa *Journal*, 6 May 1938
53 Nelles, 'Ontario's Objection to Rowell-Sirois,' 20
54 PAC, King papers, Hepburn to Dunning, 15 June 1938, 214323
55 Ibid., Hepburn to King, 29 June 1938; King to Hepburn, 30 June 1938; 214327-8, 214329-30
56 Ibid., memorandum from J.W. Pickersgill to King re Mr Hepburn and the federal government, 23 Sept. 1938, C121438-53; *Globe and Mail*, 17 Aug. 1938
57 PAC, King papers, memorandum from O.D. Skelton to King, 16 July 1938, confidential, C114360-3
58 Ibid., memorandum from E.A. Pickering to King, 26 July 1938; T.D. Pattullo to King, 5 Aug. 1938, personal; memorandum from J.W. Pickersgill to King, 10 Aug. 1938; C142401-2, 218503-4, C142412
59 W.C. Clark wanted W.A. Mackintosh to succeed Rowell, and O.D. Skelton suggested Chief Justice Lyman P. Duff or, possibly, R.B. Bennett; see PAC, external affairs department records, series D1, vol. 718, memorandum from Skelton to King, 1 June, 16, July 1938. King vetoed Mackintosh and Bennett and chose Sirois.
60 Ibid., King papers, King to Lapointe, 9 Oct. 1938, 215229-34
61 Ibid., memorandum re Mr Hepburn and the federal government, C121456-516; 'Present Day Problems, an Address by the Honourable Mitchell F. Hepburn,' Empire Club of Canada, *Addresses, 1938-9* (Toronto, 1939), 160
62 PAC, King papers, King to Vincent Massey, 15 Aug. 1939, personal and confidential, 232076-81
63 Ibid., Ian Mackenzie to King, 27 Dec. 1939, confidential; King to N.A. McLarty, 5 Jan. 1940, immediate and strictly confidential; 230588-9, 37983-6. The King papers for 1940 on had been only provisionally numbered when I consulted them.
64 McKenty, *Mitch Hepburn*, 209-10

65 RCDPR, *Report*, vol. II, *Recommendations* is summarized in the following paragraphs.
66 PAC, J.W. Dafoe papers, vol. 12, Dafoe to R.M. Fowler, 18 Dec. 1940; ibid., vol. 11, Dafoe to J.M. Macdonnell, 16 Sept. 1940
67 Ibid., King papers, King to Bracken, 23 Sept. 1940, 30771
68 Granatstein, *Canada's War*, 160–4; PAC, finance department records, vol. 2701, Graham Towers to J.L. Ilsley, 24 Sept. 1940, confidential; memorandum re Sirois report and the war, 24 July 1940, confidential
69 Ibid., King papers, Graham Towers to King, 15 Aug. 1940, confidential, 43667–72
70 Ibid., finance department records, vol. 2701, memorandum on the report of the Sirois Commission [by W.C. Clark], 11 Sept. 1940; A.D.P. Heeney to J.L. Ilsley, 23 Sept. 1940, confidential, enclosing minutes of special Cabinet committee on Dominion-provincial relations report and emergency measures (financial and economic), 20 Sept. 1940, secret. This committee also considered what Canada should do if it was cut off from Britain by the war.
71 Toronto *Daily Star*, 16 May 1940; PAO, Hepburn papers, observations regarding the report and recommendations of the Royal Commission of Dominion-Provincial Relations, Public Health, Province of Ontario, n.d.
72 Granatstein, *Canada's War*, 164–6; PAC, finance department records, vol. 2701, report of the cabinet subcommittee appointed to consider the report of the Royal Commission on Dominion Provincial Relations, n.d.; Ilsley to Hepburn, 1 Nov. 1940, persoanl and confidential; ibid., Dafoe papers, vol. 12, Grant Dexter to Dafoe, 25 Oct. 1941
73 Ibid., King papers, King to Sir William Mulock, 13 Jan. 1941, 55574–5
74 Granatstein, *Canada's War*, 167–9; Pickersgill, *Mackenzie King Record*, vol. I, 160–1
75 PAC, King papers, Hepburn to King, 8 Nov. 1940, 35229; ibid., dominion-provincial conference records, vol. 76, memorandum from James C. Thompson, 27 Dec. 1940
76 Ibid., finance department records, vol. 2701, R.M. Fowler to J.L. Ilsley, 6 Jan. 1941; C.G. Power, *A Party Politician, the Memoirs of Chubby Power*, Norman Ward, ed. (Toronto: Macmillan, 1966), 193
77 Granatstein, *Canada's War*, 169–72; 'Dominion-Provincial Conference, Tuesday, January 14, 1941 and Wednesday, January 15, 1941,' *Dominion-Provincial Conferences, 1927, 1935–41*, 1–10
78 Ibid., 10–16
79 *Globe and Mail*, 15 Jan. 1941; PAO, Hepburn papers, draft of speech, n.d.
80 'Dominion-Provincial Conference, 1941,' *Dominion-Provincial Conferences, 1927, 1935, 1941*, 16–61
81 PAC, Dafoe papers, vol. 12, Alexander Skelton to Dafoe, 8 Feb. 1941; T.A. Crerar to Dafoe, 16 Jan. 1941, personal and confidential; no transcript of this session was kept and the quotations are from Hepburn's address to the second session of the Conference, where he reportedly used words identical in substance to those of the earlier session; see 'Dominion-Provincial Conference, 1941,' *Dominion-Provincial Conferences, 1927, 1935, 1941*, 101–2.
82 Ibid., 69–75
83 Ibid., 75–9
84 Ibid., 79–80
85 Ibid., 92–102
86 Ibid., 103–8; among those who wanted to continue was A.L. Macdonald of Nova Scotia who wrote a note to King saying, 'Mr. Aberhart is willing to consider the Sirois Report along with other matters. Hepburn is willing to talk about the war. If we accepted the idea of discussing *something* could we by degrees get to a consideration of the Report'; PAC, King papers, Macdonald to King, 16 Jan. 1941, 52207
87 King to A.C. Hardy, 19 Jan. 1941, personal, 49842
88 McKenty, *Mitch Hepburn*, 230–1; PAC, finance department records, vol. 2701, press release, 20 Jan. 1941
89 Granatstein, *Canada's War*, 172–4; Pickersgill, *Mackenzie King Record*, vol. I, 176–7
90 Walter Gordon has claimed responsibility for devising these fiscal arrangements, although it seems unlikely that he alone deserves credit for them; see Denis Smith, *Gentle Patriot, a Biography of Walter Gordon* (Edmonton: Hurtig, 1973), 22–4.

91 PAC, finance department records, vol. 2697, press release re summary of offer to provinces, April 1941
92 Ibid., King papers, Hepburn to King, 21 May 1941; King to Hepburn, 26 May 1941, 50031-4, 50035-9; PAO, Hepburn papers, Hepburn to King, 28 May 1941
93 PAC, King papers, King to Hepburn, 30 May, 6 June 1941; Hepburn to King, 5 June 1941; 50052-4, 50059-60, 50058
94 Walter Gordon, *A Political Memoir* (Toronto: McClelland and Stewart, 1977), 38-9, records that Hepburn came to Ottawa with his entourage, and seeing that he was cornered, said to Gordon, 'Walter, does this mean you've got us by the - - - ?', to which Gordon replied, 'Yes, Mitch, and we intend to keep on squeezing until you sign.' Hepburn laughed, saying their predicament would eventually dawn on his colleagues, which it evidently did.
95 PAC, finance department records, vol. 2702, minutes of meeting of provincial treasurers with the dominion government, 18 and 19 Dec. 1941
96 Ibid., draft of statement by Ilsley, possibly to be released re Hepburn, 31 Jan. 1942
97 Ibid., Ian Mackenzie to Ilsley, 18 Feb. 1942, confidential

CONCLUSION

1 John Richards and Larry Pratt, *Prairie Capitalism: Power and Influence in the New West* (Toronto: McClelland and Stewart, 1979), 8
2 For a review of the writings of historians and legal scholars on federalism see Alan C. Cairns, 'The Judicial Committee and Its Critics,' *Canadian Journal of Political Science* IV (1971), 301-45. The refusal to take federalism seriously is perhaps typified by Frank Underhill's remark in 1931 that 'The only province which has not been subject to regular alternation between short periods of comparatively good government and long periods of decay is Quebec. In Quebec they enjoy bad government all the time.' Quoted in Cairns, 339-40.
3 Can., H. of C., *Deb.*, 1889, 851-2
4 Burke is quoted in Richard H. Rovere, *Arrivals and Departures, a Journalist's Memoirs* (New York: Macmillan, 1976), 8
5 David M. Potter, 'The Historian's Use of Nationalism and Vice Versa,' *American Historical Review* 67 (1972), 931
6 *Globe*, 5 Feb. 1883
7 Alan Cairns remarks that, 'It is impossible to believe that a few elderly men in London deciding two or three constitutional cases a year precipitated, sustained and caused the development of Canada in a federalist direction the country would not otherwise have taken.' 'The Judicial Committee and Its Critics,' 319
8 See Christopher Armstrong, 'Federalism, Continentalism and Economic Development in Canada,' paper presented to the International Congress of Historical Sciences, Bucharest, 1980.

Index

Aberhart, William 204, 225, 226, 227, 228
Acheson, T.W. xiii
Adams, Thomas 131
Aeronautics in Canada, In re regulation and control of (1932) 157
Aluminum Company of America 73
American Cyanamid Company 82
American Super Power Corporation 164
Angus, H.F. 208, 215, 216
Aylesworth, A.B. 72, 76, 97, 98; on disallowance 48, 51–3, 58–63, 66, 182; electricity exports 70–1; on incorporation 103–5

Backus, E.W. 92, 162
Balfour Declaration (1926) 146
Bayly, Edward 104, 105, 106, 107, 108
Beauharnois Power Company 172, 173, 175–6, 181, 182, 183, 185
Beck, Sir Adam 74, 77, 117, 162, 166, 179; creation of HEPC 56–8, 60, 65; on electricity exports 70–2, 76, 180, 188; wartime electricity shortages 78, 80–4
Bennett, R.B. 133, 145, 156, 161, 179, 181, 198, 217, 236; insurance legislation 109–12; dominion-provincial conferences (1931) 146–8, (1933) 149–52, (January 1934) 152–3, (July 1934) 153–5; New Deal 157–9, 203; St Lawrence Deep Waterway 175–7
Better terms 4, 13–14, 28–9, 117, 121
Bertram, John 36, 45
Blair, A.G. 45, 87, 89, 90
Blackstock, G.T. 98
Blake, Edward 8, 13–14, 15, 21, 25, 27, 28, 30, 31, 61
Blue, Archibald 43
'BNA Committee' (Ontario 1934) 156
Board of Railway Commissioners 89, 90, 94
Bonanza Creek Gold Mining Company v. the King (1916) 106, 107

Borden, Sir Frederick 66
Borden, Sir Robert 61, 66, 71, 74, 76, 77, 88, 92, 97, 99, 100, 105, 135; relations with Whitney 122, 124–8, 132, 234; wartime electricity shortages 80, 82; dominion-provincial conference (November 1918) 130
Boundary dispute: *see* North-western boundary
Boundary Waters Treaty (1909) 71–2, 97, 162, 182, 184, 195
Bowell, Sir Mackenzie 99
Boyce, A.C. 52, 98
Boyd, Caldwell and Company 25–6
Bracken, John 208, 222, 225
British North America Act 8, 10, 24, 29–30, 51, 66–7, 85–6, 103, 104, 110–1, 121–2, 129, 138, 151, 161, 167, 197, 209, 220, 234; amending formula 133, 142, 143–4, 146, 147, 148, 155–7, 197, 199, 202–3, 205–6, 236; amendment re provincial sales tax 204, 205; special Commons committee on (1935) 203; treaty-making power 135–7, 139, 157, 159
Broder, Andrew 61
Bronson, E.H. 87
Brown, George 3, 8, 9, 10, 11, 12, 13, 229
Brown, R.C. xiii
Bryce, James 71
Bulkley, R.J. 82
Bureaucrats, competition for jurisdiction by 5, 85, 101, 107–13, 131–2
Burke, Edmund 237
Burke, Stevenson 45, 46
Burrell, Martin 124, 125

Caldwell, William C. 26
Campbell, Thane 225
Canadian Bankers' Association 62
Canadian Copper Company 42, 44, 45, 46, 47, 50

274 Index

Canadian Deep Waterways and Power Association 174
Canadian Life Insurance Officers Association 109, 111, 207
Canadian Manufacturers' Association 56, 82–3, 102, 157
Canadian Mining and Metallurgical Company 42
Canadian Niagara Power Company 55, 76, 77, 78, 80, 81, 82, 99
Canadian Pacific Railway Company v. Ottawa Fire Insurance Company (1907) 103, 104
Canadian Union of Municipalities 91
Cannon, Lucien 108
Carborundum Company 79
Cardin, P.J.A. 193
Cartier, George-Etienne 9, 10
Cartwright, J.R. 70
Cartwright, Sir Richard 45, 120, 122, 125
Cauchon, J.E. 18
Chamberlain, Joseph 38, 39
Chandler, E.B. 10
Charlottetown Conference of 1864 9
Charlton, John 40, 41
Charlton, William 41
Chrysler, F.H. 59
Clark, J.M. 45, 50, 51
Clark, W.C. 199, 201, 202, 208
Clarke, E.F. 89, 90, 91
Clouston, E.S. 45, 50
Cobalt Lake Mining Company 48
Cochrane, Frank 66, 67, 74, 75, 100, 105, 122, 123, 124, 125
Code, R.G. 92, 93, 95, 98, 99
Colonial Laws Validity Act 146
Commission of Conservation 74, 131
Compact theory of Confederation 4–5, 13–14, 28, 31–2, 133, 143–4, 147–8, 211, 235, 236
Companies Act (Ontario 1897) 102
Companies: federal powers of incorporation of 85–6, 93–4; provincial powers of incorporation of 85–6, 100–7; provincial regulation of 101–7
Company law, American 112–3
Company law, federal-provincial conflict re 85–113
Conant, Gordon 211, 216, 217, 231
Conditional grants: agricultural education 124–5, 126, 132, 234; employment service 131; highway construction 125, 130–1, 132, 234; immigration 124; technical education 131; venereal disease 131
Conmee, James 93, 96–100
'Conmee' clause of Municipal Act 56
Cook, Ramsay xiii
Cooke, J.R. 176

Credit of Canada ..., The (pamphlet) 59
Crerar, T.A. 201–2, 203, 225, 227, 228
Croll, David 154, 202
Crooks, Adam 17, 26
Cross, E.W. 216
Crothers, T.W. 96
Crown Timber Act (Ontario 1898) 37, 39

Dafoe, J.W. 208, 222
Davies, Sir Louis 38, 44, 50
Davis, E.J. 46
Day, Secretary of State William R. 38, 39
Depression, impact on federalism (of 1920–1) 137–8; (of 1930s) 133, 159, 197, 199, 232, 234, 237
Dewart, Hartley 163
Dicey, A.V. 59
Dickenson, Don M. 38
Dingley, Nelson 35
Dingley tariff (1897) 35, 38, 39, 40, 41, 43
Disallowance, power of 9, 10, 24–7, 29, 31, 38, 40, 44–7, 48–51, 58–65, 67, 75–6, 77–8, 78–9, 181–2, 237
Dohert, C.J. 75, 78, 79, 106, 137
Dominion-provincial commission on uniformity of labour law, 1920 137
Dominion-provincial conference (February 1918) 129; (October 1918) 130–1; re unemployment (1922–3) 138–9; re unemployment (1924) 139; re taxation (1924) 141; (1927) 108, 141–4, 171, 234; (1931) 147–8; (1932) 149; (1933) 110, 150–2; (January 1934) 152–3; (July 1934) 153–4, 202; (1935) 199–203, 205, 206; (1941) 3, 198, 225, 225–30, 231, 236
Drayton, Sir Henry 80, 81, 82, 83, 168
Drew, George 191, 192
Drury, E.C. 137, 138, 162, 163, 164
Duff, Mr Justice Lyman 172
Dunning, Charles 199, 201, 202, 204, 205, 217
Duplessis, Maurice 186, 187, 209, 210, 222
Dysart, A.A. 206

Eastern Ontario Municipal Power Union 162
The Economist 59
Elections, federal (1911) 122; (1930) 145, 148, 175; (1935) 158, 198; (1940) 192, 193, 199, 220
Electrical companies, incorporation of 92–3, 96–100
Electrical Development Company 56, 57, 60, 77, 78, 79, 80, 83, 88
Electricity: *see* Water-power
Electricity and Fluid Exportation Act (1907) 69–71, 188
Electricity shortages in wartime 78–83

Index 275

Electric railways, incorporation of 86–92, 93–6
Electricity Exportation Act (federal 1938) 188
Electricity exports 68–84, 160, 186–9, 195, 208, 210, 233; American opposition to 69, 188
Electric Railway Act (Ontario 1895) 87
Ellis, J.A. 131, 145, 148, 152
Emmerson, H.R. 93
Export duty on natural resources (1897) 35, 43
Extra-Provincial Corporations Act (Ontario) 102, 105

Falconbridge, Chief Justice J.D. 64
Farrer, Edward 40
Fathers of Confederation, aims of 9–12, 23, 25, 119, 126, 209, 216, 236, 237
Federal-provincial 'game' 5, 85–113, 233
Ferguson, Howard 6, 129, 139, 140, 145, 182, 185, 234; insurance regulation 108–9; Dominion-Provincial Conference (1927) 141–4; water-power jurisdiction 160, 164–76, 178; on compact theory of Confederation 146–7, 236
Fielding, W.S. 58, 99, 121
Finlay, Sir Robert 103
Finlayson, George D. 107–12
Finlayson, R.K. 149
Fitzpatrick, Charles 70, 87, 88, 102–3
'Five-cent piece' speech (Mackenzie King 1930) 144
Flavelle, Sir Joseph 80, 81, 82, 83
Florence Mining Company 34, 48–53, 55, 57, 58, 85, 182
Foster, Sir George 83
Foster, R. Leighton 108–9, 150
Fowler, R.M. 225
Foy, J.J. 60, 71, 75, 99, 103, 104, 121
Fraser, Christopher 28–9
Free Press, Winnipeg 155

Gage, Secretary of the Treasury Lyman J. 40
Gardiner, James 229
Gatineau Power Company 165, 168, 181
Geoffrion, Aimé 170
General advantage of Canada, declarations of 29, 74, 86–100, 237
Gibbons, George 70, 71, 72, 73, 75
Gibson, Sir John M. 37, 43, 44, 46, 47, 88, 89, 91, 94–6, 100, 102, 103
Gift taxes, federal 217–8
Globe 36, 37, 50, 95
Godbout, Adelard 225–6
Gordon, the Rev. C.W. (Ralph Connor) 49
Gordon, Wesley 150, 153
Gouin, Sir Lomer 120, 121, 126, 127, 129
Graham, George 49, 94, 95, 96, 97, 166

Granatstein, J.L. xiii
Grand Trunk Railway 94
Great Coalition of 1864 9, 13, 14
Great Lakes–St Lawrence Basin Agreement (Canada-U.S. 1941) 194
Grey, Governor-General Earl 63–4
Green, W.J. 48, 50, 52
Gunboat, protection of investors by 49

Haggart, John 87
Halifax Platform 100, 122
Hamilton Radial Electric Railway 94–6
Hanna, W.J. 62, 104
Hardy, Arthur S. 18, 33, 36, 37, 38, 39, 40, 41, 101
Harrison, Chief Justice Robert A. 18
Hazen, Douglas 122
Heaps, A.A. 141
Hearst, Sir William H. 76, 78, 80, 82, 84, 125, 128, 129, 130, 131, 136
Heenan, Peter 144
Hendrie, J.S. 71
Henry, George S. 111, 147, 148, 150, 152, 153, 155, 159, 175, 176, 177, 178, 179, 185
Hepburn, Mitchell 6, 159, 235; St Lawrence, water-power 178–80, 182–5, 189–96; electricity exports 186–9; Quebec contracts 180–2, 183–4, 185; dominion-provincial conference (July 1934) 153–5; Bennett New Deal 156–8; dominion-provincial conference (1935) 197, 199–203; constitutional amending formula 205–6; debt refunding 203–5; relations with Mackenzie King 185, 192, 197–9, 207–8, 217–8, 232; Royal Commission on Dominion-Provincial Relations 208–17, 218–9, 220, 222–4; dominion-provincial conference (1941) 3, 224–30, 236; Wartime Tax Agreements 230–2
Herridge, W.D. 176
Hewson v. Ontario Power Company (1905) 103
Hilliard, Irwin 74
Hincks, Sir Francis 17
Hitler, Adolf 215
Hogg, Dr T.H. 185, 191, 192, 193, 194
Holt, Sir Herbert 167, 170, 177
Hoover, Herbert 176
Housing, federal loans for (1919) 131–2
Howe, C.D. 192
Howe, Joseph 15
Hull and Aylmer Railway Company 87
Hull, Secretary of State Cordell 189, 190, 191
Hunter, J.H. 101
Hydro-Electric Power Commission of Ontario (HEPC) 56, 57, 58, 59, 63, 68, 70, 74, 76, 77, 78, 83, 85, 96, 117, 160, 161, 163, 165, 167, 170, 172, 175, 176, 177, 178, 180, 182, 185,

276   Index

188, 189, 194; power purchases from Quebec by 161, 165, 172–3, 179, 186, 189, 195, cancellation of 180–2, 183, 185

Ilsley, J.L. 223, 224, 228, 229, 230, 231
Imperial Munitions Board 79–80, 83
Income tax: federal 128–30, 132, 133, 137, 141, 142–3, 150, 156, 157, 201, 205, 212, 214–15, 219, 228, 235; Ontario 205, 214–15, 216, 221, 235
Industrial Disputes Investigation Act 139
Insurance Act, federal (1910) 104, 105; (1917) 107; (1927) 109; (1934) 111
Insurance: federal regulation of 104, 105–6, 107–13, 234; provincial regulation of 86, 104, 107–13, 234; superintendent of, federal 104, 105–6, 107–12; superintendent of, Ontario 108–9
Insurance Superintendents, Association of Provincial 108
Insull, Samuel 168
International Labour Organization, conventions of 135–7, 138, 139, 140, 157
International Joint Commission (Canada–U.S.) 162, 163, 164
International Nickel Company (Inco) 42, 48
International Waterways Commission 70, 73, 75
Interprovincial Conferences (1887) 9, 27–30, 31, 119, 234, 235; (1902) 119–20; (1906) 93–4, 120–1, 148, 234, 235–6; (1910) 104–5; (1913) 126–7; (1929) 107, 141
Irving, Aemilius 70, 89, 91

James, C.C. 124
John Deere Plough Company v. Wharton (1915) 106
Johnston, J.T. 176
Joint High Commission (Canada–U.S. 1898–9) 37, 39–40, 41
Judicial Committee of the Privy Council 9, 15, 16, 21, 22, 24, 26, 30, 31, 32, 42, 52, 64, 72–3, 86, 105, 106, 107, 109, 111, 139, 148, 157, 159, 163, 236, 237

Kaiser, Dr T.E. 56
Keefer, F.H. 174
Kilmer, G.H. 79
King, W.L. Mackenzie 6, 108, 133, 146, 158, 206, 236; on unemployment relief 138–40, 144–5; dominion-provincial conference (1927) 141–4; water-power jurisdiction 160–1, 163–95, 234; dominion-provincial conference (1935) 199–203; relations with Hepburn 197–9, 207–8, 210, 217–19; Royal Commission on Dominion-Provincial Relations 197–8, 208–10, 218–19, 222–4; unemployment insurance 209, 219–20; dominion-provincial conference (1941) 3, 198, 225–30; Wartime Tax Agreements 198, 230–2, 235

Lake of the Woods Control Board 161–4
Lake of the Woods Regulation Act (federal 1921) 163
Lang, D.W. 213, 216
Lansing, Robert 38, 77
Lapointe, Ernest 139, 143, 146, 148, 159, 167, 169, 174, 181, 182, 203, 207, 219, 224, 227, 228, 236
Lash, Zebulon A. 101
Latchford, F.R. 50, 118, 119
Laurier, Sir Wilfrid 32, 84, 122, 123; manufacturing condition on sawlogs 36–7, 39–41; manufacturing condition on nickel 34, 43–7; disallowance 49–51, 53, 55, 57–8, 61–3, 65–7; electricity exports 71, 73–5; incorporation of companies 88, 91, 94–5, 97–101, 104–5; provincial subsidies 117–19; interprovincial conferences (1902) 119, (1906) 120–1, 235
Leduc, Paul 205
Lennox, Haughton 98
Lieutenant-governor, powers of 9, 22–4, 30
Liquidators of the Maritime Bank of Canada v. Receiver-General of New Brunswick 24, 31, 32
Liquor licensing 27, 28
Lloyd's of London 110, 111
Lobbyists, cloud of 90
Long Lac diversion: *see* Water-power, Long Lac
Lucas, I.B. 77, 78, 127, 129
Lynch-Staunton, George 74
Lyon, Stewart 179, 182, 183, 185

McBride, Richard 121
McCarthy, D'Alton 236, 237
McCarthy, D.L. 78
McCully, Jonathan 11
McDonald, James 19
Macdonald, Sir John A. 6, 15, 31, 122; view of federalism 9, 11–14; Ontario boundary 8–9, 15–22, 34; powers of lieutenant-governor 23–4; disallowance 24–7, 64–5, 67; interprovincial conference (1887) 28–30, 117, 235
Macdonald, John Sandfield 13, 14, 15, 25, 28
McDougald, W.L. 161, 166, 167, 177
McDougall, William 15
McGeachy, J.B. 213
MacKay, A.G. 92, 97
Mackay, R.A. 208, 216
Mackenzie, Alexander 9, 14, 17, 19, 25
McKenzie, D.D. 124

Mackenzie, Ian 207, 231
Mackenzie, Sir William 55, 57, 58, 60, 77, 79, 83, 88, 90, 91
McKinley, President William 35, 36
McLaren, Peter 25-6
Maclaren-Quebec Power Company 173, 181
McLarty, Norman 220
Maclean, W.F. 90
MacMahon, Hugh 18
MacMillan, A.S. 225
McNair, J.B. 226
McNaught, W.K. 71
McQuesten, T.B. 179, 208, 224, 228-9
'Made in Washington' policy 187
Magrath, C.A. 165, 168, 173
Major, W.J. 203, 205
Manitoba-Ontario boundary: see North-western boundary of Ontario
Manufacturing condition: nickel 34, 42-8, 233; pulpwood 42, 233; sawlogs 33-42, 46, 233
Markey, Fred 90
Marlborough, Duchess of, estate manager 59
Matheson, A.J. 93, 118-19, 121
Matthews, Albert 191
Maw, H.H. 49
Meighen, Arthur 109, 110, 111, 132, 138, 140, 145, 163, 168, 204
Mercier, Honoré 27, 29, 235
Meredith, W.R. 19, 36
Mills, David 17, 38, 46, 47, 48, 101, 102
Minerals, federal taxation of 201-2, 214
Mines Act (Ontario 1900) 43, 44, 45, 46
Miscampbell, Andrew 36
Mond, Dr. Ludwig 45
Monk, E.C. 18
Montreal, Ottawa and Georgian Bay Canal Company 168-70
Moore, W.H. 210
Moss, Chief Justice Sir Chalres 52
Mowat, Sir Oliver 4, 6, 36, 53, 87, 114, 117; view of federalism 9-11, 31-2, 61, 233-7; compact theory of Confederation 5, 13-14; disallowance 9, 24-7, 34; powers of lieutenant-governor 9, 22-4; Ontario boundary 8, 14, 17-22; interprovincial conference (1887) 9, 27-30; incorporation of companies 101-2
Mulock, Sir William 66, 91, 92
Municipal franchises 86-7, 88, 93, 94
Municipal Power Union of Western Ontario 57
Murdock, James 138, 139
Murphy, Charles 104
Murray, George 129
'Mushroom government' (at Ottawa) 227

National Employment Commission 202

National Finance Committee 204-5
National Hydro-Electric Company 166, 167, 168, 169, 170
National Transcontinental Railway 118
Natural resources, provincial control of 4, 31, 33-53, 54-55, 111, 214, 233, 238
Navigation, federal jurisdiction over 60, 68, 73-4, 76, 84, 92, 97, 142, 160-1, 165, 167, 169-72, 173-5
Nelles, H.V. xiii, 65
Nesbitt, Wallace 44, 63, 104
'New Deal' of R.B. Bennett 135, 157-9, 202
'New Ontario' 118
Niagara Convention (1929) 172, 178, 179-80, 183
Niagara Development Act (Ontario 1916) 77
Nicholls, Frederic 55, 57, 58
Nickel Steel Company 43
Nickle, W.F. 107, 139
Nipigon-Albany Canal and Transportation Company 100
Nixon, Harry 205, 208, 244
North Shore Power, Railway and Navigation Company 88
North-western boundary of Ontario 8, 14-22, 25, 29-30, 31, 122-3, 126, 132, 233

O'Brien, Henry 62
Ogoki diversion: see Water-power, Ogoki River
Oliver, Peter, xiii
Ontario expenditures 114-17, 133-5, 140, 146, 199-200, 213, 230; provincial debt 133-5, 140, 199
Ontario and Michigan Power Company 97-9
Ontario and Minnesota Power Company 92
Ontario Lumbermen's Association 36, 37
Ontario Municipal Electric Association 77
Ontario Power Commission 56
Ontario Power Company 55, 57, 77, 78, 80, 81, 117
Ontario Railway and Municipal Board 93, 94, 95, 96, 131
Ontario Union of Municipalities 90
Orford Refining Company 42, 44
Oshawa Strike (1937) 185, 207, 209
Ottawa Street Railway 87
Ottawa Valley Power Company 173, 181, 182

Pardee, F.F. 74
Parent, S.N. 119
Parker, W.R.P. 44
Patterson, John 43
Patterson, W.J. 225
Pattullo, Andrew 32
Pattullo, T.D. 207, 226, 227, 228
Pauncefote, Sir Julian 38

278 Index

Peace, order, and good government 10, 61, 136, 139, 157
Pellatt, Sir Henry 48, 50, 55, 57, 58, 88, 90, 91
Pensions, old age 138, 141, 158, 213, 215
Perley, Sir George 156
Petawawa lands 66-7
Pope, Joseph 102
Population, Ontario 114
Port Arthur Power and Development Company 96-7
Potter, David 237
Power controller 81-3
Price, W.H. 108, 109, 110, 141, 142, 148, 151, 175
Private property, sacredness of 66, 92
Protective tariff 4, 33, 117, 126-7
Public debt, refunding of 197, 199-201, 204-5, 206
Public power movement 54-7
Pugsley, William 74, 100

Quebec Conference of 1864 8, 9, 10, 11, 30, 235
Quebec-New England Company 166
Quebec power contracts: see Hydro-Electric Power Commission
Queen's Counsel, powers to create 23-4
Queen Victoria Niagara Falls Parks Commission 68, 70, 77
Question of Disallowance ... A (pamphlet) 59-60

Radio communication in Canada, in re regulation and control of (1932) 157
Railway Act (federal) 87, 88, 89, 90, 91
Rathbun, E.W. 36
Rat Portage (Kenora) 19, 21
Reference cases 24, 29, 30-1, 47, 103, 109, 136, 138, 158-9; companies (1916) 31, 104-7; fisheries (1898) 31; insurance (1916) 104-7; prohibition (1896) 31; water-power (1929) 161, 171-2
Reid, J.D. 81, 82
Relief: *see* Unemployment relief
Rhodes, E.N. 109, 181
Richards, Chief Justice W.B. 17
Riddell, Mr Justice W.R. 51
Rinfret, Thibaudeau 208
Riparian rights 73, 75
Ritchie, Samuel J. 43
Rivers and Streams Act 25-7, 28, 46, 64
Robb, J.A. 143
Robertson, Gideon 137, 138, 145
Roblin, Rodmond 122, 123
Roebuck, Arthur 154, 156, 158, 159, 179, 180, 183, 203, 205
Rogers, Norman 143, 202, 207, 210

Rollo, Walter 137, 138
Roosevelt, President Franklin D. 179, 180, 182, 183, 188, 190, 192, 193, 194, 195
Roosevelt, President Theodore 69
Root, Secretary of State Elihu 69
Ross, Sir George 34, 36, 39, 43, 44, 45, 46, 47, 48, 49, 56, 72, 91, 92, 102, 103, 117, 118, 119, 120, 124, 125
Rowell, Newton 83, 190, 111, 136, 163, 171, 208, 209, 212, 215, 216, 219, 226
Royal Commission on Dominion-Provincial Relations 3, 197-8, 205, 208-17, 218-19, 220-2, 223, 224, 225, 226, 227, 228, 232, 235, 236; Ontario submission to 210-15; Plan I 221-2, 224, 228-9; Plan II 222
Royal Ontario Nickel Commission 54

St Catharines' Milling Company 22, 30
St Lawrence Deep Waterway 177, 178, 179, 180, 182-3, 185, 188, 189-96; National Advisory Committee re 165
St Lawrence Deep Waterway Treaty (Canada-U.S. 1932) 177
St Lawrence Power Company 73, 74
Scott, Sir Richard 38, 39, 97
Senate, role of 11-12, 29, 141
Shawinigan Power Company 167, 168
Sifton, Sir Clifford 45, 100, 161, 168, 169, 170, 177
Sifton, Harry 168, 169
Sifton, Winfield 168, 169
Sirois, Dr Joseph 208, 219
Skelton, Alexander 218
Skelton, O.D. 141, 149, 156, 173, 182, 183, 189, 190, 191, 192, 193
Slaght, Arthur 198
Smith, Goldwin 59
Social Welfare, division of jurisdiction over 142, 146, 149-52, 156-9, 215, 220-1
Sproule, Dr T.S. 89, 96
Statute of Westminster (1931) 146-8
Statute Law Amendment Act (Ontario 1903) 102-3, 104
Stewart, Charles 165
Stone and Webster 181
Subsidies to provinces 10, 28, 29, 30, 31, 117, 119-21, 126-8, 130, 132, 140, 141, 142, 144, 212, 213, 214, 218, 221, 234, 236
Supreme Court 21, 24, 30, 47, 103, 104, 105, 106, 136, 138, 142, 158, 171
Sweezey, R.O. 172

Taché, E.E. 15
Taschereau, L.A. 60-1, 109, 110, 141, 142, 144, 148, 164, 166, 168, 170, 171, 172, 173, 174, 175, 203

Tawney, Congressman 40
Taxation of interest on provincial bonds 230–1
Tax Rental Agreements 235
Taylor, Kenneth 210, 213, 216, 217
Temiskaming and Northern Ontario Railway 48, 117, 118–19, 123–4, 126, 132
Thompson, Sir John 24, 27, 30, 31, 101
Thompson, R.M. 42, 43, 44, 45
Thornton, Sir Edward 18
Tilley, W.N. 170, 171
Toronto and Hamilton Railway Company 90–1
Toronto and Niagara Power Company 88
Toronto Electric Light Company 88
Toronto Power Company 82
Toronto Railway Company 88
Towers, Graham 205, 208, 223
Trade and Commerce, federal jurisdiction over 68, 86, 101, 113
Trades and Labour Congress 138, 157

Unemployment and Farm Relief Act (federal 1934) 148–9
Unemployment, Bennett's promise to end (1930) 145
Unemployment insurance 133, 138, 149, 150–2, 156, 157, 158, 159, 209–10, 213, 219–20, 223, 232, 236
Unemployment relief 133, 135, 137, 138, 139–40, 142, 144–6, 148–50, 152–5, 199, 202, 206, 216, 217, 234, 235; block grants 154–5, 202, 206, 207, 210, 220; matching grants 137, 138, 139–40, 145–6, 149, 150, 152, 155, 237
Unemployment Relief Act (federal 1930) 145
Urquhart, Thomas 91

Vivian Company, H.H. 45

Walker, Sir Edmund 64
Walters, Chester 204, 205, 208, 210, 213, 214, 215, 216, 217, 224, 225
War Measures Act 81, 84, 129, 131, 227
Wartime Tax Agreements 198, 230–2, 235

'Waste paper,' bill to make the BNA Act 125
Water-power: division of jurisdiction over 55, 59, 60, 68, 70, 72–6, 83–4, 92–3, 97, 99, 103, 142, 144, 160–77; Great Lakes–St Lawrence basin committee (Canada–U.S. 1940) re 193, 194; Long Lac diversion for 184, 187, 189, 191, 193, 194, 195; Niagara River diversion for 70, 77, 165, 172, 178, 179–80, 182, 183, 184, 189, 193–4, 195, 207; Ogoki River diversion for 165, 182, 183, 184, 189, 191, 193, 194, 195; Ontario–Quebec co-operation re 142, 166, 171, 173–5; Ottawa River 166–70, 192; St Lawrence River 73–5, 160–2, 164–5, 172–3, 175–7, 178, 180, 185–6, 192, 194, 195, 199, 207, 209, 219, 233, 234, Canada–Ontario Agreement (1932) 177, 192, (1941) 192, 194, 195; see also Navigation
Water Power Regulation Acts (Ontario 1916, 1917) 78–9
Watson, Lord 24
White, Sir Thomas 125, 127, 128, 129, 130, 131
Whitney, Sir James 6, 37, 84; disallowance 34, 48–53; creation of HEPC 54–66, 179, 180; electricity exports 69–76; Petawawa lands 66–7; incorporation of companies 103, 105; regulation of utilities 92–100; relations with Borden 122; provincial subsidies 118–20, 123–4, 132; conditional grants 124–6; northwestern boundary 123–4; interprovincial conferences (1906) 120–1, 234, (1913) 126–7
Willison, Sir John 37, 131
Wilmot, Lemuel A. 17
Wood, A.T. 43, 44
Wood, E.R. 58
Woodsworth, J.S. 141, 157, 202
World War, First: closure of capital markets in 129–30; impact on federal system 128–32, 136–7, 235; Victory Loans 129
World War, Second, impact on federal system 191, 198, 222, 223, 235

www.ingramcontent.com/pod-product-compliance
Lightning Source LLC
Chambersburg PA
CBHW030219100526
44584CB00014BA/1073